# ZBrush® Creature Design

CW00539108

# ZBrush® Creature Design

## Creating Dynamic Concept Imagery for Film and Games

Scott Spencer

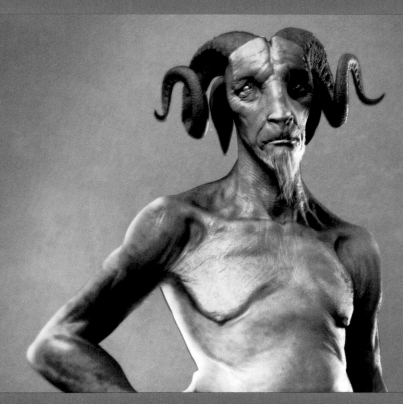

John Wiley & Sons, Inc.

Acquisitions Editor: Mariann Barsolo
Development Editor: Amy Breguet
Technical Editor: Eric Keller
Production Editor: Dassi Zeidel
Copy Editor: Adept Content Solutions
Editorial Manager: Pete Gaughan
Production Manager: Tim Tate
Vice President and Executive Group Publisher: Richard Swadley
Vice President and Publisher: Neil Edde
Media Associate Project Manager: Jenny Swisher
Media Associate Producer: Josh Frank
Media Quality Assurance: Shawn Patrick
Book Designer: Mark Ong, Side By Side Studios
Compositor: James D. Kramer, Happenstance Type-O-Rama
Proofreader: Sara Wilson
Indexer: Ted Laux
Project Coordinator, Cover: Katherine Crocker
Cover Designer: Ryan Sneed
Cover Image: Scott Spencer

Copyright © 2012 by John Wiley & Sons, Inc., Indianapolis, Indiana

Published simultaneously in Canada

ISBN: 978-1-118-02433-1
ISBN: 978-1-118-22206-5 (ebk.)
ISBN: 978-1-118-23626-0 (ebk.)
ISBN: 978-1-118-26067-8 (ebk.)

For general information on our other products and services or to obtain technical support, please contact our Customer Care Department within the U.S. at (877) 762-2974, outside the U.S. at (317) 572-3993 or fax (317) 572-4002.

Wiley publishes in a variety of print and electronic formats and by print-on-demand. Some material included with standard print versions of this book may not be included in e-books or in print-on-demand. If this book refers to media such as a CD or DVD that is not included in the version you purchased, you may download this material at http://booksupport.wiley.com. For more information about Wiley products, visit www.wiley.com.

**Library of Congress Control Number: 2011945017**

10 9 8 7 6 5 4 3 2 1

Dear Reader,

Thank you for choosing *ZBrush® Creature Design: Creating Dynamic Concept Imagery for Film and Games*. This book is part of a family of premium-quality Sybex books, all of which are written by outstanding authors who combine practical experience with a gift for teaching.

Sybex was founded in 1976. More than 30 years later, we're still committed to producing consistently exceptional books. With each of our titles, we're working hard to set a new standard for the industry. From the paper we print on, to the authors we work with, our goal is to bring you the best books available.

I hope you see all that reflected in these pages. I'd be very interested to hear your comments and get your feedback on how we're doing. Feel free to let me know what you think about this or any other Sybex book by sending me an email at nedde@wiley.com. If you think you've found a technical error in this book, please visit http://sybex.custhelp.com. Customer feedback is critical to our efforts at Sybex.

Best regards,

Neil Edde
Vice President and Publisher
Sybex, an Imprint of Wiley

*To my partner Meredith Yayanos, whose love, friendship, and inspiration I cherish.*

# Acknowledgments

There are so many people who bring a book like this to life. I would like to try to thank each of them here. This includes those with a direct hand in the editing and layout as well as those whose support makes this kind of endeavor possible. First, I'd like to thank my partner Meredith Yayanos for her loving support, and Richard Taylor and Tania Rodger for their friendship and support. I must thank Richard for giving me such a unique opportunity to travel across the globe and work every day with so many amazingly talented people. I also want to thank Karl Meyer, Brian Sunderlin, and Gentle Giant Studios for giving me a place to start my journey and remaining close and valued friends and mentors to this day.

Thanks also to all the talented artists I have the good fortune to work with at Weta. Thanks to Eric Keller for serving as technical editor and for sharing his expertise by writing on the ZBrush Materials system. Were it not for his experience and knowledge in this area, we would be missing out on a whole range of techniques. Thank you to Ofer Alon, Jaime Labelle, and Paul Gaboury at Pixologic; and to Alex Alvarez, Eric Miller, and everyone else at Gnomon.

A huge thanks to Desmoda and the team at Ownage for the exceptional, quick, and high-quality 3-D printing they did for this book. I encourage anyone with an interest in printing 3-D models from their ZBrush designs to seek out ownage.com and send Desmoda an email. There is nothing quite like holding a physical copy of your maquette in hand in the real world.

Thanks go as well to 3d.sk for allowing me to use their reference images in this book. I have used 3d.sk as a reference site for the past six years and they are an invaluable resource. I cannot express how important it has been to have constant access to an almost unlimited number of royalty-free, high-res, reference images of all kinds of humans, animals, props, and costumes. Please check them out if you haven't already at www.3d.sk.

I'd also like to thank some of the artists whose tools and techniques have inspired and informed my own process: Neville Page, Zack Petroc, Bryan Wynia, Tristan Schane, Alterton, Paul Tobin, Jerad Marantz, Aaron Simms, Scott Patton, Cesar Dacol, Ian Joyner, and JP Targete. Thank you to Tristan Crane for use of his exceptional photography to illustrate depth of field. I cannot possibly list everyone by name and I apologize to anyone who I have left out. I would also like to thank those incredibly talented artists I am fortunate to work with every day and whose work never ceases to inspire and inform me: David Meng, Greg Tozer, Will Furneaux, Paul Tobin, Gary Hunt, Jamie Beswarick, Mike Asquith, Daniel Falconer, Greg Broadmore, Christian Pierce, Daniel Cockersell, Kim Beaton, Warren Beaton, Steve Lambert, and the many other Weta artists who surround me.

I also must thank the wonderful team at Wiley who helped me through the process and were always professional, patient, attentive, and helpful. Thanks to Mariann Barsolo for managing the process and helping it along. Thanks to Amy Breguet for her expert developmental editing and to Pete Gaughan for guiding the direction of the book and helping to keep it on track and clear. Thanks to Dassi Zeidel and her production team for their masterful copyediting and layout, bringing the final product to light. Thank you all for your exceptional patience with this book and with me.

# About the Author

Scott Spencer is a digital sculptor and concept designer at Weta Workshop in Wellington, New Zealand. He uses ZBrush every day as a tool for creating creature and character concept art. His most recent and exciting project is Peter Jackson's *The Hobbit*. His background is originally physical sculpture for the makeup effects world. Over the years he has worked in various media, creating digital characters for film, broadcast, and games as well as physical sculptures for concept design, promotion, and other applications. Over the past few years Scott has worked on various film projects in the Weta Workshop design department. Scott is fortunate to work as a designer as well as a sculptor, painter, and fabricator on many of the films that come through the workshop. This allows him to remain excited and stimulated by working in various stages of the creative process.

## About the Guest Artists

Huge thanks to those artists who loaned me their expertise and agreed to share their tools and techniques in the book. The presence of industry professionals like them raises the overall quality of the book and exposes readers to more than just one artist's perception on this creature and character design process. I want to thank all of these talented folks for their time and effort.

### Alterton

Born in Trelew City, Chubut province, in the cold lands of the Argentinean Patagonia, Alterton quit a prominent career in orthodontia to become a full-time sculptor for the collectibles business. As a traditional sculptor he has worked for companies such as DCDirect, Art Asylum, and Diamond Select Toys, and as digital artist he has done work for McFarlane Toys, Pop Culture Shock Collectibles, Hollywood Collectors Group, and Disney Development.

### Eric Keller

Eric Keller has been a professional 3-D artist and high-end animator for film, commercials, and TV for over twelve years, creating animations and effects for films and commercials at the leading studios in Hollywood. He is currently visual effects supervisor working on E. O. Wilson's *Life on Earth* project. Keller got his start developing animations for scientific visualization at the prestigious Howard Hughes Medical Institute, where he worked with some of the world's leading researchers. He is the author of *Mastering Maya 2011*, *Maya Visual Effects: The Innovator's Guide*, and *Introducing ZBrush*, all from Sybex. He has also written numerous tutorials for industry magazines and websites.

## Jerad S. Marantz

Jerad S. Marantz has been obsessed with creature design for as long as he can remember. As a child he was always seen hunched over a sketch pad, drawing away. Marantz started his career at the early age of 14 by interning for low-budget practical FX houses with an emphasis in studying sculpture. Originally, he wanted to become a practical FX artist, but as he pursued that line of work, he discovered his true passion was designing. After graduating from Pasadena Art Center College of Design in 2005, Marantz was hired as a freelance concept artist for Stan Winston's Studio. Marantz has since designed for several practical FX houses, visual FX studios, and video game companies. He is currently the lead artist at The Aaron Sims Company.

Marantz's credits include the films *Clash of the Titans*, *Suckerpunch*, *Rise of the Planet of the Apes*, *Avatar*, *Green Lantern*, *Transformers 3*, and *X-Men First Class*. He has also worked on the television shows *American Horror Story*, *Grimm*, and *Falling Skies*, and several games, including *Infamous 2*, *Tabla Rasa*, and *Guild Wars*.

His work can be seen at jeradsmarantz.blogspot.com/

## Zack Petroc

Zack Petroc is CEO of Zack Petroc Studios and Model Supervisor at Disney Feature Animation.

With a commitment to driving the digital entertainment industry forward, Petroc continues to develop new techniques that redefine how digital tools impact the art and design of storytelling. In 2005 he opened Zack Petroc Studios to focus on the development of unique new content and one-of-a-kind training tools. The Studios' first independent project, Adaboy, gives viewers direct access to behind-the-scenes story development techniques, allowing them to follow along as it evolves from concept to completed project. See www.theadaboy.com.

Additionally, his studio has worked on the development of several feature films and video games with a recent client list that includes Disney Interactive, Scott Free Productions, SCEA, Walt Disney Imagineering, Snoot Entertainment, Hasbro, and Paramount Pictures.

In addition to lecturing at universities across the United States and abroad, Petroc has headed several workshops and training seminars at leading industry companies. Recently he began creating and distributing advanced training tools available for purchase and instant download via his website www.zackpetroc.com.

## Tristan Schane

Born and raised in New York City, Tristan Schane started his professional career at age 15 as a comic book artist, which was his boyhood fantasy. He has been a full-time working artist since he was 19. After several years in the comics business, he started doing fine arts oil painting and sculpture and also moved to book cover illustration for sci-fi and fantasy novels. Schane has done concept art for *DragonBall*, *The Mist*, *Thor*, and the TV series *Numb3rs* and *Teen Wolf*. His most recent ZBrush creature work includes *Green Lantern* and *Terra Nova*. His fine artwork can be seen at www.TristanSchane.com and his concept work can be seen at www.TristanArtForm.com.

## Paul Tobin

Paul Tobin graduated from Massey College of Creative Arts, in Wellington, New Zealand, in 2002 and has been a concept designer at Weta Workshop since 2003. He has worked on *The Hobbit*, *The Lion the Witch and the Wardrobe*, *Prince Caspian*, *King Kong*, *Avatar*, *District 9*, and *The Adventures of Tintin: The Secret of the Unicorn*. In addition to his role as a concept designer, Tobin is a freelance illustrator, and in 2010 created *White Cloud Worlds*, an anthology of sci-fi and fantasy artwork from New Zealand, with foreword by Guillermo del Toro. See www.whitecloudworlds.com.

Tobin also teaches Digital Illustration at Massey College of Creative Arts and runs Whitecloud Workshops. You can see Tobin's portfolio at www.paultobin.co.nz.

## Bryan Wynia

Bryan Wynia is a Senior Character Artist at Sony Santa Monica. Previously he worked at Naughty Dog where he contributed on *Uncharted 2* and *Uncharted 3*. He also works as a freelance character designer and sculptor. Some of his clients include The Aaron Sims Company, Gentle Giant Studios, Electric Tiki, and Masked Avenger Studios.

His work has been featured in *Famous Monsters of Filmland*, *Imagine FX*, *3D Artist*, and *3D World*. Wynia has a passion for teaching and sharing his creative process. He has taught classes and workshops at The Concept Design Academy, Gnomon School of Visual Effects, and Art Center College of Design. You can find out more about his artwork at bryanwynia.blogspot.com.

# Contents

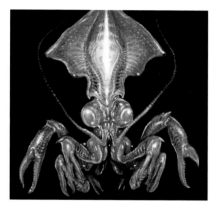

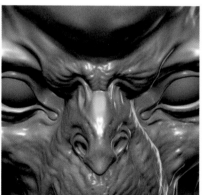

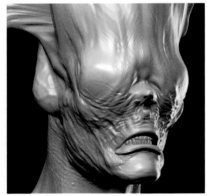

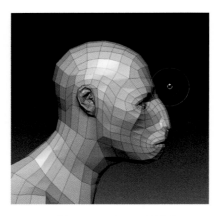
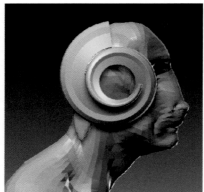

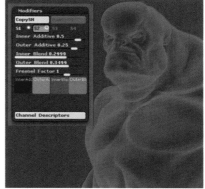

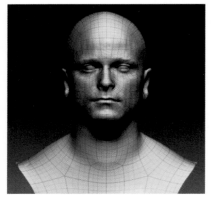

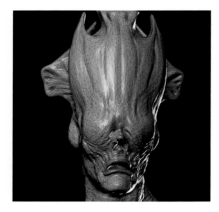

# Introduction

Welcome to *ZBrush Character Design*. In this book, we will take an in-depth look at the tools and thought processes behind creating compelling character designs using ZBrush and Photoshop as our primary tools. We will be using ZBrush not just as a modeling or painting program but as a fully featured conceptual design tool, like many creature and character designers do for the film and game industries. The point of these lessons is to create compelling and evocative images of characters with assets that can be further developed by a digital team in a production pipeline. This mirrors the production techniques used in many studios today. By learning how to use ZBrush and Photoshop together as concept illustration tools, you will discover ways to create exciting characters quickly in an evocative style that excites viewers and gives them an idea of how the final character may appear on screen. These tutorials also focus on the design process—the thoughts and motivations that go into guiding the decisions I make while creating a specific character. We will look at compositional concerns, structural and proportional judgments, color language choices, as well as how to exploit the rules of basic 2-D design with shape relationships to communicate character traits. We will even look at how to influence the viewer's perception of an alien character by utilizing visual cues in the face and body shape based on human preconceptions. These are extremely useful things to understand and I rarely see them discussed in one place. I hope that pulling together some of my own thoughts in the form of these projects may help other artists expand their own process when it comes to creating new characters.

## Who Should Read This Book

This book is for anyone who wants to sculpt creatures and characters in ZBrush and take them to a final-image finish. It is best to work from the first exercises through the book because many of these chapters are project-based. These projects span several chapters so that we can address the concerns inherent to each stage. The Forest Spirit, for example, is broken into sculpting, posing, and painting stages. This allows us to give specific attention to the concerns of each stage in development.

Because this is a visual process and a series of still images can show only so much, I have included most of the exercises on the DVD/download files in video form. You can watch these and see the steps performed in real time to get the clearest possible picture of the steps shown.

This book, is for the intermediate ZBrush user. I assume a certain amount of experience, but I have also been careful to include enough information so that a new user can grasp the topics quickly. For a more foundational introduction to the tools, I recommend looking at Eric Keller's *Introducing ZBrush*, also from Sybex.

## What You Will Learn

In this book, we will be looking at a series of design projects using a combination of ZBrush *and* Photoshop. Just like in my previous books *ZBrush Character Creation* and *ZBrush Digital Sculpting Human Anatomy*, we will focus on the artistic considerations as well as the technical applications. In this book, I move deeper into exploring how I approach a variety of different design problems. We have already covered the ZBrush program in the two aforementioned books. In this title, we will set up a series of projects and look at how to approach them using the specialized toolsets of ZBrush and Photoshop with the intention of creating a final character design suitable for film, television, games, or the collectibles market or even your own fine art.

By approaching the projects in this way, I will illustrate the thought process behind the decisions made when creating a character. Most concepts don't spring from nowhere; on some level decisions are made to hopefully create the most compelling images possible. I will share with you some of the ways I approach creating characters for film, games, and just for fun.

We will look at several different character projects. Each project is presented as a design problem or a "brief." This brief is then resolved using various techniques combining ZBrush and Photoshop. This is intended to show a more holistic approach to using ZBrush as a character-design tool rather than focus in on specific technical elements. In my previous two books, I have shown the program in depth as well as a workflow for sculpting a human figure. Here I will illustrate how to use the tools we already have in a logical way. We will look at why we make some decisions in designing the character—for example, why some shapes are placed as they are. Finally we will look at some unique workflows to illustrate how we use ZBrush and Photoshop to move from an idea to a final image. This is an exciting journey because we will learn much more than just how to sculpt or how to use ZBrush. As we work on these projects, I hope to help you see how I personally think about a design while I work. I have found that it's very helpful to understand how other artists approach the thought process of sculpting and design. For example, I work with a very talented sculptor and designer named Jamie Beswarek. Jamie shared with me his design theory that when you look at a maquette, it should represent your first encounter with a character. The look on his face, the posture, the attitude should all be carefully designed to inspire the feelings you want associated with the character. This applies to digital maquettes and painted imagery as well.

It is my hope that by sharing my own process in this book I may inspire some new considerations in your own workflow. Thank you for giving me the opportunity to share these lessons with you!

## How to Use This Book

I have structured the text to be entirely project based. We begin with basic design sculpting and then quickly move into gradually larger projects. All the chapters are self-contained lessons and result in a finished piece. Many chapters feed into each other—for example, "Sculpting the Interdimensional Traveler" naturally flows into a chapter on posing the figure, which then leads to a chapter that focuses entirely on the painting process. For this reason, I think it is important to start at the beginning of the book and work through each lesson.

This book will be especially useful to those who have some ZBrush experience but want to find ways to explore the sculpting and painting process in more detail. Once we know where the tools are in a program, we enter into an exciting phase where we start to want to find ways to effectively use them together. This is less a book about technicalities and more a book on technique. I hope those artists eager to find new and exciting ways of creating imagery with ZBrush will find these lessons helpful.

## Hardware and Software Requirements

To complete the core exercises of this book, you need ZBrush 4R2 or higher. Some sections also include material related to Photoshop and Maya and using these programs together with ZBrush. Hardware requirements are a PC or Mac running ZBrush with a gigabyte or more of RAM. The more RAM you have, the better the results you can get with ZBrush.

It is also imperative that you have a Wacom tablet. While it is possible to use a mouse with ZBrush, it is like drawing with a brick. A Wacom or other digital tablet will open the doors for you to paint and sculpt naturally. Personally, I recommend a Wacom Cintiq. There are two variations of this tablet screen available as of this writing: the desktop model with a 21-inch screen as well as a smaller portable model. The Cintiq allows you to sculpt and paint directly on the screen and can vastly improve the speed and accuracy with which you can use ZBrush. It is essential to use some form of Wacom tablet, be it a Cintiq or a standard Intuos, with ZBrush.

## The Companion DVD and Downloads

On the DVD, I have included several support files for each chapter. Many exercises have video files accompanying them. The video files were recorded using the TechSmith screen capture codes (www.techsmith.com) and compressed with H.264 compression. The videos will, I hope, help further illustrate the sculptural approach I take in ZBrush. Being able to see a tool in use can better illustrate the concepts than still images alone. In addition to videos, I have included supplementary materials such as sample meshes, materials, and brushes. There is more material than we can fit on one DVD so some material is available on the book's website, www.sybex.com/go/zbrushcreaturedesign.

### For e-book Readers

If you purchased an e-edition of this book, you may download the project files by going to wiley.booksupport.com and entering the book's ISBN.

## A Special Deal for Readers

Zack Petroc and 3d.sk (mentioned before) are offering promotions to readers of this book. Zack Petroc is offering a discount on membership to his tutorial site, www.zackpetroc.com, and 3d.sk is also offering a discount on membership to the photo reference site www.3d.sk. Please see the respective websites or the DVD or download files for more details.

## How to Contact the Author

I welcome feedback from you about this book or about books you'd like to see from me in the future. You can reach me by writing to scott@scottspencer.com. For more information about my work, please visit my website, www.scottspencer.com.

Sybex strives to keep you supplied with the latest tools and information you need for your work. Please check www.sybex.com/go/zbrushcreaturedesign, where we'll post additional content and updates that supplement this book if the need arises.

Thank you for buying this book. I hope you enjoy the exercises within as much as I have enjoyed putting this book together. Being surrounded by like-minded artists who all have something to contribute makes every day a learning experience. It is an honor for me to share some of what I have learned with you. I hope you enjoy this book. Happy sculpting!

# First Things First: Some Notes on Conceptualization

Before we jump into the examples and lessons of this book, let's take a look at some useful guideliness to help you make design decisions. The following are a selection of guidelines and helpful considerations I try to keep in mind as I work. The idea is to familiarize yourself with thinking in these terms so these questions and approaches come naturally when you try to solve a design problem.

## Realism and Expectations

One of the things I always try to do when creating a character is to anchor as much as possible in reality. This usually manifests as basing creature anatomy on real-world animal or human anatomy. When working on a creature, I will often try to draw elements from real world sources to ground the design in a sense of reality. Figure 1.2, for example, is a design by Paul Komoda that pulls elements from a variety of real-world seal life to create an intimidating new design. The same approach holds true for biped physiology as well. This helps make the creature more believable to the viewer. We recognize what an actual body looks like, and when confronted with a distorted form, it makes the character seem all the more compelling if there are elements we recognize from ourselves. Figure 1.3 shows a biomech with physiology based on the human shoulder girdle. You can see that there are recognizable shoulder muscles such as the pecs and deltoids as well as the mechanical forms molded into the shapes of collar bones and a rib cage.

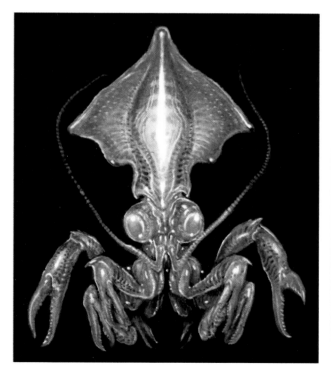

*Figure 1.2: This creature carries many elements pulled from various natural sources to help ground the design in reality; the parts are unified by being arranged into a strong overall design or silhouette. (*Krishnu *by Paul Komoda)*

*Figure 1.3: The shoulder structure of this biomechanical character is based on human anatomy.*

*Figure 1.4: Here the mouth of Sauron shows how expectations in the proportions and placement of features can be broken to great effect. Image courtesy of Weta Workshop*

## Breaking Expectations

Try to break from the viewer's expectations as much as possible. There have been thousands of creatures and characters made for film in the past 100 years. If you want to be a successful designer, you must not only capture the audience's attention, you also must show them something that is appealing and looks new. This is best accomplished by deciding what the expectations are and what the clichés are, and then finding ways to break those expectations. The triangle of the face is one example we use in the book as well as stretching the space between the facial features to subtly play on audience expectations. One of my favorite examples of breaking expectations is The mouth of Sauron from *The Lord of the Rings* (Figure 1.4). This character breaks the audience expectation about the size and placement of the mouth and removes any other facial features that would allow us to relate to the character.

## Creature vs. Character

When working on a design, it is often important to ask yourself whether this is a *creature* or a *character*. Is this an animal with emotions we can relate to, and does it have an internal life to which the audience is privy? If it does, it is a *character* with drives and emotions. A *creature* is more of a monster or an animal the viewer cannot relate to. These tend to be motivated by basic needs such as food, hunting, power, or the desire to simply be left in peace. A peaceful beast of burden and a ferocious hunting beast are both examples of creatures, whereas an alien who wants to communicate with our race, for good or bad ends, is a character. This is important because it helps us understand what we need to communicate with the design. A character (good or bad) needs some way for the audience to connect and empathize. This usually occurs in the eyes. A creature only needs to appear to be a viable life-form that is suited to the task it is portrayed to undertake. A beast of burden needs to appear to be bred to carry packs across the land, while a ferocious hunter beast needs to look like a powerful, fast, and dangerous predator. When finding a point of reference for the viewer, we have already said how familiar anatomical details can create a sense of veracity, but this won't help us relate. I find the key to relating to a character is in the eyes (Figure 1.5). If you give your character deep eyes with a sense of emotion or inner dialog, the audience will be

*Figure 1.5: The eyes will be a natural focal point for the viewer. Eyes that communicate humanity will inspire empathy, while eyes that veer away from human traits will inspire distrust or fear.*

drawn in and, hopefully, interested in what's happening in the mind of the character. Consider creatures like E.T., Gollum, and the Na'vi: they all have eyes that communicate. Creatures like those in *Alien*, *Predator*, and *Jaws* have eyes that are impossible to relate to—they lack humanity and are therefore even more terrifying as a force of nature you cannot reason with! We will take special care to look at techniques to paint realistic eyes on our characters that communicate emotion.

## Visual Development in Thumbnails and Quicksketch

As you start working up ideas, try to avoid jumping right into the final sculpture. Allow yourself the time and space to explore thumbnails and see where the design journey may lead. You will find your best ideas come not in the first 10 or even 20 attempts. You may hit on ideas of great originality 30 or 40 ideas in. You cannot do 40 finished ZBrush sculptings in a day so you must explore in thumbnails. This can be accomplished as quick sketches in ZBrush, as we will do in Chapter 2, "The Character Portrait: Sculpting the Alien Mystic" (see Figure 1.6). Thumbnails don't need to be finished drawings; they can be messy little sketches for your own use only. The point is to get ideas and shapes done so you can evaluate them against each other. You may also do this in pencil on paper or even with a small ball of clay. The important point here is to not jump into your first idea—explore and take a design journey to the best solution to the problem. Figure 1.7 shows a series of design explorations by Bryan Wynia. Bryan uses grayscale values to paint over a ZBrush sculpture and create several striking character options quickly.

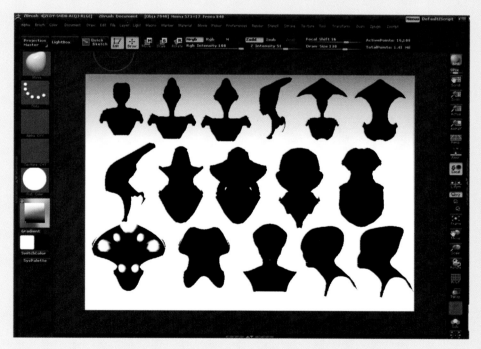

*Figure 1.6: Silhouette thumbnails created in ZBrush*

*continues*

*continued*

*Figure 1.7: A series of character concept options by Bryan Wynia. Bryan paints in grayscale over a ZBrush sculpture to generate multiple characters quickly.*

## Some Key Design Concepts

In this section we will look at some of the major design considerations that we will revisit over the course of this book. These are just a few of the important lessons we can use to inform our choices as we work on a design. I hope reading over these tenets will help you understand why I make some of the choices I do as we work through the lessons. I will often refer back to these concepts, and when I work, I try to keep them in the back of my mind as a set of guidelines to help steer the artistic decision-making process.

These tenets represent concepts drawn from the varied disciplines of graphic design, sculpture, and painting, and each of which will come up as we work through the projects in this book. Ultimately these all apply across multiple media because the rules of good art are consistent whether you are using clay, pixels, Pixols, or paint. That's why we have so much to gain by looking back at the art instruction of painters, sculptors, and photographers. Just because we are using a computer doesn't mean those lessons are invalid. Rather, it's even more important now to understand how artists arrive at pleasing images. When I approach a design, I try to keep these tenets in mind at each stage of the sculpture or painting. They represent some fundamental concepts in art and design, and you will benefit from trying to remember them as you work on your own designs.

## Sculptural Considerations

ZBrush is the primary tool used in this book. In almost all of these lessons we finish the design illustration in Photoshop, but the primary toolset remains sculptural. For this reason, I think it is important to revisit some of the sculptural lessons we discussed in my other books. These concepts apply even when you are painting because the same rules for making good art apply across all media.

In my previous two books we discussed the three tenets of sculpture: gesture, form, and proportion. These are so important that I want to reiterate them here. When working up a sculpture (or any image for that matter), you want to ensure that the figure retains a clear and compelling gesture. Second to gesture is form, and last is proportion. Before we explore other key sculptural concepts, let's review these three.

### Gesture

Gesture represents the life or motion inherent in a figure. It can be expressed in the action line drawn through a figure that communicates the thrust of its pose. When working on a figure, instill a sense of life in the pose by maintaining a strong gesture. Figure 1.8 shows a neutrally posed figure with a good gesture sketched in. Many of you may be familiar with the concept of gesture drawing. This is an invaluable exercise where you try to capture the figure with a series of action lines rather than the outlines of the figure. It's very effective for training yourself to see the life in a pose (Figure 1.9). By practicing life drawing as much as possible from both humans and live animals, you will develop a keen eye for the short pose. This means you will be able to quickly recognize and capture the lines of action in a figure. Sensitivity like this helps designers keep life in their work.

Gesture is important because it instills a figure with a sense of spring or life. It can mean the difference between what looks like a lifeless, stiff 3-D model and a living character. Gesture is especially important when posing figures. By being aware of the direction or thrust of the pose, you can effectively set up a dynamic composition for your final image (Figure 1.10 and Figure 1.11). Figure 1.12 shows a character that has been posed in a dynamic position with special attention paid to maintaining exciting lines of action throughout the body.

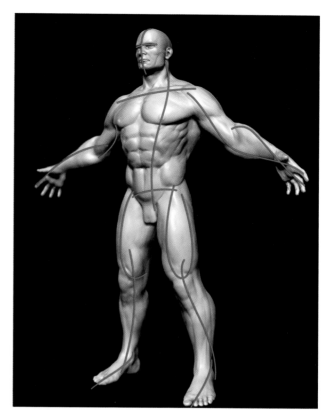

*Figure 1.8: A neutrally posed figure with gesture lines drawn in shows that even a figure at rest should have some gesture in the pose.*

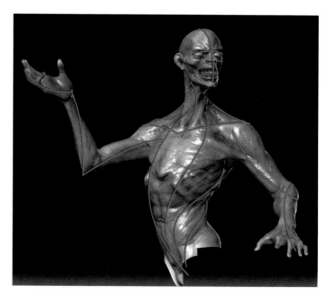

*Figure 1.9: Be aware of the gesture or lines of action in the figure.*

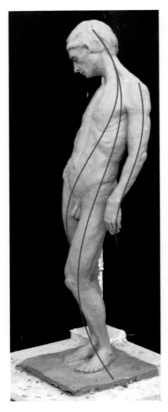

*Figure 1.10: Gesture lines drawn over a sculpture to illustrate the action in the pose*

*Figure 1.11: This figure drawing was created by first trying to capture the gesture of the pose.*

*Figure 1.12: A character in a dynamic pose*

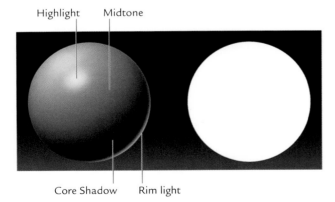

*Figure 1.13: Form is defined by light and shadow.*

## Form

Form represents the shape of a thing as defined by light and shadow playing across the surface. In Figure 1.13 you can see how removing all light and shadow reduces the sculpture to just the silhouette. When working on a character, you want to define form as fully as possible, making sure it is resolved before you must move on to the next stages. Form is the difference between a soft-looking character and one that feels like it has structure and anatomy. One example of how well-resolved form is important is when you need to represent the contrast between bony, hard shapes under skin and soft, fleshy ones (Figure 1.14).

There are often cases when you are working under an extremely tight timeline, and you must finish the sculpture and have it painted in a matter of hours. If you skip any step in the process, do not skip refining the form. Given the choice between form and detail, sacrifice the details, as they do little to sell the realism or beauty of the sculpture, while the form is part of what makes it come to life. A colleague of mine from the Gnomon School of Visual Effects, John Brown, one of the best figurative sculpture professors I have ever met, has a wonderful method of breaking down the hierarchy of form. I will try to do it justice here but I highly recommend his DVD series, available from `www.figuresandfocus.com`, which has some of the best sculpting educational material on the market! John considers form in three classes: primary, secondary, and tertiary. Primary forms are the biggest shapes of the character—the skull, nose, and ears for example. Primary forms are those most basic shapes that make a recognizable head. Secondary forms are things like folds of flesh and fat rolls (Figure 1.15). These are details that add character to the face. Tertiary forms are the fine details, such as pores and wrinkles.

### Proportion

Proportion is the relative size between the parts of a figure. Proportion can help define how we perceive a figure. Notice how the figure with a larger head naturally appears shorter in silhouette (Figure 1.16). Proportion plays an important role in character design in that the same rules that apply to a human also apply to creatures. That means that a large head on a body tends to make that creature look shorter or younger, while a smaller head makes the body look massive and more imposing. You can subtly influence how the character is perceived by being cognizant of the rules of proportions and deliberately manipulating them.

*Figure 1.14: In this detail, you can see how the soft, fleshy forms of the cheek and eye contrast against the hard, angled forms of the cheekbone.*

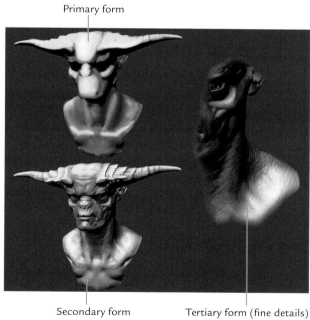

*Figure 1.15: Primary, secondary, and tertiary forms examined*

*Figure 1.16: In silhouette it becomes clear that altering the head size changes the perception of the relative size of the figure.*

## Shape Considerations

In this section we will look at how to intelligently use shapes and their interactions as a tool in design. By being aware of how shapes interplay through rhythm, balance, contrast, and other aspects of shape language, we can be sensitive to the overall appearance of our characters. In this section we will learn how the silhouette or overall shape of the character is the most important element in the design. By learning how to look at and manipulate shapes, we will have more control over creating compelling creatures and characters.

### Silhouette: The Overall Shape Outline

One of the most important aspects of the overall character design is the silhouette. This is the outline of the character, the overall shape. Some designers call this "the first read" because it is the first impression the viewer gets of the character or object when looking at the image.

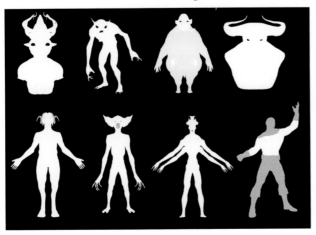

*Figure 1.17: A selection of character designs in silhouette*

The eye registers the outline first, then fills in the internal details. For this reason it is important to create an iconic silhouette. By "iconic silhouette" I mean a graphic outline that is bold and memorable enough to become iconic. Picture the shape of Darth Vader's helmet or Gandalf's hat. The images spring easily to your mind because those are iconic shapes. Figure 1.17 shows several characters in silhouette. Notice how each has a character and interesting form, which is communicated even in this black-and-white shape.

The silhouette must be strong to create a sense of the iconic. Iconic silhouettes lead to memorable characters. If the silhouette is plain or uninspired, the character may not leave a strong impression. Take, for example, the silhouettes in Figure 1.18. There is no question as to who the illustrated characters are. This is why iconic silhouettes are so important. They allow you to identify a character at a glance, and they imprint on the consciousness. It's the same principle in logo design and graphic design. As a matter of fact, some of the best designers I know have extensive experience in graphic design. This attention to big graphic shapes informs their design work, enabling them to create strong iconic designs.

## Shape Language

When I talk about shape language I am referring to how the shapes of a character relate when broken down into their simplest forms. It can also be called shape relationships. Most characters can be resolved to spheres, ovoids, boxes, or cylinders. Look at these shapes and observe how they are stacked in space. Are the proportions between them appealing? Do the relative sizes change or are they consistent? It is usually best to try for variation (Figure 1.19).

*Figure 1.18: Because of the iconic nature of their designs, these silhouettes should remind you of other characters.*

   The concept of shape language is often found in graphic design. By "shape language" I mean the type of shapes you use and how they relate to one another. For example, are you using predominately ovoid shapes and are they contrasted with a more rectangular shape? This represents a use of contrast in your shape language. Alternately, you could compose a creature of predominantly a single kind of shape. The image in Figure 1.20, for example, represents an alien head composed entirely of ovoid forms. This approach can be a bit dull because there is no sense of contrast or tension beyond the variation in size and rotation of the ovoid shapes. Adding contrasting angled shapes creates a different and interesting shape relationship. You have contrast between the ovoid forms and the angular forms (Figure 1.21). You can see this in practice in Figure 1.22.

*Figure 1.19: Basic shape relationships and interlocking of forms in a character*

*Figure 1.20: A head in silhouette composed of all ovoids*

*Figure 1.21: Here we see contrast with ovoid shapes by the introduction of angular shapes.*

*Figure 1.22: Here you can see this kind of contrast applied in the combination of soft, spherical and hard, angular forms in this character.*

The concept of shape language extends to more than just the silhouette of the figure. I will often try to visualize the character as being composed of basic forms. Then I will examine how those basic shapes interact. Figure 1.23 shows a character broken into simple volumes, while Figure 1.24 shows the same for a human figure. Understanding how to recognize and manipulate the graphic shapes in your characters is an important step to being able to control how you communicate with your designs.

The following are some things I keep in the back of my mind while I work on the shapes and forms of a character. These don't need to be conscious considerations on a checklist as you work. It's best to read this section and be aware of how these structures manifest. Look for them in other work, and they will inevitably creep into your own design language.

You may also seek inspiration from nature. Collect as many photos of plant, animal, fungus, and landscape formations. Nature has devised every combination of shape and color at some point, and you can do no better than to reference and evaluate from this resource. I keep a very large folder of photo references divided by subject. This is in addition to the reference library of books and magazines that I often page through for general inspiration.

*Figure 1.23: A character broken into simple volumes to examine the shape relationships*

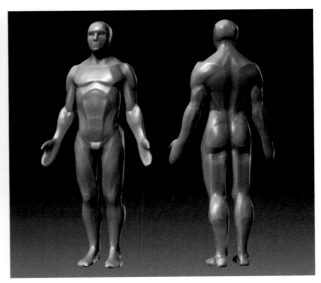

*Figure 1.24: A human figure broken into simple volumes and planes*

## Organizing Shapes

Shapes can be organized in different ways to different effects. Here we will look at how shapes are organized into configurations of rythym, balance, and contrast, and how shapes can take on visual weight.

## Rhythm

When working with a character, I will sometimes look for interesting rhythms within the placement of the shapes. Rhythms create a sense of structure and balance through repetition. Figure 1.25 shows an abstract design created by the rhythmic repetition of elements. For a practical look at this in action, Figure 1.26 shows a character with a repetition of shapes throughout the design. Notice how the large curved forms echo throughout the bust. This creates an appealing visual motif that repeats through the form and unifies it into a single visual composition. It is not a coincidence that rhythm is a musical term in most minds. When used effectively, it creates the same sense of underlying structure that a solid drumbeat maintains in a song.

*Figure 1.25:  Shape rhythm explained with basic shapes*

*Figure 1.26:  A character with a rhythmic repetition of shapes*

Designer John Mahoney suggests a great tip for using music while you work. Pick a specific piece of music that fits the character and keep it playing while you sculpt and paint. This helps keep your mind "in character" and focused on the mood and attitude of the character you are designing.

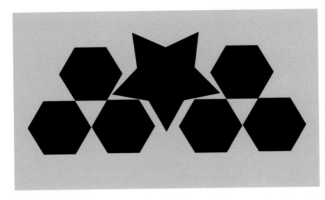

*Figure 1.27:  The principle of balance illustrated with simple geometric shapes*

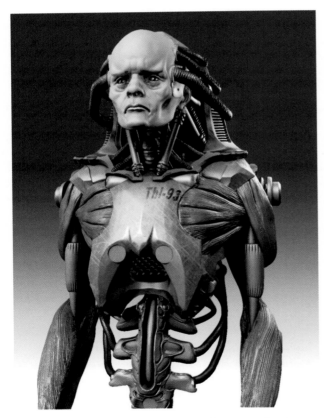

*Figure 1.28:  Balance was used to add a sense of industrial coldness and strength to this biomechanical design.*

## Balance

Balance is the equal distribution of elements (Figure 1.27). You may also find that some designs require a sense of balance. Balance works well in some situations, but too much balance can be very boring. In nature nothing is ever symmetrical: there are always subtle variations. There are situations where symmetry and balance may be desired to communicate something cold, brutal, or immobile such as a robot or biomech perhaps (Figure 1.28). Balance can also imply strength and stability.

## Contrast

You can get interesting effects if you break from balance by introducing the principle of contrast. Depending on the effect you want, you can either balance or contrast your forms. I find it's best to contrast and try to avoid perfect balance in most cases. The degree of contrast will, of course, impact the effect you get. Balance is rarely interesting, as it does not create any sense of tension. Figure 1.29 shows contrast and tension by clustering the shapes in an asymmetrical manner. One practical example of where contrast is useful is when experimenting with proportional variations in a character. Interesting effects can be achieved by contrasting a large upper body with a smaller lower body, for example (Figure 1.30). This represents a contrast of forms.

## Visual Weight

Visual weight is a very important consideration. The relative size and placement of a shape can give it more visual weight than others on the screen (Figure 1.31). This can accentuate a design element for good or bad effect. For example, the shapes of these horns in Figure 1.32 carry more visual weight the larger they get. When the horns are smallest, as they are in image A, they serve no real purpose on the design; they add little to the overall effect. In image B they carry a little visual weight but not enough to make the overall effect feel special. They read as just decoration. When the horns are at their largest, as in image C, they become a design statement. This is a bolder approach to the horns that creates an interesting character bust because there is a dynamic tension between the character's head and the massive sweeping horns.

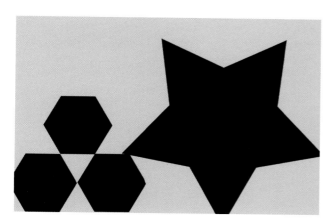

Figure 1.29: *Contrast in basic forms*

Figure 1.30: *Contrast between body forms is seen here with the large torso and small legs.*

Figure 1.31: *The concept of visual weight illustrated with basic geometric shapes*

Figure 1.32: *Visual weight applied to the horns of a character*

Many of the best designers I know have a graphic design background. They have a solid and thorough understanding of how basic 2-D shapes interact and create compelling combinations. They use this information to inform their designs of creatures, characters, and costumes. These basic lessons of art and design apply to everything from the simplest shape to the most complex creature design. In the end, we are always just moving shapes and color to influence the perceptions and feelings of the viewer. Collect examples of strong, easily read graphic design to add to your reference folder. Just the act of learning to recognize good abstract design is valuable. It's even better to analyze why you respond to some designs over others. This helps you determine what makes a particular layout appealing.

## Design Statements and Features

A design statement is an element of the design that can be considered key, or part of what makes that particular design unique. The term is sometimes interchangeable with *design feature*. You want to make sure every design has at least one statement. You can have multiple statements, but if you get too many, you end up with elements fighting each other. Determine the design statement in your favorite characters. Frankenstein's monster's flat head is a statement; Predator's mandibles and dreadlocks are statements. By these examples you can see how it is important to pick out elements and make them features that will make the design special rather than just decorate it.

## Anatomical Considerations

When working up a creature, I consider the physiology and biology in terms of its natural world counterparts. A powerful carnivore, for example, will tend to have large, crushing masseter muscles in the jaw. Figure 1.33 shows the substantial surface area given over to the jaw muscles of a carnivore.

This physiological detail is important because we subconsciously pick up on those shapes and cues. By creating a character with large, powerful jaw muscles, we tell the viewer that the character or creature is strong and potentially dangerous. This is because we are cued into those kinds of subtle details when we observe other animals, including people.

Look at the highly developed masseter muscles on a muscular male (Figure 1.34). These are a result of intensive training of the neck and shoulders as well as low body fat. Typically, a strong jawline is partially created by pronounced masseter muscles: this tends to denote strength.

*Figure 1.33: This skull shows the large surface area given over to the jaw muscles of a carnivore.*

*Figure 1.34: The masseters on this muscular male are pronounced, which add to his strong jawline and appearance of strength.*

Strong effects can be achieved by breaking the norms of the proportions of the face or body. For example, eye spacing has been used to great effect in several recent character designs to break with norms (see Figure 1.35).

*Figure 1.35: This figure shows the uncanny effect created by breaking the normal proportions of the face.*

## Culture and Lifestyle Considerations

Lastly, it is equally important to get an idea of how your character lives. What is his world like? How does he prepare food? Does he hunt or farm? Is he peaceful or warlike? As many details as you can gather or invent will inform the decisions you make with a design.

Figure 1.36 is an illustration by designer Paul Tobin. Notice how the design is filled with small, unique details that communicate a sense of culture and place. From the tattoos to the choice of weaponry, the character looks like he comes from a specific culture with a specific level of technology. Visual cues like these are important to consider and include whenever possible. These same considerations can be extended to the manner in which a creature interacts with its environment. A quadrupedal alien with opposable thumbs on all four limbs will interact differently with his world from a biped with two hands.

Even if the viewer is not aware of the backstory, consistent details like this inspire a sense of cohesion and reality to the design. The viewer will pick up on these details, and nothing will feel contrived or out of place. These kinds of considerations help to sell the character and make it feel real.

## About Color

In the course of many of the lessons we will be painting color on the character. Color will come into play when we make skin markings as well as when we light and place the figure in an environment. Don't panic at the thought of color theory. It may seem complex, but there are a few simple concepts we will be using here. When gathering reference materials

*Figure 1.36: This character design by Paul Tobin features many details that portray the character's culture and backstory.*

for your personal library, don't neglect books and magazines such as *National Geographic*. Anthropologists who study the development of human cultures often document beautiful and expressive color languages that are unique to different cultures across the planet. Tasteful color designs can be created by sampling from the existing palettes in use by any number of peoples. For creature design you may also sample color directly from an existing skin texture. Aquatic animals have vibrant and interesting skin colorations that lend themselves to use in alien life.

### The Color Wheel

The color wheel is the basic tool for using and understanding color (Figure 1.37). The wheel is read by finding the primary colors red, yellow, and blue (Figure 1.38). These colors cannot be mixed from other sources; they are pure primary colors. The secondary colors, green, violet, and orange, are created by mixing primaries (Figure 1.39).

Tertiary color is created by mixing two secondary colors together (Figure 1.40).

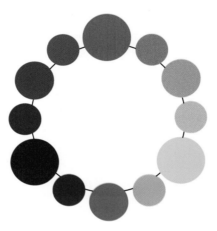

*Figure 1.37: The color wheel*

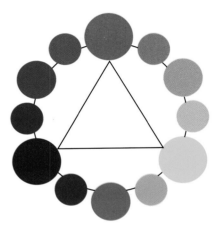

*Figure 1.38: The primary colors*

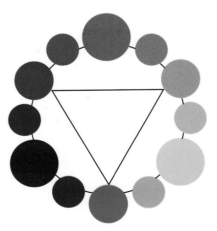

*Figure 1.39: The secondary colors*

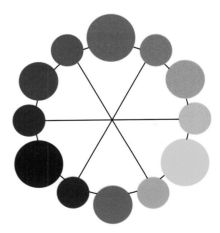

*Figure 1.40: The tertiary colors*

You will rarely have to "mix" color on your computer screen. You will merely select it from the color picker. It is important to understand the color wheel because it shows us what colors are complements to each other, meaning what color is directly opposite on the color wheel. These complements create color contrasts that can be useful when trying to create visual interest. Mixing a complementary color into a composition can create a focal point and draw the eye or simply help make a very dull paint scheme more vibrant. One of my favorite complements is violet and green. If you add the complement to a color you will desaturate it. We will talk more about saturation below.

### Temperature

Temperature refers to the relative warmth or coolness of a color. Figure 1.41 shows the color wheel broken into warm and cool. Notice, though, that even when dealing with a "warm" color such as red, you can move toward a cool or warm hue depending on the side of the wheel you move toward. Remember that color temperature is relative. You can have warm and cool reds or cool and warm blues.

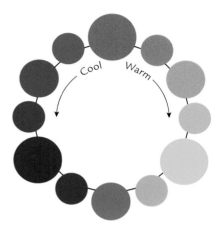

Temperature is most valuable in that warm colors tend to look like they are advancing toward the viewer while cool colors recede (Figure 1.42). I use this tenet when working on the background of the design. I try to keep my backgrounds cool and my figures warm or vice versa. That way there is a temperature contrast that helps separate the character from the backdrop (Figure 1.43). This concept can also help when defining rim light on a character. In Figure 1.44 you can see the key light or main light on the figure is warm while the rim light is a cooler blue hue. This helps create visual interest though contrast, and it also uses the rim light to help carve out the figure from the background. Always avoid broad flat lighting with no temperature contrast or rim lights, as it creates a very bland image with little depth.

*Figure 1.41: Reading temperature on the color wheel. Moving toward red is warm and moving toward blue is cool.*

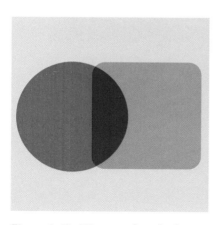

*Figure 1.42: Warm and cool advance and recede with basic shapes.*

*Figure 1.43: Using temperature contrast to pull the character from the background*

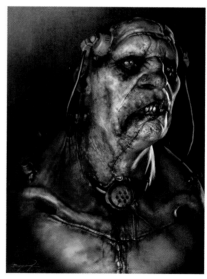

*Figure 1.44: Cool rim light example by Bryan Wynia*

### Saturation

In the course of the book, we will often be altering the saturation of a color. Saturation is the relative vibrancy or purity of a hue. Figure 1.45 shows a color through various stages of desaturation. Desaturating the colors of a design has a calming effect on the eye: it can make the image easier to look at by reducing the vibrant nature of the digital color and provides the same slightly neutralized look of a traditional paint palette. Remember that mixing the complement into a color will desaturate it. Many painters will slightly neutralize their colors to get this effect.

Color saturation is also a function of perspective. A color will lose saturation the further it gets from the eye. This is useful when trying to separate a figure from the background to create a sense of depth in the image. Parts of a character that are receding from the viewer can be desaturated further to make them recede from view. (Figure 1.46). This also means that areas closer to the viewer will have a higher color saturation and therefore be a natural focal point for the eye, drawing the viewer's attention. By being aware of this aspect of color saturation, you can hold the viewer's gaze in certain areas of the image based on where the color is most saturated.

Figure 1.45: Here you can see red at full saturation at the top of the strip. As you move down, the color desaturates.

Figure 1.46: An example of receding areas losing color saturation. The top image is fully saturated while the bottom has a gradual falloff in saturation as the figure recedes from the viewer.

## Composition

In this section, we will touch on some considerations for how to compose the image in the picture plane. We will look at focal points and how to arrange them in an image. This is a brief introduction to these concepts. We will be looking at composition in far more depth in the lessons themselves.

### Focal points

Once you are ready to light and render your character to take it into Photoshop for the final painting passes, it's time to consider how the character will be experienced by the viewer. When creating the final image of your character, you should consider the moment when the viewer first encounters the subject in the image. Seek to create a dramatic and exciting moment in time. You will need a focal point for the image. This is arguably the most important placement in the image—the first point the viewer should look when they see the image. I often keep the character's eyes as a focal point by their placement in the picture plane. Some of the methods to draw the viewer's attention to a focal point are with light, placement, color contrast, or the placement of details. You can call the viewer's attention to a spot in the image by simply making it the brightest point.

In Figure 1.47 I have the center of the key light as the focal point. Notice how attention naturally is pulled to this area away from the darker areas. You can use this technique to paint less of the image if you allow some areas to fall into shadow and silhouette (Figure 1.48). This can save valuable time by allowing you to illustrate just enough of a character to get the idea across, freeing you to move on to create other options. Often your success depends on how quickly you can work and how many different designs you can execute in a day. Lastly you can guide the eye by placing the character in a certain way on the screen. We will look at this in more detail in the next section, composition.

### Composition and the Rule of Thirds

When composing the final image, we take some considerations to mind: the aspect ratio of the final image and the placement of the figure on the plane. One of the easiest ways to place the figure is to use the rule of thirds, seen here in Figure 1.49.

The eye naturally tends to be drawn to a horizon line two-thirds above the base of the image. By placing points of interest at the intersection of any of these lines, you keep the focal point away from the center of the image and make a more interesting composition. Remember how balance does not create tension. By placing the focus at the center of the image, you create a symmetrical, balanced image, which tends to be less exciting than one with tension. We will look more closely at the rule

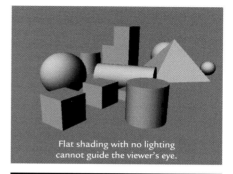

Flat shading with no lighting cannot guide the viewer's eye.

Spotlight trained on sphere helps guide the eye to the brightest point.

*Figure 1.47: Guiding the eye with light*

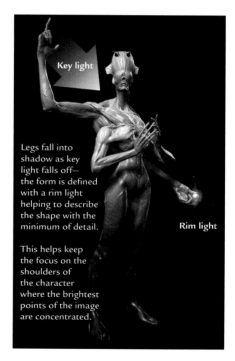

*Figure 1.48: Guiding the eye with detail and lost edges*

*Figure 1.49: Divide the picture pane into nine frames.*

of thirds as well as the mysterious and highly useful Golden Rectangle in Chapter 9, "Painting the Forest Spirit."

### Demonstrating Composition: *The White Fox vs Sherlock Holmes*

*Thanks to Paul Tobin for contributing this section! Paul is a senior concept designer at Weta Workshop whose credits include* The Hobbit, King Kong, Chronicles of Narnia, District 9, *and* Avatar.

No matter how beautifully rendered or detailed, a picture with a poor or confused use of composition will undermine all later work. So putting that extra time into getting your composition right is time well spent.

When I first start to explore an idea for a picture, I begin with roughs and these initial forays often evolve at an intuitive level. In these early roughs, I want to identify the various pieces of my picture and how they relate to each other. By assigning focal points and a hierarchy to your pieces, you can then start to build a composition that supports your concept and communicates it efficiently. It's not unlike completing a jigsaw puzzle: the first step is to just concentrate on finding your edges and the rest will follow. Start simple with clearly identifiable shapes and then build depth and detail later.

This illustration, titled *The White Fox vs. Sherlock Holmes*, appeared in *Coilhouse Magazine* Issue 5 and illustrated a story about Chinese pulp fiction at the turn of the century. In some of these stories, China actually appropriated the Victorian Sherlock Holmes and integrated him into Chinese folklore, with one of his chief adversaries being the mystical White Fox. After working through a number of roughs, the central idea unfolded, which was that the White Fox and the protagonist Sherlock Holmes would be literally on a stage, not unlike actors in a Chinese Opera. In terms of compositional pieces there were primarily just the three, the two characters and the stage. In terms of hierarchy it's the White Fox, followed by Sherlock Holmes, and finally the stage itself, which is intentionally a sparse and simple backdrop for the drama to unfold upon. I always imagined that this picture caught that moment when the curtain raises and the characters are revealed for the first time in dramatic poses: the beautiful White Fox with her sword and fan, defiant and deadly, and Holmes, intent upon the clues, his pose a play upon the iconic depiction found in the classic illustrated books of the period. Figure 1.50 shows my compositional breakdown of this image.

If I had placed White Fox in the middle of the picture, it would have forced Holmes uncomfortably off to one side. As I had to overlap these figures, it was important to find a solution that allowed the partially obscured Holmes to still be a strong secondary element. By using the rule of thirds (the blue grid), I tweaked my initial rough to make sure that the White Fox was on the left one-third line and Holmes's face and hand on the right one-third line. This was done by eye without literally putting down a grid, but with an understanding of how the rule of thirds can be applied.

The second compositional device I employed was the triangle (in yellow). I wanted the White Fox to be a dominant and formidable character, so by splaying her dress and positioning the arms, I created a triangle composition that gives a sense of physical strength and stability. It also serves the purpose of leading the eye to the primary focal point of the picture, the White Fox's face.

I also made sure that the horizon line (in orange) was perfectly horizontal to emphasize this stability, and by adding in receding floorboards, I was able to build a sense of depth into the picture.

The last main device I employed was the use of diagonals, often offset to one another to build a degree of dynamism into what was becoming a very static picture. These diagonals would also help lead the viewer's eye to my focal points. The line of the sword and arm combined with the inward tilt on the fan all help lead to the White Fox's face. The same is also true of my hair design for this character. Not only do the two main points symbolize fox ears, but they also angle toward the face.

In the case of Holmes, having him bent forward dramatically angles him away from the body of the White Fox. His arm matches the angle of his back to really sell this thrusting, intent pose, and the long line of his opium pipe leads to his face, which is the secondary point of focus for the picture. A late addition to the painting was the drifting cherry blos-

*Figure 1.50: Compositional breakdown:* The White Fox vs Sherlock Holmes

soms, which are also angled to create more energy to the picture, rather than just having them drift vertically from above. Once all these elements were in place I slowly started to work up the detailing and used color and lighting to build upon the compositional effects.

## ZBrush to Photoshop Design Process

In this book we will use a variety of tools and techniques. ZBrush will be the core program used in all the tutorials. In many lessons, we will take our models to Photoshop for a final painting pass to help "sell" the character. Oftentimes you will want to work out the overall shape of a character in 3-D from all angles, then pick a dramatic angle to render in Photoshop with color and atmosphere. This allows you to show a director or art director the character both as a sculpture and as a dramatic living being as they may look on film. Figure 1.51 shows a character in both grayscale and a painted presentation.

This is standard practice in concept design for many artists today. The benefit of using ZBrush to generate a base on which to Photoshop paint is that you have a consistent base model that can be further edited in real time for the director. New views are easy to generate, and most importantly, when the design is approved, the 3-D model already exists and can be passed on to departments and then fed into a production pipeline.

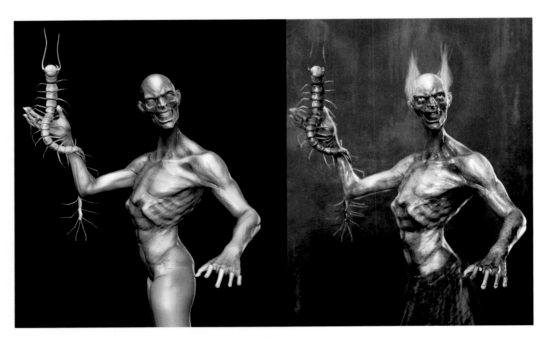

*Figure 1.51: Character as grayscale and painted*

We will also look at other techniques, such as designing for 3-D printing. Many times a design is printed on a 3-D printer to generate a physical maquette that can be held and experienced (Figure 1.52). This is a common practice as well, and it is quite rewarding to see your work in the real world. Luckily the price of 3-D printing is dropping substantially, so it is accessible to most consumers now.

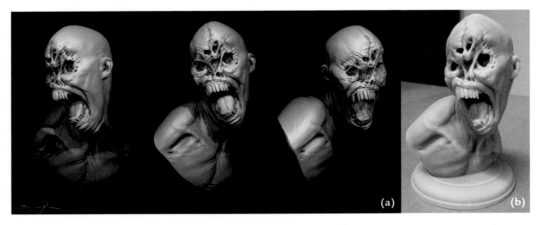

*Figure 1.52: This digital sculpture by Bryan Wynia was printed on a 3-D printer to create the physical maquette in image B.*

Another powerful aspect of this process is that your underlying model is reusable. It has never been easier to grow and create variations on a character than now with ZBrush. In a matter of minutes, multiple versions of a character can be worked up and put before a director for evaluation. This kind of immediate feedback allows artists to get the character exactly as the director wishes faster than even before (Figure 1.53). It also allows far more possibilities to be explored in less time.

*Figure 1.53: Variations on a character can be created quickly.*

We have taken an in-depth look at the various tenets of design I try to keep in mind as I work. We will refer back to many of the concepts in this chapter throughout the rest of the tutorials in this book. The lessons in this chapter will serve you well as you develop ideas for creature and character concepts. Let's move on now and put these lessons into practice.

In the next chapter I will illustrate the process of designing an alien character bust. Throughout the process, we will refer back to many concepts from this chapter such as gesture, shape language, and rhythm. Let's get started!

two

# The Character Portrait: Sculpting the Alien Mystic

In this chapter we will look *at the process I take to design a character I call the alien Mystic. We will look at how I create this character based on instructions from a director called "a brief." In the process of designing, we will see how basic shape language is used to create an interesting silhouette, which in turns helps to create an interesting character design. We will see how natural human anatomy can be pushed into the uncanny valley to create an alien face that has a basis in reality. This anchoring of fantasy characters in real-world anatomy helps the viewer accept the creature as a biologically viable creature and not just a blob of fantastic shapes with no physiological veracity. Over the course of this chapter, you will see the design process we have discussed so far in action as it unfolds within ZBrush. It is my hope that by seeing what changes I make to the character head at various points in the process, you will come to understand how I employ many of the design concepts we discussed in Chapter 1, "ZBrush as a Character Design Tool." In this design, we will be particularly focused on silhouette, shape language as expressed between the various masses of the head, creative manipulation of human facial anatomy, and how the lines of the sculpture flow and guide the eye through the design.*

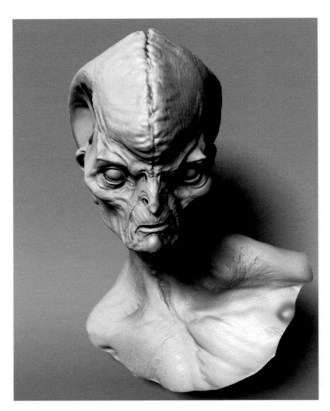

*Figure 2.1: The final Alien Mystic design bust*

You may recognize this character (Figure 2.1) from the cover of my book *ZBrush Character Creation*, 2nd edition. I am excited to now be able to show you how I went about designing this character in ZBrush. Instead of focusing on the technical aspects of sculpting and working in the program, we will look at the design methodology I used to guide my process while sculpting this character.

This chapter is intended to focus on the considerations to keep I mind when sculpting a design. We will not be concerned with color and paint yet—that's for our next character. This lesson is intended to help you see how I think about a character design when it is in it sculptural stages. How shape language, silhouette, form, and proportion are used to help communicate a dynamic and interesting character.

## The Importance of Reference

Throughout this book we will be creating a variety of different kinds of characters and creatures. As mentioned in Chapter 1, it is of paramount importance to always have a reference. A professor of mine in college, Paul Hudson, explained the need for reference well. He said, "Never lie. A viewer can tell when you are lying and making up details with no reference, and they will judge the work harshly for it."

Keep a reference folder of images from the Internet: people, faces, animals, textures—any interesting thing that you can file away for future use. When you are working on a face or body part, having a reference can be the difference between a plain and uninspiring sculpture and a really interesting shape that has details in flesh and weight that you just wouldn't have considered without that photo reference.

I recommende 3d.sk as a fantastic reference source. The 3d.sk site and its sister sites are the largest collection of photo references for artists on the Internet. I highly recommend a membership for any artist professional or student. The easy access to high-resolution reference imagery will improve your work immediately. Less time seeking out good references means more time you can spend using them. Figures 2.2 and 2.3 show prime examples of available imagery.

# Designing a Character Bust: Getting Started

I often find that you can start a character design by working on a bust. This allows you to define the attitude and presence of the character quickly without getting lost in the body details. By bringing the viewer in to a close-up, you also give them a more intimate picture of the individual. Busts are quick to sculpt, and I can generally finish a design in about a day from sculpt to finished paint up. For this reason, we will start the book by doing a bust design. If you find the bust is successful, you can then move on to designing a body for the character.

© Peter Levius www.3D.sk

© Photo-Reference-for-Comic-Artists.com

*Figure 2.2: These human figures were downloaded from the exceptional reference site 3d.sk and its sister site photo-reference-for-comic-artists.com.*

© Peter Levius www.3D.sk

*Figure 2.3: The 3d.sk site also offers animal reference images from various angles as well as armor and weapons references.*

## The Brief: A Character Study

The brief for this lesson is a character study of an ancient alien being. He is extremely intelligent with advanced technology. This character feels no allegiance to humanity, but he is not at war with Earth. This character seems to display a general contempt for humans and should be considered dangerous. He needs to appear to have evolved along similar lines to humans, but perhaps with advanced senses or mental abilities.

## Thumbnails

One of the first steps to a good design is sketching ideas. You should always sketch in some form, such as a ZBrush doodle or even a series of thumbnails on a piece of paper at your desk. This allows you to work out ideas and poses quickly so that you don't waste time at the computer. Figure 2.4 shows a finished image and the original sketches. Notice that the sketches can be very rough. The idea is to work out the rough ideas on paper, where you can think quickly and are not bogged down in technical considerations.

Thumbnail sketches are an important part of the design process. Thumbnails help to dial in the silhouette of the figure quickly. They also allow you to work through a variety of ideas very quickly. I consistently find that my first ideas are the weakest and only after I spend some time doing the "expected," conventional approaches in my sketches do I come upon a new and fresh idea. It usually takes some time to work to this point in ZBrush, but if you work this process out on paper, you will start further ahead in your sculpting. I have also found that in the last hour of work on a piece I sometimes make a sudden and drastic change that pushes the design into a new realm.

Thumbnail sketches are often created with a chisel tip marker in black and white.

## A Thumbnail Process for ZBrush

This same approach of creating black-and-white thumbnails is possible within ZBrush as well. It allows you to explore several options quickly in thumbnail form. This kind of approach is important because 3-D makes it easier to get locked into an idea too early because you are often starting from an existing mesh or volume.

The thumbnail approach has the added benefit of introducing a level of spontaneity or "happy accident" to the sculpting process, which is often absent from digital workflows.

One plug-in that will be useful in this lesson, as well as throughout the book, is Svengali's QuickSave plug-in. This can be found on the DVD or downloaded from zbrushcentral.com. This plug-in allows you to save iterations of your model with a numerical file extension by pressing a hot key. This means you can

*Figure 2.4: Here you can see my* Centipede Magus *illustration next to the original thumbnail. The ideation sketch need not be elaborate. A simple rough figure will do to work out big ideas.*

save models with a three-digit numerical extension such as _001, _002, and _003 by simply pressing your save hot key. As you will see, this functionality can speed work along nicely. I highly recommend that you download and install this plug-in. I have included the plug-in on the DVD or download files, but you should check the forum at `www.zbrushcentral.com` to be sure you have the newest version. Svengali updates his plug-ins. Follow these steps to add the plug-in to ZBrush:

1. From the DVD or download files, browse to the file `QuickSave4.zsc`. This is the QuickSave plug-in file. Copy this into the ZBrush scripts folder so that it will load when ZBrush starts.
2. Right click and copy the file. Now browse to the root ZBrush plug-in folder. This folder is located at `C:\program files\pixologic\ZBrush4\Zstartup\ ZPlugs`. Paste the file into the ZPlugs folder. Be sure it is not in a sub-folder. It must remain in the root ZPlugs directory. For a Mac, this will be `Applications/ZBrush 4/ZStartup/ZPlugs`.
3. Restart ZBrush. If it was open, be sure to shut it down completely and restart. When ZBrush opens again, a new menu will be found under the Zplugin menu. This menu will be titled Svengali.
4. Click on the Svengali menu to open it. This is where the QuickSave options will be found (Figure 2.5).

*Figure 2.5: The QuickSave plug-in*

The plug-in functions by using two buttons for each thing that can be saved. Project will save your initial project file. This is where you specify the filename you want to save the project as. For example, press the Project button and name your file **thumbnails_001**. Now when you press the P+ button, the script will save a new version of your file, appending the next digit onto the filename. If you press P+, it will automatically save a new project as `thumbnails_002`. This protects against file corruption because you are not saving the same file over itself. We will use the Model save function to save automatic increments of our model as we create silhouette variations of it. Before we move on, we will set a hot key for the save button to speed workflow.

1. Press and hold the Ctrl and Alt keys and click the M+ button. ZBrush will prompt you for a hot key assignment (Figure 2.6).
2. Any key you press now will be assigned as the QuickSave model hot key. I chose Alt S. I try to keep my hot keys clustered around the Alt key and the left side of the keyboard so that I can press them quickly while I work.

*Figure 2.6: ZBrush prompts for a hot key assignment.*

We are now ready to move into the process of making a thumbnail sheet. Follow the steps below to start generating thumbnails using ZBrush:

1. In ZBrush, set a large document size. In this case, I have set the document window to 1920 × 1440. This larger document size will allow us to create several thumbnails on the same page (Figure 2.7).

2. Select the color white from your color picker and press the Back button under the Document menu to set white as the background color of the document. This will allow us to see our thumbnail studies as black on white (Figure 2.8).

3. On the upper right sidebar, click the AAHalf button. This will cause the full screen to be visible. You can also use the Zoom button to make sure the whole document is visible. This will make it easier to place our thumbnails as we work.

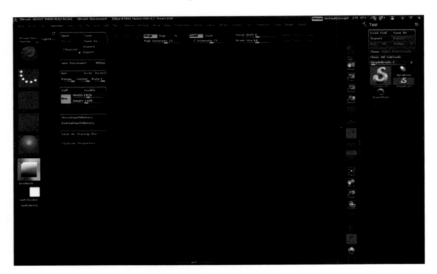

*Figure 2.7: Set your document size to 1920 × 1440.*

*Figure 2.8: The background set as white.*

The document is now prepared. In the next steps we will open a generic head ZTool and change its material to a black silhouette. By removing all details from the inner forms, we are forced to look only at the silhouette. By using the Move brush, we will then quickly shape the character into a variety of interesting shapes. Each one will be dropped to the canvas as a snapshot and the model saved. In this way, we will build up a selection of thumbnails and associated models.

1. For this section, we will use the generic ZBrush bust I have covered in my previous book, *ZBrush Character Creation*. You will find this ZTool on the DVD or download files. Load the tool and draw it on the canvas. Press T to enter edit mode (Figure 2.9).

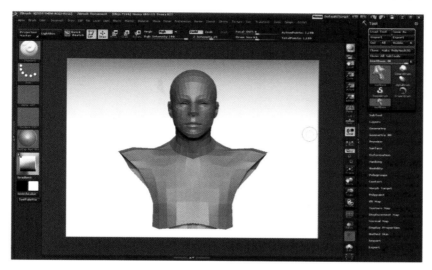

*Figure 2.9: The generic head ZTool on the canvas in edit mode*

2. In default mode, the material is a red wax shader. We want to change this to a solid black material so that we can manipulate the model with the silhouette as our only concern. To do this, we will change to the flat color material. Open the Material menu and select Flat Color (Figure 2.10). Set the active SwitchColor to black (Figure 2.11). If the model's material does not change, that means the material channel has been filled. To correct this, select the flat color material, turn on the M button at the top of the screen, and then click Color ➤ Fill Object. This will clear the material channel so that whatever material is selected will display on the ZTool. This technique will also correct models that have material applied to some areas and not others.

3. Now the model will display as a black silhouette on screen (Figure 2.12). Save the model using the QuickSave Model button as **thumbnail _000**. This will set a base filename and allow you to increment numbers as you save.

4. Select the Move brush and start changing the shape of the model. You will see how interesting forms can be created by merely dealing with the outline of the character (Figure 2.13).

5. When you have a new shape, size the model down and snapshot it to the canvas by pressing the Shift S hot key. Shift S will take a snapshot image of the ZTool in its current position and display it in the document window. Once you have snapshot the image to the canvas, press the QuickSave hot key, Alt S. This will save your model with a 001 extension.

You can also save images with the hot key, but this does not allow you to compare the thumbnails on a sheet together, which is an important part of the process.

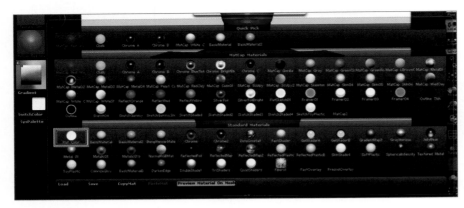

*Figure 2.10: Set the material to Flat Color.*

*Figure 2.11: Select black as the active SwitchColor.*

6. Continue to work your way across the page, making new shapes with the Move brush. You may also add new subdivision levels while you work if you need more resolution in the silhouette. As you work your way across, save new versions of the model for each snapshot you drop to the canvas so that you can easily recover the corresponding model later. Alternately, you can create a new layer for each thumbnail (Figure 2.14). Because you are using the QuickSave plug-in, you can find the model that corresponds to a thumbnail by comparing the number of its filename with the thumbnail on the page: the fifth thumbnail across will correspond with file_005.

7. While you work, you can switch to the basic material again to see what strange internal forms your Move brush has created. In Figure 2.15, I find that some strange wing forms have been created entirely by accident on the sides of the head.

Also remember you can still add geometry or step down the Subdivision levels as needed while you sculpt these silhouettes. Stepping down subdivision levels can be accomplished with the Shift D hot key.

*Figure 2.12: The bust in silhouette*

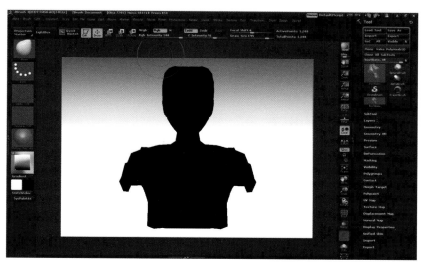

*Figure 2.13: Using the Move brush, shift the model around and create new and interesting silhouettes.*

*Figure 2.14: A selection of thumbnails. There is a model saved for each version, from left to right.*

At this stage I often walk away from my work and come back after a short break or a night's sleep. This allows me to evaluate the silhouettes with fresh eyes. When you come back, determine what shapes are the most interesting. Look for new ideas in the sheet. This is not unlike Rorschach inkblot tests. Try to find something new and interesting. I made my choice based partly on the silhouette and partly on the interesting ear/skull form created randomly by my use of the Move brush. With the model selected, we are ready to move on to sculpting our character portrait.

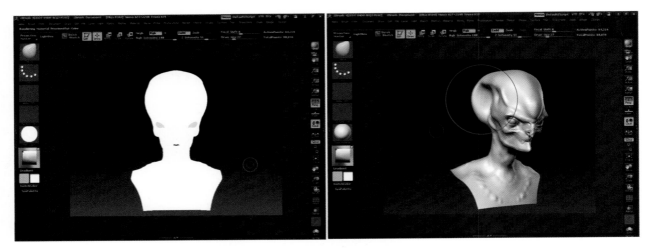

*Figure 2.15: Happy accidents can be encouraged by sculpting these rough shapes with the flat color material on. The ear structures seen here were a random occurrence but they carry over into the design.*

## Another Approach to Thumbnail Ideation with Guest Artist Bryan Wynia

*In this section, Los Angeles–based character artist Bryan Wynia will demonstrate his approach to thumbnail ideation in ZBrush and Photoshop. Currently working as a senior character artist at Sony Santa Monica, Bryan started his career with me at Bill Johnson's Lone Wolf Effects in Atlanta, Georgia.*

I will share my techniques for generating ideation drawings, or thumbnails, using ZBrush and Photoshop. Figure 2.16 shows a selection of character designs based on an amphibious monster theme. When designing a character or creature, I find it very useful to use thumbnails to explore my designs. I can quickly generate new ideas and steer my design down a successful path. It's rare that the first idea you have is the best idea. Take the time to explore and evolve the character.

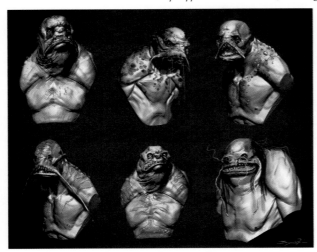

*Figure 2.16: A selection of design variations generated quickly in ZBrush and Photoshop*

1. When I receive a character description, I will quickly gather reference and jump right into ZBrush. Starting from a simple mesh, I create a design sculpture, also known as a speed sculpt (Figure 2.17).

2. Depending on the time frame and project, I will create multiple speed sculpts. Each sculpt allows me to explore new silhouettes, shapes, and characteristics. Using the Best Preview Render function, I do a simple render of each speed sculpt.

3. I then bring the renders into Photoshop to start the thumbnail process (Figure 2.18).
4. I will create a row for each speed sculpt. You can hold Ctrl+Alt+Shift to quickly duplicate each layer in Photoshop. The first render will remain similar to the speed sculpt. I
   usually paint only eyes, hair, and accessories. Figure 2.19 shows an example of a quick
   paintover as well as the final illustration further developed in Photoshop.

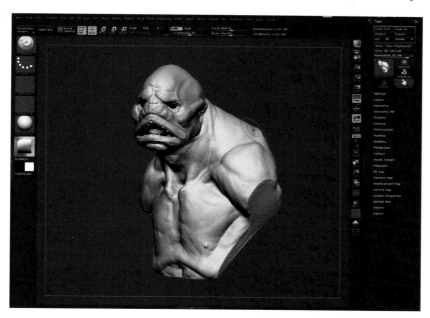

*Figure 2.17: The initial speed sculpt*

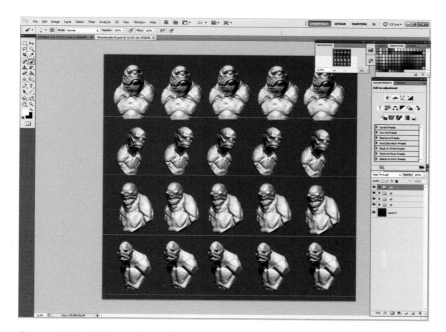

*Figure 2.18: BRP renders of each variation, ready to paint*

**5.** For the remaining layers, I will start by using the Liquify tool found in the Filter tab (Figure 2.20). I use this very much like the Move brush in ZBrush. It's a great tool for creating a new silhouette. At this point, the Transform and Warp functions are very useful as well. I'm trying to create new options with each image. Perhaps one version is thin and agile and the next is more defined and has larger eyes. Use this time to explore and expand on your character.

*Figure 2.19:  An example of a quick paintover and a final illustration developed from the same speed sculpt base*

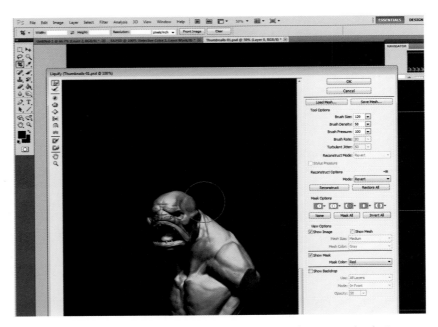

*Figure 2.20:  Using the Liquify tool to make further changes to the design*

**6.** I will sample color from the render to paint new shapes on the character (Figure 2.21). You can do everything from adjusting bone structure to extending the length of the ears, and so on. Most of the thumbnails I create are in grayscale, as I'm only focusing on the character's forms and shapes at this point. Depending on the design, I will use a simple brush to suggest hair, fur, or clothing. When painting, I also try to use value to create areas of interest on my character. For example, perhaps the skin around the eyes and mouth are darker and have more specular highlights.

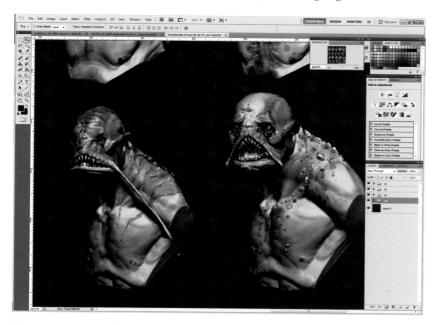

*Figure 2.21: Sampling color to paint new shapes and highlights into the image*

The more thumbnails you create, the better! I like to leave no stone unturned when it comes to ideas (Figure 2.22). Investing this time to properly explore your character can only benefit your designs and creative process.

You can find out more about Bryan and his artwork at bryanwynia.blogspot.com.

## Refining the Character Bust

With the bust base selected from the page of thumbnails, we are ready to start sculpting more refined forms from the base model. At this stage we will think about the anatomy of the character as well as the relationships between the shapes of the head, for example, how the forms of the cheekbones relate to the sphere of the head. These relationships will be different for each character. It's important to consider how the base shapes interlock and relate. One good rule of thumb is to avoid equal distributions of shapes. In this character, I make the head essentially

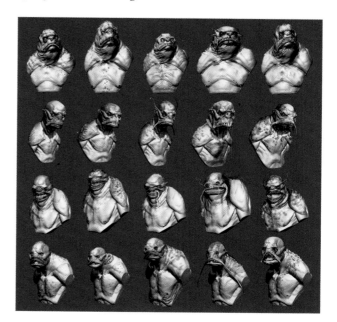

*Figure 2.22 Here is a large selection of ideas generated from the initial design mesh*

*Figure 2.23: The most simplified shape of the head is an oval and a triangle 1/3 the size of the head as a whole.*

two shapes—an oval and a triangle (Figure 2.23). The triangle is about 1/3 the size of the head as a whole.

## Shaping the Head and Facial Features

We'll start by roughing in some details to the character's head, eyes, cheekbones, and other areas:

1. Using the Move brush, continue to shape the head. I try to create a narrow facial wedge suspended under the bulbous head. Immediately, I am thinking about how the head is broken into at least two shapes and how those two shapes will relate. At this stage I am almost entirely using the Move brush to create these shapes. (See Figure 2.24.)

2. Using the Standard brush I sketch in cheekbones (Figure 2.25). This is a very quick, rough stroke. The only point is to start to define the edges of the face and its shape. Don't spend too much time working on skeletal anatomy yet. We are too early in the process to think about secondary anatomical forms in detail. Right now, we want big shapes and their relationships to each other.

3. Add a sphere for the eye by appending a Polysphere into the SubTool stack. Use the Transpose Move tool to place the eye where you want it. I chose to place them wide and just below the midpoint of the head. Place the spheres for the eyes early so that you can be sure as you sculpt the anatomy of the eye, both the bony and fatty forms, that they will be relating back to the eye's spherical shape. Otherwise you will make it far harder on yourself to be accurate because you have no point of reference. Changing their position later is extremely easy with Transpose and the Move brush.

When the eye is roughly placed, use the ZScript SubTool Master to mirror it across the X axis. Press the Mirror button and choose the options Across X axis and Merge into one SubTool. SubTool master must be installed and is available for free from www.pixologic.com. Here we see the eye after mirroring with the ZScript SubTool Master (Figure 2.26).

Using the Standard brush in conjunction with Clay Tubes and Polish, refine the shape of the eyelids and cheekbones (Figure 2.27). Be sure to use Transparency mode as you work, With Transparency and Ghost buttons turned on, you will be able to see both the eyelid and the shape of the sphere beneath it. This is invaluable to help conform the eyelids around the sphere of the eyeball. If you cannot see through the SubTools as shown in the image below, be sure to turn on Ghost mode. The button is located on the right of the screen just below the Transp button.

*Figure 2.24: The base forms of the head roughed in*

*Figure 2.25: Sketching in the shape of the cheekbones*

Position the eye with Transpose Move | Mirror the eye across the X axis with SubTool Master | The mirrored eyes are merged into one SubTool

*Figure 2.26: Placing the eyes*

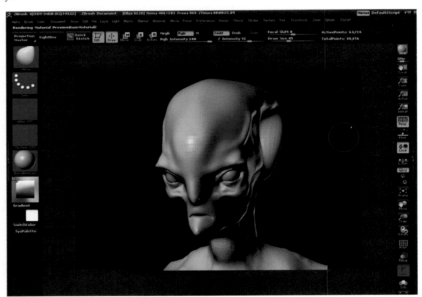

*Figure 2.27: Work the shape of the eyelids.*

4. I continue working the head and face. At this stage a theme is emerging of sharp angles pointing downward. These can be seen here in the shape of the nose mouth and chin. This repetition creates a rhythm between the elements. It is not something I necessarily consciously chose, but a development of arranging the forms until they felt more appealing. Notice also how the eyes are slightly tilted, giving an air of malevolence to the head. This effect is lessened considerably before the head is completed. Little touches such as the tilt of the eye and angle of the upper lid can communicate so much about a personality (Figure 2.28).

At this point I want to create an interesting nose shape (Figure 2.29). Because this head is based on a human face, we want to break as many conventions as we can: adding extra nostrils and enlarging and shrinking elements will help. The hope is to push it away from human while retaining enough elements that it is relatable as a humanoid character.

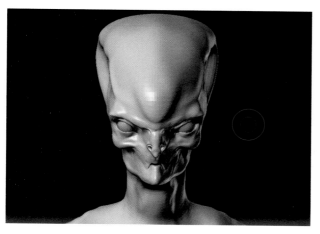

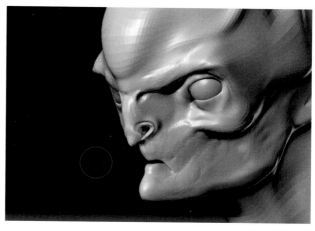

*Figure 2.28: The eyes of the character modified. With these angles in the facial features, he takes on a sense of malicious intent.*

*Figure 2.29: Working on the shape of the nose*

5. We have enough of the head's primary forms now that we can start to think about smaller shapes. I further break up the shapes of the head by adding some secondary forms. Here you can see how the structure of the cheekbones have been brought out from the skull and further refined. I use these forms to both frame the large eyes and create a sense of tension in the face. Skin can stretch from these sharp cheekbones down to the mouth, creating some dynamic lines later in the sculpture. These two facial landmarks also serve to be a point of reference between human and alien anatomy (Figure 2.30).

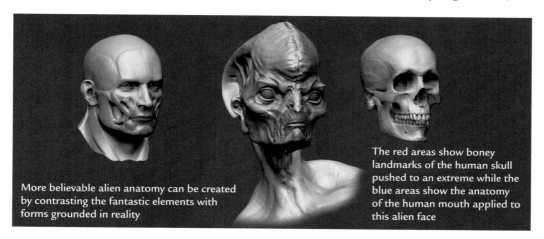

More believable alien anatomy can be created by contrasting the fantastic elements with forms grounded in reality

The red areas show boney landmarks of the human skull pushed to an extreme while the blue areas show the anatomy of the human mouth applied to this alien face

*Figure 2.30: By relating the anatomy of the human face to the alien cheekbone and facial muscle structure, you can add a sense of veracity to the design.*

6. At this stage, you can see some implied lines developing in the head. I will use these lines to guide the eye through the design. (See Figure 2.31.) It's like pictorial composition but in three dimensions. Just like a painting or illustration has lines that guide

you through the design of the picture plane, you can use implied lies in your sculpture to create interesting shapes and guide the eye along the forms. Remember that, in most cases, this sculpture will be seen as a painted 2-D image, so thinking in compositional terms early on will help.

Changes to the overall shape create a more interesting look. In Figure 2.32, you can see the head at this stage from the front view. I have sought to use the lessons we have learned so far to make sure the head is composed of basic shapes that relate together in interesting ways. The facial anatomy is suitably removed from human while retaining humanoid elements, and the overall silhouette is strong (Figure 2.33).

7. Returning to anatomical considerations, we look at the mouth. I want to give the mouth a sense of being an actual orifice with skin and folds. The best way to approach this is to look at the anatomy of a human mouth and push those elements. The mouth is defined by the forms of the zygomaticus major and minor and the orbicularis oris muscles (Figure 2.34). I push these shapes to fit the extremely tapered jaw line and to accentuate their prominence to create some variation in the shape around the mouth.

At this point, I zoom back and take inventory of the changes I have made. Figure 2.35 shows the character from the front and three-fourths views. Notice how the face wedge is subordinate to the great sweeping arc of the cranium in the second image. Shape relationships like this, while abstract, can make the character more interesting if you are aware of them and try to explore and exploit them. Notice also that I make sure the cheekbones break the silhouette from the front view. This creates variety and interest in what would otherwise be an egg shape.

Remember that the mouth and eye areas are based on very human shapes (Figure 2.36). This is intended to ground the character in some elements the viewer may find empathy with. By giving an alien some human aspects, it can more easily communicate emotion or calculated menace to the viewer.

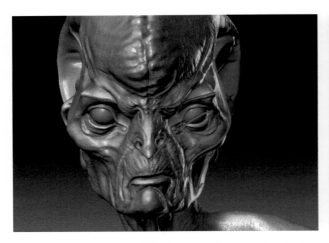

*Figure 2.31: Be aware of the internal, implied lines in the shapes of the sculpture.*

*Figure 2.32: Working on the shape of the head from the front*

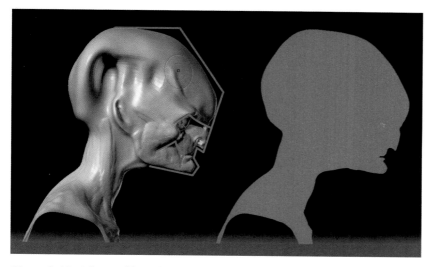

*Figure 2.33: The profile includes several strong graphic forms with the angles shown here.*

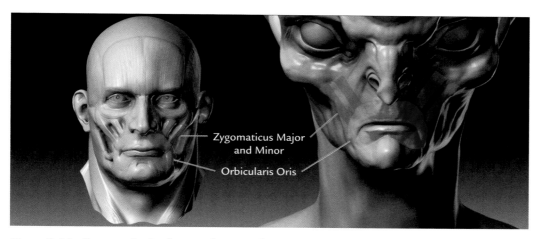

*Figure 2.34: Once again, I reference the muscular anatomy of the face to create the shapes seen here around the mouth.*

To add a sense of fleshiness, I use the Clay Tubes brush. One of the secrets to creating a soft fleshy feeling in a sculpt is to avoid deep, dark divisions between all your forms. The Clay Tubes brush is chosen because it adds into the recesses first and makes the undulations on the surface of the sculpture more subtle. Figure 2.37 shows a fold at the side of the mouth before and after being softened with the Clay Tubes brush. Make sure to turn off the Alpha on the brush to get the softening effect (Figure 2.38).

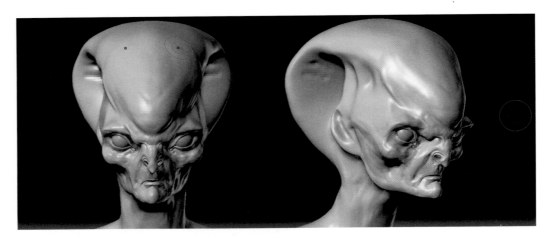

*Figure 2.35: Front and three-fourths views*

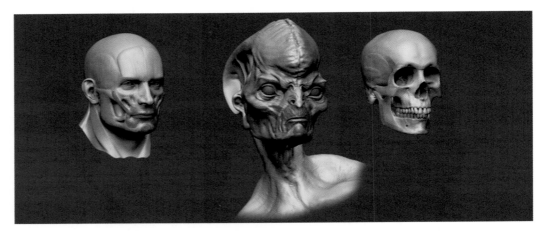

*Figure 2.36: The mouth and eyes are based on very human shapes to help the viewer relate to the character.*

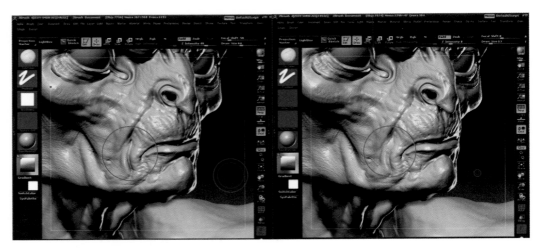

*Figure 2.37: By brushing into the spaces between folds with the Clay Tubes brush, you can accentuate the appearance of soft flesh.*

## Further Refining

Now I will rough in most of the angles and forms. At this stage in the tutorial, I hope you are getting an idea of how I am considering these shapes and what I am going for with the mesh as I move it. For me, the design process is a constant push and pull of shapes as I try to make each decision serve the overall look and intention of the character. In Figure 2.39, you can see how I am considering the triangular shapes that make up the whole character head and the overall silhouette as well as the basic form language, or how the volumes of the head interrelate.

Using the Clay Tubes brush, I quickly stroke some folds into the face (Figure 2.40). These are intentionally sketched in a quick, gestural manner so that they draw the eye down into the angles of the mouth and chin. The lower portion of this creature's face is all about tightening angles and points. I also suggest the anatomy of the neck and collarbones (Figure 2.41). Notice how I have just quickly suggested these with two strokes of the brush. I think that this kind of quick, confident approach is important in ZBrush, just like it is in drawing and painting. If you have a clear idea where a muscle starts and ends, you can easily sketch its form on the surface. If you are able to learn about the anatomy enough that you can suggest muscles and bones with short, confident strokes, your sculpture will appear less overworked and more spontaneous. I always try to be confident when I sculpt, even when I am not confident in where it is going. In the end, a bold sculpture will look better than a weak and overworked one.

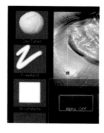

*Figure 2.38: Be sure to turn off the Alpha on the Clay Tubes brush to get the maximum softening effect of the brush.*

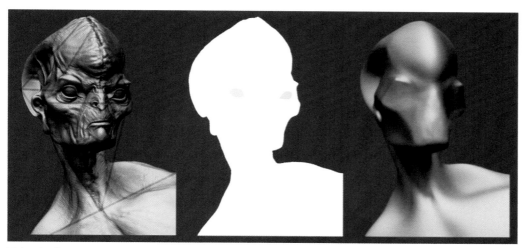

**Major Angles**
The red and blue lines in this image trace the major triangular shapes I used to design this character bust.

**Design Silhouette**
The silhouette or outline of the character is important as it is one of the first things the mind registers about the character. It should be bold and striking to create an immediate impact.

**Basic Forms**
Any complex shape can be broken down into its basic forms. Here you can see this alien is an oval shape stacked on top of an inverted trapezoid.

*Figure 2.39: This image illustrates the interplay of angles in this character head.*

With the Standard brush, I sketch in some negative spaces in the temple area and deepen the large ear wings. These large auditory organs are photosensitive and translate color into sound. This alien being can actually hear the harmonies of color around us. This kind of organ is a complex construct, and I suggest these kinds of complexities with narrow pits along the side of his head (Figure 2.42). Using the Standard and Inflate brushes, I further refine these forms and add radiating lines from the pits out along the wing shapes on the sides of the head.

*Figure 2.40: Face folds sketched in. The overlay shows the flow.*

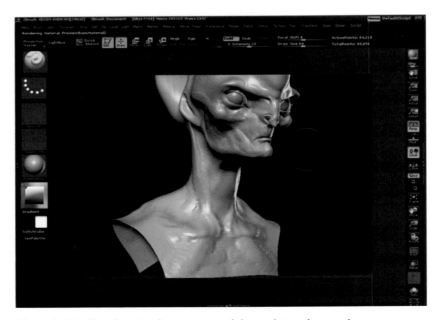

*Figure 2.41: Sketching in the anatomy of the neck in a few strokes*

This structure is inspired by the abstract form of a clamshell, but the organic function of these lines represents rows of photosensitive cells that gather color information from the creature's surroundings. You will notice I also add a more natural-looking ear shape where the human ear might be found. This is shaped using the Standard and Inflate brushes. I add this more traditional ear structure to keep the head from looking unpleasantly odd (a humanoid head lacking any kind of ear shape might be unusually truncated on the sides of the head) and to suggest that the character is capable of hearing sounds as well.

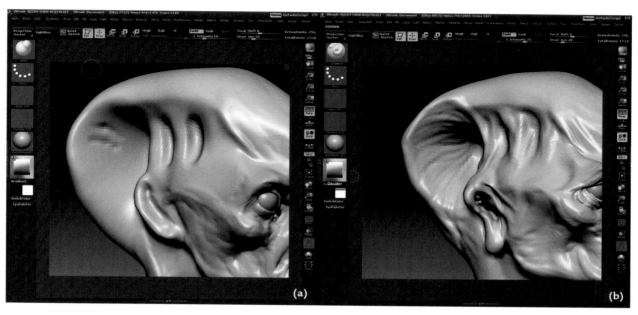

*Figure 2.42: Etching in narrow trenches on the sides of the head for the auditory organ of the head. Figure b shows the ear itself further refined with the Inflate brush to create the shape of the lobes.*

At this stage, I want to give the flesh of the face more character. To do this, I will sketch in a pattern of wrinkles freehand. I will use these wrinkles to follow the overall flow of the face to suggest the kinds of expressions the character makes by defining where the skin is folding from use. Select the Standard brush and Alpha 01 for this wrinkle pass. Sketch in lines that radiate out from the mouth as seen in Figure 2.43. Use the Inflate brush with a low ZIntensity setting on the spaces between the lines to pucker up the mesh into folds of flesh.

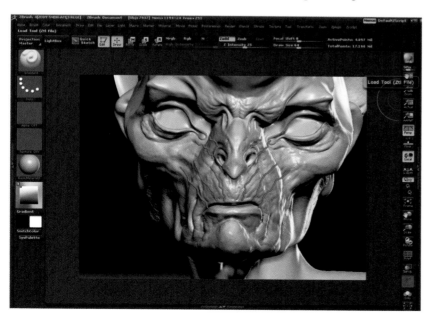

*Figure 2.43: Sketch in the wrinkles of the face with the Standard brush.*

I now stretch the eye shape further by changing the shape of the tear duct, or medial canthus (Figure 2.44). By elongating and enlarging this shape, I can change the size of the eye without changing the eyeball. It's also a way to make the eye seem more alien while retaining human characteristics. This is essentially accentuating and misshaping human anatomy, unlike the next step where we add new anatomy.

At the bridge of the nose, I add a new nasal structure. This is actually a somewhat subtle addition, but these extra breathing passages are not at all human. They introduce an entirely fantastic element to the face, and I like how they are subtle enough that they may slip past the initial viewing (Figure 2.45).

Figure 2.44: *Elongate the medial canthus of the eye to give it an otherworldly feel.*

Figure 2.45: *The new nasal structure*

## The Final Design

The design sculpt is now complete. I chose to offset the head and shoulders to give a sense of attitude and make the image more interesting before I paint over it in Photoshop. This character represents my interpretation of the design brief, a slightly menacing, highly intelligent alien. This creature has highly developed chromasensitive wings on his head that translate color wavelengths to sound. This allows him to hear color and, therefore, combine his superior vision with his ability to hear and locate objects and individuals via color sound—an interesting take on evolved senses.

We will now move on to another design problem. This chapter has set down many of the basic tenets that will inform the rest of our decisions in the book. We will consistently refer back to the concepts and ideas put into practice in this lesson.

Figure 2.46 shows the final design with color applied and post processing in Photoshop. I have included the layered PDF files on the DVD or download files for this book for your reference as well as the ZTools. We will now move on to a full body character. This next design we will take from sculpt to pose, and all the way to final painting!

## DVD Bonus Content

As a bonus for Chapter 2, please see the DVD or download files, where I have included ZTools, Photoshop files, and videos on the creation of my Centipede Magus image (Figure 2.47). It was originally offered as a Gnomon Master Class. I have included materials to help you understand the creation process using many of the same ideas and concepts from this chapter from initial concept through to final painting.

*Figure 2.46: The final design sculpt with Photoshop paintover*

*Figure 2.47:  See the DVD or download files for extra materials on the Centipede Magus character design seen here.*

Always be thinking while you work, and whenever possible make changes for a reason. Have a clear idea in your mind of where you are headed as opposed to blindly moving shapes until it "looks right." Starting with a clear and basic graphic idea of the character will be a huge benefit to the process.

three

# The Interdimensional Traveler: A Full Body Character Design

**In this chapter we will design** *and sculpt a bipedal character. This character walks on two legs—upright like a human— but we want to make sure that, even though he is a biped, his nature is entirely alien to human. As we talked about in Chapter 1, "ZBrush as a Character Design Tool," this design is a character more than a creature: he has personality and character as well as an internal life. This will be somewhat malevolent in atmosphere, but it is important that this design inspire awe and some trepidation rather than total revulsion or fear. We will look at ways to break convention in silhouette, proportion, and structure to create a character that is new and interesting within the confines of being humanoid in overall appearance.*

*This lesson focuses on how to manipulate the viewer's expectations by breaking the normal placement of humanoid features and proportions. By lengthening the figure and giving it a sweeping gesture, you create a beautiful form that is then contrasted with grossly emaciated forms and skeletal shapes, both of which inspire some degree of fear. These contrasts, combined with breaking the normal expectations of the figure, create a sense of trepidation in the viewer when looking at the design.*

*From a technical standpoint, we will look at how to adjust proportions, develop ideas quickly with the sculpting brushes, and add entirely new limbs to an existing model without having to rework the mesh. We will glue new pieces on to the model. Figure 3.1 shows the final character.*

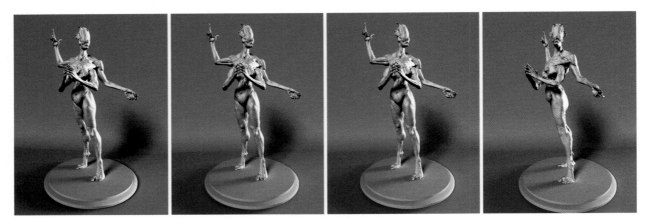

*Figure 3.1:  Here we see the final character after the sculpting and posing process as well as the finishing pass detailed in Chapters 4 and 11.*

## The Brief: Archon

The character we will create in this chapter is an interdimensional traveler called "The Archon." He is a high-ranking member of a caste of beings that travel between worlds, colonizing them for their own needs. His motivations are to promote the interests of his own alien race and therefore may run counter to those of humanity. He considers humans to be like cattle, and his awesome power combined with his aristocratic arrogance make a dangerous combination. The character should communicate regality and strength without being a brute or animalistic force. He is magical in his presence and uses his ability to manipulate space and time to subjugate the beings he encounters. Ancient cultures may have feared and worshiped these creatures as gods.

## Design Journey

The brief we just read contains much information about the character we are being asked to design. You will notice it is full of keywords such as *alien*, *powerful*, *regal*, and *arrogant*. These are points that will help us define the attitude and presence of the character though the design process.

You may also note this brief has no information about the visual look of the character. Briefs like this will be given when a director is interested in exploring a vast array of possibilities to find the best solution to his character. We call this process a *design journey*, and it involves traveling down various concept paths with the expectation that most of them will not be selected as the final design. Each one will give some insight into the best possible solution to the character design.

Even though there are no visual descriptions, we can intuit some elements from the director's description. *Regal*, *high-ranking*, and *god* imply a tall, muscular character, like Zeus, perhaps. Or maybe he is a valiant warrior who has battled his way to the top. Here is where you can choose to be creative. Try to find ways to confound your own expectations and instincts. If you immediately think tall, what happens if you try to communicate these traits in a small fat character? This is where the excitement and originality for design come in. In this chapter we will create a lithe, slender character that has the presence of a decadent king or a strange high priest. Remember, this is an alien that travels between dimensions. It is a perfect opportunity to twist the expectations of a human body in strange ways.

# Establishing Your Basic Figure

We will begin by considering the most basic aspects of the figure. These aspects are gesture, form, and proportion. I will often begin working on a character by thinking of the overall gesture of the figure. I will think about the attitude of the character and how it is communicated through his stance. I find that I can get into the mind-set of the character by standing up and assuming the posture or stance of the character. It is much like acting, and a good designer needs to be able to get into the head of his subject, to be able to assume its identity and communicate it to the viewer.

Proportion is another key element, especially in humanoid figures. A figure with an eight-head or ten-head proportion will appear massive while a six- or five-head figure will appear diminutive and small. The proportions of the figure can quickly lead the viewer to make all kinds of assumptions about the character, including its relative size, age, demeanor, and mobility. Variations in proportion can greatly impact how we view a character. A larger head-to-body ratio can appear less graceful and imposing while a smaller head-to-body ratio appears taller and, in some cases, more imposing. Later in this book you will see how a larger head-to-body ratio is used for the Forest Spirit character design in Chapter 8, "Sculpting the Forest Spirit." We touched on these topics in Chapter 1, but these concepts are so important that I would like to touch on them again here.

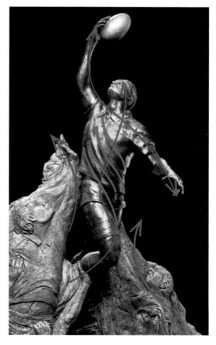

*Figure 3.2:  Here we see a sculpture of a rugby player with the gesture lines indicated.*

## Gesture

We talked about gesture in Chapter 1, and it has come up many times over the various projects. We will reference gesture a few times in this chapter, and many of the decisions we make will be informed by the desire to create an appealing gesture in the figure. If you have read my previous two books, the concept of gesture should be familiar. It is, in my estimation, one of the three tenets of sculpture: gesture, form, and proportion.

Gesture is the implied line or life of a figure. If you were to draw a line through a figure that represented its overall stance or thrust, this would be the gesture line (Figure 3.2). A poor gesture results in a stiff or lifeless figure. Figure 3.3 shows the final figure from this chapter with gesture lines overlaid. Notice how the gesture lines work even on a neutrally posed figure. In any position, the model needs to display some sense of life and spring in its limbs.

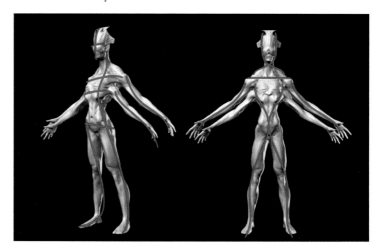

*Figure 3.3:  Here is the final figure with gesture lines overlaid.*

## Form

As we develop this character, we will be thinking of the forms he is composed of and how those forms interrelate. When we design a fantasy character, dealing with form is much different than when we work on a representational sculpture of a human figure. For this character, we are able to exploit the form language, the way the various shapes make the viewer feel. We can experiment with creative combinations of the shapes and push them in new and exciting ways. As we have already seen in previous projects, it's important to consider the character in its most basic forms and evaluate how those forms interrelate.

## Proportion

As we saw in Chapter 1, proportion refers to the relative sizes between the parts of a figure. Proportion is very important in this particular design as we make a conscious effort to move far away from human proportions to elongate this character to an extreme degree. These longer proportions communicate an elegance and grace and, when combined with the more menacing shape language of the head and bony anatomy, also malevolence or danger.

How will we know how to manipulate proportions to get effects like this? Well, we need to understand a baseline guide to human proportion first. When we have this as a fundamental measure of a "normal" human, we can then make educated decisions on how to break those rules. A fundamental measure is often referred to as a *canon*. A canon is merely a set of rules used to measure a figure. The human body has several, but one of the most popular is the eight-head canon (Figure 3.4).

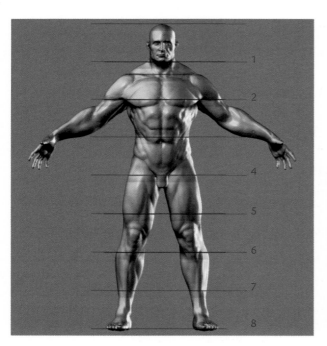

The eight-head canon helps you measure the figure by breaking it into eight equal head measurements. By knowing where each body landmark falls at each head measure, you can quickly and accurately construct a figure in a convincing proportion. The eight-head canon is popular because it is a very heroic proportion that results in a large body and long legs. There is a degree of elegance to the figure, and you often find this measurement used in comic book art.

Table 3.1 shows how to break a figure down into the eight-head canon and where the major landmarks fall in Figure 3.4. We will be using these measurements as a basis to depart from the form of the human body to create a more alien figure. For example, when we lengthen the arms, we will use the canonical rule that the body length equals the arm-span width to help us create an accurate-looking arm span. Figure 3.5 shows how the total head measure of the body also applies to the normal arm span of a human. By breaking rules like this, you can subtly or more drastically affect the manner in which a character is perceived.

*Figure 3.4: This image shows a heroic male figure divided into eight head measures. This is the eight-head proportional canon.*

**Table 3.1: Eight-head Canon for Figure Breakdown**

| Landmark | Head Measure |
|---|---|
| Chin | Head 1 |
| Nipples | Head 2 |
| Navel | Head 3 |
| Pubic bone | Head 4 (midpoint of figure) |
| Lower thigh | Head 5 |
| Bony protrusion of knee (tibial tuberosity) | Head 6 |
| Lower shin | Head 7 |
| Bottom of feet | Head 8 |

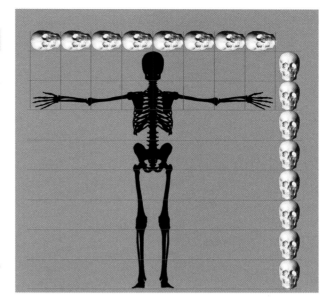

*Figure 3.5: Here you can see how the total head length of the figure also applies to its arm span.*

Understanding proportion allows you to break the rules in an educated way. For example, if you enlarge the head and hands of a normal-sized figure, the resulting proportion appears adolescent. If you enlarge them too much, they can start to feel childlike or even overly stylized. Knowing how proportions work allows you the freedom as an artist to manipulate them. This section will give you the basic information you need to understand the eight-head proportional canon. For more information on creating a full human figure in the eight-head canon, see my book *ZBrush Digital Sculpting Human Anatomy*.

## Roughing in the Body Proportions

We will begin this character by working in an existing human ZTool. This gives us the benefit of having the most basic forms sculpted in already as well as having a standard human form and proportion to start from (Figure 3.6). These will all be changed significantly in the final piece, but I always find it is nice to have a baseline to begin from that is more than a simple box model. This can greatly help in terms of speed if you need to get designs out quickly. I don't consider this a cheat, especially if you created the base models. I have included a basic human body model on the DVD or download files. This model is from *ZBrush Digital Sculpting Human Anatomy*. If you want to create your own, the entire process is there. The book also offers more information on human anatomy.

For this creature, we will be breaking and accentuating certain anatomical elements to give it a sense of emaciation.

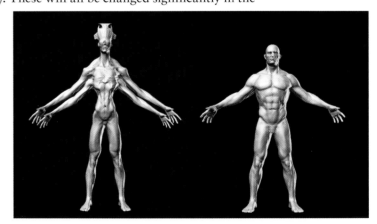

*Figure 3.6: The standard human model and the final creature together*

## Changing the Proportions

We will use a combination of the Transpose tools and the Move brush to shift the body portions on this mesh. Follow the steps below to start changing the shape of the human mesh into something far more alien. If you want more in-depth information on the Transpose tools, see my book *ZBrush Character Creation: Advanced Digital Sculpting*.

1. Load the human ZTool into ZBrush by opening the Tool menu and clicking the Load button. Browse to the human.ztl file on the DVD or download files. Draw the model on the canvas and press the T hot key to enter edit mode (Figure 3.7).

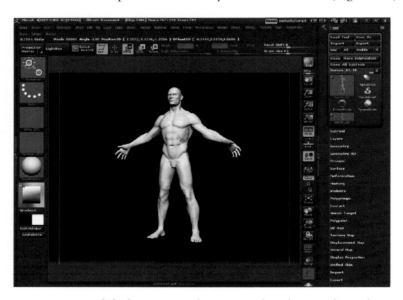

*Figure 3.7: Load the human ZTool into ZBrush and enter edit mode.*

*Figure 3.8: The Transpose Move button at the top of the screen*

*Figure 3.9: The Transpose brush is also found in the Brush menu.*

2. With the human model in edit mode, we are now ready to shift the forms around. The first and most basic changes come first. We know the figure will have a much more elongated proportion, so we will begin by stretching the central core of the figure as well as his arms and legs. Select the Move button from the top of the screen to enter Transpose Move mode (Figure 3.8). You can also enter Transpose Move mode by pressing the W hot key. Alternately, you could select the Transpose brush from the Brush menu (Figure 3.9).

3. We will use Transpose masking to mask the upper body from the lower body. Transpose masking works by pressing the Ctrl button and click dragging along the body. The mesh will mask based on the underlying topology. You want to mask the body from the waist up. If you need to manually adjust the mask, feel free to use the mask pen tool or the masking rectangle; both are under the Brush menu.

4. To stretch the length of the body, click and drag from the ZTool off to the background. If you hold Shift while you do this, the transpose line will draw in a straight line. Release the mouse and the key when the line is drawn.

5. Hold Shift again and click and drag in the center circle of the line. Because you are holding Shift, the movement will constrain to the axis of the transpose line. Move the lower body down, stretching the length of the torso. Compare Figure 3.10 to the previous image to see this effect.

6. We will now extend the arm length as well. Transpose mask the body so that the arms are unmasked. Again you can manually adjust the masking using the mask pen and rectangle brushes. Draw a transpose move line from the shoulder to the elbow. Once this line is in place, while holding Alt, click and drag in the circle at the elbow (Figure 3.11). This will lengthen the arm.

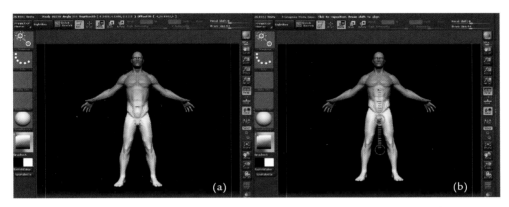

*Figure 3.10: Mask the upper body as in image A, then lengthen the torso with the Transpose Move brush as in image B.*

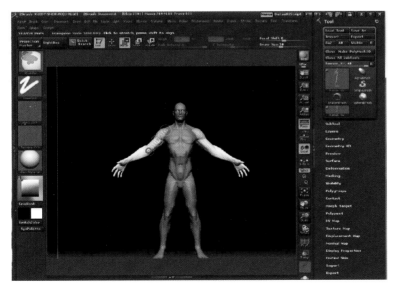

*Figure 3.11: Mask the body to isolate it from the arms to facilitate lengthening them. Then lengthen the arms using Transpose Move by Alt click dragging in the circle at the elbow.*

7. This stretches the upper arm but not the lower, so it will not complete the effect we want. I want to give the forearm a slightly longer proportion relative to the upper arm. To do this, mask to the elbow and use Transpose again to stretch just the forearm. Click at the elbow and draw the line to the wrist. Then click and drag the last circle to stretch the forearm (Figure 3.12).

8. The final effect is seen in Figure 3.13. Based on what we know about human proportions, we want the fingertips to fall almost halfway down the thigh. If you make the arms look too short, it will give the character a squat compact appearance, which is unappealing.

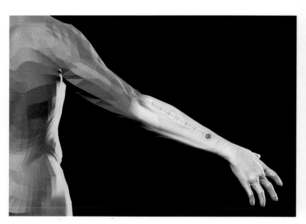

Figure 3.12: *Stretch the forearms by masking to the elbow and using Transpose Move to stretch the limb as in the previous step.*

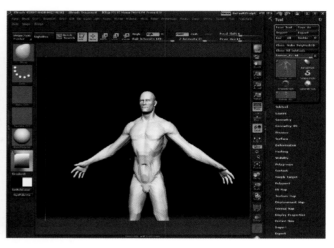

Figure 3.13: *The arms on this figure have been lengthened at both the upper and lower arm bones.*

A rule of thumb I use with my students in class is, when in doubt, elongate the proportion slightly because long limbs will look like a stylization where short ones tend to look like a mistake. This also works for the sizes of hands and feet. Common errors are to make hands and feet too small, which always looks like a mistake. If you make them slightly larger, it looks like a stylistic choice, and the view is far more forgiving. But do this within reason; you don't want all your characters to have cartoon character mitten hands!

## Accentuating the Bony Landmarks

In the next stage we will accentuate the skeletal landmarks to add a sense of emaciation as well as a jagged, angular skeleton beneath thin, leathery skin.

1. Use the select Rectangle or select Lasso brush to hide the arms so that you can see and work on just the central core of the figure.

2. Rotate to a side view and with the Move brush pull the points of the pelvis and ribcage forward, as shown in Figure 3.14.

I am pulling these points forward because they are common bony landmarks on the human body and important to note when trying to place the surrounding muscular and skeletal anatomy. Figure 3.15 shows these on a skinned human model. The hip points are called the anterior superior iliac crests, and the ribs represent the inferior border of the thoracic arch. Both can be seen on the skeleton in Figure 3.16.

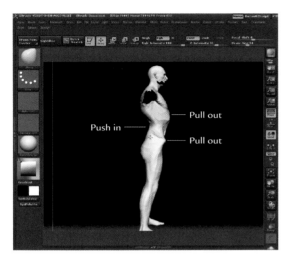

Figure 3.14: *Use the visibility rectangle to hide the arms so that you can work on the gesture of the figure's core.*

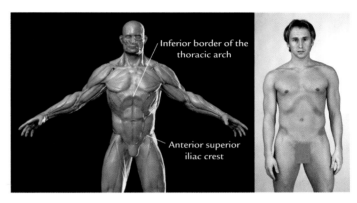

Figure 3.15: *The bony landmarks called out on a human figure*

People have a very sharp eye for human anatomy, even if they have no artistic training whatsoever. We know human bodies because we see them every day and live in one. This is why someone with no artistic training can see when something is "off" on a human model. Viewers have a sense of what looks natural, so they know when it looks "wrong" on your figure. The difference between a conscious decision to break proportion and a mistake is that decisions made on the proportion will be harmonious with the rest of the figure in terms of its overall look of the character. A mistake will not work in concert with other elements of the character design, which is why it sticks out to the viewer. Mistakes are not decisions, so they do not combine harmoni-

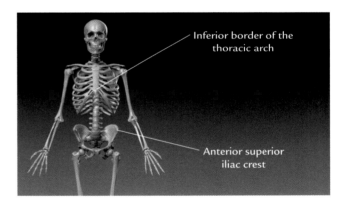

Figure 3.16: *The bony landmarks on a skeleton model*

ously with the other design choices. If you make a conscious decision to break with the rules of anatomy, this decision tends to be reflected and harmonious with the design. For this reason the viewer will accept them.

For example, people will typically recognize that the skeleton is close to the surface at the points of the pelvis we just sculpted, even if they do not know the name of the part of the skeleton they are seeing. By pulling these bony landmarks forward, it creates a jagged, aggressive quality to the very physiology of the character. We have taken points on the skeleton that the viewer will remember seeing on a normal body and pulled them out to create a sharp, aggressive shape. Psychologically, this creates a sense of surprise in the viewer because he expected those points but not in that shape. This effect is further compounded because the shapes created are aggressive ones as opposed to rounded softer shapes that communicate less aggression. I also use the Move brush to tuck in the lower back, giving the waist a very narrow wasplike quality. This gives the impression of a more emaciated figure with a more prominent skeletal structure.

At this point I decided to adjust the gesture of the figure to give it a more sweeping S-curve. Mask the torso, and using Transpose, shift the hips forward (Figure 3.17). This gives the figure's stance a lithe quality leading with the hips. It is almost serpentine. To accentuate this, use Transpose Rotate to rotate the legs back from the hip and forward from the knee to create the S shape seen in Figure 3.18.

*Figure 3.17: Shift the hips forward with the Move brush.*

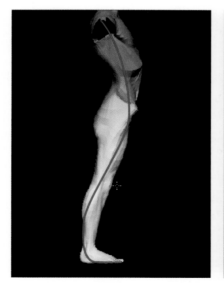

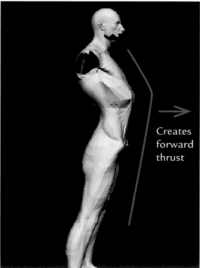

*Figure 3.18: Rotate the legs back from the hip and forward at the knee to create the S-curve seen here.*

*Figure 3.19: Here the shape of the ribs has been altered to give them more distinct character.*

I now use the Move brush to readdress the shape of the ribcage. It has gotten lost a little in the stretching, and I want to be sure the masses of the pelvis and torso remain intact. These give the long figure its sense of internal structure. Using the Move brush, I pull the thoracic arch out farther to create the sharp plane break seen in Figure 3.19. This is one of those jagged, aggressive shapes that both pulls the physiology away from human and subconsciously suggests aggression, or forward thrust, in the figure's stance.

At this point, I pull the hip bones of the iliac crest forward and narrow the waist (Figure 3.20).

In the process of stretching the legs and torso, the midline, or groin, of the figure has moved out of place. There is too much distance between it and the hips. Using the Move brush, I shift it back up. This has the effect of also lengthening the legs a bit more (Figure 3.21).

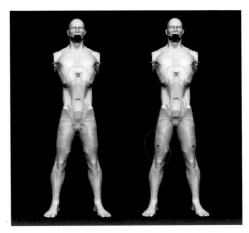

*Figure 3.20: Narrowing the waist and sharpening the bony landmarks of the hips and torso. By removing any soft forms, we add a more attenuated and disturbing feel to the anatomy.*

*Figure 3.21: Shifting the groin up lengthens the legs. In the figure on the left, you see the original groin position. In the figure on the right, you can see the effect of raising this point.*

Now we want to catch shadow in areas to suggest more attenuated sinewy muscle in the body. Select the Standard brush and at the midriff carve in some hollows beneath the thoracic arch to give the impression of tight-knit abdomen muscles extending down the torso (Figure 3.22). Again, this is based on real anatomy that has been pushed into a more extreme representation. As you can see in Figure 3.23, the abdominal muscles do indeed flow in the direction I am placing them on this figure. The idea is that I am suggesting the presence of the muscles by pulling out bits of shadow around them without having to completely sculpt the entire muscle. This helps to keep things a little more subtle. While working on the form, I will often switch to the BasicMaterial2 material because it has a specular shine that I find makes it easier to judge form.

I decide I need to lengthen the legs again. Using Transpose Move, I elongate them (Figure 3.24). This change makes the leg length closer to the length of the arm from the pit of the neck to the fingertips. You can measure this manually using the transpose line. Click and drag from the pit of the neck to the fingertips and note the value at the upper left of the screen. Draw another transpose line from the groin to the toes and compare this measurement (Figure 3.25). They should be close to equal.

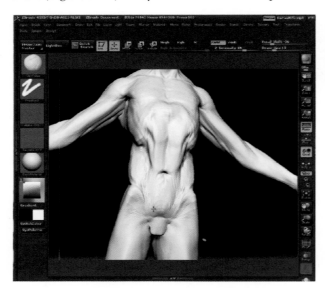

Figure 3.22: *Etching in the abdominal muscles*

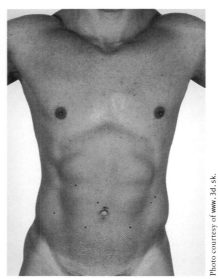

Figure 3.23: *Reference of actual human abdominal muscles*

Photo courtesy of www..3d..sk.

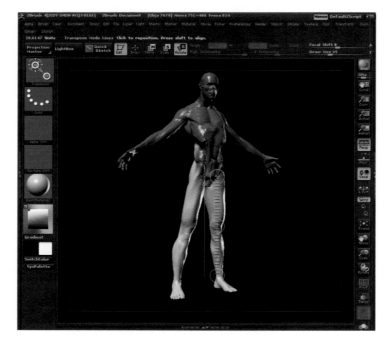

Figure 3.24: *Lengthening the leg*

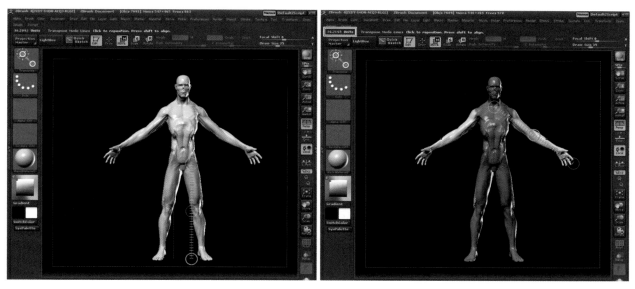

*Figure 3.25: Use a transpose line to compare the measurement from the groin to the floor with the measurement from the pit of the neck to the fingertips. The measurements should be close to equal.*

## Refining the Head and Face

At this point, we are ready to address the head in more detail. We will look for a sense of character in the head through the way in which its shapes interlock and relate to the rest of the figure. We will also look at ways to confound audience expectations and alter normal human features to create an inhuman and unsettling design.

Let's look at the head and face in more detail now.

### Position and Placement

I want to bring the head forward so that it continues the S-curve created by the body. As it stands, it sits too squarely over the shoulders. I want the stance to be more languid and long than that.

Use Transpose masking to mask the body from the head (Figure 3.26). Use a Transpose line to rotate the head forward, as shown in Figure 3.27. Note that I use the pit of the neck as my center of rotation. This is because I want to lengthen the neck, and rotating from here causes the least distortion to the neck and creates a more graceful length by extending the head out toward the front of the figure.

Remember, I want the proportions on this character to all be longer than normal. The distance from the pit of the neck to the chin is typically one-third of a head, but I will make it much longer here. When moving central parts such as the head, be sure to turn off X symmetry by pressing the X hot key. If you don't do this, you run the risk of separating the two halves of the head or making them collapse into themselves. This won't always be apparent when looking from the side view. When you have finished making the changes, turn X symmetry back on.

Using the Move brush, elongate the chin and the top of the head. I also accentuate the cheekbones using the Standard brush (Figure 3.28). The face will ultimately take on a cadaverous look, and the head will be quite longer than a normal human's. This stage is about moving the forms away from human toward something that borrows elements from the normal but carries them into strange combinations.

Step up a subdivision level and smooth out the eye details to create empty sockets. Using the Standard brush, I sketch in the nasal cavity and pull shadow out beneath the cheekbones (Figure 3.29). This is to suggest that the facial muscles extend from the cheekbones to the mouth (Figure 3.30). Again, this is playing on the human nature to recognize accurate anatomical structures on instinct. We have seen these shadows on human faces; seeing them here communicates that this is a thin, sickly body with a cadaverous face—unsettling combinations!

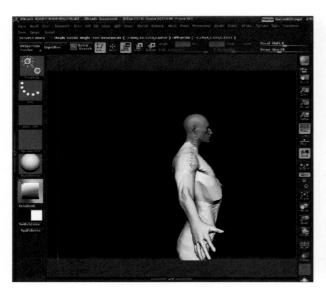

*Figure 3.26: Isolating the head with a mask*

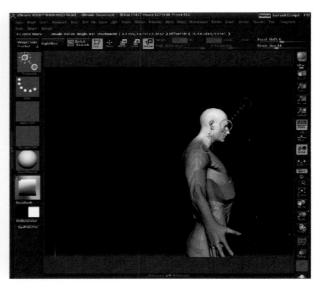

*Figure 3.27: Rotate the head forward.*

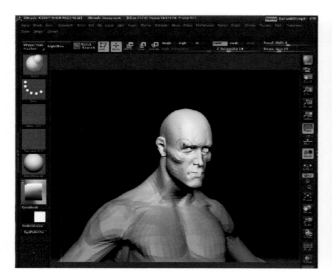

*Figure 3.28: Use the Move brush and Standard brush to alter the shape and character of the head.*

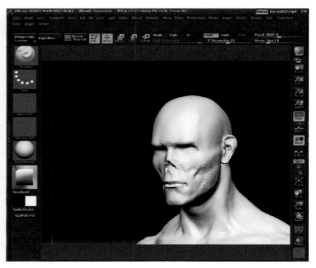

*Figure 3.29: Using the Standard brush to suggest facial anatomy. Overstating the bony structure creates a cadaverous look in the character.*

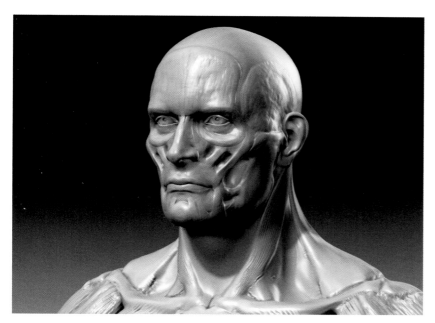

*Figure 3.30: The anatomical structure of this creature's face is based on the actual facial anatomy seen here. Note the way existing bone structure and muscles have been slightly accentuated to monstrous effect.*

## Creating the Head Crest

Now I want to create the head crest. I know that I want the shape of the creature's head to be tall and suggest the headdress of a bishop or a crown. This is to subconsciously reinforce the imposing, regal quality of the figure. Follow these steps as I build up the head crest.

Use the Move brush to pull the top of the head up (Figure 3.31). The shape I am going for should suggest a crown or a bishop's hat (Figure 3.32).

Use the Move brush to create the strange crest shape. This breaks up the form and gives it the feeling of an ornate headdress that is actually part of his anatomy (Figure 3.33). This is similar to the sagittal crest on the top of a gorilla's head (Figure 3.34).

In an attempt to make the character even more disturbing, I will remove the eyes. Because he is a god-like interdimensional traveler, it's unlikely he needs or uses normal senses the way we understand sight, sound, smell, and touch. Use the Clay Tubes brush to stroke across the bone structure of the eye sockets to fill it in

*Figure 3.31: Pull the top of the head up with the Move brush.*

with what looks like draped skin (Figure 3.35). This gives an unsettling effect because the presence of the facial anatomy suggests eye sockets but there is nothing in their place but draped skin. Again, we upset the viewer's expectation to create a strong reaction.

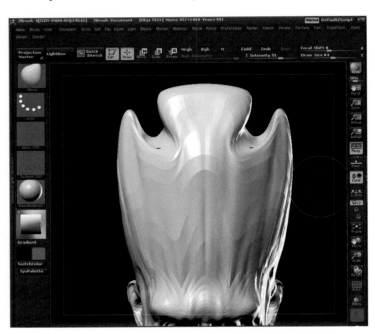

*Figure 3.33: Further shaping the crest of the head with the Move brush to create a more complex shape language*

*Figure 3.32: The head crest is based on the shape of a bishop's mitre. Using cultural references like this subtly suggests power, royalty, and solemnity to the viewer.*

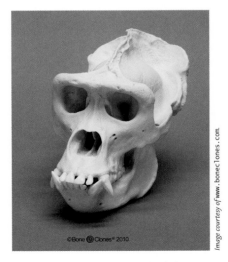

*Figure 3.34: This gorilla skull shows a pronounced sagittal crest.*

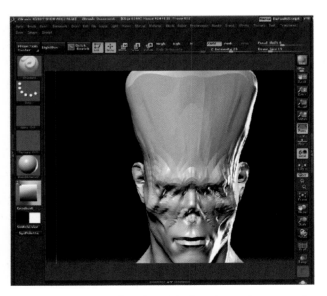

*Figure 3.35: Using the Clay Tube brush, stroke across the eye sockets to fill them in.*

We will now add teeth to the head using a SubTool. This is so that there will be teeth inside the mouth if we decide to give the face some expression later. I have included a ZTool of teeth gums and a tongue made by Jim McPherson on the DVD or download files.

From the Tool menu, load the teeth ZTool. When the teeth are loaded into ZBrush, they will appear on the canvas in place of the figure. Open the Tool library from the Tool palette and select the figure to return to the model. Now that the teeth are loaded, you can add them to the figure as a SubTool by selecting Tool then SubTool and then Append (Figure 3.36).

Use the Transpose Move and Scale tools to shift the teeth into the head. Scale them down with Transpose Scale so that they lay inside the mouth cavity (Figure 3.37). You may find it is easier to make precise movements of the teeth if you temporarily turn off Perspective with the P hot key.

*Figure 3.36: Appending the teeth ZTool into the model*

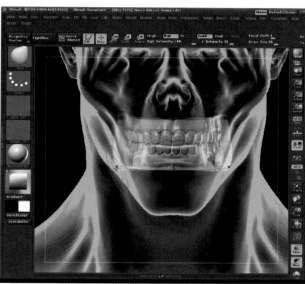

*Figure 3.37: Move the teeth into the head. Turn on Transparency to place the teeth accurately inside the head geometry.*

## Using Topological Masking

Now we want to open the lips slightly to expose the teeth. We will use the Move Topological brush to accomplish this task (Figure 3.38). You may notice that if you try to move the lips with the normal Move brush it will grab all of the faces under the red brush falloff circle, making it impossible to separate the two lips. The solution to this is to use a special variant on the Move brush called Move Topological. Move Topological will move the underlying faces with a falloff based on how close the faces are topologically instead of just moving all of the faces under the brush falloff. The model in Figure 3.39 is colored to show how the falloff of the Move brush compares with the falloff of the Move Topological brush. Follow these steps to use the Move Topological brush.

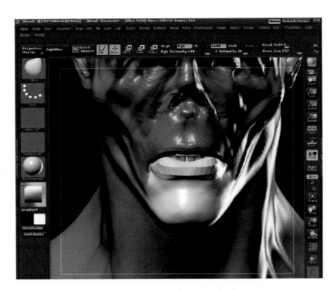

*Figure 3.38: Open the lips slightly with the Move Topological brush to reveal the teeth.*

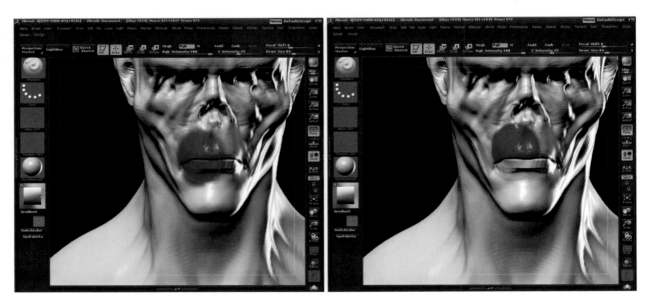

*Figure 3.39: The falloff of the Move brush compared to the Move Topological brush is illustrated with this colored region. Notice how the opposite lip remains unaffected by the Move Topological brush.*

1. Select the Move Topological brush from the Brush palette in the main Brush menu at the top of the screen.
2. Open the Auto Masking submenu and set the range slider to 0.5 (Figure 3.40). The range slider controls how much of the mesh will be affected by the Move Topological brush. This value may be different, depending on your model scale.

**3.** Click and drag the lower lip. You will find it moves just those faces close to the center of your brush that are topologically near to the falloff zone. This allows you to move the lips independently of each other. This can be used in any tight areas of the mesh such as the eyes and ears and between fingers and toes. Here we see the lips open with the teeth partially exposed (Figure 3.41). When using Topological masking on any brush, be sure to step to a lower subdivision level: the action of the brush is slower on dense models because ZBrush needs to calculate the topology of the surface with every stroke.

*Figure 3.40: Setting up Topological masking*

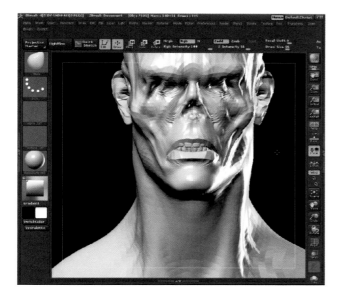

*Figure 3.41: Opening the lips*

## Continuing the Head Crest

At this point I feel the silhouette of the head is drab and needs to be revisited. Using the Move brush, I mask out a strip of faces behind the existing head crest structure.

**1.** Use the Move brush to pull the faces up as seen in Figure 3.42.

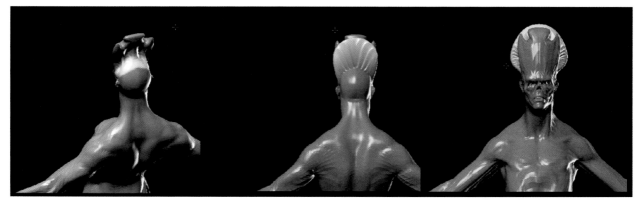

Isolate a strip behind the crest    Pull the unmasked faces up    This new crest addition seen from the front view

*Figure 3.42: Isolate a strip of mesh behind the crest with a mask, then pull the unmasked faces up.*

2. Rotate to a front view and pull the faces out into an oval shape that extends out for the outline of the front form. Shape the top of this crest into a T shape, as seen in Figure 3.43. This adds more visual interest to the crest by introducing an interesting interplay between positive and negative space.

3. I continue to refine the shape by moving parts to overlap the silhouette in interesting ways (Figure 3.44).

4. Use the Masking Pen brush to create some vent shapes down the edges of the crest. These could be hearing or some other sensory organs developed for the spaces between worlds in which these creatures dwell (Figure 3.45).

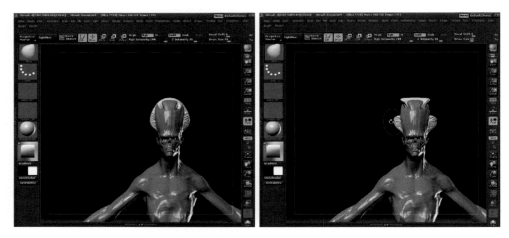

*Figure 3.43:  Further refining the shape of the crest into more complex shapes. Here we explore more contrast between positive and negative spaces in the head crest.*

*Figure 3.44:  Further refining the crest shapes*

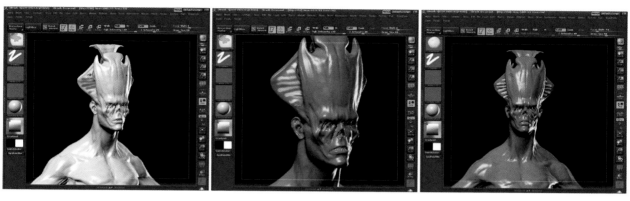

*Figure 3.45: Drawing mask lines on the sides of the head to push in vent shapes*

5. Now I make a bolder statement with the eye sockets and fill them in entirely. This creates an interesting interlocking form between the sagittal crest and the facial structure.

6. Select the Clay Tubes brush and turn off the Alpha (Figure 3.46). I fill in the eye sockets (Figure 3.47) and build up the resulting form as seen in Figure 3.48.

7. Using the Clay Tubes brush, I stroke along the head crest and bone structure of the face to unify the shapes and give the feel of skin stretching across the forms (Figure 3.49).

8. At this stage we have a figure with an extremely long, attenuated form. Up to now, we have yet to bring that same elongation into the hands and fingers. We will use the Transpose tools to lengthen the hands and give them a more graceful and slender appearance (Figure 3.50).

9. Use the Clay Tubes brush to build up the bony structure of the hands. Pick out shadow areas between the metacarpals. Metacarpals are the technical anatomical names for the bones of the hand or palm. The finger bones are called phalanges. This helps create a sense of emaciated skin over gnarled bone (Figure 3.51).

*Figure 3.46: The Clay Tubes brush with the Alpha off*

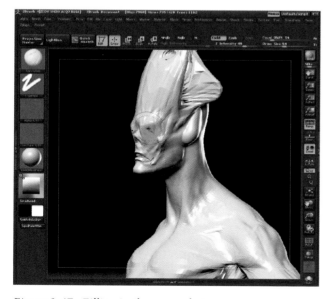

*Figure 3.47: Filling in the eye sockets*

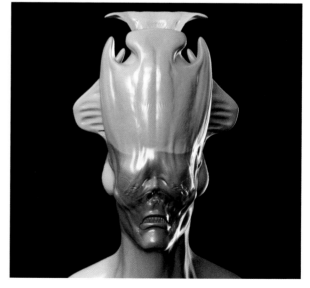

*Figure 3.48: Here you can see the individual forms of the crest, face, and eyes color coded. Notice how these shapes interlock together.*

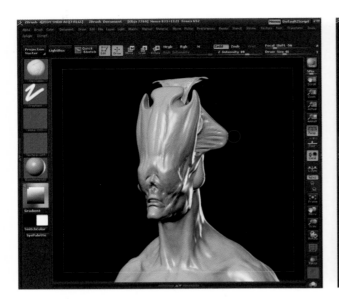

Figure 3.49: *The final filled-in eyes*

Figure 3.50: *Lengthening the hands to give them a more elegant quality*

Figure 3.51: *Here we see the gnarled hand sculpture after further detailing and posing.*

## Revising the Shoulders and Arms

Now we will make some changes to the shoulder girdle of the figure. This will include making alterations to the shape of the muscular and skeletal forms in the shoulder area. We will also be adding an entirely new set of arms later on, which will demand we have an understanding of how the anatomy of the shoulder functions; otherwise, we will not be able to incorporate the new physiology in a convincing and functional manner. Before we get too deep into these changes, let's take a look at what the shoulder girdle actually is and how it functions.

The shoulder girdle is the skeletal structure that allows the arm to move through its full rotational axis (Figure 3.52). It consists of the collarbone, the shoulder blade, and the upper arm bone. These parts are more properly known as the clavicle, scapula, and humerus (Figure 3.53). Without these skeletal components, no movement of the arm would be possible.

The shoulder girdle is manipulated by several important muscles. The most recognizable of them are the sternomastoids and trapezius in the front and the trapezius and rhomboids in the back (Figure 3.54).

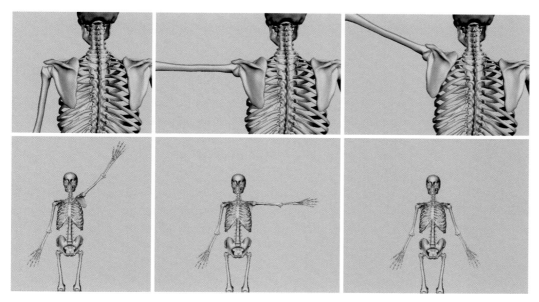

*Figure 3.52: Here you can see some of the range of motion possible with the shoulder girdle.*

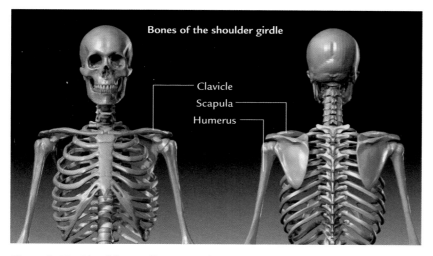

*Figure 3.53: Shoulder girdle seen in the skeleton*

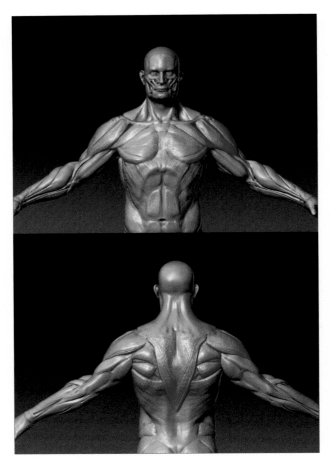

*Figure 3.54: The muscles of the shoulder girdle*

## Adding New Arms

At this stage I decide we need to break the silhouette even more daringly. I decide that such a long torso could support a second set of arms. This allows for a complex silhouette—breaking human forms. It also allows a character like this to perform more complex tasks with four limbs at his disposal. It implies the character has a different way of thinking and interacting with his environment and will allow for some striking performances on screen. On a subconscious level, this silhouette will suggest some ancient god forms that are depicted with multiple limbs. All of these elements lend themselves to the type of feeling I am trying to evoke in the viewer with this character.

There is a great challenge to adding a second set of upper appendages to a character. This applies whether you are adding a second set of arms or a pair of wings, which are very structurally similar to arms. The challenge is that any pair of arms requires a functioning shoulder girdle to be realistic physiological elements to the character. It's problematic when a design simply adds an arm coming out of the trunk of the body. This takes none of the complex anatomy of the shoulder into account and creates an arm that would never actually move and makes no physiological sense. As we have already seen, viewers have an innate sense of what appears to be anatomically viable. If your characters do not make some kind of physical sense, they will never be as convincing or compelling as characters created with attention paid to the underlying anatomical structure.

To compensate for this we need to determine a logical way to attach the arm to the body. Figure 3.55 shows my solution to this issue. Notice how I created a new sweeping clavicle that attaches to the sternum and allows the pectoralis muscles of the lower arm set to insert along the lower border of the ribs. From the back view, a second set of scapulas is clearly visible. Details like this give the impression that there are muscles there to insert in the skeleton and make motion possible. Follow the steps below to see how I added these arms.

1. First we will duplicate the body ZTool. Under the Tool and SubTool submenu click the body SubTool so it is active and then click the Duplicate button (Figure 3.56).
2. This will create a copy of the body as a SubTool. Select this copy and use Transpose to shift it down slightly (Figure 3.57).
3. Remember in the first chapter when we talked about rhythm, contrast, and avoiding symmetry? To create a nice descending rhythm of scale and to avoid perfect balance between all four arms, I want to make the lower arms slightly smaller. This will make them appear subordinate to the upper arms and will help the viewer process the shape of the character and read a pair of arms as dominant. You will notice that when all

four arms are the same, the character somehow seems less interesting or appealing because there is less variety in the forms. The repetition in size of the arms also echoes the extreme tapering of the overall design, which goes from wide shoulders down to a drastically narrowed waist (Figure 3.58).

4. Use the visibility Rectangle or Lasso brushes to hide all but the arms. This brush is accessed by pressing Ctrl + Shift and click dragging a green show marquee around the areas you want to maintain as visible (Figure 3.59). You want to isolate just the arms from the duplicate body and then delete the hidden geometry. Notice in the image that I have Transparency on for clarity so that the main body SubTool appears transparent.

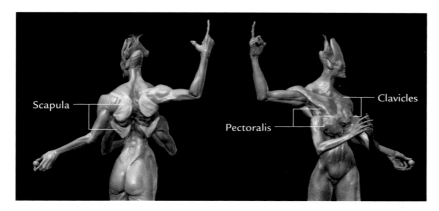

Figure 3.55: *Here you can see how I address the anatomical demands of a second set of arms by integrating the pectoralis and clavicles into the ribcage. From the back view, a second set of scapulas can be seen as well.*

Figure 3.56:
*Duplicate the body ZTool*

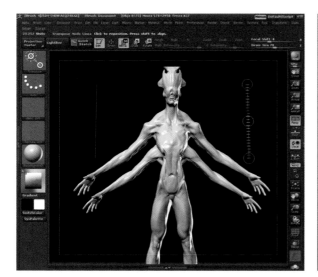

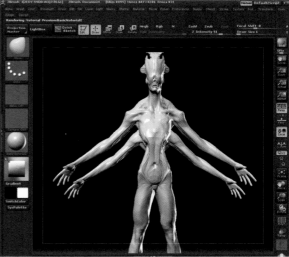

Figure 3.57: *The duplicated arms are moved down with the Transpose Move tools.*

Figure 3.58: *Scaling down the extra arms with Transpose Scale.*

5. Using the Transpose tool, shift the arms forward so that they fall in the middle of the abdomen and just forward from the upper arms in side view (Figure 3.60). You may want to use the Move brush to gently shift the shape of the shoulders to fit into the volume of the body. You want the front of the chest to fall on the front of the ribcage and the back of the new figure to fall near the back of the main body.

6. Lastly, we will push the shapes of the shoulders to be a little more stylized and extreme. I want the silhouette here to be less humanoid. I will accomplish this by accentuating the bones of the shoulders where the scapula and the collarbone meet: this is called the acromion process (Figure 3.61). With the Move brush, pull these bony landmarks out and raise the trapezius (Figure 3.62).

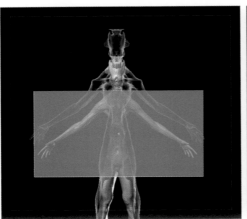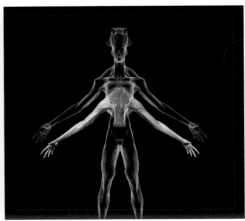

*Figure 3.59: Hiding the body from the duplicate arms so that only the arm geometry is visible (the original body SubTool is transparent in this image)*

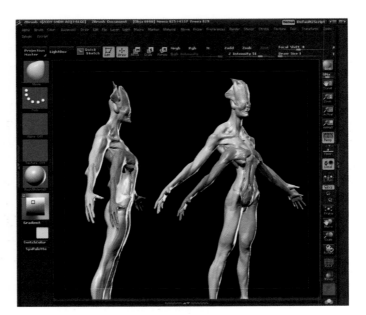

*Figure 3.60: Shift the new arms forward and use the Move brush to conform them to the shape of the lower ribcage so that they appear to attach.*

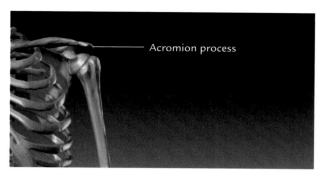

*Figure 3.61: The acromion process*

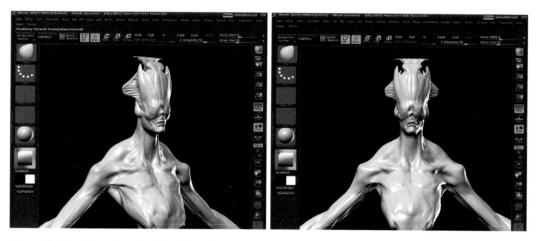

*Figure 3.62: Changing the shoulder shapes*

Giving the trapezius a more angular overall shape creates a large diamond shape from the upper body silhouette (Figure 3.63). This large diamond becomes a striking, iconic aspect of the character's overall look. Figure 3.64 shows the back anatomy.

*Figure 3.63: The shape of the trapezius in silhouette creates a strong diamond configuration.*

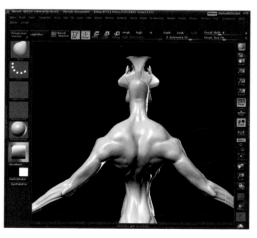

*Figure 3.64: The anatomical structure of the creature's back*

## Attaching the Arms to the Body

As it stands, the arms are just a SubTool sitting inside the body ZTool. We will want to "glue" the two SubTools together so that we can sculpt across the transition between the two models. This will allow us to effectively blend the shapes together and can be accomplished in two ways. The first uses the InsertMesh button to maintain your current ZTool, its topology, and its subdivision levels while blending the separate arm meshes into the sculpture. The second technique uses the new ZBrush 4.3 Dynamesh and InsertMesh brush technique. The drawback to this second approach is that you will lose your topology and your subdivision levels. The benefit of the second technique is that the arms and body will be joined together into a new mesh. I will demonstrate the Insert Mesh technique here, and we will use the InsertMesh brush technique to add geometry to our figure in Chapter 10, "Rendering The Enforcer."

1. Make sure the secondary arms and the main body still have the same number of subdivision levels. Both should be at the highest level.
2. We want to delete the hidden parts of the secondary arms to save geometry to sculpt on later. Select the secondary arms and mask them by Ctrl click dragging a mask marquee around the whole model (Figure 3.65). This is necessary because we will be deleting hidden faces. If you do this without masking the higher subdivision level, ZBrush will sometimes lose details from your mesh. The mask effectively frees the details while you delete hidden faces.
3. Step down to the lowest subdivision level and press the Tool ➢ Geometry ➢ Delete Hidden button to remove the hidden faces. ZBrush will preserve your details and your subdivision levels while deleting the unused body from the secondary arms (Figure 3.66).

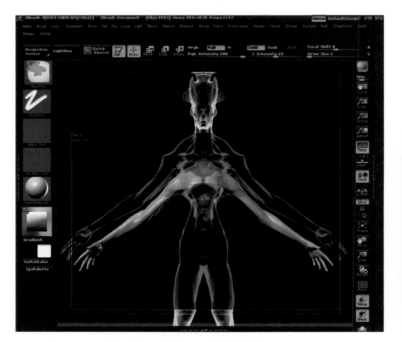

*Figure 3.65: Drawing a masking marquee around the secondary arms (transparency is on)*

*Figure 3.66: Delete hidden faces on the second set of arms to permanently remove the hidden body geometry we don't need.*

**4.** Step the arms back to the highest subdivision level. Make sure your body SubTool is also at the highest subdivision level. In the SubTool menu, select the arms SubTool. This should be just above the body in the SubTool stack. Press the MergeDown button (Figure 3.67) and click OK on the dialogue box. This will merge the arms into the body SubTool while retaining all your subdivision levels.

*Figure 3.67: The MergeDown button*

---

It is important to note that when using the InsertMesh button, as we have done here, you are able to maintain your subdivision levels and the two meshes combine into a single ZTool. Notice that the two meshes are still separate models even though we can use the Clay Tubes brush to blend across the seam. When using the InsertMesh brush, you will create an entirely new Dynamesh model that essentially shrink-wraps itself over the body and the new arms. This means you have a single mesh but will also lose your subdivision levels and your original topology. We will look at the InsertMesh brush as well as Dynamesh in Chapter 10.

---

**5.** You can now blend across the seams using the Clay Tubes brush. Select the Clay Tubes brush. From the main Brush menu, open the Modifiers submenu and set the Brush Modifier slider to –20 (Figure 3.68). This value affects the depth and level of blending accomplished with the brush when stroking across two meshes, as we will do here. You may find that this value needs to be adjusted to get the best results. Stroke along the seams between the shoulders and the torso to blend the models together (Figure 3.69).

*Figure 3.68: The Brush Modifier slider is found under the Brush and Modifiers menu as well as in the Brush palette screen.*

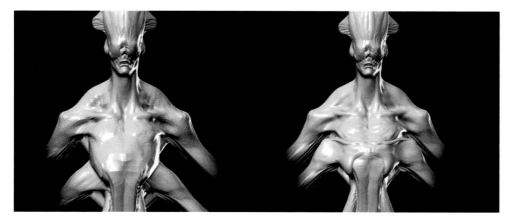

*Figure 3.69: The Clay Tubes brush can blend across the seam between two separate meshes when the SubTools have been merged into one.*

In this section we have seen how to use the InsertMesh button to add new geometry to our model while retaining detail, topology, and subdivision levels. In Chapter 10 we will look at how to add geometry using the new Dynamesh and InsertMesh brushes. Now let's move on to the final touches to this figure. Remember to check the videos on the DVD or download files for this chapter, as I have recorded the entire process of this character for absolute clarity. This way you can see each brush and technique in detail as it is used.

## Finishing Touches and Final Passes

In this last pass we will add some secondary form and some minor details to the figure. The purpose of these smaller details is to add a sense of attenuated muscle anatomy to the figure. We want it to feel like skin stretched over muscle and bone with little to no body fat. We will add some general final details, but this is really just to catch highlights in the specular shader and add interest to the form. Many of these steps are illustrated in the video on the DVD or download files. I will call out a few details that I think are the most important. Follow these steps to accentuate some of the anatomical forms of the model.

I want to suggest the ribs beneath the skin of the torso. Select the Standard brush with Alpha 01. Dial back the ZIntensity and sketch in a few depressions to suggest the ribs where the skin is stretched over the bony forms (Figure 3.70).

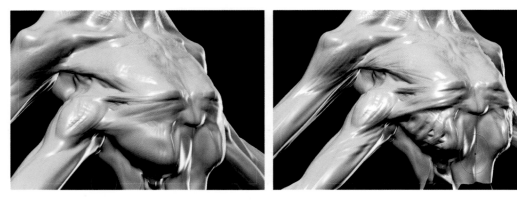

*Figure 3.70: Suggesting the ribs with the Standard brush and ZSub*

Rotate to the back view. With the Standard brush and no Alpha, I deepen some of the shadow areas around the scapulas (Figure 3.71). I also add the cervical vertebrae from between the shoulder blades and continuing up the neck (Figure 3.72). I don't spend much time here because I know the illustration will be of the figure from a front or three-fourths view. I do know we will revisit this model for a 3-D print, so I am careful to give some attention to the back view now.

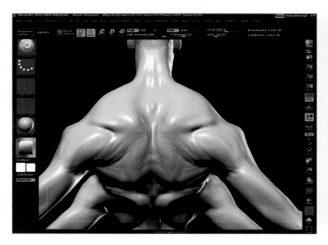

*Figure 3.71: Refining the shape of the scapulas*

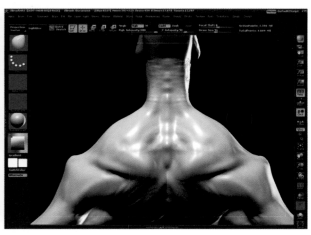

*Figure 3.72: Adding the cervical vertebrae*

Zoom into the face and use the Sandard brush with Alpha 01. Dial down your draw size to about 25 and loosely sketch raised wrinkles all around the mouth and eye areas. Try to keep these lines gestural and loose. The idea is to create the impression of raised tissue wrinkles in the skin, like wet tissue paper over bone (Figure 3.73). You may continue these wrinkles down the neck.

A quick way to add raised wrinkles like this to select Alpha 58. Figure 3.74 shows Alpha 58 applied to the model surface with ZAdd on. This helps create a fine crosshatching wrinkle pattern of raised rather than recessed lines.

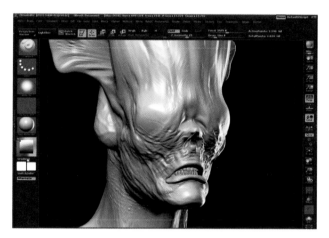

*Figure 3.73: Using the Standard brush and Alpha 1 to freehand sculpt a wrinkle pattern on the face*

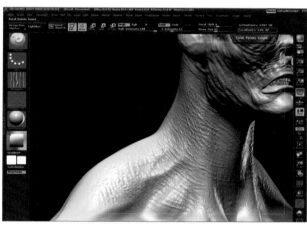

*Figure 3.74: Using Alpha 58 to create a fine wrinkle pattern*

Now we will add an overall noise pass to the skin. Do not get lost in sculpting details on this model. The idea is to communicate the concept of a character; details will never sell a concept. If it's an integral detail such as scaly skin or a certain type of skin texture, that's fine; otherwise, try to keep your surface generally detailed and remember we will be adding a lot in Photoshop in the next chapter. As long as the secular surface is broken up and does not appear plastic, this will be fine (Figure 3.75). A noise pass usually suffices to cover this. There are two ways to detail the figure, manually with brushes and automatically with the noise function. See the DVD or download files for a video detailing both approaches. In this section we will quickly add some noise with the ZBrush Noise Maker plug-in.

To add noise to the figure, first determine whether you want an overall noise pass or just want to add noise to specific areas. You can mask any area you do not want to be affected by the noise. This is

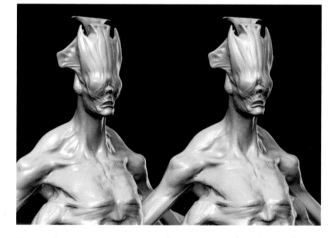

*Figure 3.75: Noise pass on skin compared to the undetailed plastic look of skin*

helpful if you want a larger noise pattern on the body and a finer one on the face. We will add an overall noise pass to the figure as a whole.

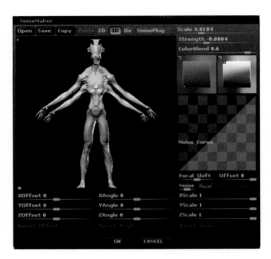

*Figure 3.76: The Noisemaker tool allows you to add finely controlled noise to your character's skin.*

1. Step up to the highest subdivision level of the figure.
2. Open Tool and Surface and press the Noise button. This will open the Noisemaker tool for ZBrush. In the Noisemaker menu, you can finely control all aspects of the surface noise (Figure 3.76).
3. Set the Scale value to 3.91 by adjusting the slider. The value need not be exact: you can judge the effects from the preview window.
4. Set the Strength slider to –.0004. If you want to zoom into the preview window, click in the upper right corner of the window. You can also rotate the model to get a better view by clicking inside the window. When you are happy with the look of the noise, click OK.
5. The noise will now display in the ZBrush document window. This is a rendering effect, though, and not actually part of the mesh detail. To "bake" the noise in as sculpted detail, press Tool, Surface, and Apply to Mesh button. The noise will now be applied to the highest subdivision level. If you lose detail or the noise is not crisp enough, you may need to undo, add a subdivision level, and try again.

That completes this section on designing the biped character. We have looked at how to interpret a character brief and how to break humanoid anatomy into new and surprising forms. We have also looked at some technical processes for adding entirely new parts to the model without losing details or subdivisions. We will now move on to Chapter 4, "Posing the Interdimensional Traveler," where we will pose and render passes from ZBrush that we will then use as a basis for illustrating the character in Photoshop.

Before we move on, I'd like to share some thoughts from a good friend and incredible artist, Zack Petroc. Zack has been a huge influence on my work as an artist for years. Zack has been developing a graphic novel created entirely with ZBrush and Photoshop. I invited Zack to share some of the details of that process in this book to show some of the unique ways you can use ZBrush to illustrate creatures and characters.

# *Adaboy and the Saints of Alchemy:* A Sculpted Novel by Zack Petroc

*Thanks to Zack Petroc for contributing this section! In 2005, Zack, a model supervisor at Disney Feature Animation, opened Zack Petroc Studios, which focuses on the development of unique new content and one-of-a-kind training. The Studios' first independent project,* Adaboy, *gives viewers direct access to behind-the-scenes story development techniques, allowing them to follow along as the story evolves from concept to completed project.*

## The Story

Long before the Age of Enlightenment, in the secluded hamlet of Addletown, the orders of religion and alchemy shared a precarious but peaceful coexistence. A deadly explosion in a rogue alchemist's lab upset the balance and gave the church leverage to outlaw alchemy once and for all.

Thirteen years later, the alchemist's first son works to secretly rebuild the alchemical order. In an attempt to destroy these new elixirs of science and quell the uprising, the town's religious elders unwittingly unleash hordes of underworld creatures and the roving dead.

As their defenseless town is sieged, a ragged band of children escape into the surrounding forest. Led by Adam Lamarck, the alchemist's second son, the children must rescue their town. Placing their faith in the alchemist's untested weapons of science and the moral code of their upbringing, each child must choose between selfless actions and self-preservation.

## The Process

The team at Zack Petroc Studios is using ZBrush in the creation process of its first media output for *Adaboy*, a downloadable animated comic. For this example we'll be looking at the creation of the Rambouillet creature as it is revealed for the first time, entering the alchemist's lab (Figure 3.77).

*Figure 3.77: The sculpted comic panel revealing Rambouillet for the first time*

At the core of every new character is a design sculpt, the product of translating the 2-D designs and other inspirational references into a 3-D asset. It represents and communicates all the design intentions of your character. "It's important for us to block in the entire design in a low-resolution form to see how all the individual pieces relate," says Zack. "We don't want to get caught up in any details until we know the overall shape and design language is working" (Figure 3.78).

At this stage, quick poses are often done using Transpose Master and other tools in ZBrush to gain a feeling of how the character might act, as well as to test movement constraints due to the design or costume. If the story calls for your character to hold a sword over his head in several scenes, now is time to make sure your costume won't prohibit that from happening (Figure 3.79).

*Figure 3.78: The character design sculpt*

*Figure 3.79: Quick poses are created with Transpose Master to ensure that the design can fulfill the pose needs for the character.*

*Figure 3.80: The Rambouillet head retopologized*

Once the design is finalized, an organized and animatable mesh can be created to allow for better deformations and overall consumption in any animation pipeline (Figure 3.80). It is not always necessary and was not used for the images highlighted in this tutorial. It's an option that can be executed at any stage in development or when deemed necessary to allow the asset to be translated to any other media. For example, the same design sculpt is used to create a mesh suitable for feature film animation and a next-generation game. The requirements of these two different model types are extremely different, but both leverage the design sculpt to dramatically cut down on their individual creation times.

For use in the animated comic, the model is posed based on a storyboard sketch to match the action dictated by the boards. In this case, Transpose Master in ZBrush is used to move the Rambouillet into position and define its pose (Figure 3.81).

A similar "rough to fine" approach is used to develop the alchemist's lab based on design intentions and story needs. A polygon modeling software is used to create many of the low-resolution base objects. They are imported into ZBrush in groups, and a high-frequency detail pass is applied (Figure 3.82). Parts of the set that are outside of the camera's view are hidden to speed up render times.

The images are rendered in individual passes using ZBrush (Figure 3.83). Separating render passes allows for easier comping of the final image in Photoshop. The same render pass and Photoshop composite process is detailed in Chapter 5, "Painting the Interdimensional Traveler."

In Photoshop, the layers are combined to create the final image. A variety of layering options are used to achieve the desired effect. For example, shadow and occlusion passes are often layered on top of base color passes using the Multiply layer setting. Figure 3.84 illustrates the in-progress compositing of the individual passes.

Next, the text boxes, dialogue, and other effects such as atmosphere and lighting are layered in. When the desired integration of all the elements is achieved, the final image is flattened and ready to be rolled into the story. In the case of an animated comic, many of the individual elements are created separately and then layered in to allow for a variety of animation techniques to be applied through proprietary software and output as a downloadable app. The final image is seen at the start of this section.

Figure 3.81: *Rambouillet in pose on the digital set*

Figure 3.82: *The alchemist's lab set*

Occlusion    Highlight    Shadow    SSS Skin

Figure 3.83: *The render passes*

Figure 3.84: *The passes composited together*

# Posing the Interdimensional Traveler

In this chapter *we will take the design from Chapter 3, "The Interdimensional Traveler: A Full Body Character Design," and begin to render it in a compelling final image. We will learn how to use Transpose to pose the figure, how to use the Layers menu to store pose data, and how to use the TimeLine to store views. We will also look at the concept of the golden rectangle to help us plan the composition and find the best image dimension for the final presentation. In Chapter 5, "Painting the Interdimensional Traveler," we will look at how to composite ZBrush renders in Photoshop, using painting tools to add the final touches to the image.*

## Considerations in Posing

We will begin by looking at how to pose the figure from Chapter 3. The design as it stands is in a neutral pose. We will add some character and personality to the figure before we start the illustration. This is our chance to act with the figure. We will determine the character and his motivations and then communicate these in the way the character holds his body.

You will recall that this character should have a regal, imposing bearing. With that in mind, we can further hone the design. Jamie Beswarick, one of the most talented designers I have ever met, told me that a design maquette, or image, should represent your first encounter with a character. It should represent a moment that sums up the character's attitude and motivations. I try to remember this when I plan my illustrations. How might the first scene where the character is introduced look? What will he be doing? How will this figure be perceived by other characters?

In this case, I have chosen to maintain the regal grace we already explored in Chapter 3. I also chose to place the viewer below the figure to give him a more imposing air. When posing the figure, I maintained a sense of grace by continuing to exploit the S-curves, bending the joints and keeping a sweeping flow between the limbs (Figure 4.1).

## Lines of Action

As we create the pose, we need to remain aware of the lines of action, or gesture lines, in the pose. As you will recall from previous chapters, this is a fundamental consideration you want to keep in mind throughout the process of sculpting, posing, and establishing the final composition. It is important that the action lines of the pose flow in a pleasing way throughout the figure because they guide the eye into and around the image itself. Once you decide on a final pose and angle of view, you want to be sure those lines flow naturally and appealingly through the picture plane. Figure 4.2 shows a few examples of poses with the lines drawn in.

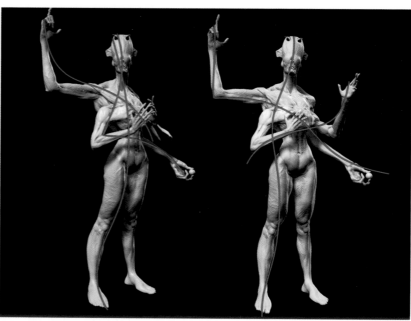

*Figure 4.1: In this pose you can see the sweeping curves implied by the limbs.*

*Figure 4.2: Here we see some pose options with the gesture lines overlaid.*

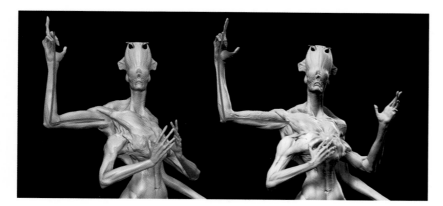

*Figure 4.3: Always try to avoid right angles as seen in the arm of the figure on the left. These tend to be static and uninteresting.*

Figure 4.3 shows a good example of something to avoid. While posing the arm I found I had created a right angle at the elbow. This introduced a hard edge in the pose and broke the rhythms I had established. You can see how I correct the right angle to give a more fluid gesture to the arm. Little subtleties like this can make a big difference in how the image reads to the viewer. An appealing design posed and presented in an unappealing way will undermine all your hard work and give it far less impact. A director or other creative decision maker will often only give your work a few seconds of attention. In these few moments, you need to make an impression.

## Tangents

Tangents are another consideration when composing the figure for the final illustration. Tangents are points where the figure crosses over itself or another object in the scene. You will recall from Chapter 2, "The Character Portrait: Sculpting the Alien Mystic," how important silhouette is in defining the character. Silhouette is also important in defining the character's pose. You want the pose to be clean in silhouette view. If it isn't, the viewers will have to stop and untangle the figure in their minds to understand what they are looking at. This will detract from the powerful initial read the viewer gets from the design. The first reaction will not be awe, but frustration and confusion.

Figure 4.4 shows a few poses in silhouette. Note the tangents of the figure's arms in some of the poses. You want to avoid areas where the arms intersect with the body and make the pose unclear. The circled areas represent areas of tangency. Pose D is the clearest because it shows the physiological structure of the creature without confusing the eye.

*Figure 4.4: Here you can evaluate some poses in silhouette.*

Before you pose the figure, you need a general idea of the angle of view you want for the final image. At this stage, we are ready to position the figure and prepare to render final images. I prefer to show the character in a three-quarter view. I find it best to avoid a straight on, front or side view, as these tend to be less dynamic and do not show the form of the figure particularly well.

In the following steps we will use the Transpose tools to pose the figure. For more in-depth looks at these tools see *ZBrush Character Creation* and *ZBrush Digital Sculpting Human Anatomy* or the video on the DVD or download files that come with this book.

1. I know I want to offset the limbs so that each pair is performing a clear action. I will begin by posing the upper right arm. I step down a couple subdivision levels so there is less geometry to work with. Posing at the higher subdivision levels makes it more difficult to control the Transpose tools.

*Figure 4.5: The Transpose Move icon*

2. I want to isolate the right arm by masking the rest of the body. The easiest way to do this is to use a Transpose mask. Press the W key to enter Transpose Move. The Move icon will now be lit at the top of the screen (Figure 4.5).

3. Hold the Ctrl key and then click drag down the arm. The mesh will mask the arm based on the underlying topology. You may need to further clean up the mask using the mask brushes.

### Brush Selection for Precision Masking

For precision masking you can use the Mask Pen or Lasso brushes. These brushes are selected from the Brush menu but are only accessible when pressing the Ctrl key. For example, you can select the Mask Pen brush to sculpt with any of the normal brushes, but when you press the Ctrl key, the brush will change to the mask pen. ZBrush has many brushes that are mapped to function keys. The smooth brushes, for example, are mapped to the Shift key, the masking brushes to Ctrl, and the visibility brushes to Ctrl + Shift. This means that you can be sculpting with any brush and then hold Shift to switch to your selected smooth brush, then hold Ctrl for your masking brush selection, and then hold Ctrl + Shift for the visibility or clipping brushes.

Select the masking brush you prefer from the Brush menu. To use this brush you will need to press and hold the Ctrl key while sculpting. The brush will convert to the masking brush you selected from the menu. When in masking mode, the cursor will become yellow. Press Ctrl to mask. Press Ctrl + Alt to erase your mask. Ctrl click on the masked area to soften the mask edges or Ctrl + Alt click on the mask to sharpen it.

4. When the arm is unmasked, make sure you are in Transpose Move mode (press W) and click drag to draw a transpose line from the shoulder to the wrist (Figure 4.6). Make sure the start of the line is at the center of the rotation of the shoulder and that the end of the line falls at the wrist. You can reposition the ends of the line by clicking and dragging *on*, not *in*, the endpoint circles or the line itself. Rotate the arm up as seen in Figure 4.7.

Click drag this circle     to rotate around this circle.

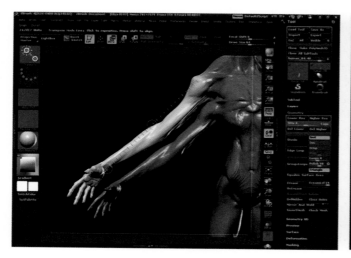

*Figure 4.6: The Transpose line is drawn from the shoulder to the wrist.*

*Figure 4.7: The arm is rotated up with the Transpose Rotate brush.*

5. Now we will rotate the elbow in a different manner. Click and drag from the shoulder to the elbow. For the elbow, we will bend the arm using bone posing. This is a built in skinning algorithm in Transpose that allows you to bend joints such as knees and elbows without causing the mesh to collapse. Hold Alt and click drag in the circle at the elbow to bend the joint. Notice that one side of the joint stretches while the other contracts. This prevents the mesh from collapsing and losing its volume (Figure 4.8).

Alt click drag this circle to bend the elbow naturally

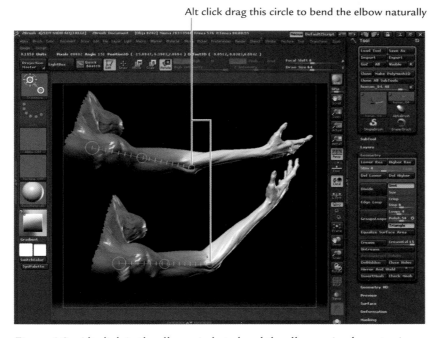

*Figure 4.8: Alt click in the elbow circle to bend the elbow using bone posing.*

6. The wrist can be posed using the same bone posing method that we used on the elbow. This ensures that the wrist maintains its volume while bending (Figure 4.9).

7. When working on the opposing arm, I decided to angle it down for contrast. Having both arms raised would create an equilibrium that is not what I am trying to achieve in posing this figure (Figure 4.10).

8. In figure 4.11, we see the fingers being posed. I decided to place a small object, in this case a sphere, into one of the hands. This allows the character to interact with an object and opens new posing possibilities to those fingers. The fingers are posed using bone posing for the most part. Be sure to rotate often as you move the fingers and use masks as you work.

9. Isolate the head from the body with a mask to rotate the neck (Figure 4.12). Draw a transpose line from the head to the center of the shoulders. Click and drag in the center circle to rotate the head around its Y axis. The process of posing the head requires a few variations of masking and Transpose. To see the process in detail, refer to the video of posing this character on the DVD or download files.

*Figure 4.9: Posing the wrist*

*Figure 4.10: Posing the opposite arm*

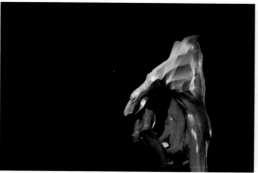

*Figure 4.11: Here the fingers are posed to lend an appealing gesture to the hand.*

## Posing the Secondary Limbs

The secondary limbs are posed in much the same way as the primary. The main difference is that I choose to group these in separate polygroups. This makes is easier to isolate one arm from the body and the other arm while I work. This is particularly important for the lower limbs because I will want them to cross over and interlock the fingers in some poses (Figure 4.13). To cross limbs over the centerline of the body and pose them in close proximity to one another I need a way to isolate the arms quickly and clearly from the rest of the body. See the video on the DVD or download files for the entire posing process in action.

At this stage the pose is ready for us to move on to compose the figure into a final image. We will make further adjustments to best serve the angle of view once the figure is placed on the image plane.

*Figure 4.12: Posing the neck*

*Figure 4.13: Here the arms cross the center-line of the body and the fingers intertwine.*

# Setting Up the ZBrush Document

Now we will set up our document and render image passes to composite and paint over in Photoshop. We will begin by creating a pleasing proportion for the overall document size by exploiting the golden rectangle. Then we will position the figure and use the TimeLine tools to store variations in angle to help pick the best view. As we position the figure on the picture plane, we will continue to consider how the lines flow through the pose and adjust the position as needed to get the best possible result.

## The Golden Rectangle: Ancient Secret, Timeless Tool

Before we position the figure on the canvas, we need to determine the proportion and resolution of that canvas. I avoid using the default ZBrush document because the resolution is too low for the best results and the overall proportion is not as pleasing as possible. We will resize the document to be a higher resolution and a more pleasing proportion and create a pleasing base document using a golden rectangle.

The golden rectangle has gone by many names: you will find it called golden section or golden ratio. The golden spiral is derived from its shape. It is one of the fundamental ratios of measurement in nature and has been a secret of designers, builders, and artists since the dawn of civilization. It is a powerful and often misunderstood tool. I hope to give you some insights in this section on how it can be applied to your work as a designer. While the golden rectangle is referenced often in graphic design, I rarely find examples of how it can be practically applied to other kinds of design—especially sculpture and figure studies. I hope to offer some examples here of how the rectangle can be used to help us proportion a figure and place it pleasingly on the image plane of an illustration.

In a nutshell, the golden rectangle is a rectangle that can be divided into a square and a smaller rectangle. The smaller rectangle has the same aspect ratio as the original larger rectangle. Figure 4.14 illustrates this. Here we see that the length of the smaller rectangle divided by its width is equal to the length of the larger rectangle divided by its width, a ÷ b = (a + b) ÷ a. The ratio of the larger to the smaller side of each rectangle is known as the golden ratio. This rectangular ratio is found in nature as well as in art and design. A 35mm film frame is very close to a golden rectangle.

The importance of this rectangle is that it provides an extremely visually pleasing ratio. This shape has been exploited by artists and designers for centuries as an internal measure for the relationship between parts of a figure or image as well as a basis for the proportion of the image plane itself. By composing inside a golden rectangle, many artists feel they are starting off with a proportionally beautiful window through which the viewer is asked to look.

It may seem like a strange thing to consider a simple ratio "beautiful." Keep in mind this proportional relationship is found throughout nature and was adopted by artists in the ancient world. They believed that perfect beauty was found in balance and harmony and that nature expressed the highest manifestations of this. By bringing the rules of proportion from the natural world into their work, these artists hoped to imbue their art with a touch of the same perfection they found in nature.

Remember that within any golden rectangle is a smaller golden rectangle, and within that rectangle is another, and so on (Figure 4.15). The smaller rectangle can be divided over and over to create an infinite nest of golden rectangles (Figure 4.16).

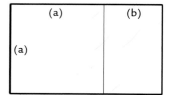

Figure 4.14: A golden rectangle in its simplest form

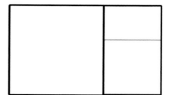

Figure 4.15: Notice how the golden rectangle contains another golden rectangle within itself.

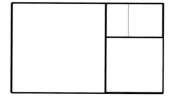

Figure 4.16: Furthermore, this second rectangle contains another copy of the golden rectangle.

This nesting effect is what gives us the golden spiral found in conch shells (Figure 4.17) and elsewhere in nature. This logarithmic spiral is called the *spira mirabilis* (Figure 4.18). This spiral can also be used as a tool to guide the placement and layout of elements in the picture plane. Figure 4.19 shows the arms laid out to fall within the spiral arm.

Figure 4.17: A golden spiral in nature

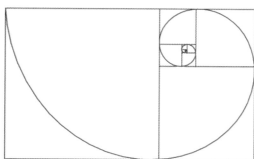

Figure 4.18: A golden rectangle with a nested rectangle and spiral in red

The most famous application of the golden rectangle to design is Leonardo da Vinci's *Vitruvian Man*. This famous image shows Leonardo applying the golden rectangle to the proportions of the human body (Figure 4.20). Here we see the height of the person was divided into two segments at the navel. By dividing the distance from the bottom of the feet to the navel by the distance from the navel to the top of the head, we get the golden mean. Renaissance artists sometimes called this number the *divine proportion* because of its presence throughout nature and close association with the depiction of beauty and proportional harmony.

 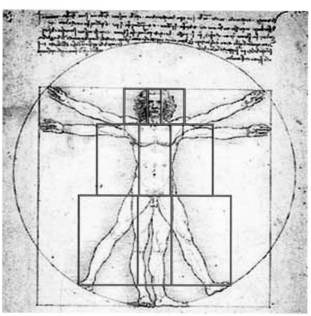

*Figure 4.19: The arms fall within the spiral.*

*Figure 4.20: Leonardo's* Vitruvian Man *illustrates the proportions of the golden rectangle found in the human body.*

The golden rectangle is found in the individual parts of the body as well. Figure 4.21 shows the ratio of measurement between the fingers of the hand. This is a 3:2 ratio. The 3:2 ratio is extremely close to the golden rectangle. I have overlaid the golden rectangle over a model of the human hand bones to illustrate this. Note how the smaller finger bone falls within the smaller proportion of the rectangle while the larger bone falls within the larger division. This ratio repeats up the bones of the hand. Try finding other instances of the golden rectangle in the human body.

The golden rectangle was originated by the Greek mathematician and philosopher Pythagoras in the sixth century BC. Since that time it has been seen in the work of various artists and architects throughout the ages. It seems that you can find applications of the golden ratio in just about any aesthetically pleasing layout, from the Parthenon (Figure 4.22) to the structure of faces in classical art (Figure 4.23).

All this begs the question, is this is a conscious decision on the part of the designer or is an intuitively created and successful design always going to follow the golden ratio? I don't think the answer actually matters. Some artists may well have an instinctual eye for pleasing proportions. Others (such as myself) need to learn from the masters and apply the techniques that appeared to guide their work. By being aware that the golden rectangle exists and represents a powerful design tool, we can exploit it in our own work.

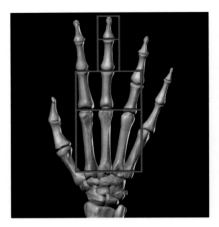

Figure 4.21: *The same nested scale of proportion is found in the parts of the body. Here you see it in the ratio of the fingers to the hands.*

Figure 4.22: *The golden rectangle is represented in the façade of the Parthenon.*

## Using the Golden Ratio in a Creature Design

So how do we apply this to our character? The most direct way to exploit the information we now have about the golden rectangle is to see whether our character's body can conform to this proportion. Figure 4.24 shows how the head fits perfectly into a golden rectangle, which is why the ratio between the facial mass and the head crest is appealing. Note how it is less successful when the proportion is changed so that the ratio between the face and crest is close to 1:1. You can check the body proportions and adjust as needed. Figure 4.25 shows the body of the character with golden proportions measured out.

Figure 4.23: *The face of the* Mona Lisa *is a contained within a perfect golden rectangle.*

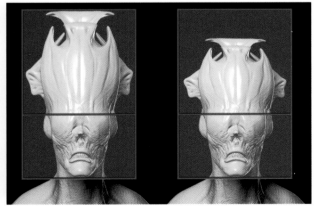

Figure 4.24: *Here the golden rectangle is applied to the character's head. Notice how the effect is much better when the ratio of the head parts fall within a golden rectangle.*

## Rule of Thirds and Golden Rectangle

A common compositional tool for creating a pleasing layout is known as the rule of thirds. The rule of thirds is derived from the idea of the golden rectangle, but it is not a golden rectangle itself. It is a quick way to create a pleasing proportion in most aspect ratios. The rule of thirds is often used in illustration and photography. This rule divides the picture plane into nine equal parts as shown in Figure 4.26.

When composing the image, make an effort to place objects of interest on the intersections of these lines. These intersections represent focal points for the image. This helps you avoid placing focal points in the center. We want to keep areas of interest outside the center for reasons already discussed in Chapter 1, "ZBrush as a Character Design Tool." Perfect symmetry and balance tend to be boring. The idea is that images composed in this manner will carry more dynamic tension than a perfectly centered composition.

Figure 4.27 shows the rule of thirds applied to an image. While the rule of thirds is not exactly the golden rectangle and will not result in the same composition, it is a close and quick approximation that is very helpful to many artists seeking a way to organize their image planes into dynamic compositions.

I hope this section has adequately explained the meaning and use of the golden rectangle. I have always been fascinated by this phenomenon in art and equally mystified by its application. Hopefully this section has helped to clarify how we can use this ratio in our work.

These are guidelines to help create better images. The idea is to understand and use them to your benefit—not to be shackled by them. As you compose your own images, you will sometimes have to adjust your approach based on multiple variables. For example, in my composition I needed to place the figure torso down the center of the picture plane. This was because of the highly complex multiple limbs and potential for

*Figure 4.25: The body with the golden rectangle overlaid*

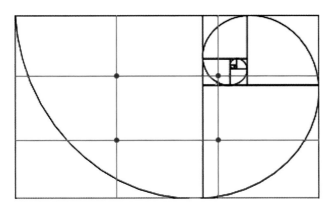

*Figure 4.26: Using the rule of thirds, the picture plane is divided into nine sections to help place points of interest.*

*Figure 4.27: Applying the rule of thirds to a composition shows how the elements are arranged (image by Paul Tobin).*

unappealing tangents. I balanced the pros and cons of each problem and decided that bringing the figure toward the center was acceptable because it allowed a more aesthetically pleasing arrangement of the limbs. I also feel the contrast between the multiple arms offsets any sense of balance created by a centered placement.

### Adjusting the Document Size

Using the golden rectangle to define our document size is a very simple process. We will create a golden mean document by changing the proportions to a ratio that represents a golden ratio. Follow these steps to create this document:

*Figure 4.28: Turn off constrain proportion.*

1. Go to Document and turn off Pro: this is the constrain proportions button. Set the document to 1600 × 2592 resolution. This is a rectangle in the golden proportion. I think you will find this allows you to create a very pleasing composition with a standing figure (Figure 4.28).

2. Disable the WSize button. This prevents ZBrush from resizing the document when you load the project again (Figure 4.29). Position the figure on the canvas and Save the project. You can upsize and downsize this document by clicking the Double and Half buttons under the Document menu (Figure 4.30).

*Figure 4.29: Disable WSize.*

## Placing the Character on the Picture Plane

Now we will look at some of the considerations when placing the character for your final illustration. This is a very important step because the position and pose you choose here will serve to either show off your hard work or hide it. You can ruin a good design with a poorly thought out composition.

*Figure 4.30: Double and Half buttons*

Remember to be aware of the silhouette and tangents as you place the figure. Figure 4.31 shows several poses in grayscale and in silhouette. The pose must be clearly readable in silhouette to be successful. These poses are unsuccessful because the areas of tangency confuse the figure. It is difficult to read how the limbs are related to the body and the pose. Figure 4.32 shows the two most successful configurations. There is tangency between the arms and the body in both options, but enough information is given from the elbow to the forearm to make these poses read easier to the eye. The rest of the limbs are extended from the body and have a clear action in silhouette.

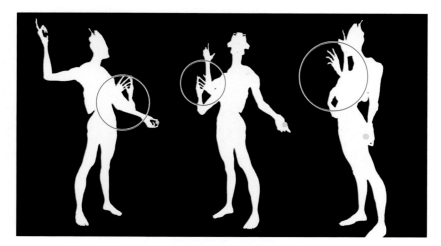

*Figure 4.31: Areas of tangency have been circled here.*

This concept of the first read has been revisiting us since the very early design. It is such an important aspect of design theory that it carries all the way through to animation. Animators will always evaluate the pose and position of the character I silhouette to make sure it reads clearly.

As you pose the figure, look for negative spaces and how they interrelate. In Figure 4.33, for example, you can see the triangular negative space created by the inside of the lower arm. This negative space shows the arm is bent and the elbow is away from the body. If I shifted the figure and lost this space, the pose would be less clear. These shapes will register to the viewer. It is part of the artist's job to be aware of them and in control of their presentation.

The area around the figure counts as negative space as well. Be sure to consider the overall outline space of the figure. In Figure 4.34 you can see how the negative space is just as important in defining the figure as the silhouette or positive space.

*Figure 4.32: A clear pose reads well, even in silhouette. Here we see two pose options that are the most successful.*

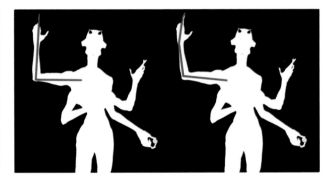

*Figure 4.33: Here you can clearly see the negative spaces around the shape of the arm.*

*Figure 4.34: The negative space around the figure*

*Figure 4.35: Note how the arm is improved by breaking the 90-degree angle and introducing more of a curve.*

While composing the image, be sure to keep the implied lines in mind. These are similar to the gesture lines of the figure. Figure 4.35, for example, shows the arm at a right angle. This creates an unnatural break in an otherwise organic form. Bend the arm out slightly to create an implied line that flows down the figure.

Also try to avoid parallel lines. Remember that symmetry can be boring as well as repetition of strictly vertical and horizontal lines (Figure 4.36). Try to keep lines on a bias to keep the work interesting (Figure 4.37).

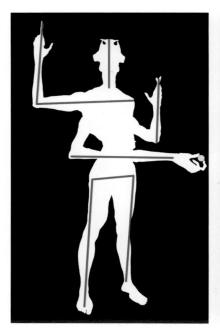 

*Figure 4.36: Notice how the straight lines here are repetitive and boring.*

*Figure 4.37: Improve the pose by breaking the repetition of verticals and horizontals.*

*Figure 4.38: Click here to show the TimeLine.*

*Figure 4.39: The TimeLine with two dots. Dots serve as keyframes on the timeline.*

## Using TimeLine to Store Options

We will use TimeLine to store variant positions. This helps us quickly evaluate a series of options to pick the best one. You may also choose to store vastly different positions and poses using TimeLine and Layers combined. This allows you to create an entire series showing off your character and store them all in one project file. To use TimeLine to store positions follow these steps:

1. Open TimeLine by going to Movie, then TimeLine, and click Show (Figure 4.38).
2. With your figure in position, click on the timeline itself to add a dot. You can now change the figure position and click farther down the timeline to create another dot. These are camera keyframes, and they will store the figure position on the canvas (Figure 4.39).
3. Continue to add new position options as needed. If you need to change the pose, create a new layer and Save the changes there. You can then keyframe the layer opacity to move the figure itself for different views (Figure 4.40).
4. Once you have your options stored, you can quickly move between them using the arrow keys. This allows you to quickly evaluate which compositions appear the strongest.

*Figure 4.40: This layer contains changes to the figure position.*

You can also use TimeLine to store changes in the pose. This is helpful in allowing you to have multiple body positions stored as well as camera positions. This makes it easier to render out multiple image options to Photoshop to paint over later. To add poses to a layer follow these steps. (Be sure to see the DVD or download files for a video illustrating the process of storing poses in layers with TimeLine.)

*Figure 4.41: Create a new layer and name it Pose Variant.*

1. Create a new layer while at the highest subdivision level.
2. Use Transpose to make changes to the figure pose. Changes will be stored on the newly created layer. Rename this layer "pose variant" by clicking the Name button (Figure 4.41).
3. You may turn visibility on or off on the pose variant layer to render the character in the original or modified position. You may store as many poses as you wish in separate layers with this method. Figure 4.42 shows a series of pose variations stored in layers. This gives you maximum freedom when going to Photoshop to pick the strongest presentation image.

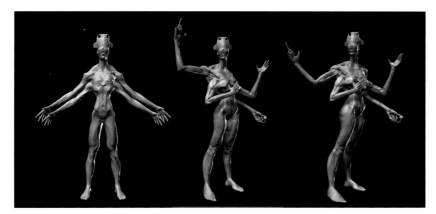

*Figure 4.42: These various pose options are stored in layers.*

## Setting up Lighting and Camera Settings

The last step before you render is setting up lighting and camera settings. Camera settings are controlled by the Focal Angle slider under the Draw menu (Figure 4.43). This is set by default based on object scale, but you can control the perspective distortion by adjusting this slider. Figure 4.44 shows the effect of a few different settings. Experiment on your own figures though, as the FocalAngle setting will always appear different depending on the original scale of the object in the document window. Remember that the focal angle is specific to the ZBrush camera and will not correspond to camera settings in other software packages or the real world.

*Figure 4.43: The FocalAngle slider adjusts the camera perspective.*

Lighting is adjusted under the Light menu. Follow the next few steps to create a key and rim light lighting setup. The key light is the main light that casts the dramatic shadows on the figure. The rim light will shine from the rear and create a bright rim of light around the edge of the forms. This will both define the shapes and bring the figure forward from the background.

1. Open the Light menu and dock it to the side of the screen.
2. Click and drag the orange light icon to adjust the key light placement (Figure 4.45).

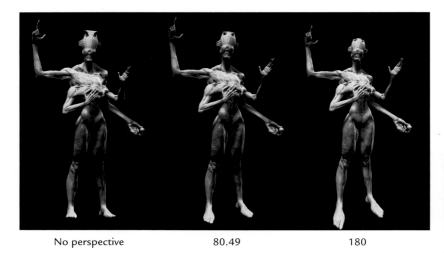

No perspective  80.49  180

*Figure 4.44: The effect of altering the perspective settings*

*Figure 4.45: Adjusting key light placement*

3. Turn on the next light by clicking the light bulb icon. Turn the Intensity all the way up and move to the center of the sphere (Figure 4.46).

4. Click on the orange placement icon to put the light behind the object. You will see the light change in the document window to appear to be lighting the object from behind (Figure 4.47). Move the light to the edge to get a nice rim light. This light setup will save by default with the ZBrush project.

*Figure 4.46: The light settings*

*Figure 4.47: Here you can see the dramatic effect of rim light on the figure. Rim light adds depth by carving the figure away from the background to better define its shape.*

## Creating Render Passes

At this stage, the figure is posed and placed on the picture plane in a composition you find appealing. Make sure you pick the pose you like best from any stored on layers. We are now ready to render some passes out of ZBrush to take into Photoshop for painting. We want to export separate passes of light, shadow, special highlight, and matte to give us the most freedom in creating our final illustration (Figure 4.48). We will render these passes using the ZBrush BPR, or Best Preview Renderer.

Render                Ambient Occlusion            Shadow

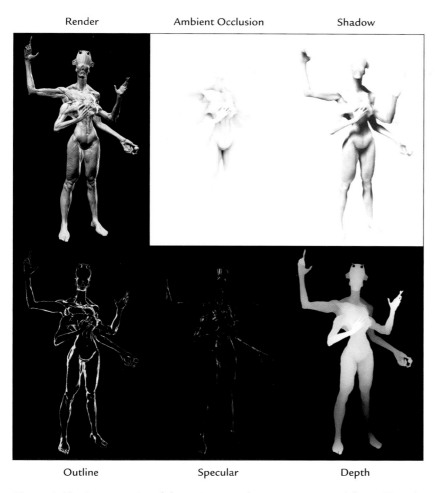

Outline                    Specular                Depth

*Figure 4.48: A composite of the various render passes exported from ZBrush*

1. Begin by setting up the shadow settings. Under the Render and Bpr Shadow settings menu, set Strength to 0.77 and Rays to 55. This will give you a strong shadow with a soft edge. Set LDepth to −8 to cast more dramatic shadows (Figure 4.49).

2. Make sure ambient occlusion is enabled under the Render menu by pressing the AOcclusion button (Figure 4.50). This ensures the ambient occlusion pass will render.

3. Next enable the render pass option under the Render menu by pressing Create Maps (Figure 4.51). This will cause the renderer to automatically generate the image, depth pass, ambient occlusion, shadow, and matte renders.

4. Make sure you selected Material BasicMaterial2 or Basic Material and pressed the BPR button to render these passes (Figure 4.52). The maps will appear in the slots under the Render menu. Click each icon and specify a file name and location to export them (Figure 4.53). When rendering the document, make sure the Actual button on the right side of the screen is pressed (Figure 4.54).

*Figure 4.49: The Bpr Shadow settings*

*Figure 4.50: The AOcclusion button under the Render menu*

*Figure 4.51: Click the Create Maps button to generate render passes automatically.*

This renders the document at actual size or full document resolution. The anti-aliasing quality of BPR renders is good enough so that the rendered image does not need to be resized when you export from ZBrush. If you do need to improve the quality, increase the SPix slider on the right of the canvas before rendering.

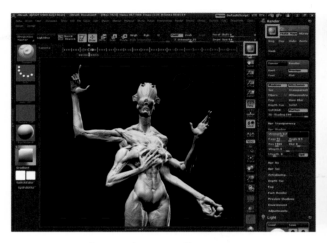

*Figure 4.52: The BPR button will execute a Best Preview Render.*

*Figure 4.53: Exporting the render passes*

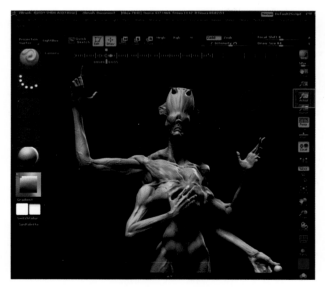

*Figure 4.54: The Actual button renders and exports the document at actual size.*

## Creating Rim Light and Specular Passes

Some useful passes are not created by default in ZBrush. You will want to manually create a pass for specular shine so that you can control the highlights on the figure. You will also want to make an outline pass to accentuate the rim lighting. Follow these steps to make these passes:

1. Make sure RGB is on at the top of the screen. Select black as the active color (Figure 4.55). Go to Color and FillObject to fill the model with black (Figure 4.56).
2. Click the Best button under the Render menu to enable Best Renderer mode (Figure 4.57). Best Renderer is the older ZBrush rendering method. We are using it for these passes because we don't need the highly realistic shadows of BPR mode. Press Render to render the document. With the black color on, the only thing that renders is the specular shine. We can composite this into our image in Photoshop to control the shininess of various parts (Figure 4.58).

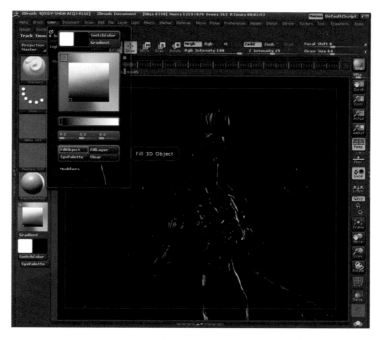

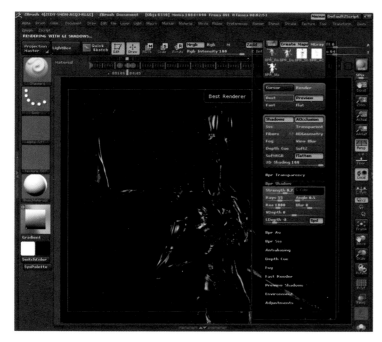

*Figure 4.55: Here the active color is black.*

*Figure 4.56: Here the figure has been filled with the color black.*

*Figure 4.57: The Best button under the Render menu*

*Figure 4.58: After rendering the figure, you will have an image that only contains the shiny highlights. This can be added as a layer in Photoshop with screen blending mode to add specular highlights.*

3. Export the map by going to Document and Export, and Save as specular.psd. Make sure the document is set to actual size by pressing the Actual button on the right of the screen; otherwise this render pass will be a different size than the previous ones.

Next we will make a rim light pass. Follow these steps:

1. Open the Material palette on the left side of the screen (Figure 4.59).

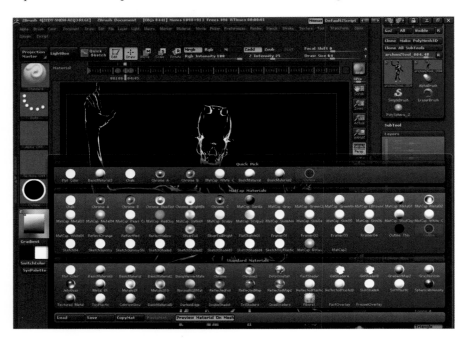

*Figure 4.59: The Material palette open*

2. Select the Outline shader (Figure 4.60). This will be useful for creating relight effects in Photoshop. Make sure Mrbg is on at the top of the screen (Figure 4.61). Make white the active color again and press the Color and FillObject button. Export this image as outline.psd.

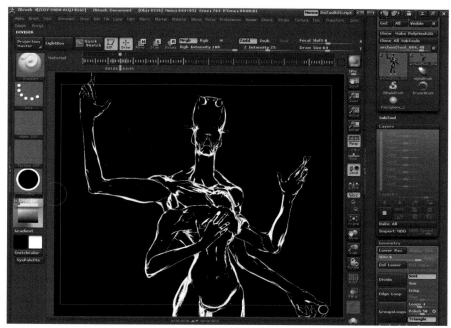

Figure 4.60: *The outline shader is useful to create rim lights in Photoshop.*

Figure 4.61: *The Mrgb button*

This concludes the process of preparing render passes to composite in Photoshop. In the next chapter we will bring all these parts together into a single file and look at how to add the final touches of light and color to create our creature illustration.

# five

# Painting the Interdimensional Traveler

**In Chapter 4,** *"Posing the Interdimensional Traveler," we looked at how to infuse our character with personality and purpose by posing its body. Now, it's time to enhance and finalize our conceptualization with with the use of Photoshop Painting tools. We will introduce color and texture, and further explore the concepts of light, shadow, depth of field, and other details to create a compelling final illustration. At the end of this chapter, you will have a finished Photoshop painting created using your ZBrush sculpture as the basis of the image (Figure 5.1).*

## Adding Color and Texture with Photoshop Paintover

We are now ready to import the images into Photoshop, composite them together, and start painting color and texture over the base design. This is where all our work comes together and we create a compelling final-presentation image. In this section, we will be using Photoshop in conjunction with some special hot keys. I highly recommend learning and using the Photoshop hot keys, as it will increase your speed. Being able to access tools via hot keys allows you to focus more on the work and less on

*Figure 5.1: In this chapter, we will create this final image of the Interdimensional Traveler.*

the process of using the software and hunting down tools. Also, be sure to check the DVD or the download files for a fully narrated video of this chapter project. You can follow along the chapter steps in real time as I work on this image.

> While I do most of my work in this chapter with basic round brushes, varying their hardness, you may want to use some of the specialty brush presets available on the DVD or download files. See the video on loading custom brush sets.

*Figure 5.2: Convert to 8 bit RGB*

## Preparing Images for Composite

Before we can composite the images together, they all need to be the same format. This facilitates using the "load files into stack" Photoshop script. All the image files need to be RGB 8 bit images. The shadow and depth passes are rendered from ZBrush as Grayscale multichannel images. These cannot be processed by the Photoshop script and therefore they need to be converted to 8 bit RGB. Follow these steps to prepare the images for composite.

1. Open the Shadow, Ambient Occlusion, Depth, and Matte passes in Photoshop.
2. For each image go to Image ➢ mode ➢ and convert to RGB. If an image is Multichannel, convert to grayscale first and then convert to RGB. Next convert each image to 8 bit under the Image ➢ mode menu (Figure 5.2).
4. Save the images.
5. The images are now ready to composite into a single document. Since they are all the same format now, the easiest way is to go to File ➢ Scripts ➢ Load Files into Stack (Figure 5.3).
6. Click the browse button and select all the image layer passes. Select the BRP_Render, BPR_AO, BPR_Shadow, BPR_Mask, BPR_Depth, specular, and rim light files. Click OK (Figure 5.4). The files are now loaded into a single Photoshop document. Each layer is named descriptively, based on the filename (Figure 5.5).

## Arranging the Layers

We are now ready to arrange the passes we imported into ZBrush. In this section we will be looking at Photoshop blending modes and the layer menu. We will also be using some Photoshop hot keys from here on. Table 5.1 shows some of the ones I use most often. Remember you can define your own Photoshop hot keys with the Keyboard Shortcuts menu under the Edit menu. You can also define what Photoshop menus are visible and what tools are accessible under the Menu tab of the same window (Figure 5.6).

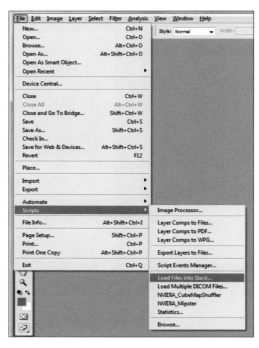

*Figure 5.3: Load files into stack*

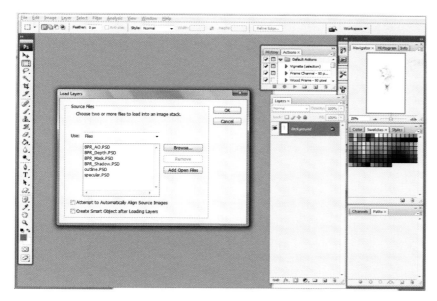

*Figure 5.4: The Load Files into Stack script UI in Photoshop*

*Figure 5.5: Layer stack*

### Table 5.1: Common Photoshop Hot keys

| Photoshop function | Hot key |
| --- | --- |
| Collapse layer Down | Ctrl + D |
| Collapse all layers into a copy | Ctrl + Alt + Shift + E |
| Show/Hide Selection Marquee | Ctrl + H |
| Jump selection up as a layer | Ctrl + J |
| Cut and jump up new layer | Ctrl + Shift + J |
| Group layers | Ctrl + G |
| Zoom | Ctrl + or Ctrl – |
| Color balance | Ctrl + B |
| Hue Saturation | Ctrl + U |
| Levels | Ctrl + L |
| New layer | Ctrl + Shift + N |
| New document | Ctrl + N |
| Create clipping mask | Ctrl + Shift + G |
| Select all | Ctrl + A |
| Fill with foreground color | Alt + Delete |
| Invert selection | Ctrl + Shift + I |
| Brush size control | [ and ] |

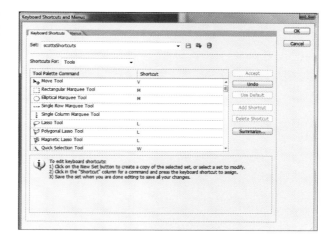

*Figure 5.6: The Keyboard Shortcuts and Menus screen in Photoshop allows you to customize hot keys as well as menu layouts. This screen is accessible under the Edit ➤ Keyboard Shortcuts menu*

ZBrush artist and author Eric Keller has a very useful technique for recalling hot keys. Eric recommends making an image that charts your hot keys and then setting it as the desktop background image on your computer. Whenever you need a quick reminder of the hot keys, simply minimize all windows (on Windows computers, press the Windows key + D to minimize all windows) and your hot key cheat sheet will be visible. See the DVD or download files for a hot key cheat sheet image of the table below. There are many more useful hot keys—see the Photoshop menu items to find the relevant hot keys or define your own in the Edit ≻ Keyboard shortcuts menu.

## Blending Modes

Before we move on, we need to fully understand the layer menu and blending modes. Figure 5.7 shows the layer menu and many of its options highlighted. Most of your time in Photoshop will be spent between the Brush menus and the Layer menus. The Layer menu functions as a stack. The topmost image in the layer stack displays above those layers below it. Changes made to the top layers usually obscure the layers below when the blending mode is set to normal. If you alter the blending mode, it changes the way the layers blend, in many cases allowing the bottom layers to show through, modified by the pixels of the upper layers.

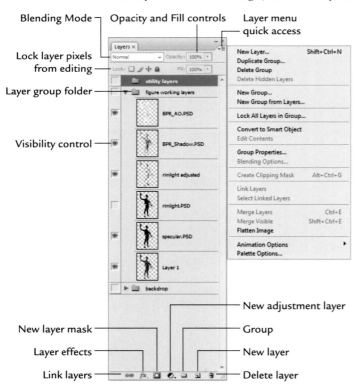

*Figure 5.7: The Layer menu contains many options for controlling layer appearance and how each layer interacts with those below it. This image calls out many of those options for your reference*

Table 5.2 shows some of the most common blending modes and their function. These are the blending modes I use on a regular basis. The verbal description of blending modes can be tricky to grasp. I recommend checking the example images as well as experimenting on your own. Blending modes are powerful in their ability to help you create "happy accidents" in your work. Their impact will always be a little different depending on the contents of the layers you are working with. This element of randomness and unpredictability makes experimenting with layers a lot of fun. While understanding the various modes will give you a technical understanding of what each one can accomplish, I often find I get surprises that lead my painting into new directions as I experiment with blending modes in my painting. Also, don't be afraid to hue shift or change the values of your layers to alter the way the blending mode affects them. Experimentation will bring interesting results. See the video for this chapter to see several instances where blending modes Overlay and Soft Light are used to influence the impact of a texture on the image (Figure 5.8).

### Table 5.2: Common Blending Modes

| Blending mode | Function |
| --- | --- |
| Normal | The default blending mode—the two layers do not interact and the top layer will overlap the lower ones |
| Multiply | Darken the lower layers based on the relative value of the selected layer. White will be transparent while darker values will darken the layers below. |
| Lighten | Lighten evaluates the pixels of both the selected layer and the one beneath and uses the lighter pixels value between the two. |
| Linear Dodge (Add) | Lightens the lower layers based on the lightness values of the pixels in the selected layer. |
| Overlay | This blending mode multiplies the light colors and screens the dark colors. |
| Soft Light | Soft Light is the reverse of Overlay—it will multiply the dark colors and screen the light ones. Its effect tends to appear subtler. |
| Screen | Screen brightens lower layers based on the lightness of the selected layer. |

|  Normal  |  Multiply  |  Screen  |  Soft Light  |  Overlay  |

*Figure 5.8: Here we see the same texture overlay applied with different blending modes.*

Blending modes can have a powerful effect on an image. One very common use is adding noise to an image. Noise is a random pattern of color or value that can be used to break up the perfect digital look of the illustration and create a sense of dirt or randomness. Noise manifests in the real world as dust on a lens, grain in the film stock, or scratches and dirt on an image or screen. The world is full of visual imperfections, so it's important that we introduce these kinds of low-fidelity details to our digital images. We are trying to create atmospheric illustrative images of our characters—not crystal-clear 3-D renders where every detail is in perfect focus. Adding noise and losing detail is an important part of creating that painterly look. Figure 5.9 shows an image before and after noise is added.

Noise can also be used to add texture to a surface. By using an image of random patterns as an overlay, you can give the impression of texture variation on a surface. Figure 5.10 shows a swatch applied as an overlay layer to create the impression of detailed skin.

Overlay texture

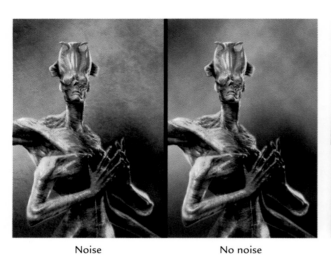

Noise          No noise

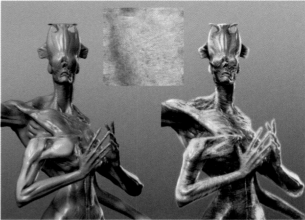

No texture overlay applied     Texture overlay applied

*Figure 5.9: Here you can see an image before and after adding a layer of noise. Noise can help degrade the extreme crispness for a 3-D render and help give it a more suggestive and atmospheric look.*

*Figure 5.10: Here you can see a texture swatch applied as an overlay to give variation to the skin.*

## Organizing the Layer Stack

Now that we have the layers imported and we have a basic understanding of how to use layer modes to change the way the layers relate, we are now ready to organize the image. We will arrange the various render layers in order so the stack will allow us to let the lighting passes, like Ambient occlusion and Shadow, impact the render layers. Follow the steps below to organize the render layers and prepare the file for painting.

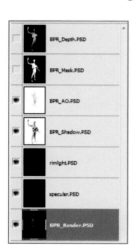

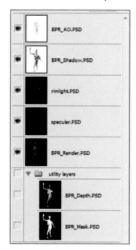

*Figure 5.11: the layer stack*

*Figure 5.12: Group the Depth and Mask layers in a folder called Utility Layers. Turn off visibility and move them to the top or bottom of the stack.*

Follow these steps to organize the working layers.

1. BPR_Render.PSD is your base layer render. This is the sculpture with no shadow or ambient occlusion passes applied. Make this the bottom layer. Click and drag the rim light and specular layers so they sit above the BPR_Render layer. Above these, place BPR_Shadow.PSD and BPR_AO.PSD at the top of the stack (Figure 5.11).

2. The Depth and Mask will be special-use layers. You can turn off visibility on those. I tend to keep them off at the top or bottom of the stack. Shift-select the two layers and press Ctrl + G to group them into a folder. Name this folder "Utility Layers." You can drag this to the top or bottom of the stack. Turn off visibility by disabling the eyeball icon (Figure 5.12).

3. Set both BPR_AO.PSD and BPR_Shadow.PSD to Multiply blending mode (Figure 5.13). This causes the darker areas to be multiplied into the image, effectively darkening the shadow areas defined by the AO and Shadow layers.

**4.** For the specular pass to read correctly, the layer needs to be set to screen blending mode. Figure 5.14 shows the before and after effect of this change. Remember that screen will lighten the layers beneath based on the white areas of a black-and-white image. Black will have no effect while white will lighten. At this stage your layer stack should look like Figure 5.15. I have the utility layers (Depth and Mask) in a group at the bottom of the stack.

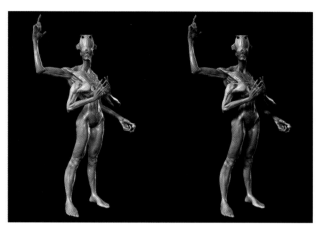

No lighting layers          Ambient Occlusion and Shadow
                            applied as Multiply layers

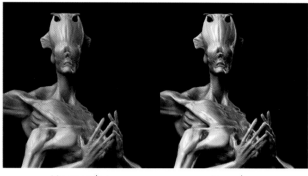

No specular          Specular
pass                 applied

*Figure 5.13: The image on the left has no Shadow or Ambient occlusion passes applied. On the right, the two lighting passes are applied as Multiply layers.*

*Figure 5.14: The effect of setting the specular layer to Screen blending mode is to punch up the shiny qualities.*

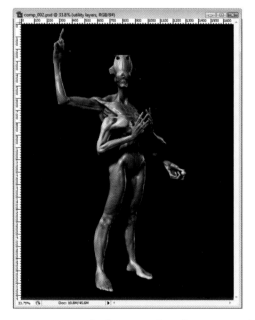

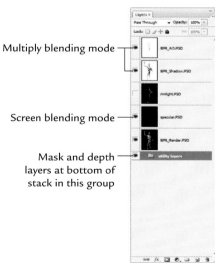

Multiply blending mode

Screen blending mode

Mask and depth
layers at bottom of
stack in this group

*Figure 5.15: The layer stack at this stage with the lighting and specular passes in correct order and the utility layers at the bottom of the stack*

*Figure 5.16: Open the utility layers group by clicking the arrow next to the folder to access the mask layer.*

Next we will knock out the backdrop using the mask layer. This section will show you how to quickly create selections from the contents of a layer. It will also show you how to isolate elements on a transparent layer by deleting the background.

1. Open the Utility Layers group by clicking the arrow next to the folder. This will unfold it and grant you access to the layers inside (Figure 5.16).
2. Select the mask layer and with the magic wand tool select the white area of the image. The layer need not be visible to do this; Photoshop will know what to select as long as you click in the area of the figure while the Mask layer is active. Once the selection is made, the outline of the figure will be surrounded with the "marching ants marquee" (Figure 5.17).
3. Select the BPR_render layer and press Ctrl + J to jump the figure selection up. This creates a copy of the figure with no background (Figure 5.18). Name this new layer "figure"

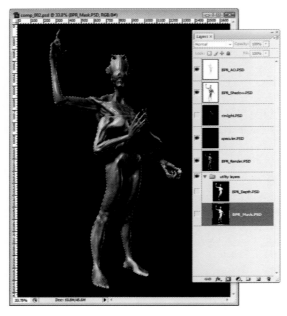

*Figure 5.17: Selecting the mask*

*Figure 5.18: Jump figure up with the Ctrl + J hot key to create a new layer*

4. We will now delete the background for all the layer renders. This will allow us to add a new backdrop and have total control over its color and value. Had we not deleted the background, we would have extra, unnecessary pixels in each layer getting in the way. By deleting the backgrounds, we now have only the figure on every layer except the bottom layer, where we keep the background itself. It makes for a much more organized and easy to manage image. Hold down the Ctrl key and click on the image for the figure layer to automatically select the figure outline. Make sure you click the image thumbnail and not the layer name. Ctrl + Click will create a selection that conforms to a layer's contents.
5. Once you have the figure pixels selected, press Ctrl + Shift + I to invert that selection so the background, not the figure, is selected. Alternatively, you can invert the selection under the menu Select ➢ Inverse.
6. Now select each layer and press delete. Because the pixels on the outside of the figure are selected, this will remove the background from each layer. When you are done, you will see only the figure on a checkered backdrop (Figure 5.19).

### Create a Backdrop Layer

Now we will create a new background for the image. We want to create a backdrop, over which we have the most control, allowing us to adjust the value relationship between the foreground and background by adjusting the levels and gradient of the backdrop image. This will be very helpful as we work since you may find that you need to make changes to the background to make the figure more visible. It is harder to do this if the backdrop is part of the same image as the figure or if the background is just a simple gradient bitmap.

1. Create a new layer by pressing Ctrl + Shift + N. Name this new layer "Backdrop" in the dialogue box that appears. Click OK to create the layer. Move the layer under the figure layer. From the color palette at the left of the screen, select a middle gray (Figure 5.20).

2. Fill the layer by pressing Ctrl + A to select all, then Alt + delete to fill with foreground color. This will create a flayed gray backdrop for the figure. We want to create something with more depth, like the gradient falloff of a photo studio backdrop. To accomplish this, we will add an adjustment layer.

3. With the backdrop layer selected, press the adjustment layer icon at the bottom of the Layer menu and select levels (Figure 5.21). This will open the layers adjustment sliders on the right side of the screen (Figure 5.22).

4. Darken the image by dragging the middle point to the right. This will have the effect of darkening the overall background. We now want to add a gradient falloff to his effect. Click in the white box next to the levels layer in the Layer menu (Figure 5.23). This mask controls what part of the image is affected by the levels control. Areas of black are masked while areas of white will be impacted by the adjustment layer. Shades of gray in the mask layer will have an effect in proportion to how close the shade is to black.

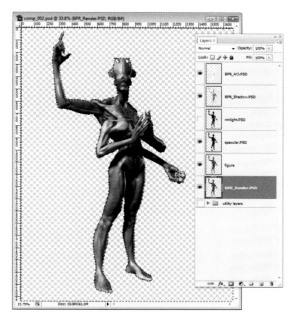

*Figure 5.19: Background deleted and checkered backdrop visible*

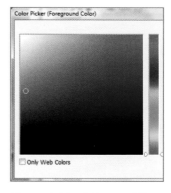

*Figure 5.20: Select middle gray from the palette.*

## Benefits of Using Adjustment Layers

At this stage you could just fill the layer with a simple gradient between a lighter and darker value of gray. This is an acceptable approach, but by using an adjustment layer and a mask we get to learn how to use layer masks, adjustment layers, and we also gain a much greater level of control over the backdrop.

With this configuration, at any point later in the painting process you can easily double click the layer to access the level controls to adjust the lightness or darkness of the falloff. You can easily change the color of the background or even replace it with an image. You can also manipulate the layer mask to change the rate or the gradient. This is much more control than you would have available with a simple gradient bitmap. We also want to learn how to use adjustment layers, as we will revisit them to create a lighting effect on the figure itself later in this tutorial.

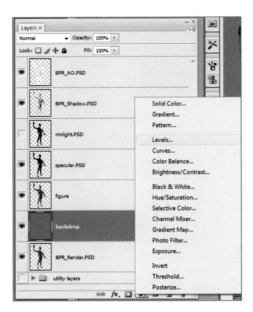

*Figure 5.22: The levels control sliders*

*Figure 5.21: Adding an adjustment layer to control the backdrop levels*

*Figure 5.23: The white box next to the adjustment layer icon is the layer mask.*

5. This is the mask associated with the adjustment layer. It's plain white now, which means all of the image is affected by the layer control. We will add a gradient to this mask to obscure some of the effect, creating a gradual falloff to dark. Select the gradient tool from the left side of the screen (Figure 5.24).

6. Make sure the gradient is set to opaque (Figure 5.25) and your colors are set to black and white. Click and drag to draw a gradient. This should be in the mask layer, so if you see an actual gradient on screen, undo and click on the mask layer. This gradient will cause the effect of the levels control to fade from no impact to full impact (Figure 5.26). You can then adjust the mask to further tweak the background falloff.

7. Lastly Shift-select all the backdrop layers (the adjustment layer and the backdrop itself) and press Ctrl + G to group them together. Name this group "Backdrop." This will just make it easier to navigate and manage your document by keeping the layers organized.

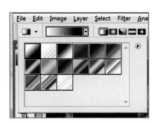

The final effect should be a gradual falloff to dark. You can adjust the rate and the direction of the falloff by adjusting which direction you draw the gradient line and how far it extends. Longer gradient lines create a more gradual falloff. Remember that this approach gives you far more control than a simple gradient backdrop. If you prefer a more simple approach, you may use it, but be aware we will need to use and understand Layer masks and adjustment layers for the lighting effects we paint later in this chapter.

*Figure 5.24: The gradient tool*

*Figure 5.25: The gradient settings*

## Adjust Specular and Collapse Layers

So far we have been combining the render passes from ZBrush into a suitable base upon which to add color and texture. When we have that image, we will hide the original working layers to keep the document as simple as possible. In this section, we will adjust the specular and add the rim light layer before collapsing into a simpler set of working layers.

Select the specular layer. Adjust the opacity to get the best effect. You may choose to erase some parts of the layer to reduce the shine in some areas compared to others. You can increase the shininess by adding another instance of the specular layer. Simply select the whole specular layer with the Ctrl + A hot key, then press Ctrl + J to jump a new copy up. This will immediately have a visible effect on the image (Figure 5.27). Adjust the opacity and erase as needed. Another useful trick is to use the Dodge tool to brighten areas of the specular layer you want to accentuate (Figure 5.28). Set the tool to highlights with a high opacity. This will brighten highlights as you brush over them. Press Alt to darken as you paint.

Now we are ready to collapse in to a few simple layers to continue working. Follow the steps below to consolidate the layers into a more manageable working file. This will allow us to simplify the number of currently active layers we have to deal with while retaining the original layers in group, in case we need them later.

1. Turn off visibility on the backdrop and utility layers groups. The figure should be visible against a transparent checkerboard background (Figure 5.29).
2. Select the topmost layer and press the hot key Ctrl + Shift + Alt + E. This will collapse all visible layers into a new layer copy. This retains all the other layers underneath (Figure 5.30).
3. Turn off visibility on all layers but the backdrop group. Again press Ctrl + Shift + Alt + E to collapse the backdrop into a new copy. Move the backdrop up beneath the figure copy layer.
4. Select the individual figure layers and group them together with the Ctrl + G hot key. Name this group figure "Working Layers" and move it to the bottom of the stack. Your layer stack should look like Figure 5.31. Be sure to see the video on the DVD or download files where this process is fully narrated.

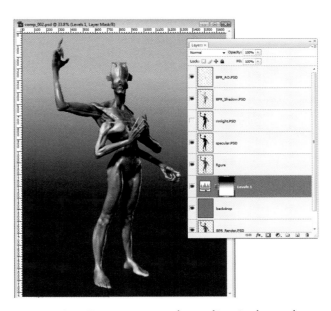

*Figure 5.26: Here we can see the gradient in the mask layer as well as its effect on the appearance of the background image.*

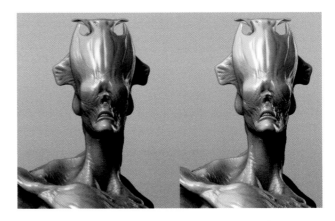

*Figure 5.27: Adjusting the specular shine. The figure on the right has two instances of the specular layer applied to increase the level of shininess.*

*Figure 5.28: Dodge tool settings*

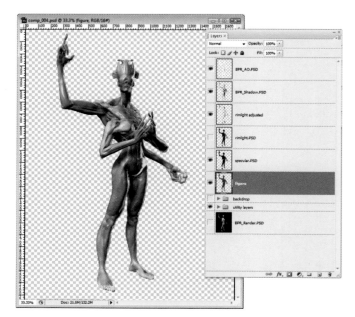

Figure 5.29: Turn off visibility on all groups
but the figure layers.

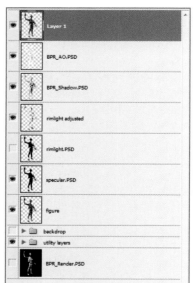

Figure 5.30: Collapse the figure layers into a
new copy with the Ctrl + Shift + Alt + E hot key.

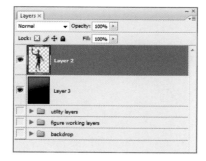

Figure 5.31: The layer stack at
this stage has the background and
figure collapsed into two separate
layers. The original working layers
are grouped together and stored
at the bottom of the stack in case
they are needed.

## Painting Some Corrections

At this stage, I can make some corrections using the Paint Brush tools.
We will use the eyedropper to sample color directly from the grayscale
image and paint out any errors or artifacts in the sculpture. We can correct errors or paint in highlights in areas we may have missed before. In
the steps below, I will show you how I paint out a rendering artifact in the
abdomen.

1. I zoom into the image with base layer selected. I focused on the
   abdominal area where the geometry has a faceting effect that is
   distracting (Figure 5.32).
2. We always want to avoid painting directly into a layer whenever possible. This allows us more freedom to revert from changes or turn
   them off entirely. Create a new layer by pressing the Ctrl + Shift + N
   hot key. Name this layer "Corrections." We will paint our corrections into this layer rather than the original figure layer.
3. From the Brush menu, select a round brush and turn the hardness all
   the way down so the edges are as soft as possible. Turn down opacity
   to about 60%.
4. While the brush is selected, hold the Alt key. Your brush will now
   become an eyedropper tool 🖉. This allows you to sample color
   directly from the image itself. This is a huge benefit when trying
   to paint into an image. It allows you to use the image itself as your
   color palette rather than try to use the color picker to find accurate
   hues and values.

5. Sample color from the immediate area of the artifact and start brushing over the problem areas. Remember to sample often from the areas of highlight and shadow already present in the image to maintain a more natural gradation of values. In Figure 5.33 you can see the effect of sampling color and painting out the problem areas.

---

As you paint with most Photoshop tools, you can control the opacity by pressing the numbers 1 through 0 at the top of your keyboard. This will change the opacity setting in multiples of 10.

---

6. The forearm has a similar problem area where the geometry folded in an unappealing manner. Using the same techniques of sampling values directly from the image, paint the forearm extensor muscles in, to correct this area (Figure 5.34). You can see this correction painted in real time on the DVD or download files. The process is one of sampling the highlight, midrange, and shadow tones directly from the area you are painting. Be sure to vary your brush hardness as needed.

7. Some areas may have noticeable polygon faceting. In Figure 5.35 you can see this faceting on the pectoral muscles. I need to add some more detail to this area to suggest striations in the muscles that fan from the sternum to the lower arms. Using the same technique of direct sampling, I paint these details in. I also stroke lighter marks across the muscles of the arm to suggest a bit more texture in this area.

8. You can also use the Blur brush to smooth out polygon faceting. Set the Blur brush strength to 50% and touch the areas of faceting. Very little application is needed to render these artifacts invisible (Figure 5.36).

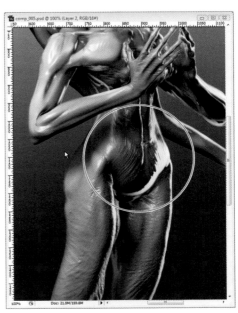

*Figure 5.32: We can see the geometry in the abdomen has some faceting that needs to be corrected.*

 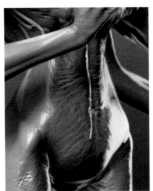 

Abdominal artifacting    Paint over artifacts in a new layer

Highlight, midtone, and shadow are sampled directly from the image to help paint corrections to the forearm extensor muscles

*Figure 5.33: Sample color directly from the image to paint out the artifact on the abdomen*

*Figure 5.34: Here I use the same technique to correct this error in the forearm*

## Using the Color Picker Sample Size

The color picker tool has some options that can make your work more accurate. When the color picker tool is selected, there will be a tool option at the top of the screen defining sample size. This is read in pixel-by-pixel radius. The larger this radius the closer your sampled color will be to what you spot by eye on screen. This is because your eye blends the color of several pixels in close proximity. By using a larger sample size of the color picker, you will sample a color closer to the one you are seeing rather than the exact color of the pixel on which you happen to click as with a single point setting.

*Figure 5.35: The chest is given more detail in the pectoral region by painting in muscle striations and areas of light and shadow.*

*Figure 5.36: The polygon faceting is easily removed with the Blur brush.*

Continue to correct any problem areas in this manner. On small areas like this, I try to sample color directly and paint in. I avoid the Clone brush at this point because it tends to create repetitive stamped patterns unless used very carefully.

### Create Color and Texture Overlays

In this section, we will give the skin a sense of color modulation by using overlay images. This is my favorite approach to creating a skin texture, as it is quick, effective, and helps foster those surprising "happy accidents" as you start to tinker with color balance and blending modes. As we apply images of skin directly to the model, we will use the hue and saturation controls to adjust their appearance on the model. These layers will be applied as overlay or soft light blending mode.

This approach allows us to quickly build up a sense of skin texture without having to painstakingly paint a texture map for the character. Remember that speed is important in creating a concept image like this, so the faster you can generate multiple ideas, the better. With this approach to creating skin texture you are only rendering a single view of the character using evocative texture and color passes. This creates the impression of skin without having to paint it explicitly. Figure 5.37 shows a selection of skin sample images that can be used as overlays to create texture on the character. The following steps illustrate the process of adding skin texture overlays from reference photos.

1. From the DVD or download files, load skinswatch2.psd (Figure 5.38). Select the image with the Ctrl + A hot key and copy it to the memory buffer with Ctrl + C. Switch to the creature illustration and paste this skin swatch in as a new layer by pressing Ctrl + V (Figure 5.39).

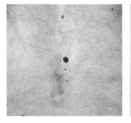   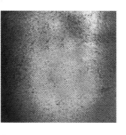 

*Figure 5.37: These skin swatches can be used as overlay images to quickly introduce skin texture and color variation to the character.*

*Figure 5.38: Load skinswatch2.psd from the DVD or download files.*

2. Press Ctrl + T to transform this skin swatch layer. Scale it up to cover the entire body. Set the layer blending mode to Overlay.
3. Ctrl + Click on the figure layer to select the pixels of the figure. With the skin swatch layer selected, press Ctrl + Shift + I to invert the selection and then press delete to clear any image that does not cover the figure (Figure 5.40).
4. Zoom into the head and select the eraser tool. Dial down the opacity and erase out areas of the face. We are doing this because we want there to be texture variation in the figure and some areas will be textured by different overlay images than others (Figure 5.41).

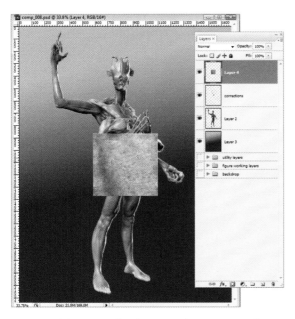 

*Figure 5.39: Paste the skin swatch in as a new layer.*

*Figure 5.40: Set the skin swatch layer as overlay and delete any pixels not covering the figure.*

5. The effect of the overlay image can be tweaked by changing the color hue and saturation. With the overlay layer selected, press the Ctrl + U hot key to bring up the Hue Saturation menu. Alternatively, you could go to Image ➢ Adjustment ➢ Hue/Saturation (Figure 5.42).

6. From the DVD or download files, open the file skinswatch.psd. Copy and paste it into the illustration. Move the layer to cover the character's head and change the blending mode to Overlay (Figure 5.43).

7. Open the Hue/Saturation menu again with the Ctrl + U hot key. Hue shift the overlay image toward a purple to unify it with the body textures (Figure 5.44). Delete any unneeded pixels from the head overlay as in previous steps.

*Figure 5.41: Erase the overlay texture in some areas to help create variation.*

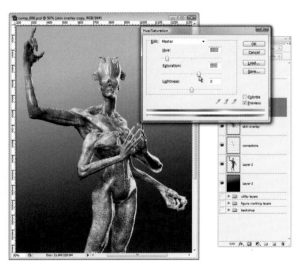

*Figure 5.42: Open the Hue/Saturation menu to shift the values of the overlay image, changing its effect. Here we see it pushed toward a more purple skin tone.*

*Figure 5.43: For variation, the head will be textured using skinswatch.psd. Here we see it as an overlay layer over the figure.*

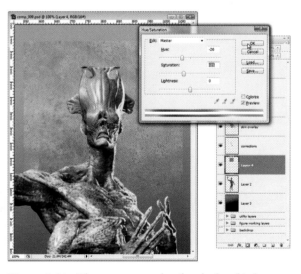

*Figure 5.44: The texture overlay for the head is hue shifted toward purple to unify it with the body textures.*

8. Duplicate a copy of the head overlay by pressing the Ctrl + J hot key while the head overlay layer is active. You will see the intensity of the texture increase (Figure 5.45). We will create texture variation by erasing out areas from the top layer so some portions of the head texture are more saturated than others (Figure 5.46).

9. To simplify the layer stack again, we will now turn off visibility on the background and collapse all visible layers into a new layer. Name this layer "Collapsed Skin." This will create a new layer with all the skin overlays and figure merged together (Figure 5.47). Group the skin overlay images together in a group called "Skin Overlays," in case you need them later.

10. Turn on visibility again on the background layer and with the new figure layer selected, I adjust the hue and saturation to get an overall look I am happy with (Figure 5.48).

Figure 5.45: Duplicate a copy of the head overlay layer with the Ctrl + J hot key.

Figure 5.46: Erase out areas of the topmost layer to create variation in intensity and saturation within the head texture overlays.

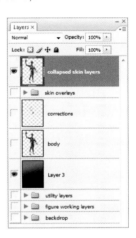

Figure 5.47: Collapse the skin overlays and figure into a new layer. Group the overlay files in case you need them later.

Be sure to check the fully narrated video on the DVD or download files, for this full process in real time. On this video, we discuss a few more concepts and considerations that we just don't have the space to address in print. Be sure to check your media files or the download link for E-reader versions of this book.

# Beyond Color: Lighting Effects

In this section, we will look at how to create dynamic and atmospheric lighting for our image. We will use gradients to create dramatic lighting. We will look at how to paint rim lighting directly into the image.

We will also create the look of a colored key and fill light on the character. Lastly, we will add a fog to create a sense of atmospheric perspective. This gives a mysterious feeling to the figure and also lets us drop part of it into a deep shadow.

Figure 5.48: Adjust the hue and saturation on the collapsed figure layer to get the best look possible.

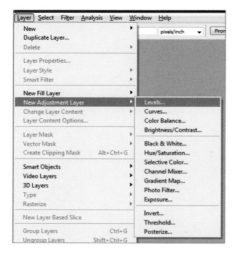

*Figure 5.49: Create a new Levels adjustment layer*

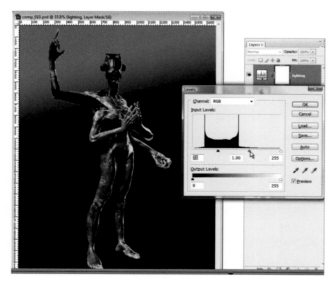

*Figure 5.50: Adjust the levels controls to darken the image.*

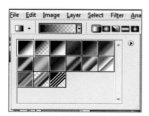

*Figure 5.51: Make sure to select the Foreground to background solid gradient preset for the gradient tool.*

*Figure 5.52: Make sure the layer mask is selected before drawing the gradient on the image. That way the gradient will be applied to the mask and not the image itself.*

## Adding Dynamic Lighting Falloff to the Image

In this section, we will see how to create a dramatic key light that lights the figure from the upper left and falls off into shadow at the feet. This technique of massing areas of light around the key point of the image (the head and chest) while letting the lower body fall into shadow is a common design trick. By showing just the legs in shadow we describe their shape in silhouette without having to spend time painting the details. This is a huge timesaver when working under a tight deadline. Make sure you have the legs visible in rim light and shadow. This allows the viewer to read the forms and place them in their mental picture. If these areas fall into darkness, it will call attention to their absence and just look like you didn't finish the figure.

1. As we did before, when setting up the backdrop layer, we will be using an adjustment layer. Go to the Layer menu and select new Adjustment Layer ➢ Levels (Figure 5.49). This will create a new adjustment layer at the top of the layer stack. Adjust the levels controls to darken the overall image as seen in Figure 5.50.

2. We will now add a gradient into the layer mask to create a falloff, where the levels are normal at the upper left of the image but fall off to darkness toward the bottom of the figure. Select the gradient tool. From the tool options at the top of the screen, make sure that the Foreground to background solid gradient is selected (Figure 5.51).

3. Click on the layer mask so it is active. You can tell the layer mask is active when there is a small rectangle around the white square of the mask (Figure 5.52).

4. Draw the gradient from the upper left to lower right of the screen. The levels will adjust to gradually fall off across the image, giving the impression of dramatic lighting (Figure 5.53).

5. We can further adjust the lighting by painting directly into the layer mask. Painting lighter values into the mask with the paintbrush will darken areas while painting black will lighten them (within the limits of the original levels adjustment). Figure 5.54 shows the effect of painting directly into the layer mask with a soft round brush and the color black to pick out areas of light. The rim light along the arm in the right-hand image was created in this manner as well as the various highlights in the arm.

6. Further details can be added by using the same technique of sampling color directly from the image and painting into a normal layer. Figure 5.55 shows the before and after images of the head after some skin striations and highlights have been painted in to add interest to the area.

*Figure 5.53: The gradient creates the impression of dramatic lighting by adjusting the falloff of the levels adjustment.*

*Figure 5.54: Painting black into the layer mask will brighten areas that have been darkened. This is useful to pick out highlights in the dark areas.*

## Painting Glows with Linear Dodge

The glow effect is created on the sphere using a Linear Dodge (Add) layer blending mode. The same Linear Dodge (Add) layer is used to create the impression of translucency in the skin. A common Subsurface Scattering effect is to see the scattering of light in the material along its edge. This is most commonly seen in backlit ears. Subsurface scattering also manifests as a radiance or glow to the skin. We will create a similar translucency effect to the shell of this character's head. Follow these steps to create the glowing sphere and backlight effects.

*Figure 5.55: Sample values directly from the figure layer to further detail the head and neck. The idea is to pick out areas of shadow and highlight to create visual interest.*

1. Create a new layer and name it "Sphere Color."
2. Select a soft round brush and from the color picker select a purple hue (Figure 5.56).
3. Set the layer blending mode to Linear Dodge (Add) and start to paint the purple over the sphere. It will take on a luminescent quality as a result of the layer blending mode. Adjust the layer opacity as needed to get the proper intensity for the effect (Figure 5.57).
4. We will now select the whole sphere layer with Ctrl + A and press Ctrl + J to duplicate the layer up. Name this layer "Sphere Color copy." This will increase the power of the glow effect (Figure 5.58).
5. Set the blending mode for sphere color to Overlay. You may want to adjust the levels on this layer to get the best glow effect. Leave the sphere glow copy layer blending mode as Linear Dodge (Add). Use the Smudge tool to drag tendrils off the sphere (Figure 5.59). The Smudge tool is located under the Blur tool. Figure 5.60 shows the image at this stage of the tutorial.

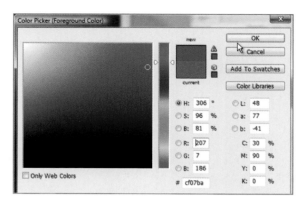

*Figure 5.56 Select a soft round brush and a purple hue from the color picker.*

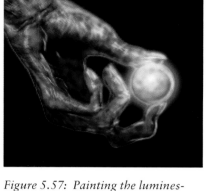

*Figure 5.57: Painting the luminescent sphere using a purple hue on a Linear Dodge (Add) layer*

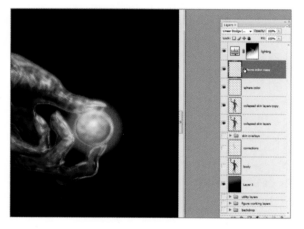

*Figure 5.58: Duplicate the sphere color layer to increase the intensity of its effect.*

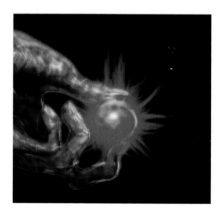

*Figure 5.59: Use the Smudge tool to drag fine tendrils off the sphere.*

6. Lastly, we want to create the sense that the glow of the sphere is casting a purple rim light along the leg of the figure. Create a new layer and call it "Sphere Reflected Light." Set this layer to Overlay. With the same purple hue, stroke along the outer edge of the leg and abdomen as seen in Figure 5.61. Adjust the levels and opacity as needed until the glow seems to be cast from the sphere onto the leg. I also add a soft, cast purple light to the undersides of the arms and to any area that would catch a glow from the sphere. Remember the light will be stronger the closer it is to the sphere, and it should fall off in intensity as you get farther from the source.

7. To help keep the image organized, group the glow layers together and name this group "Spherelight" (Figure 5.62).

*Figure 5.60: The figure with the glowing sphere at this stage of the tutorial*

*Figure 5.61: Painting in a glow from the sphere shining on the body*

*Figure 5.62: Group the sphere glow layers together in a group called "Spherelight".*

In the previous steps, you can see what a unique and powerful effect the Linear Dodge (Add) blending mode has. We will now use it to create the impression of subsurface scattering along the crest of the creature's head. We want to recreate the effect of light refracting within the translucent material of the skin, giving it a signature soft glow. We will replicate that effect on the large organic crest of the creature's head. This will help make the creature feel fleshy and more alive because it suggests a translucent material for the head rather than an opaque form.

1. First we will create a new layer. Call this layer "Backlighting" and set the blending mode to Linear Dodge (Add). Zoom into the head of the figure (Figure 5.63).
2. From the color picker, select a dark purple hue that's slightly unsaturated. In this case, I chose RGB 127 53 93.
3. Stroke this color over the edges of the head crest. This will start to give the forms a slightly translucent glow (Figure 5.64).
4. Once you have painted in some of the areas, you may want to adjust the levels on the layer to tweak the effect. Changing the levels will shift the color of the backlight glow (Figure 5.65). Figure 5.66 shows the final head and crest after adding a few more passes of color to the layer.

*Figure 5.63: We will paint backlighting into the crests to give a sense of translucency.*

*Figure 5.64: Painting into the backlight layer to create a translucent glow*

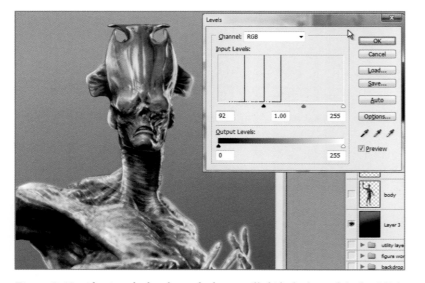

*Figure 5.65: Altering the levels on the layer will shift the hue of the backlight*

*Figure 5.66: The final translucency effect on the head crest*

## Creating Light Gradients

Now we want to create some more visual interest by creating a warm and cool color contrast in the lighting of the image. The image as it stands is lit with a single white key light, a white rim light, and a purple incidental glow. To create a more interesting image, we will introduce a cool cast to the key light and a purple cast to the fill. By breaking up the color temperature across the image, we give the eye more variation and generally create a far more interesting final image. To create the appearance of colored key and fill lights, follow these steps.

1. First we need to determine the color contrast we will use between the two lights. We will have one light shining from the upper left and another from the lower right. I choose to contrast a cool blue light from the upper left and a purple light from the lower right.

2. Create a new layer at the top of the layer stack by pressing Ctrl + Shift + N. Name this layer "key light."

3. Open the color picker and choose a warm red orange such as RGB 137 213 190.

4. Select the gradient tool and select Foreground to transparency as the gradient type (Figure 5.67).

5. Draw a gradient from the upper left across to the middle of the figure. Adjust the layer opacity and levels until you have a suitable cool blue light effect (Figure 5.68). Set the layer blending mode to Soft Light.

6. Repeat this process for the purple light. Create a new layer called "purple light." Select a purple hue from the color picker (RGB 203 88 202) and draw a gradient from the lower right corner of the image. Set the blending mode to Overlay and dial back the opacity on this layer so it's a more subtle lighting effect (Figure 5.69).

The final effect is the impression of colored spotlights shining on the figure from two angles (Figure 5.70). The color temperature contrast helps add interest to the image.

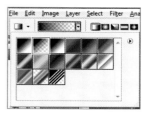

*Figure 5.67 Select Foreground to transparency as the gradient style.*

## Adding Atmospheric Clouds

To create a sense of atmosphere, we will add a cloud layer. This will allow us to create the impression of space around the figure. A misty atmosphere helps

*Figure 5.68:  A cool blue light effect before and after setting the layer to soft light blending mode*

*Figure 5.69:  The purple gradient before and after setting the layer blending mode to Overlay*

*Figure 5.70:  The final lighting effect*

in creating a sense of the dramatic and mysterious. Fog such as this also helps create atmospheric perspective and depth of the image.

1. Create a new layer at the top of the stack. Name this layer "fog."
2. Go to Filter ➢ Render Clouds to fill the layer with clouds (Figure 5.71).
3. Select the layer and scale it up. This will give a larger noise pattern to the fog so it feels more misty and airy rather than the more high-frequency cloud pattern generated by default (Figure 5.72).
4. Dial back opacity on this layer to about 80%. Set the blending mode to Overlay and move the fog layer between the figure and the colored light layers (Figure 5.73).
5. Duplicate the fog layer by selecting all with Ctrl + A and pressing Ctrl + J to jump copy the layer up. This will create a new instance of the fog layer named "fog copy." (Figure 5.74). Make sure the blending mode on this fog layer is set to Normal.

*Figure 5.71: Layer filed with clouds*

*Figure 5.72: Scale up the cloud layer for a larger cloud pattern.*

*Figure 5.73: Set the blending mode on the fog layer to Overlay and move the layer to sit between the colored gradients and the figure.*

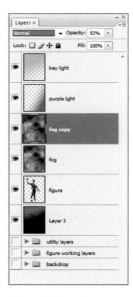

*Figure 5.74: Create a copy of the fog layer.*

6. Use the Eraser brush at 40% opacity to knock out the majority of the fog from the focal point of the image. You want this layer of fog to serve as a framing element, to help keep the eye focused on the upper half of the figure (Figure 5.75).
7. We will soften the fog layers by using the Gaussian Blur filter. Click Filter ➢ Blur ➢ Gaussian Blur and set the radius to approximately 3.2 (Figure 5.76). You can see the final effect of the fog layers in Figure 5.77. The fog serves to add atmosphere as well as create visual interest with a layer of noise that helps fill in background dead space.

*Figure 5.75: Erase the fog from the focal point of the image so the majority of the effect serves to frame the figure.*

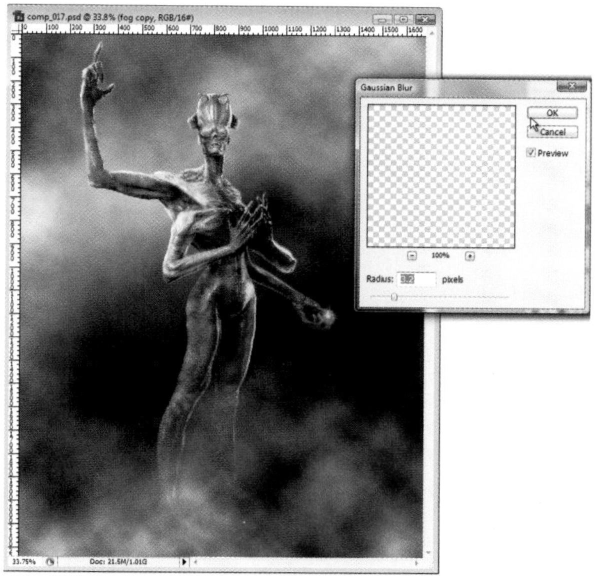

*Figure 5.76: Apply a Gaussian Blur effect to the fog layer.*

# Final Effects: Noise and Depth of Field

We have nearly completed this illustration. Now we will add the final touches to help pull the image together. This section will look at how to add a layer of noise to the image as well as create the impression of depth of field. Both of these effects are borrowed from the discipline of photography where noise and depth of field are natural occurrences in all photos and help create a sense of realism. Noise is a random pattern that can be applied to the image as an overlay. The purpose of noise is to subtly introduce visual irregularities that mimic film grain or other imperfections. These imperfections tend to soften the perfectly crisp lines and images of 3-D art. Adding noise layers helps to unify the various renders, paint strokes, and textures of the image into a single whole.

Depth of field refers to the tendency of a photographic lens to hold only a certain depth of image in sharp focus. The term is from photography but the best way to illustrate is to pick a point in space and stare at it. Notice how the rest of the room that is closer and farther away is less focused than the center of your attention. This is the focal depth of your eye.

*Figure 5.77: Final cloud effect*

By mimicking this effect we are able to recreate the look of a photograph as well as draw the viewers' attention to focal points in the image that remain in sharp focus. Figure 5.78 shows two examples of depth of field (DOF). In the first image, there is a deep focal depth, as only the background falls into a blur. In the second image, we have a shallower focal depth as the figure's face is in sharp focus with elements of the figure, foreground, and background falling out of focus.

Photos by Tristan Crane, www.tristancrane.com

*Figure 5.78: Examples of shallow and deep depths of field.*

To create this effect, we will use the depth pass rendered by ZBrush. The Depth image represents the relative distance from the camera to the figure. White areas are closer while darker areas are receding. This data can be read by Photoshop's lens blur filter to introduce the effect of depth of field. DOF helps sell an image as real because it mimics the effect of an actual camera as well as the human eye. Areas that fall outside the range of focus fall into a blur. This is a stark contrast to default digital images where all aspects are in unrealistically sharp focus. We create a lot of atmosphere and interest by allowing the image to lose detail as much as by adding details. The legs falling into shadow, with areas lost in darkness or becoming blurred by depth of field, all add up to a suggestive image.

Follow the steps below to create a depth of field effect for the image.

1. Select the figure layer. Create a new layer mask by going to Layer ➤ New Layer Mask ➤ Reveal All (Figure 5.79). This will create a white layer mask attached to the figure layer (Figure 5.80). We will add the depth pass into the layer mask because the Photoshop lens blur filter reads from the layer mask to create an accurate depth of field.

*Figure 5.79: Create a new layer mask for the figure layer*

2. Open the utility layers group and select the depth layer. Turn on visibility on the layer (Figure 5.81). Press Ctrl + A to select all and then Ctrl + C to copy the depth layer into memory.

3. Select the figure layer again while holding Alt-click on the layer mask. The image will now appear white, as this makes the mask visible. Press Ctrl + V to paste the depth pass into the layer mask. Click the icon for the figure image in the layer menu to return to image view from mask view. The figure will appear transparent in the areas that are farther from the camera (Figure 5.82). That is because the depth pass is in the layer mask. We will disable the mask after we use it to define the depth of field, so ignore this effect. We will delete the mask by the end of this section.

*Figure 5.80: This creates a layer mask attached to the figure layer*

4. Open the Filter ➤ Blur ➤ LensBlur menu (Figure 5.83). This opens the Lens blur plug-in window.

5. Set the depth map setting to layer mask. This will read the depth from the mask we just created form the ZBrush depth image. This allows Photoshop to make accurate calculations on how the blur should be applied across the image as if it were a photo of a three-dimensional object. Adjust the Blur focal distance slider or alternatively click in the image on the area you want in sharpest focus. Photoshop will calculate for that point. The rest of the figure should become somewhat fuzzy. If the face becomes blurry, click the Invert checkbox.

6. The level of blur can be controlled by adjusting the radius slider. Find the right look for your image and click OK. When you return to the Photoshop window, the blur effect will not yet be visible because the layer mask is still active. Right click on the layer mask and select Delete Layer Mask from the popup menu (Figure 5.84). Figure 5.85 shows the final depth of field effect.

7. You can manually accentuate the blur effect with the Blur brush as needed. In Figure 5.86, I am adding a soft edge to the underside of the arm to help remove some of the sharp hard edges of the render and give the image a more painterly look.

*Figure 5.81: Select the depth layer from the utility layers group.*

*Figure 5.82: The layer mask will temporarily give the image a partially transparent look.*

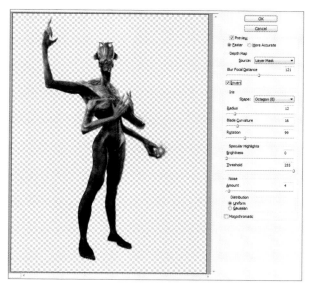

*Figure 5.83: Adjust the Lens Blur settings to read from the layer mask. Click in the image itself to define the focal center.*

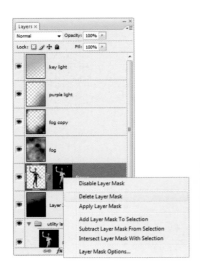

*Figure 5.84: Delete the layer mask to see the Lens Blur effect.*

*Figure 5.85: DOF effect applied*

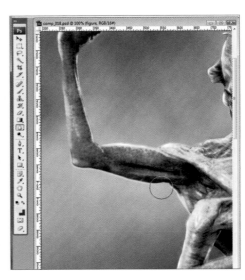

*Figure 5.86: Manually accentuate the blur using the Blur brush as needed.*

8. At this stage, for added grime and realism I add one more overlay layer of noise. Open the file Overlay8.jpg from the DVD or download files (Figure 5.87).
9. Copy and paste it into a new layer at the top of the document (Figure 5.88). Set the blending mode to soft light.
10. Adjust the opacity on the noise layer until it is a very subtle overly effect (Figure 5.89).

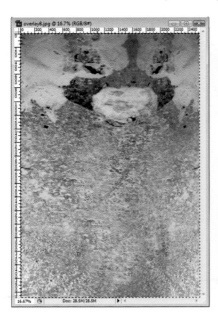

*Figure 5.87: Open the image Overlay8 from the DVD or download files for use as a noise layer.*

*Figure 5.88: Paste the noise layer into the image and set the blending mode to soft light.*

*Figure 5.89: Adjust the layer opacity until the noise overlay is suitably subtle. You don't want it to overpower the image.*

The final step is to crop the image to the correct golden rectangle proportion. Along the way, my image got wider than it needs to be. You will recall from the last chapter we discussed the benefit of composing within a golden rectangle. Figure 5.90 shows the image cropped and resized to the correct proportion of 1600 × 2592.

That concludes this first look at painting over our sculptures in Photoshop. This chapter has introduced several very important points, from composition to the mechanics of working in Photoshop with layers and blending modes, as well as how to use texture overlays and level adjustments to quickly create interesting light and color effects on the skin. Before we move on, I would like to share some tips from a good friend and fantastic artist, Tristan Schane.

# Speculative Anatomy and Creature Design with Tristan Schane

*I am thrilled to share this chapter with New York-based concept designer, illustrator, sculptor, and painter Tristan Schane. Here, Tristan shares a few tips as he walks through his creation of an insectoid alien creature.*

Whenever designing a character for myself or for a client, I always have two fundamentals of design in mind. I try to consider the basic type of character and then, based on that, the physiognomy of that character. Physiognomy can be interpreted to mean how the physical appearance influences our perception of character.

*Figure 5.90: The final image cropped to the golden proportion*

## Concept and Design

Firstly, I imagine an overall character type—is it reptilian, insect-like, a bone or rock creature? What type of creature is it? I try to give the character a comprehensive concept. Unless the character is described as being some kind of a hodge-podge of disparate elements, each aspect of the creature—limbs, head, tail, antennae, etc.—must work within the whole conceptual framework. When creating a creature, I can't help myself imagining my design like it must have evolved somewhere. Its entire form would result from an imagined environment. This helps me visualize the character better. What type of claws might it have? Where does it fit in the imagined ecosystem's food chain? What's the creature's general level of intelligence (more intelligent creatures might need a design that enables the use of tools, for example)?

The other fundamental is the physiognomy—how the musculature and skeletal structure (if it's to have one) works. For me, the fun of creature design is creating a strange limb or a complex facial structure, and then defining the anatomy to show how these body parts will likely move. The term I use when describing this process is **Speculative Anatomy**. I should say when talking of anatomy I am also thinking of skin and fatty tissue, which also—when rendered realistically—add to the quality of a creature's design. Here you can see how I have taken care to determine how the exoskeletal plates of this character interlock and articulate from the back view (Figure 5.91).

I have a traditional arts background and have spent a great deal of time working with anatomies of all types, real and imagined. This was especially true in traditional sculpture where you recognize how muscles and joints function. I love taking this information and applying it to the speculative anatomy of creature design.

Often I am trying to design a being whose limbs or other body parts don't exist anywhere in nature. However, even for a static two-dimensional concept painting, the anatomy of this creation must look like it works. I like to design this speculative anatomy so that when someone sees the concept, in their mind they are already seeing it move and recognizing how the muscular and skeletal (or exoskeletal) structure enables this movement. Simply having big muscles or odd and interesting textures and body parts is nothing. Good creature designers are masters at creating believable speculative anatomy that ties all these elements together and gives them the realism that sells the concept. This is what appeals to me as a concept artist. Sometimes the idea for a character is inspired by images of real creatures, like insects or animals. Other times I try not to look at reference images and just design without any reference. This character was done like this. The only two thoughts I had in starting was I wanted him to be insect-like and I wanted him to have some sort of flap/valve organs to show an unconventional respiratory system (Figure 5.92).

I started with a base mesh in Maya (Figure 5.93) and then sent it in to ZBrush to begin sculpting. I usually start with base meshes rather than using ZSpheres, but I really don't have one set way of working that I follow for every piece. After a little bit of work, I finally have a basic design for the silhouettes and overall form of the character. I then do some quick retopologizing back in Maya and then shoot him back in ZBrush to get to the actual sculpting.

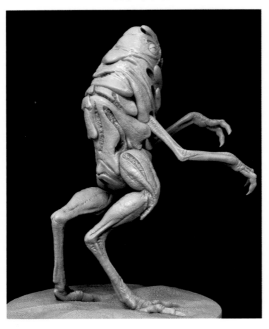

*Figure 5.91: The exoskeletal articulations as seen from behind*

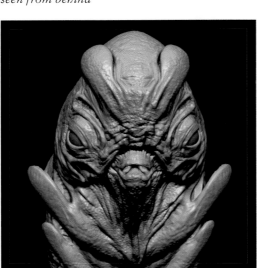

*Figure 5.92: The flaps in the exoskeleton serve as a design feature and imply a kind of alien respiratory system.*

*Figure 5.93: The base mesh*

## The Importance of Working Globally

With all art pieces, I feel it's important to work globally, meaning working on the piece over-all rather than focusing on one section of the piece and getting that to an advanced stage before moving to another area. Working globally is especially important for characters so that you can evenly apply the level of detail and anatomy to all the parts. For this character, while he walks upright, his fore limbs don't let him handle tools, so I imagine him as being at something around the intelligence of a dog or a dolphin. If I wanted to suggest a more feral mentality, I would have made him less humanoid in structure. If I wanted to suggest greater intelligence, I might have changed the design of his "hands" (and feet).

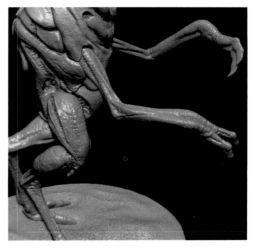

*Figure 5.94: The arms of the character are insectoid and spindly.*

When I'm working on a character's musculoskeletal system, I am imagining how tendons and muscles would contract to animate the character. I flesh out anatomy with an idea of how muscles and tendons function, contracting in one area to bend a joint, while an opposing muscle group is in place to extend it, and supplemental musculature is also identifiable to stabilize or provide more dynamic movements. For this character, as I wanted him to have an insect-like quality, his limbs are spindly and the movement is characterized by gangly sinews and well-delineated joints. Figures 5.94 and 5.95 show the creature's arms and legs, respectively.

After I've sculpted in all the muscle, sinew, joints, and skeletal plates, I start to think about surface detail (Figures 5.96 and 5.97). Again, I am going for something insect-like. I didn't want it to be too noisy a texture. I was very happy with the detail of the body shapes with their interlocking, puzzle-like formations, and the semi-open, fibrous slitted areas and didn't want to bury this behind a super busy surface detail. For surface detail, I do a lot of freehand sculpting and then supplement with custom

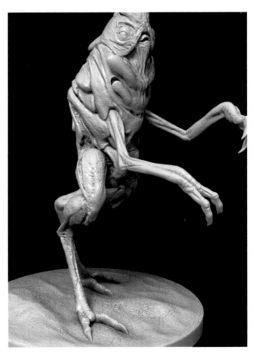

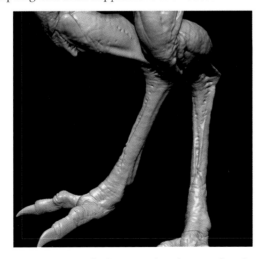

*Figure 5.95: The legs are also elongated and sinewy.*

*Figure 5.96: The surface texture is coarse but understated so as not to overpower the design.*

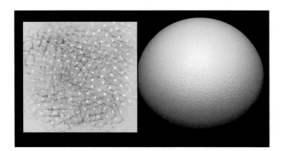

*Figure 5.97: The Ostrich Skin alpha below is a favorite for bumpy skin textures. This alpha is available on the DVD or download files.*

brushes, which use my own alphas rather than using straight alphas. Each time I use an alpha, I go in and customize the settings on the alpha as well as tweak the settings of the brush (almost always a Standard brush). So, rather than doing this over and over, I make a new brush with all the custom settings in place. I also prefer to make my own alphas, but there are a few from the Pixologic Download Center that I employ straight out of the box.

The main brushes I use for my sculpting are the Clay Tubes brush, the Standard with a soft fall off alpha, the Move brush, the Form brush, the Flatten brush (for flattening and also for smoothing), the Inflate brush and the Damian Standard; lowering the ZIntensity on the Dam Standard to around 10 makes it excellent for gentle wrinkles or light cracking in chitinous surfaces (Figure 5.98). I almost never use any of the other brushes for organic character work.

*Figure 5.98: The Dam Standard brush with ZIntensity set to 10 works well for freehand sculpting light wrinkle patterns.*

With the sculpting all done, it's time to get some renders, then bring it in to Photoshop to composite, and then paint the sucker.

## Adding Color and Other Details

I don't have one set technique I use repeatedly for each concept painting. Rather, I have a set of tools, which I utilize in different ways depending on the piece and on my mood. I am always experimenting with my own technique and also looking at the techniques of other artists.

In general, I use Multiply mode layers to add color and shadow. I use Color and Overlay mode layers to further play with colors and Normal mode layers to add highlights, details, and to define or redefine the creature. Occasionally I will also use a Screen mode layer for an effect, but I rarely at all use any of the other mode layers.

I use Liquefy and the Transform functions regularly, as well as play with the various level and color adjustments settings as I work.

To begin, I quickly create a background color and texture. This is simply a layer placed behind the figure layer in Photoshop (Figure 5.99). Sometimes I start building up the character's colors before I add something in the background, but here I wanted something to give contrast early on.

Then I do a little more work on the character using Multiply and Color layers (Figure 5.100). Color sections are painted into Multiply layers to tint the underlying gray model. Highlights are painted into a layer set to Normal blending mode. The highlights are painted with a small round brush set to about 80% opacity. These will be the specular highlights.

Color, Overlay, and Multiply layers are used to build up color with normal layers adding highlight and fleshing out the smaller anatomical details (Figure 5.101).

Now I cool off the image by giving it a bluish tint. This is accomplished by painting blue and green hues into a layer set to Overlay blending mode. I also play with the saturation of different layers till I get what I want. I'm using Overlay mode layers to add some orange high-light around the edges of his body plates to add a crustacean-like look to the insect-like structure (Figure 5.102).

*Figure 5.99: The background tex-ture is applied in a separate layer to quickly help create contrast.*

*Figure 5.100: Basing in the initial color passes*

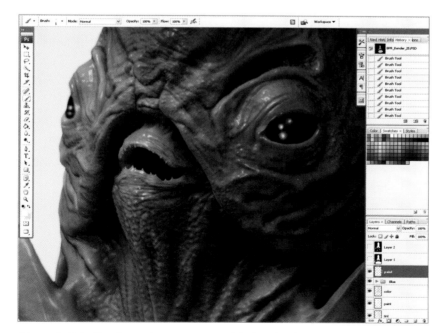

*Figure 5.101: Further color passes are added in the form of green washes.*

I want to intensify the lighting on the creature's right side (the left side of the painting). I press the Ctrl + Alt + Shift + E hot key to create a flattened copy of all the layers on top of the layer stack. I then intensify the levels and lower the saturation of the flattened, top layer. Now I erase most of the image, leaving a border area, giving a look of a more intense light from that side (See Figure 5.103).

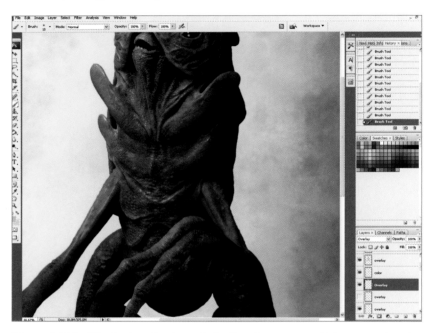

*Figure 5.102: The body color is cooled off and orange rim lights are painted in along the edges of the plates.*

*Figure 5.103: Intensifying the rim lighting*

I add a little motion blur (Figure 5.104) on the background for dramatic effect and ... *Voilà!* The final image (Figure 5.105).

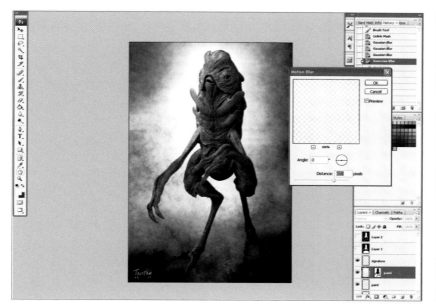

*Figure 5.104: Adding motion blur to soften edges and add a sense of depth*     *Figure 5.105: The final image*

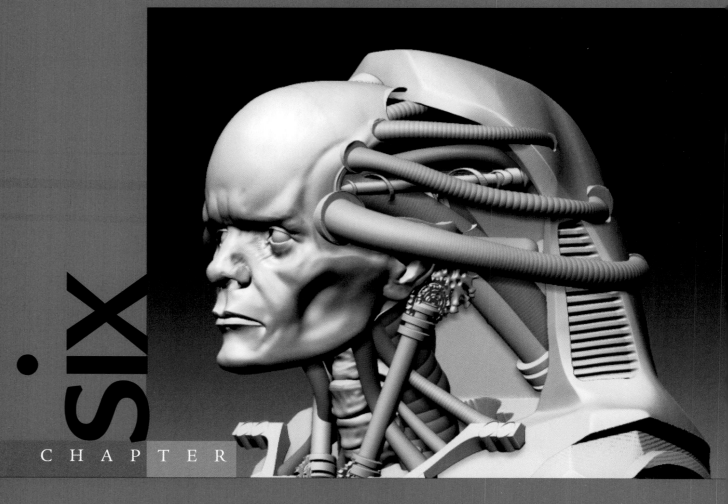

# six

CHAPTER

# A Biomechanical Character

## In this chapter, we will *depart from working with more organic forms and examine how to conceptualize and create a more machined or manufactured shape. ZBrush typically lends itself to working out organic shapes quickly and intuitively. This presents a problem when the design called for industrial shapes, which are obviously manufactured.*

*In this chapter, we will execute a biomechanical design using some of the new hard surface and form sketching tools available since ZBrush 4.0. ZBrush includes an entire suite of brushes intended to let the artist sketch mechanical shapes much in the same way they might sketch organic forms. This has opened a new vista for using ZBrush as a concept design tool because it frees designers to explore industrial forms in 3-D freely, when before such form exploration would require the planned, careful use of Maya. Until now it was difficult, if not impossible, to "sketch" 3-D form explorations of hard surface models with any degree of accuracy without a high degree of expertise in polygon or NURBS modeling. We will explore tools like the Planar brushes, Clip brushes, Shadowbox, and we will even incorporate Maya into your workflow with GoZ.*

*The purpose of this chapter is to illustrate how mechanical forms can be quickly conceptualized using the right combination of tools. By taking this approach, you can avoid the "modeling quagmire," where you are too busy worrying about proper edgeflow and polygon geometry to be freely creative.*

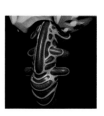

As we work through this character, I also want to show the considerations that went into this particular design. His mechanical structures are based firmly on human physiology, and I attempt to use interesting shape combinations, contrast between organic and mechanical forms, and a strong silhouette with interesting use of negative spaces. I want to show how I consider all these topics to help create an interesting character design.

---

### The Brief: Biomechanical Character

The brief for this character is a human-machine hybrid—a cyborg—with more mechanical parts than human. The robotic anatomy should mirror the form and functionality of the human skeleton and muscle system with flesh incorporated into the mechanical structure. The design should have a laboratory feel, meaning this is not a finished "showroom ready" robot but rather a prototype with some exposed elements. It should appear to have been constructed from parts in a lab. I want the character to have a strong mass of an upper body to denote a core strength, but I thought more spindly or skinned arms might be an interesting contrast. Most importantly, I wanted to explore the use of negative spaces in unexpected areas to drive home that this is not a man in a suit but rather human parts grafted into a mechanical structure.

---

# Creating the Cyborg Design

We will now begin the process of bringing our biomechanical character to digital design. I will begin by pulling some elements from my library of shapes. After a short time working in ZBrush, you will develop a back catalog of old designs, sculptures, and forms that sit on your hard drive. Don't be afraid to revisit and reuse these for other projects. Speed is one of the keys in concept design—you must produce strong ideas but you need to do them fast. By taking advantage of your shape library, you will always be able to cut down on time and quickly reform an old part into something entirely new. As we work on the rest of the body, we will try to relate shapes back to human anatomical forms. This is for two reasons. Firstly, we want to engage audience recognition of humanoid forms within this cyborg creature. Secondly, the design of a robot will tend to follow the same biomechanics as the human body. This is simply because the human machine is time tested and well designed. It tends to be the point of departure for robotics designers. When we create structures like the shoulder apparatus, we will be using the actual shoulder girdle of the human skeleton as a reference point.

## Creating the Head

In this case, I will use the basic head we created from a Polysphere in my book *ZBrush Creature Creation*. We will use this as the base to sculpt the cyborg's face. As you follow this tutorial, be aware this is a very involved process, which I have documented fully on video. I have highlighted steps here to call attention to some of the most important parts of the process. Be sure to watch the complete video of the process supplied on the DVD or download files to get the most from this lesson.

## Negative Spaces

Negative spaces are those areas between shapes. Here you see the white shapes are distinct from the spaces in black. I have inverted the color in two distinct images to help you see the two different shapes (the positive and negative). Notice how both create interesting shapes that define the overall look. These negative shapes are often just as important as the shape of the figure itself. We see both when we observe an object and the negative spaces can either help reinforce or detract from the design, depending on how they are treated. In life drawing and sculpture, when artists work from a model, they are taught to observe the negative space to help understand the actual form or outer contour of the figure. By always being aware of what you are saying with both your shapes and the negative space around your shapes, you are exerting more control over the effect of your design. You can see how both positive and negative shapes can be interesting.

For this character, I want to let the negative spaces infringe on areas where the viewer will expect there to be body. By knocking out negative space behind the head or in the waist, it creates a surprise for the viewer. They register a humanoid form but one with holes where they should not be. This creates a sense of the unexpected and hopefully helps generate interest in the design. The viewer will have their expectations upset, which should make the character more appealing to look at closer.

Negative spaces
marked in red

We will begin by working on the Head ZTool. We will use this as the base on which to create the emaciated human head fixed into the mechanical shell of the robot body. We will need to use some of the standard sculpting brushes to take the character away from the heroic strong-jawed bionic man and into the realm of a more unsettling, sickly looking cyborg.

1. From the DVD or download files, load the generic head ZTool.
2. Using the Move brush, shift the shape of the head around to give it a more sickly character. I begin by reducing the mass beneath the cheekbones to give the face a more gaunt appearance (Figure 6.1).
3. Using the Clay Tubes brush, build up the skeletal structure of the zygomatic bones (commonly called the cheekbones) as well as the temporal ridge of the skull and the frontal eminence. This helps accentuate the skeletal landmarks beneath the skin, adding a sense of anatomical realism as well as a malnourished, creepy quality to the face.

*Figure 6.1: A generic human head ZTool. Using the Move brush, change the shape of the generic head, accentuating the bony landmarks of the skull.*

4. Returning to the Move brush, enlarge the cranium as well as the eyes to suggest a more fetal proportion to the head (Figure 6.2). Perhaps this character was never a normal human but a genetic experiment grown for this very purpose. As a result, the skeletal development would be skewed. The slightly disturbed head proportion will also have a more unsettling effect on the viewer. By understanding head and facial proportions, you are able to make informed decisions like this in how to break the rules for your own needs. We will also be carving out the back of the head and filling the skull with mechanical tubes and pistons, so the extra space will be useful. To the viewer, a slightly oversized infantile head connected to a massive robotic body implies a strength that is not tempered by rational thought.

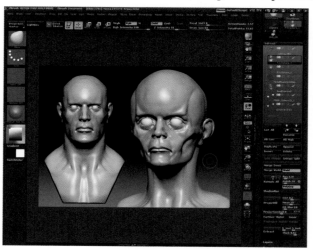

*Figure 6.2: Create a more infantile proportion to the head.*

At this stage, I want to isolate the face and cranium as well as carve away a negative space in the back of the skull. To do this, we will use the Clip brushes to slice sway the neck geometry. The Clip brushes are available under the ZBrush Brush menu. There are a few variants, but here we are using the ClipCurve brush. Later in this lesson we will use the ClipCircle brush briefly to detail some mechanical elements.

1. Step down to a lower subdivision level and, using the Move brush, compress the unneeded shoulder geometry up into the neck. Smooth and shift the faces to gather them beneath the head, where they can easily be clipped (Figure 6.3).

2. Press the B key to open the Brush menu and then the C key to show the brushes that start with the letter C. Select the ClipCurve brush from the menu and rotate to view the head from the side.

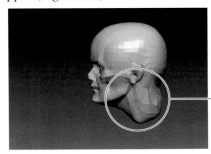

Compress the neck and shoulder geometry under the head

3. Ctrl + Shift + Click drag to create a clipping line. When drawing a clipping line, any geometry that falls on the shaded side of the line will be clipped while the unshaded side will remain untouched. Figure 6.4 shows the process of slicing the neck away. Remember to press Alt once to create a curve and twice to create a hard angle.

*Figure 6.3: With the Move brush, compress the neck and shoulder geometry beneath the head, where it can easily be clipped.*

Use the Alt key to change the shape of the ClipCurve

Press Alt twice to make an angle

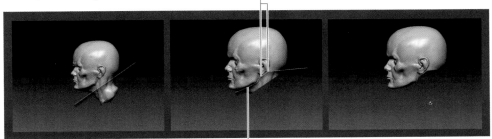

Trim the neck down to the underside of the skull using the ClipCurve brush

Press Alt once for curve

*Figure 6.4: Use the Clip brushes to slice the neck geometry*

The ClipCurve brushes work by pressing Ctrl + Shift + Click and dragging a line. The shaded side of the line will be "clipped" from the geometry on the unshaded side of the line, which will remain unchanged. When you are drawing a clipping line, press spacebar to reposition the line, press Alt once to insert a curve anchor point in your line, and press Alt twice to insert a hard angle anchor point.

4. At this point, we will carve away some negative space at the back of the skull (Figure 6.5). This will help interrupt the viewer's expectation that the cranium will be a solid mass and allow us to play with adding some interesting mechanical shapes inside to suggest some complex life support system. We will use the ClipCurve again for this cut.

**5.** As a final touch, we will add come cylindrical details using the ClipCircle brush. From the Brush menu, select the ClipCircle brush. This brush differs from the ClipCurve brush in that it draws a circular clipping area. Notice there is a crosshair in the center of this circle. We will now use the ClipCircle brush to add some points on the head where tubes will later insert (Figure 6.6). The ClipCircle brush has two interesting effects. If the circle is drawn so the center crosshair is outside the geometry, it will carve away a circular shape. If the crosshair is inside the geometry, it will create a countersunk cylinder shape. Draw the ClipCircle and make sure the center point is within the geometry to create the tube connectors as shown (Figure 6.7).

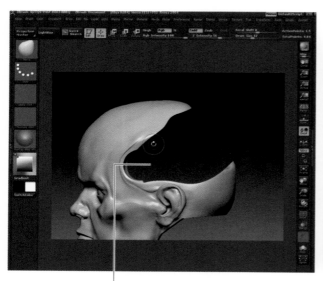

The ClipCurve brush is used to carve away the back of the cranium

*Figure 6.5: Carve away the back of head.*

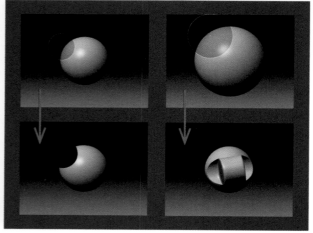

Using the ClipCircle brush, keep the center crosshair outside the surface

Let the crosshair overlap the model

to slice out a clean circular shape

to create a cylinder shape like this

*Figure 6.6: The ClipCircle in use*

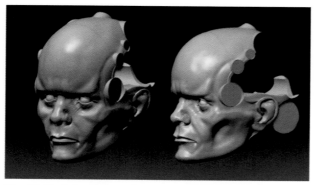

The ClipCircle brush is used to create these cylindrical shapes through the head—we will attach pipes here later

*Figure 6.7: Pipe attachment points made with clip circle*

## Avoiding Undercuts

Something to be careful of when working with the Clip brushes is undercuts. The Clip brush is actually a flattening effect, so you want to avoid any geometry that extends out beyond the volume of the head. The feathered edge of the curve does not actually cut, but rather it flattens the existing geometry into a place that corresponds to the curve. The graphic below shows how this can create thin wings of edges if you slice an area that is curving back and away.

Head curves back around here

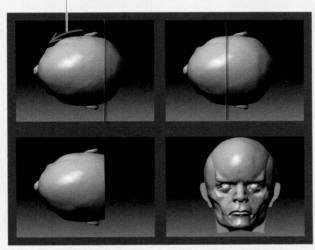

Always slice before the          Slicing at the curve results in
surface curves back             undesirable flattened faces

## Creating the Body

We will now create the torso mass for the cyborg character. We will do this by sculpting a basic Polysphere primitive. The Polysphere is a very versatile shape that can be manipulated into all manner of forms using the standard ZBrush sculpting tools. In my book *ZBrush Character Creation*, I illustrated how to create a complex creature bust using just such a polygon sphere. In this case, we will create the torso structure of our character from the sphere using a combination of the Move brush, Trim brushes, and Clip brushes. We will then use a combination of ZBrush hardsurface tools such as the Polish and Clip brushes to further refine the shape.

### Creating the Torso

Here we will look at the steps to create the torso. This will be created by using the Polysphere ZBrush model to create a basic ribcage form. From this base shape, we will build the rest of the mechanical elements of the body.

1. Open the Lightbox browser and under the ZTool menu select the Polysphere tool. This is an all quad sphere form with no poles. These are ideal balls of digital clay for all manner of forms and I use them often. Once the Polysphere is selected and loaded into

ZBrush, return to the head ZTool and append the Polysphere as a SubTool using Tool ➤ SubTool ➤ Append.

2. This Polysphere will be the basis of the torso. Use the Move brush to shape it into the egg form of a ribcage (Figure 6.8).

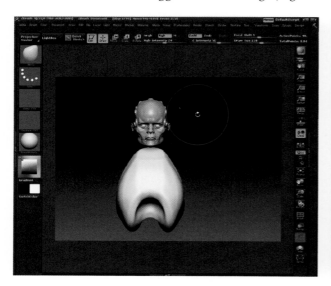 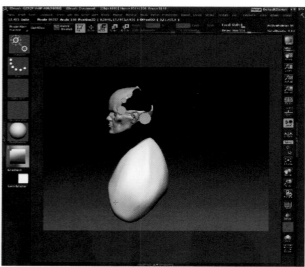

*Figure 6.8: Shape the sphere into an egg form to create the ribcage.*

### The Mechanical Details of the Neck

With the basic torso created, we will now look at how to create some detailed mechanical details for the cyborg. We will begin by creating some mechanism to move the head and neck. These pieces will be based on the natural shape of the anatomy of this area. To create these pieces, we will use ZBrush primitives as well as some new mesh generation tools that have been added to ZBrush 4. One of the methods we will use is called Shadowbox. Shadowbox is a unique new mesh generation technique that allows you to create new geometry by drawing it in front, side, and top views. This is an incredibly fast way to create complex forms for further sculpting. We will also use ZSpheres to quickly generate section of mesh to sculpt into a spinal cord. This section is intended to illustrate how complex new pieces of geometry can be created on the fly.

## Greebles

*Greebles* may be an unfamiliar term to many of you. It dates back to the days of physical model making for film when many miniatures were built from both custom parts and pieces of old model kits, toys, scrap, and whatever else might be handy. Greebles were small mechanical details that served no real purpose other than to break up a surface and make it appear to be mechanically functional. Greebles are an important part of design. While it is often important to understand the form and function of each piece you design, there are times when "greeble" detail is appropriate. In this section, we will create the neck anatomy of the cyborg. This will include both visually functional parts that mirror human anatomy as well as smaller greeble details to add visual interest to the area with texture and shape contrasts.

## The Mechanical Shoulder Apparatus

We will begin by creating some mechanisms to move the head. I want to base these parts on the actual sternomastoid muscles of the human neck (Figure 6.9). I believe the anatomy of the neck is imprinted on the mind of the average viewer because they see human heads and necks every day. It's something that we understand even if not on a technical level. Most people have a sense of the two large muscles of their neck. Creating mechanical parts that mirror the form and function of human anatomy will help the viewer understand the function of the parts when they see them. It also helps keep a humanoid look to the head and neck while using non-human elements. The viewer should assume the structure would work because it subconsciously implies the anatomy of the neck visible on most people. This will help create both visual interest and character.

*Figure 6.9: The finished neck structure should mirror human anatomy.*

1. From the Tool menu, select a cylinder 3-D tool. Under the Tool ➢ Initialize menu, set X and Y size to 20. Click Make PolyMesh3D to convert this primitive to an editable 3-D mesh (Figure 6.10).
2. Append this into the cyborg tool. We will now create some greeble detail on the ends of the pistons. *Greebles* is a term from physical model making. It means any mechanical detail shape that serves no purpose other than to increase the visual interest and complexity of the surface. From the Brush menu, select the Mask Rectangle brush and mask some strips along the ends of the cylinder. Invert the mask, then use Tool ➢ Deformation ➢ Inflate to offset these details (Figure 6.11).
3. Use the Transpose tools to move the piston into place and mirror it across with the SubTool master ZScript (Figure 6.12).

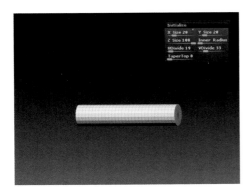
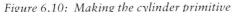

*Figure 6.10: Making the cylinder primitive*    *Figure 6.11: Detailing the piston with ridge details from a combination of masking and the inflate slider*

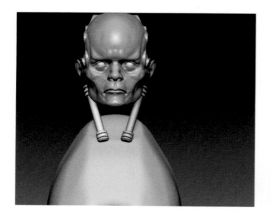

Figure 6.12: Mirrored pistons—notice the geometry has been duplicated and positioned behind the head as well to add complexity

We will now create the clavicles (or collarbones) for the character using Shadowbox. Shadowbox is a tool that allows you to create complex shapes by simply drawing them in front, side, and top views using the masking brushes. It's an incredibly fast technique for making editable meshes of complex forms that would be far more difficult to model under other circumstances. If you can sketch it, you can create 3-D geometry of it in Shadowbox. ZBrush has several Shadowbox tools available in the Lightbox ZTool menu (Figure 6.13).

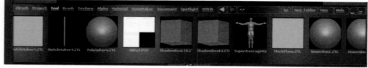

Figure 6.13: Shadowboxes are loaded via the Lightbox.

1. Open Lightbox and select Shadowbox 64. There are two Shadowbox tools here and each one will generate geometry in the resolution notes in the filename—Shadowbox 64 being the lowest res and Shadowbox 128 the highest. Since we will want to divide and detail the geometry more before the model is complete, we will use the lowest res Shadowbox since we can then just add geometry as we need it.

2. The Shadowbox will now be the active tool in ZBrush. Return to the cyborg ZTool and append the Shadowbox as a SubTool under the Tool ➤ SubTool menu. Append this Shadowbox into your Cyborg as a SubTool and use the Transpose tools to place it in the vicinity of the clavicle or collarbone (Figure 6.14).

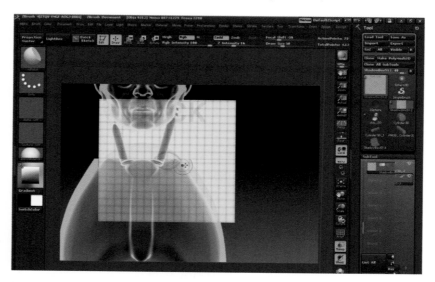

Figure 6.14: The Shadowbox placed in the area where we will build the collarbone

3. From the Brush menu, select the Mask Pen brush and draw the shape of the clavicle from above. This will instantly create the shape you draw. You can further refine the form by rotating to the front and drawing the shape in the front profile. When you are satisfied with the shape, exit Shadowbox by pressing Tool ➤ SubTool ➤ Shadowbox.

This will place the new geometry in our SubTool menu (Figure 6.15). The clavicle can be further shaped and refined with the ZBrush sculpting tools, as it is now a polymesh, which is fully sculptable.

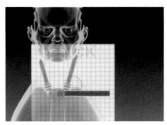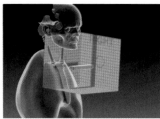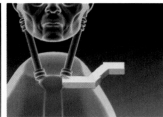

Use Shadowbox to sketch up a clavicle shape

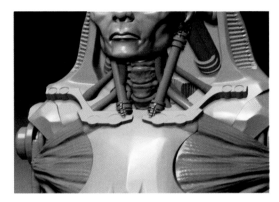

The final clavicle after further work with the Clip brush

*Figure 6.15: Shadowbox in use to make clavicles*

Further details are created in the neck area with Shadowbox as well as by duplicating and repositioning repeating elements. Figure 6.16, for example, shows a gear structure created entirely with Shadowbox. See the video on the DVD or download files for this process in full. A complex character like this can be built by duplicating and layering a selection of relatively simple base parts.

## Shaping the Torso

We have now established the basic torso structure, including the mechanical details of the neck and shoulders. Next, it's time to add shape.

1. First, move to the side vide and pull the shoulder area up so it sits behind the head like a carapace (Figure 6.17).

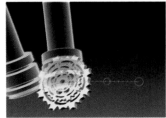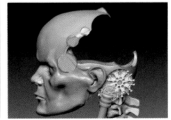

*Figure 6.16: This complex gear structure was created with Shadowbox and is viewable on the DVD or download files.*

2. Use the ClipCurve brush to shape the front and back of the carapace as seen in Figure 6.18.
3. Make sure to place the torso back from the head, leaving a good space between the two forms. Note the negative space from the side view between the head and shoulder/carapace structure (Figure 6.19). This area will be filled with mechanical parts later to add interest to the space and give the impression of mechanization. By allowing the negative spaces to remain here, it reinforces the fact that this is a head attached to a machine and not a man in a suit.

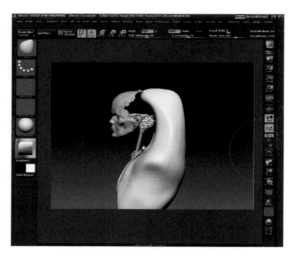

*Figure 6.17: Pull the back of the ribcage up into a carapace behind the head.*

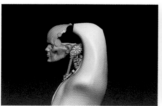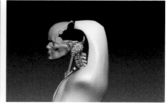

*Figure 6.18: Shaping the carapace with the ClipCurve brushes*

*Figure 6.19: Negative space between the head and shoulders from side view*

## Man in a Suit

In creature design, it is often important to avoid the man-in-a-suit look. Decades of monster movies have created an audience familiarity with the look of a performer inside a rubber suit. There are proportional points that cannot be easily changed, just like the proportions of the face are locked in even for prosthetic makeup unless some digital alteration can take place. Many directors will stress they want a creature design which obviously cannot be accomplished with a suit since it will best exploit the power of CGI and create a creature the audience has most likely not encountered before. Some effective designs from the past include Geiger's Alien, Pumpkinhead, and more recently Wink from *Hellboy 2*, the Pale Man and the Faun from *Pan's Labyrinth* as well as many of the robots from the film *A.I.* Part of the reason these are so successful is because the artists, designer, and director are experienced creature designers and know what visual cues create the man-in-a-suit look. Through clever design, these conventions were broken and exploited to make memorable characters. They understand what the audience expects and then try to confound those expectations.

### Refine the Torso Details

When creating the mechanical details of the torso, we will take advantage of the Trim Dynamic brush, the Planar brush, and the Polish brush. Some basic planes are created using the Trim Dynamic brush. The Trim Dynamic brush allows you to polish and flatten the surface along a curved path. This helps create machined surfaces like car bodies and other semi-organic machined surfaces. Use this brush to polish the curves of the torso. The Planar brush will trim to a specific depth along the surface normal. This depth is set under the Brush menu by controlling the depth mask imbed slider. Any areas that appear noisy or lumpy can be easily flattened by using the MPolish brush. The MPolish brush will polish out imperfections in the surface leaving a smooth refined surface.

1. At this stage, the torso shape is roughed in, but it appears soft and unrefined. There is very little machined or mechanical about it. We will use the Planar Cut brush to slice in the small flat planes on the torso sculpt (Figure 6.20). The Planar Cut brush depends on the Depth mask to control how deep into the surface it slices. The Depth control is found under the Brush ➢ Depth menu. The circle represents the brush's area of effect and the dot at the center represents the depth into the surface it will cut (Figure 6.21). Lower this dot slightly beneath the surface of the sculpt and when you use the planar cut brush it will cut into the sculpture to the depth measure you specify here. This process can be seen on the associated video.

2. In addition to the flat planes on the torso, there are dynamic curves that, while appearing flat and machined, follow a contour much like the machines lines in a car body for example. Figure 6.22 shows these areas. These are created using the Trim Dynamic brush. Trim Dynamic will flatten the area beneath the brush by

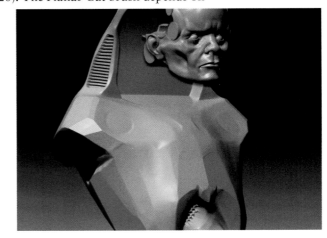

*Figure 6.20: The planes shown here are created with the Planar Cut brush.*

dynamically sampling the brush position and surface normal beneath the center of influence. This allows you to create curved machined contours.

3. Build up areas slightly with the Clay Tubes brush, then knock back the plane using the Trim Dynamic brush as seen in Figure 6.23

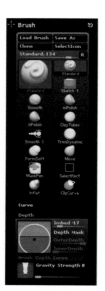

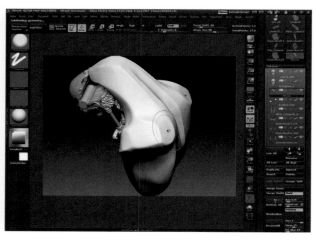

*Figure 6.21: The brush depth control menu*

*Figure 6.22: The Trim Dynamic planes*

*Figure 6.23: Using the Trim Dynamic brush*

*Figure 6.24: Isolate an area for the vent structure.*

4. The intake vent on the side of the shoulder structure is created with a simple mask. Use the Masking brush to isolate the area for the vent (Figure 6.24), invert the mask, and from the alpha menu select alpha 28. Adjust the V Tiles slider to 32 to create the vent alpha. Using a dragRect stroke, draw the vent alpha over the unmasked area (Figure 6.25).

That completes the torso section. Figure 6.26 shows the stages from start to finish. You may also refer to Figure 6.27 for a summary of each part of the torso and how it was created. We will now move into some more detailed mechanical structures of the anatomy of the character.

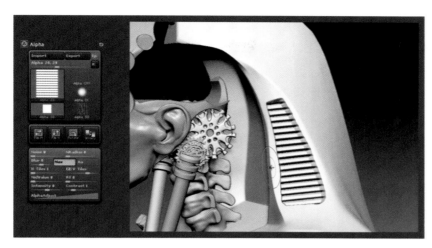

*Figure 6.25: Modify the alpha and draw the vent.*

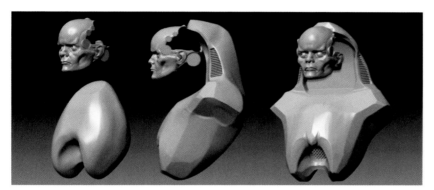

Progression of shaping the torso carapace

*Figure 6.26: From start to finish, this image shows the progression of the torso planes.*

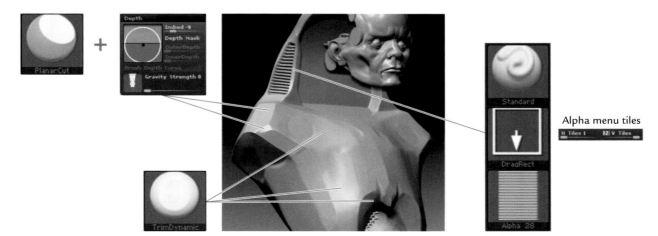

*Figure 6.27: The mechanical details summarized*

## Create a Spinal Cord and Pipes

Here we will add a length of spinal cord to give some more organic elements to the neck. We will also create some pipes that suggest coolant, oxygen, or other important materials being circulated around the cyborg's body. These kinds of details really add visual interest and can also be design elements in themselves, especially when creating the gesture and sweep of the pipes. Parts like these can help guide the eye through the design if you treat them as more than items just "stuck on" the final form. The spine is created by using ZSpheres while the pipes will be created using ZSketch. Be sure to check the video for an in-depth look at the process of making these parts.

1. Append a ZSphere into the SubTool stack and position it in the neck area (Figure 6.28). Draw a ZSphere chain to create the cervical (neck) spine.

2. Rotate to a back view and draw a series of child ZSpheres off the side to represent the transverse processes of the spinal cord (Figure 6.29). The transverse process is the protrusion on each side of the vertebrae (Figure 6.30).

3. Draw child spheres off each link in the center of the chain that extends toward the back (Figure 6.31). These will be the spinous processes, or the bony protrusions that come off the back of the spine.

4. Convert the ZSphere chain into a polymesh using the Make Adaptive Skin button under the Tool ➢ Adaptive Skin menu and append it into your SubTool stack. You may choose to delete the ZSphere chain now or hide it by turning off the eyeball icon in the SubTool menu. Use your favorite brushes to sculpt the spinal section. I used Standard, Move, and Inflate. Remember to take advantage of the polygroups created by the ZSpheres to easily mask parts close together and create tight spaces where the vertebrae come into contact with each other (Figure 6.32). As a final touch, I use the ClipCurve brush to slice an arc down the length of the transverse processes of the spinal cord. Figure 6.33 shows the spinal cord in position.

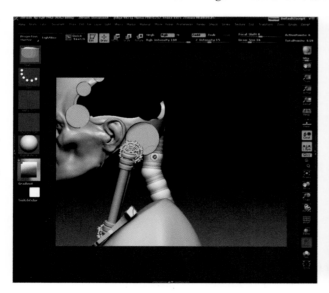

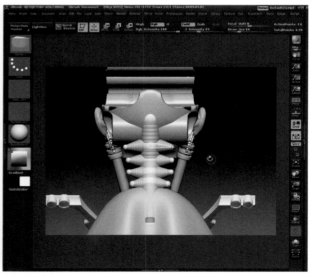

*Figure 6.28: Append a ZSphere into the neck area and draw a short chain the length of the spinal section you want.*

*Figure 6.29: Draw a series of child ZSpheres off the side to represent the transverse processes of the spinal cord.*

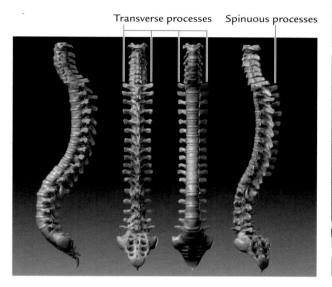

Transverse processes    Spinuous processes

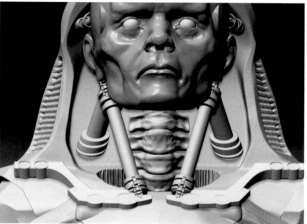

*Figure 6.30:  The components of the spine labeled*    *Figure 6.31:  The spinous processes*

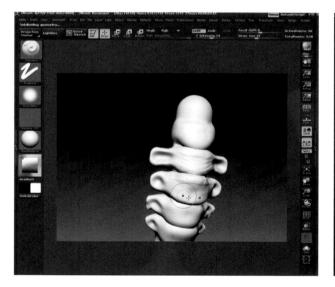

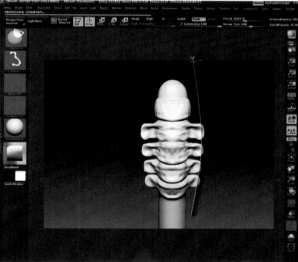

*Figure 6.32:  Making the spine*

We will now create a system of pipes that connect the cranium to the carapace of the body suit. This will break up the negative space between the head and the body as well as create the impression of body fluids, fuels, and other supply conduits connecting the body to the head.

*Figure 6.33: The final spine*

The piping is created with ZSketch. ZSketch is a stroke-based modeling tool that allows you to build up geometry by creating strokes with a Sculpting Brush. These strokes are well suited to creating vines and tubes quickly and easily.

1. Append a ZSphere into the Cyborg tool and Transpose Move it to the center of the head.
2. Enable ZSketch under Tool ➤ ZSketch ➤ Edit Sketch (Figure 6.34). You will automatically be ready to start drawing strokes with the ZSketch brushes. Create the tubes as seen in Figure 6.35.

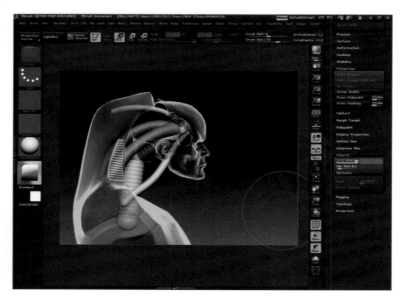

*Figure 6.35: Pipes created in ZSketch*

*Figure 6.34: The Edit Sketch button*

3. When you are ready to convert them to geometry, set the Tool ➤ Unified Skin value to 512 and press Make Unified Skin. Append this new skin into the cyborg ZTool.

You may now delete the ZSketch SubTool, leaving the Unified Skin. The ribbed pipe texture is created with the Stitch brush. Replace the alpha with Alpha 59 rotated once with the Alpha Rotate button. This will create a repeating rib texture along the length of the brush stroke (Figure 6.36). Simply drag it down the length of the tube to create the conduit-style surface.

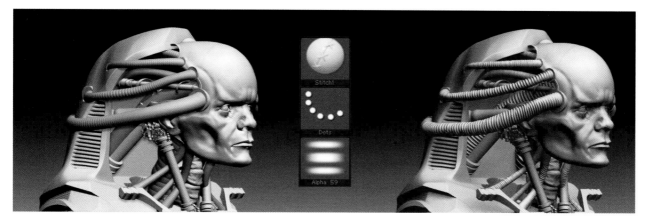

*Figure 6.36: Using the modified Stitch brush to create a ribbed texture on the conduit pipes*

## Create the Arms and Chest Muscles

In this section, we will look at ways to add new geometry to the cyborg model with third party modeling tools. We will use the new ZBrush plug-in GoZ, which allows a seamless integration of outside 3-D modeling software with ZBrush. GoZ supports Maya, 3D Studio Max, Modo, Cinema 4d, and others, but we will be specifically using it with Maya. The plug-in allows us to export our ZTool to Maya, where new geometry can be added and then brought back into ZBrush seamlessly. This adds a new level of flexibility to the ZBrush workflow, which leverages the strengths of the Maya modeling toolset with ZBrush.

GoZ is a tool to link ZBrush with any number of third party modeling and animation packages. We will use it to transfer models to and from Maya. When you press the GoZ button, ZBrush exports your current SubTools to a Maya scene file. Once in Maya, you can make changes to the topology or even add new objects and return them to ZBrush. We will use GoZ to add basic arm structures using Maya primitives.

1. Turn on visibility on the torso and head. Make sure all the other SubTools are hidden. Press the Visible button under the File menu (Figure 6.37). This will export just those visible SubTools to Maya using GoZ. Maya will automatically open with the SubTools visible in the scene file.

*Figure 6.37: Press the Visible button to export the visible SubTools to GoZ.*

2. The visible SubTools will export to your GoZ-enabled application. In this instance I use Maya as my GoZ app. Figure 6.38 shows the torso and head base subdivision levels exported to Maya. I can now build new geometry in scale and relationship to these parts and transfer them back to ZBrush.
3. The shoulder mechanism is built by scaling and duplicating a series of cylinders at the socket for the arm. These should appear to be rotational elements for the arm (Figure 6.39).

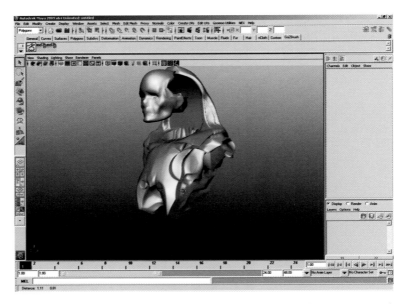

Figure 6.38: *The base subdivision level for the head and torso exported to Maya with GoZ*

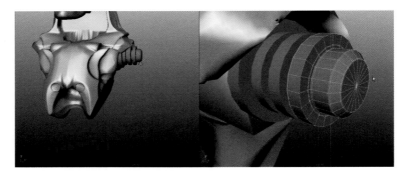

Figure 6.39: *The arm is started by duplicating and scaling a series of cylinders at the shoulder.*

**4.** The arm is constructed from basic box and cylinder primitives, as seen in Figure 6.40. A polygon box is created and positioned to serve as the basis for the humerus bone. Since I know these arms will be covered in organic tissue, I'm not too concerned with details outside the joint and articulation areas.

Figure 6.40: *Continuing to develop the arm by adding primitive boxes and cylinders*

**5.** When the structure is complete, select all the parts with a marquee and group them together with the Ctrl + G hot key. Duplicate them across the X axis by going to Edit ➤ Duplicate Special ➤ ❑. Reset the settings and then set scale X to –1 to flip the copy across the X axis. Click OK (Figure 6.41). This is basic polygon modeling and is documented fully on the video on the DVD or download files.

When you are done modeling, select all the parts. From the shelf marked GoZ, press the GoZ button to transfer the new parts back to ZBrush (Figure 6.42). Back in ZBrush, append the new arm geometry into the cyborg ZTool (Figure 6.43).

## Adding Muscle Tissue

At this stage, I want to add some muscle tissue to the rest of the body that is intertwined with the mechanical parts. As it stands, the head is the only organic element in the biomechanical character. Using a Polysphere, we will sculpt the pectoral muscles connecting the mechanical arms to the chest chassis (Figure 6.44).

**1.** Append a Polysphere into the ZTool and using the Move brush, shape it into a form consistent with the pectoralis muscle. Notice how the muscle is shaped like a large fan extending from the arm bone. I try and mimic the forms

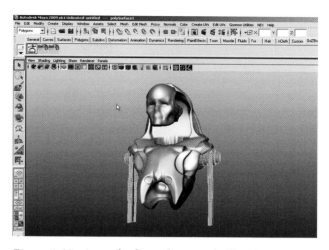

*Figure 6.41: Arms duplicated across the X axis*

*Figure 6.42: Press the GoZ shelf button when the parts are selected to transfer them back to ZBrush.*

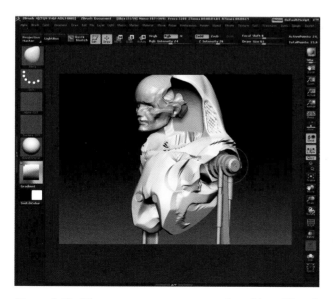

*Figure 6.43: The new arm geometry transferred into ZBrush*

*Figure 6.44: This illustrates the human anatomy we are trying to suggest with these biomechanical structures.*

of the natural body as much as possible when building these biomechanical elements (Figure 6.45).

2. I repeat this process to add deltoid muscles (Figure 6.46), making sure they weave over the pectoralis and around the mechanical articulation of the shoulder (Figure 6.47).

3. The muscles of the bicep and forearm are created with ZSketch. First append a ZSphere into the tool and draw a chain down the length of the forearm (Figure 6.48).

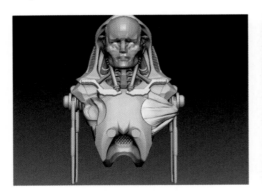

Figure 6.45: *Create the chest muscles.*

Figure 6.46: *Create the deltoid muscle.*

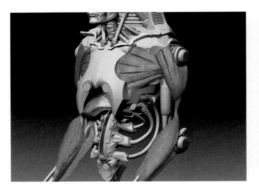

Figure 6.47: *Interweaving of muscles*

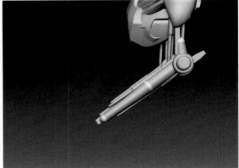

Figure 6.48: *Draw a ZSphere chain down the forearm to facilitate the ZSketch strokes for the flexor and extensor muscles.*

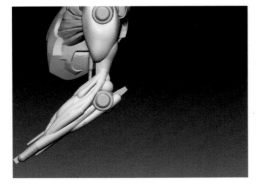

Figure 6.49: *Use ZSketch strokes to build up the volume of the forearm muscles.*

4. Enable edit sketch under Tool ➢ ZSketch and draw strokes down the forearm to build up the shapes of the muscle forms (Figure 6.49). I leave the bicep muscle out because its function is almost identical to a piston pulling on the lower arm. In its place I leave the pneumatic piston geometry visible.

5. To add the striations of the muscle tissue, add a few subdivisions to the mesh. Select the Rake brush and turn on lazymouse by pressing the l hot key. This will help you make long, even strokes along the muscle surface (Figure 6.50).

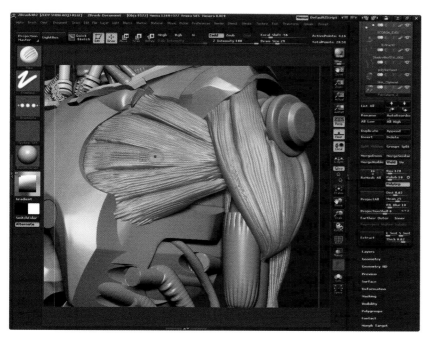

*Figure 6.50: Adding muscle striations*

## Character Accessories in ZBrush

Since ZBrush's hardsurface modeling tools are so useful for creating character accessories, I have also included a video on making a sci-fi gun using ZBrush. Please look on the DVD or download files for this bonus content. (The gun seen here was designed by Christian Pierce.)

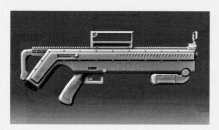

## Create the Lower Body

The lower body spinal section and pipes are created using a combination of tools. The pipes are generated with ZSketch, using the same technique as before. The lumbar (lower) spinal section is created using ZSketch and the Group Loops function to create the more intricate details. Follow these steps to create the lower body section. Be sure to check the DVD or download files for a video that details how to use ZSketch in conjunction with Group Loops to create unique forms like this.

1. Append a ZSphere into the SubTool stack. Draw a chain that extends from the torso down toward the hip area. Make sure it is long enough to feel like a functional waist and spine for the character. You will want to use this form to balance the upper body. Draw a few branches off the central ZSphere chain as seen in Figure 6.51. This structure is designed to mirror the configuration of the lumbar vertebrae, only larger and mechanical in nature (Figure 6.52).

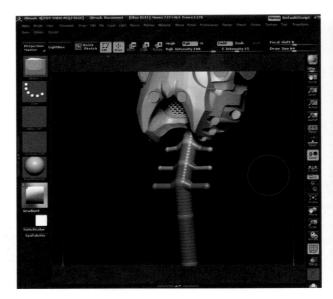 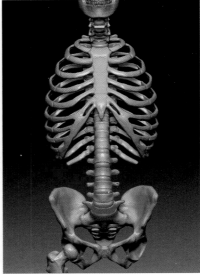

*Figure 6.51: The ZSphere chain for the lumbar section*

*Figure 6.52: The lumbar spine of the skeleton*

2. Enable edit sketch under Tool ➢ ZSketch. Using the Sketch 1 and Sketch A brushes, build up the form into an interesting shape. Try to consider how the mechanical structure will look when it is complete. Each ZSketch stroke will be a polygroup and later in this section we will isolate and extrude each stroke. Keep this in mind as you draw the stokes (Figure 6.53). There are other stroke brushes available in the Lightbox under the Brush ➢ ZSketch menu. I encourage you to experiment with the Sketch 2 and Sketch 3 brushes as well as Sketch B and Sketch C. These brushes build up form in different degrees of intensity.

*Figure 6.53: Strokes are polygrouped by default.*

3. When you have completed building up the general form of the lower body, create a Unified Skin by pressing Tool ➢ Unified Skin ➢ Make Unified Skin (Figure 6.54). This will create a new skin tool in the tool palette that represents an editable mesh of your ZSketch.

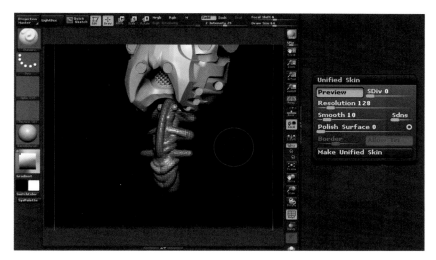

*Figure 6.54: Create an editable object from the ZSketch with the Make Unified Skin button.*

4. Append the Unified Skin into the SubTool stack. You will now delete the ZSketch now or hide it from view.
5. At this stage, we will use a tool called Group Loops to isolate each polygrouped stroke with an edgeloop (Figure 6.55). This will allow us to create some interesting and intricate surface details with sharp machined edges. Group Loop the mesh by pressing the Tool ➢ Geometry ➢ GroupLoop button. Notice how this slightly smoothes the mesh and adds a defining edgeloop around each polygroup.
6. Isolate the main loop seen in yellow here by Ctrl + Shift + Clicking on the polygroup. This will isolate the polygroup and allow you to mask it independently of the rest of the model. Ctrl + Click on the background to mask all. Ctrl + Shift + Click on the background to reveal the full mesh again and invert the mask by Ctrl + Clicking on the background.

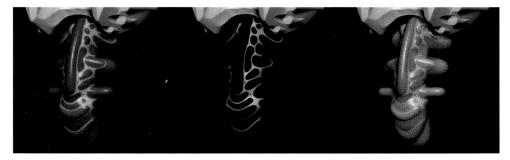

*Figure 6.55: The lower body with Groups Loops applied. The main edgeloop is isolated. The model is masked, with the main loop unmasked.*

7. You may now extrude just the edgeloop by opening Tool ➤ Deformation and dragging the inflate slider. This will offset the unmasked areas from the rest of the model creating a very interesting surface detail. You may further offset groups by selectively masking and using the inflate slider or the move tools (Figure 6.56).

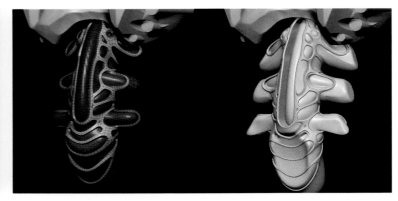

*Figure 6.56: Use the inflate slider to alter the unmasked edgeloop and add an interesting surface detail. This is the result of inflating the edgeloop to offset it from the rest of the surface*

8. The pipes are created with ZSketch. I appended a single ZSphere into the torso and then drew the strokes from the torso to the contact points on the spine. Use the Move brush to shift the pipes around and make it flow in the direction you wish. Create a Unified Skin and then mirror the structure across the X axis using the SubTool Master Mirror function (Figure 6.57). Check the DVD or download files for a video of this process in action.

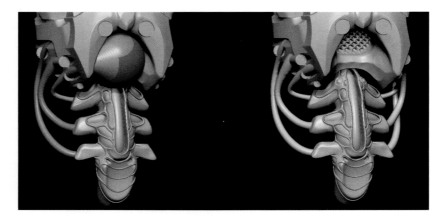

*Figure 6.57: Adding the pipes to the lower body using ZSketch and then converting to a skin and mirroring the resulting geometry*

This completes the modeling and design of this figure. In this chapter we have seen how to use ZBrush's hard surface modeling tools to sketch mechanical forms much in the same way organics are created easily in ZBrush. These tools free the designer to think in different kinds of shapes with the same loose and freeform approach. Usually mechanical designs must be planned painstakingly before being approached in 3-D. Using these techniques, a much more "sketch" oriented approach is possible. Please be sure to see the DVD or download files for a video of this design process.

The final image is created by compositing images from the BPR render passes. Noise textures were laid in as overlay layers to add a sense of grime to the image (Figure 6.58).

*Figure 6.58: The final image*

seven

# Sculpting a Mermaid Character with Dynamesh

**In this chapter, we will** *create an ichthyoid character, a different take on the mermaid archetype. Ichthyoid is the technical term for a fish or fishlike vertebrate animal. We will execute this design using a different ZBrush tool for generating base meshes. Previously, we have worked with imported models, generic meshes, or ZSketch strokes. In this chapter we will explore a new development in ZBrush 4 R2 called Dynamesh. Dynamesh allows you to dynamically build up a character using what essentially amounts to a ball of dynamically updating clay. We will be able to push and pull a single ZBrush Polysphere and even add new parts—seamlessly incorporating them*

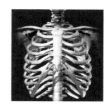

*into the original volume. This is a groundbreaking new approach to sculpting and I am excited to share the technique with you here. It allows a seamless creative process to take place in ZBrush in ways never before possible. Figure 7.1 shows the character we will create in this chapter.*

*Figure 7.1: The mermaid character*

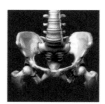

## The Brief: Creating the Aquatic Female Character

Our design brief for this chapter is to create an aquatic female character, a new take on the mermaid. The mermaid should not follow the typical archetype of female torso on a fish body; rather, look for ways to create an appealing feminine character while combining humanoid and fish form language. The character need not appear helpless or vulnerable; instead she should seem fully capable of self-defense in an underwater environment while retaining beauty, sense of grace, and elegance. The character should appear much more ichthyoid than human.

We will execute this brief using dynamesh as our primary design tool. This will allow us to build up the volumes of the character with no concern for the underlying base mesh. Dynamesh allows us to approach this figure just like we would a traditional clay sculpture, by adding and removing mass when and how we need to, rather than trying to push an existing volume into the shapes we need.

# Using Visual Cues to Communicate Character

In the process of working this brief, we will need to create an undoubtedly alien character—in this case, an undersea being with ichthyoid qualities that reads to the audience as being female. How do we accomplish this? To successfully communicate humanoid and aquatic qualities, we need to find real world touchstones we can incorporate into the design. These visual cues serve to subconsciously push the viewer's mind to make the assumptions we want them to make about the character. We have seen this already in how we treat the jawline of an aggressive character or how we use shape language to communicate malicious intent as opposed to kindness. In this case, we will look for typically female qualities we can incorporate into the design.

Since we know this character needs to appear more alien than human, we know we will need to rely on the body proportions and the shape and relationship between the facial features to communicate a sense of the feminine. Without being able to rely on cultural gender cues like hair and costume, we will rely instead on a generalized baseline of skeletal and facial shape relationships that will lead the mind to read the figure as female.

### Stereotypes and Tropes in Design

In design we sometimes have to play with stereotypes as a visual shorthand to communicate some things to the audience. For example, when creating this feminine-looking creature, we will rely on some facial structural cues that are stereotypically feminine within a narrow band of western culture. It is important to keep in mind there are vast variations of female and male faces in the human population just like there are variations in body types, skin tones, and costume. When we try and shape the viewer's perceptions while relying on generalized perceptions, keep in mind the elements we rely on in this chapter are exactly that, generalizations and not a barometer for any kind of visual standard of "beauty."

## Skeletal and Morphological Differences Between the Sexes

Since we will need to create the impression this character is female rather than male while retaining a distinctly alien anatomy, we will need to understand the common general visual cues that help us sex the skeleton. From a skeletal standpoint, the female skeleton tends to be smaller and lighter than the male's. The humerus bones, in the upper arms, are typically longer than in the male. The ribcage is narrower and the thoracic arch is not as widely set

(Figure 7.2). The torso in the female is slightly longer than the male, while the lower extremities (legs) are shorter and the shoulders and ribs are narrower. There is a common myth that women have one less rib than men. This is not so, as both men and women have 24 ribs including the two "floating" ribs.

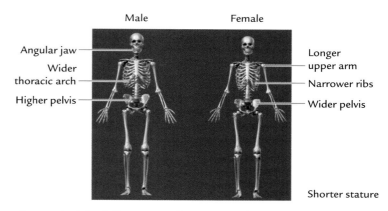

Figure 7.2: *The differences in the male and female skeleton are illustrated here.*

The female pelvis is wider than and not as high as the male pelvis. The inguinal ligament is not as defined in the joint between the hips and the lower extremities. The pelvis may appear to have a slight inclination forward compared to the typical male pelvis. The wider pubic arch creates a larger space for the abductors of the thigh to attach. This leaves an opening between the legs in a more slender figure where the inner thighs are not padded with fatty tissue. This is because the origins of these muscles will be farther from the midline of the body than in the male (Figure 7.3).

The measuring point used on the skeleton, the great trochanter of the femur, is generally considered the widest point of the male hips. On the female, this widest point appears lower due to the differences in the way fat tissues are distributed (Figure 7.4).

The face is where we will try to incorporate many of the more subtle visual cues. Figure 7.5 shows a female face of European descent with some typical features called out that feminize the forms. We will incorporate elements like the shape of the chin, the more acute angle of the jaw, and the rounder structure of the cheeks into this mermaid character. The addition of these visual cues should cause the viewer to perceive the face as feminine despite its absolutely alien nature.

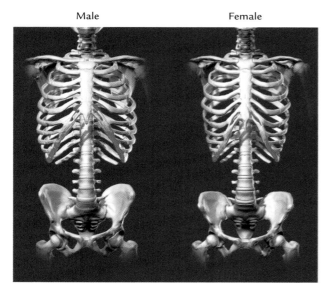

Figure 7.3: *The thoracic arch (in red) is wider in the male ribcage and narrower in the female. Also note how the pelvis is lower and wider in the female.*

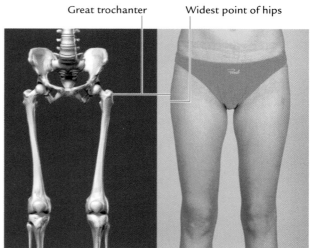

Figure 7.4: *Here you can see the great trochanter on the skeleton and the fat pad of the hips, which create the widest point on the hips.*

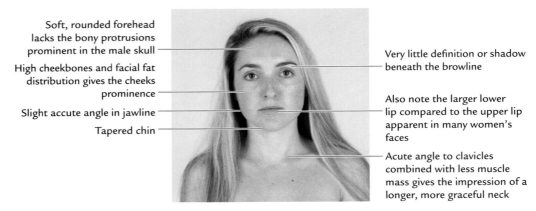

Soft, rounded forehead lacks the bony protrusions prominent in the male skull

High cheekbones and facial fat distribution gives the cheeks prominence

Slight accute angle in jawline

Tapered chin

Very little definition or shadow beneath the browline

Also note the larger lower lip compared to the upper lip apparent in many women's faces

Acute angle to clavicles combined with less muscle mass gives the impression of a longer, more graceful neck

*Figure 7.5: Here we can see some of the key feminine facial features we will try to incorporate into our character design.*

Remember that human and animal anatomy are two powerful tools in your arsenal as a designer. An understanding of how skeletal and muscular anatomy are arranged in nature allows you to combine natural structures from various sources in new and viable ways. This level of understanding also helps you influence the audience's perceptions by exploiting key shape relationships that communicate things on a instinctual level about the character. This mermaid is a perfect example. We will combine a ichthyoid face with humanoid elements and by playing on the audience's expectations of what is a stereotypically feminine, you can communicate that this completely nonhuman creature is female, graceful, and potentially dangerous due to her spiny fins.

By understanding how the viewer will react to various combinations of shape language and proportion, you can influence the audience's perceptions of your character on a deeper level. When you are thinking about your characters in this level, it becomes less a question of "how do I put neat shapes together?" and more of a case of "how do I combine shapes that tell the story I want to communicate about this creature?"

## Introduction to Dynamesh

Dynamesh is a new tool developed for ZBrush 4 R2. Essentially, Dynamesh tries to replicate the feel of sculpting in practical clay by allowing you to continually pull new forms from the base shape, interactively combine new meshes into the existing volume, and even carve away negative spaces, all the while maintaining an easily workable even quad mesh layout. This frees you from really having to think about the underlying topology as you work. It also allows you to create any kind of volume for sculpting without having to be tied to the limits of a base mesh. This is highly beneficial in cases where you might want to carve out a large negative space in a model. In previous workflows this was not easily accomplished. With Dynamesh, the mesh will update to accommodate any new shapes you create or remove from the model.

## Getting a Feel for Dynamesh

In this section, we will look at a basic demonstration of Dynamesh using basic primitives. We will create an abstract organic shape as an opportunity to experiment with the Dynamesh workflow before we dive into creating a figure sculpture.

1. Open ZBrush or create a new project. Open the Lightbox and from the Tool section load the Polysphere ZTool. Step down to the lowest Subdivision level and under Tool ➢ Geometry, click the Del Higher button to remove the higher subdivision levels.

2. From the Brush menu, select the Move brush. Turn on X symmetry and start to pull the sphere out into a larger shape. Don't be afraid to stretch the mesh beyond its normal limits. You will see the mesh starts to distort as the underlying polygons are stretched (Figure 7.6).

3. At this stage it is impossible to alter the shape of the sphere further without adding new sub-division levels because the underlying mesh is stretched beyond its limits. Using Dynamesh, we will now rebuild the underlying mesh to support the new form. Click Tool ➢ Geometry and set the Dynamesh Resolution slider to 32.

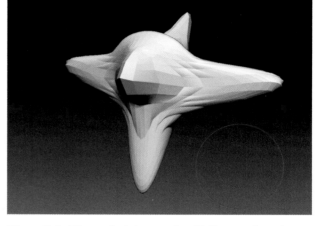

*Figure 7.6: The underlying mesh will distort when the Polysphere is stretched beyond the limits of its underlying topology.*

Press the Dynamesh button (Figure 7.7). If you forgot to delete the higher subdivision levels, ZBrush will ask if you want to freeze subdivision levels—if so, press no. ZBrush will now rebuild the mesh into an evenly spaced all-quads topology that supports the current shape (Figure 7.8).

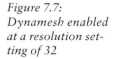

*Figure 7.7: Dynamesh enabled at a resolution setting of 32*

4. Using the Move brush, continue to shift the geometry—stretching it into new directions. You may also try using the Snakehook brush, which often pulls the geometry beyond the limits of the mesh (Figure 7.9). When you are satisfied with the new shape, we will dynamesh again to correct the geometry to better support the form.

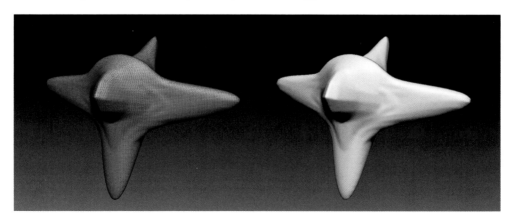

*Figure 7.8: The dynameshed geometry*

5. To re-dynamesh the model, hold down the Ctrl key and click and drag a masking marquee on the document window—do not mask the model, simply Ctrl + Click + Drag somewhere off the model (Figure 7.10). ZBrush will again apply dynamesh and rebuild the underlying geometry to support the shapes you have created (Figure 7.11).

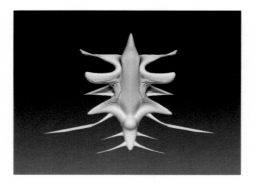

Figure 7.9: *Stretching the shape further*

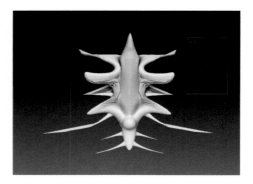

Figure 7.10: *Drag a masking marquee some-where off the model with Ctrl + Click + Drag while in Dynamesh mode to re-dynamesh.*

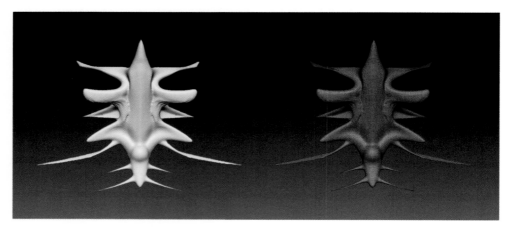

Figure 7.11: *The new form dynameshed to rebuild the underlying topology*

It is not necessary to add subdivisions when Dynamesh is on because they will be deleted whenever you Ctrl + Drag to execute Dynamesh. If you want to increase the resolution of your Dynamesh, you can adjust the resolution slider under Dynamesh in the Geometry menu. It is best to consider it a blocking in or rough-form building tool. Once you get the general form in, you will exit Dynamesh mode and begin to add subdivision levels and sculpt as you normally would in ZBrush. For this reason, I avoid setting the resolution slider too high. I use Dynamesh to establish the overall forms while maintaining a workable lower resolution mesh. To exit Dynamesh mode, simply press the Dynamesh button under Tool ➤ Geometry.

Now that we understand the basic approach to Dynamesh, let us look at some of the added functionality of the Insert Mesh brushes.

## Insert Mesh Brushes

ZBrush 4 R2 has further developed the insert mesh functionality to incorporate it into a set of brushes called the Insert Mesh brushes. We will look now at how these brushes are used to incorporate new geometry into the model seamlessly.

1. Enable Dynamesh again if you have turned off Dynamesh mode. From the Brush menu, select the Insert Sphere brush (Figure 7.12). Click and drag on the ZTool in the document window to insert a sphere.

2. The model will automatically mask. This allows you to manipulate the sphere with the Sculpting or Transpose tools. Position the sphere where it intersects the model and clear the mask by Ctrl + Click dragging a marquee of the model. At this point the mask is merely cleared—the model has yet to be dynameshed. Draw another masking marquee of the model again to update the Dynamesh. The spheres will now be incorporated into the rest of the model (Figure 7.13).

4. The Mesh Insert brushes can also be used in a subtractive manner. That means you can add volume with them as well as subtract. From the Brush menu, select the Insert Cylinder brush. Click and draw a cylinder on the mesh while holding down the Alt key. Any time you draw a mesh with the Mesh Insert brush while holding Alt, it will subtract that volume rather than add it (Figure 7.14).

5. Clear the mesh and then draw a second mask marquee to apply Dynamesh. The cylinders will disappear and their volume will be subtracted from the model (Figure 7.15).

*Figure 7.12:  Using the InsertSphere brush*

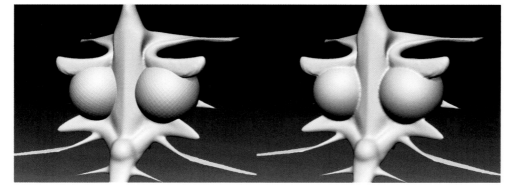

*Figure 7.13:  The sphere is placed and then the sphere is incorporated with Dynamesh.*

**6.** Mesh Insert allows you to incorporate multiple copies of a mesh at one time. Select the Insert Sphere brush and draw a new sphere on the model. Scale and position the mesh (Figure 7.16). Press W to enter Transpose Move mode. Draw a transpose line and while holding down Ctrl + Click, drag in the center circle to drag the spheres. If you hold Ctrl, this will actually drag a new copy of the sphere (Figure 7.17).

**7.** Drag multiple copies of the spheres along the model (Figure 7.18). When you are done, clear the mask then execute a Dynamesh by control-click dragging again on the document window. The spheres will be incorporated into the model (Figure 7.19).

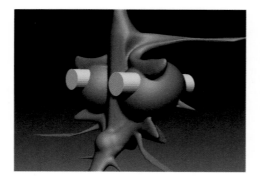

*Figure 7.14: Draw a cylinder with the Insert Cylinder brush while holding Alt.*

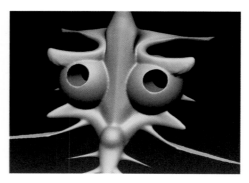

*Figure 7.15: The cylinder volumes subtracted from the mesh*

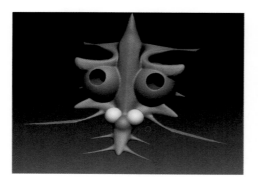

*Figure 7.16: A new sphere scaled and positioned*

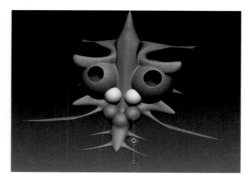

*Figure 7.17: Ctrl + Click drag in the center circle of the transpose move line to make copies of the sphere.*

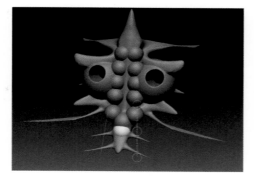

*Figure 7.18: Placing copies of the sphere up the length of the model*

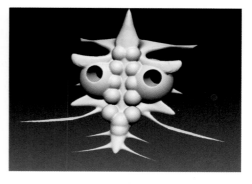

*Figure 7.19: Dynamesh combines all the meshes into one volume.*

Now we have a general overview of the Dynamesh tools. We are ready to start using them to create an actual character.

# Creating the Figure

In the following sections, we will build up a figure from basic volumes using the same techniques demonstrated above. We will also use the Mesh Insert brush to add arms from an entirely different model. Let's get started.

## Start the Figure: Base Shapes

We will use a Polysphere to start this figure. Beginning with the head, we will create the major forms of the head, neck, torso, shoulders, waist, and arms by inserting basic primitives. Follow the steps below to block in the figure.

1. Initialize ZBrush. From the Lightbox, select the Polysphere ZTool. Draw it on the canvas and enter edit mode.
2. Select the Move brush and rough in the general shape of the head (Figure 7.20). This will be a feminine character so try to focus on keeping a more acute angle to the jaw and a smaller chin. A more masculine figure head would have a wider jawline and a more pronounced chin.
3. Isolate the area for the neck with a mask (Figure 7.21). Select the Move brush and turn up the Draw size so you can move the whole unmasked area with one stroke. Pull the neck geometry down from the head form (Figure 7.22).

*Figure 7.20: Start to shape the head with the Move brush.*

*Figure 7.21: Isolate the neck with a mask.*

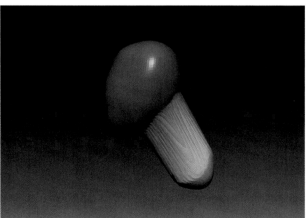

*Figure 7.22: Use the Move brush to pull the neck down from the head.*

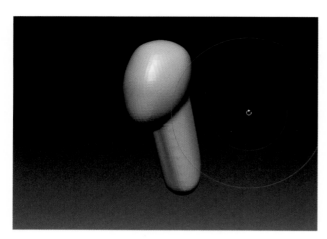

*Figure 7.23: Dynamesh used to resurface the head and neck form*

4. We are now ready to apply Dynamesh. Open Tool ➢ Geometry and set the resolution slider to 24. Drag a masking marquee to apply the Dynamesh (Figure 7.23).

5. We will now add the torso. Rather than try to stretch the neck into a torso shape, we will simply use Insert Sphere to add a sphere. This is the best approach since the torso will take on an egg form from the ribcage and it simply makes good sense to add a primitive sphere form and then shape that into the torso mass. From the Brush menu, select the Insert Sphere brush

6. Insert a sphere into the mesh and then switch to the Move brush. Shift the sphere into an egg form. Using the Move brush, I suggest the hollow area in the ribs known as the thoracic arch. Dynamesh to merge the pieces into one mesh (Figure 7.24).

When making this ribcage, I am trying to keep in mind this is intended to be a feminine creature. This should be reflected in the shape of the ribcage. As we saw earlier, the male ribcage is larger and wider set—the thoracic arch is more open, while on the female ribcage the arch is narrower and the overall size of the mass is smaller (Figure 7.21). The ratio of size between the ribcage-shoulders and hips will all help to immediately lead the viewer to ascribe feminine traits to the character even if she has several overwhelming ichthyoid qualities as well.

7. Using the Mesh Insert brush, draw two spheres for the shoulders (Figure 7.25). With the Move brush, shape them to help create the scapulas from behind and the trapezius muscles from the front (Figure 7.26).

8. Dynamesh to combine the shapes into one (Figure 7.27).

9. Rotate to a side view and with the Move brush, check the gesture of the neck. I adjust this slightly to give a more graceful curve from the head to the shoulders. As I work, even at this early stage, I am trying to remain aware of the need to maintain graceful feminine forms (Figure 7.28).

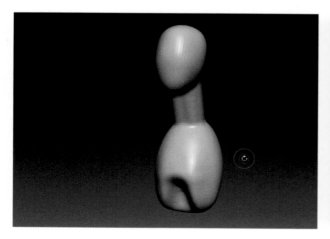

*Figure 7.24: Create an egg shape for the torso.*

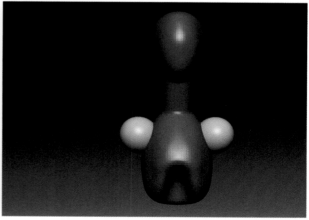

*Figure 7.25: Insert spheres for shoulders.*

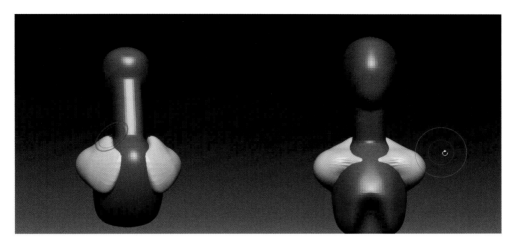

*Figure 7.26: Shaping the spheres into the trapezius muscle and scapulae*

10. Insert another sphere for the waist. Shift it into position and using the Move brush, give it the general shape of the pelvis, the abdominal muscles, as well as the muscles of the lower back (Figure 7.29). Try and be aware of how the masses of the body interlock and interrelate. They are not just stacked shapes—rather, they are puzzle parts that interlock (Figure 7.30).

11. Add two more spheres to serve as the buttocks. Shape them with the Move brush as shown in Figure 7.31. Use the Inflate brush with a low ZIntensity setting to inflate the two spheres against each other to create the illusion of the gluteal cleft where the two glutes meet. Dynamesh to combine these parts.

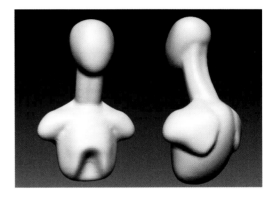

*Figure 7.27: Shoulders dynameshed*

12. Select the Insert Cylinder brush. Draw two cylinders into the mesh and position them with transpose move. These will serve as the base shapes from the upper arms (Figure 7.32). I will insert the lower arms in a later step. Dynamesh to combine the parts (Figure 7.33).

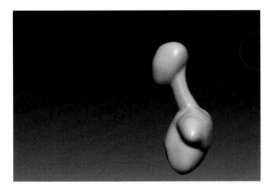

*Figure 7.28: Adjusting the gesture of the neck for a more graceful curve*

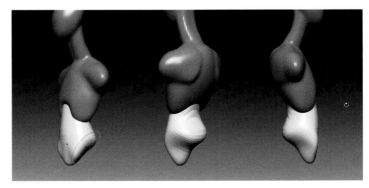

*Figure 7.29: Add a sphere for the waist.*

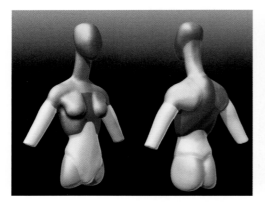

*Figure 7.30: Here you can see the interlocking volumes of the body color coded. Remember that the forms are not simply stacked in space—rather, they interlock like a puzzle.*

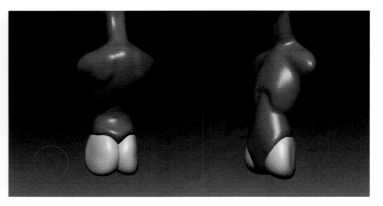

*Figure 7.31: Add two spheres for buttocks.*

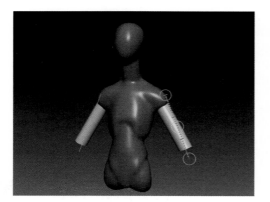

*Figure 7.32: The upper arms are created from inserting cylinders.*

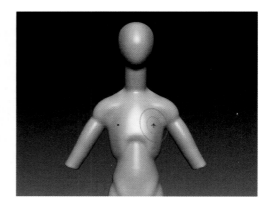

*Figure 7.33: The arms combined with Dynamesh*

13. Since this is a "mermaid" and a feminine character, we will add a major secondary sexual characteristic by giving the figure a bustline. This will immediately convey to most viewers that the figure is female as opposed to male. The breasts are added by placing two Mesh Insert spheres on the ribcage (Figure 7.34). Be careful when placing the breasts that you do not treat them like spheres stuck on the front of the body. These forms lay against the cylinder of the ribcage and should have a sense of weight.

14. Rotate to the side view and with the Move brush, bring the top of the breasts up to the collar bone. They should take on a teardrop shape where the weight is in the bottom of the form. There should be a definite sense of the tissue laying against the ribcage rather than being a large unnatural volume stuck on the body (Figure 7.35).

15. Remember that the muscles of the chest lay beneath the breast. The pectoral muscle needs to be apparent where it extends from under the breast to attach to the upper arm (Figure 7.36). Use the Move brush to create this form, which also serves as the front wall of the armpit. Dynamesh to combine the forms.

16. Using the Standard brush, sketch in the shape of the clavicles. At this stage, I also suggest the placement of the eyes by creating two depressions on the head. These are not final details, just landmarks to help me see while I work (Figure 7.37).

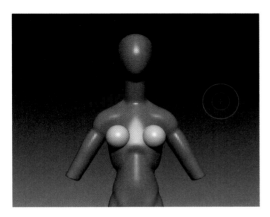

Figure 7.34: *Insert spheres to serve as the basis for the bust*

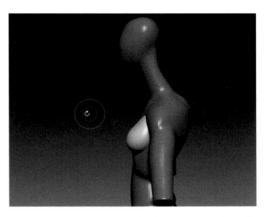

Figure 7.35: *Adjusting the breast from the side*

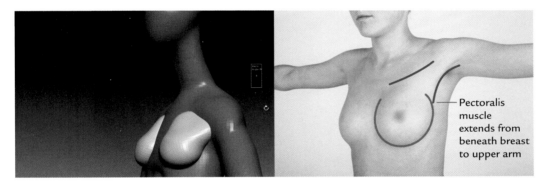

Pectoralis muscle extends from beneath breast to upper arm

Figure 7.36: *The pectoralis muscle extends from beneath the breast to the upper arm, forming the front wall of the armpit.*

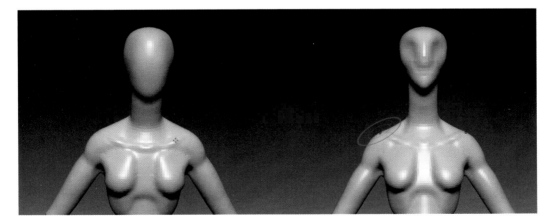

Figure 7.37: *Sketch in the shape of the clavicles with the Standard brush.*

At this point, the primary shapes of the figure are completed. We are now ready to start to address secondary forms.

## Working with Secondary Forms

In this section, we will address the figure's various body parts, adding details that will infuse character and complexity. We will add the arms and hands as well as several fin forms. The idea behind the fins will be to break up the silhouette with fin forms, creating a more complex and interesting shape.

### Create the Neck Fins

The neck fins will be created by inserting a sphere, changing its shape, and then duplicating it up the length of the neck. The form is intended to suggest both a fin structure as well as a high ruff collar as seen on fashions in the seventeenth century.

1. Begin by inserting a sphere with the Insert Sphere brush. Turn off X symmetry so only one instance of the sphere is drawn. Use the Move brush to flatten the sphere into a fin shape, as seen in Figure 7.38. Once you are satisfied with the shape of the initial fin form, draw a transpose move line. While holding down Ctrl + Click, drag the center circle to duplicate a new instance of the neck fin and position it slightly above the first. I scale this new fin down slightly.

2. Use the Move brush to alter the shape of the front of the fin so it incorporates into the neckline, as seen in Figure 7.39.

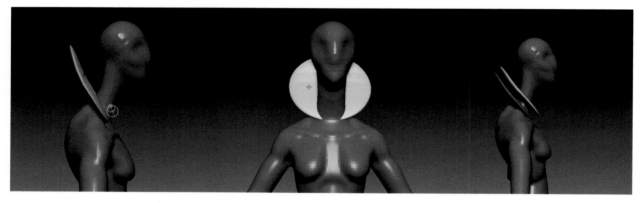

*Figure 7.38: Insert neck sphere and change the shape. Then duplicate it by Ctrl + Click dragging the transpose line.*

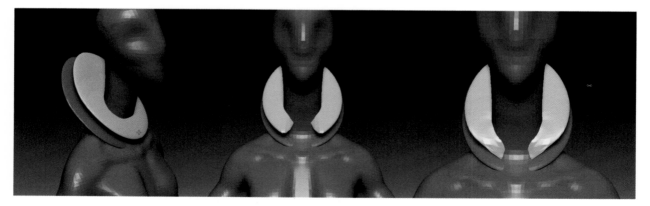

*Figure 7.39: With the Move brush, shape the front of the fin so it integrates into the neck in an interesting way.*

3. Duplicate 3 more instances of the fins up the neck. Be sure to change the scale as you go, so the shape will taper toward the head (Figure 7.40).

4. Using the Move brush, I add a kick to the uppermost fin. This helps to add some character to the shape (Figure 7.41).

5. Duplicate the fin again and bring it down to the shoulders. I widen this instance and give it a wide flared quality like a collar or short shawl. The fins are intended to suggest the flowing fin of a manta ray (Figure 7.42). Clear the mask and update the Dynamesh to combine the fins into the body (Figure 7.43).

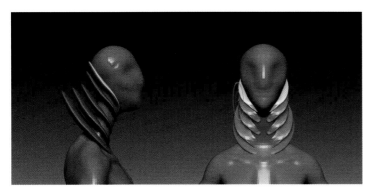

*Figure 7.40: Duplicate the neck fins up toward the head.*

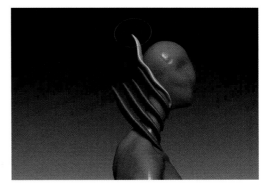

*Figure 7.41: Adding a visual twist to the tip of one fin*

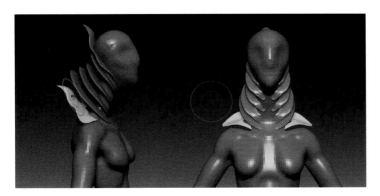

*Figure 7.42: The fins ready to dynamesh*

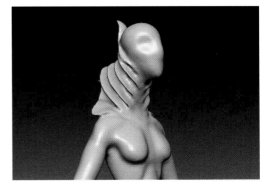

*Figure 7.43: The fins dynameshed into the sculpture*

6. At this stage, the fins are simply concentric rings leading up the neck. I want to add some interest to them by changing the negative spaces they create. I will do this by subtracting some volume from the fins and thereby giving some complexity to their form. Select the InsertSphere brush. Turn on Z symmetry and draw two spheres while holding down Alt. Transpose scale them to intersect with the neck fins as shown in Figure 7.44. Remember that when we dynamesh, the volume of the spheres will be subtracted form the fins. Update the dynamesh by drawing a marquee off the model (Figure 7.45).

7. At this point, I want to add a cowl or cloak structure which will suggest both a draped cape as well as a fin in the manner of a manta ray. This is intended to break up the back of the figure silhouette and give the impression of a sweeping beautiful drapery.

8. Turn off X symmetry. Insert a sphere in the back as seen in Figure 7.46. With the Move brush, shape it as seen in Figure 7.47, so it extends from the neck fins down to the hips.
9. Dynamesh to combine the parts together by clearing the mask and then drawing another masking marquee off the model (Figure 7.48).

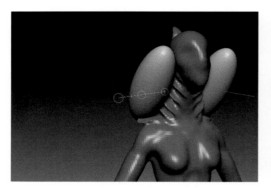

Figure 7.44: Inserting spheres to the neck for use as a subtractive object

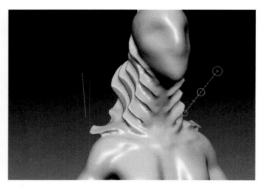

Figure 7.45: The sphere volumes subtracted from the fin forms

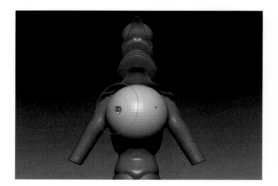

Figure 7.46: Insert a sphere into the back to create the cowl.

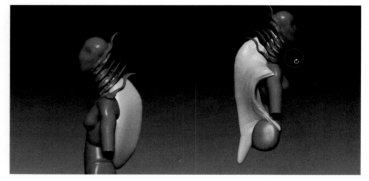

Figure 7.47: Shape the sphere so it conforms to the back and creates a large draping fin shape, similar to a manta ray.

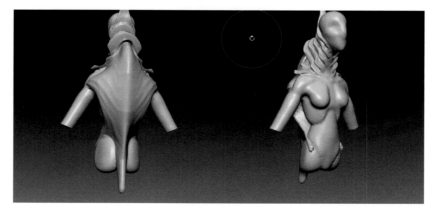

Figure 7.48: The back fins dynameshed

Next we will use MeshInsert to create a series of vents down the sides of the figure. This adds both visual interest as well as the impression of a biological function to the flaring membranes at the sides of the body. I feel these may serve as a method of locomotion where water may be taken in and then expelled, much in a manner similar to squid locomotion.

1. Turn on X symmetry and add two spheres to the mesh. Using the Move brush, flatten them into disk shapes. Place them in the armpits of the figure.
2. Draw a transpose line and while holding Ctrl + Click, drag the center circle to create a second pair of vents below the first pair. Shape these and scale them to follow the contours of the cowl form. Again, duplicate several instances down the length of the body, as seen in Figure 7.49. Combine the mesh with Dynamesh (Figure 7.50).

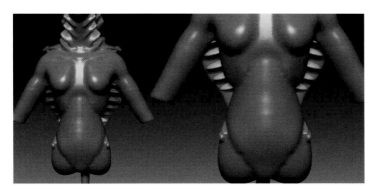

*Figure 7.49: Adding vents to the back fin structure*

*Figure 7.50: The vents dynameshed into the whole*

## Head Details

In this section, we will start to add some more details to the head of the figure. Starting with the crest fin and moving on to eyes, lips, and details. We are nearly done with the Dynamesh phase and are ready to move into traditional ZBrush sculpting.

1. Mask the top of the mesh with a marquee. Isolate a strip of faces, which we will use to create the top fin (Figure 7.51).
2. Using the Move brush, pull the fin faces up and shape them as seen in Figure 7.52.

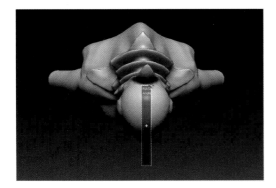

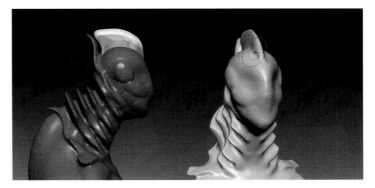

*Figure 7.51: Mask the top of the head to cre-ate a cranial fin.*

*Figure 7.52: Use the Move brush to shift the faces up from the top of the head to create the fin shape.*

3. We will now add eyeballs to the mesh. Append a Polysphere into the ZTool and place it with Transpose Move and Scale. Mirror it across the X axis using the SubTool master plug-in (Figure 7.53).

*Figure 7.53: Add spheres for eyes.*

4. Using the Clay Tubes brush, reinforce the basic forms of the face (Figure 7.54). I intend to keep this face as simple as possible while still communicating an appealing feminine quality. The less detail I put in here, the more soft and streamlined it should appear. It is a tricky balancing act to get that right. Turn on Transparency mode and isolate the faces behind the eye with a mask (Figure 7.55). Next, pull those faces out to the surface of the eyeball. We will use these to sculpt eyelids and other membranes around the sphere of the eye (Figure 7.56). Even though fish do not have eyelids, we want to give her some humanoid characteristics to the eyes since these are key to creating a sense of empathy with the character.

5. Use the Move brush to shift the lids around and create a tear duct (Figure 7.57). Here, the cheekbone is masked to help protect that form from the Move brush while we work the eye area. At this stage, I use the Standard brush to suggest the lips by etching in the gesture of the lip line.

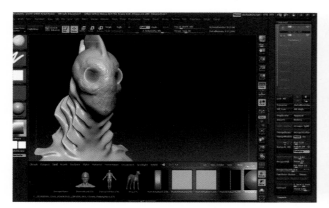 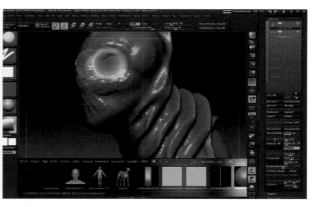

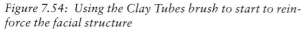

*Figure 7.54: Using the Clay Tubes brush to start to reinforce the facial structure*

*Figure 7.55: Isolate the faces behind the eye with a mask.*

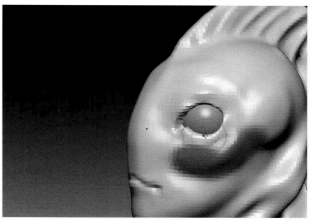

*Figure 7.56: Bring those isolated faces to the surface of the eye and suggest eyelids.*

*Figure 7.57: Create the tear duct. The cheekbone is masked to protect the form from being inadvertently changed with the Move brush as we work this area.*

6. The eyes are refined with the Move brush. Using the Standard brush, start to suggest the shape of the lips. The lips are further refined by gently inflating the upper and lower lip forms (Figure 7.58). We will return to the lips later after we exit Dynamesh mode. At this stage, they require more resolution than we are able to provide without dividing the mesh again.

*Figure 7.58: Sculpting the eyes and lips*

## Adding the Forearms and Hands

We will add the forearms and hands by cutting them off an existing mesh. One of the strengths of the Insert Mesh brushes is that they are capable of inserting any mesh that can be loaded into ZBrush, so long as it has only one subdivision level. For the arms, we will use the forearms off the SuperAverageMan tool.

1. Open the Lightbox ➤ Tool menu and select the SuperAverageMan ZTool. Double click to select it. It will replace the current model displayed on screen as the active ZTool. Press the F key to center the model in the document window.
2. From the Brush menu, select the SelectLasso brush. ZBrush will notify you that this brush is now the active selection brush—Click OK and make sure X symmetry is off.
3. Draw a selection marquee around the forearm, isolating it from the rest of the model (Figure 7.59).
4. With the arm isolated, click on Tool ➤ Geometry ➤ delete hidden, to remove the body, which we will not need.
5. The arm is very thick and masculine. We will want to reduce its mass slightly so it will fit better with the mermaid character. Open the Tool ➤ Deformation menu and set the inflate slider to −2. This will cause an overall shrinkage in the arm, thinning the fingers and hand (Figure 7.60).

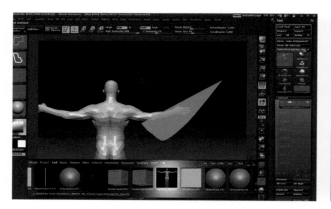 

*Figure 7.59: Isolating the forearms with a select lasso*

*Figure 7.60: Thin the arm with inflate set to −2. Here the arm has been deflated by −2 to thin the fingers. The slider automatically resets to 0 after each use.*

6. The arm is now ready to be inserted into the mermaid model. From the Tool menu, select the character mesh. It will replace the arm on screen as the active ZTool. Press F to refocus the model to the center of the document window.
7. From the Brush menu, select the InsertEar brush. Open the Brush ➤ Modifiers menu and Click on the little window that shows the ear. When you do this, the pop-up tool library opens and you can select from any of the 3-D meshes. Here you may browse to any loaded ZTool and select it as the inserting mesh. From this tool menu, select the forearm in its place (Figure 7.61).
8. The arms are now set to be the meshes inserted by the InsertEar brush. This will only be for this session and the brush will reset when you restart or initialize ZBrush. Turn on X symmetry and draw the arms into the model (Figure 7.62).
9. Use the Transpose Move and Scale tools to position the arms and scale them to the body (Figure 7.63). Dynamesh to combine them into the body (Figure 7.64).

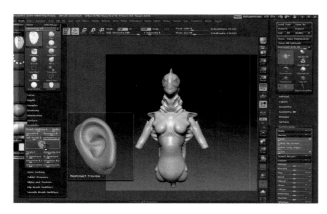

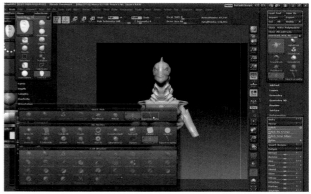

*Figure 7.61: Selecting the forearm to insert*

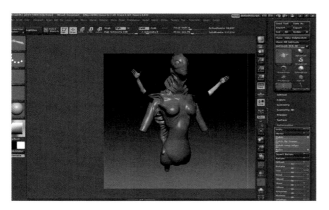

*Figure 7.62: Arms drawn with the MeshInsert brush*

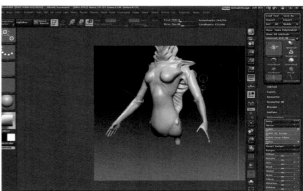

*Figure 7.63: Arm inserted and positioned*

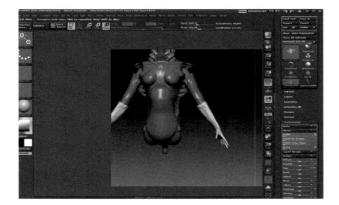

*Figure 7.64: The arms combined with Dynamesh*

10. The elbow joints are isolated with a mask and pressed in to create a sharp lip on the upper and lower arms. This helps suggest a hard carapace around the limbs, like a shell (Figure 7.65).

11. At this point, I pull a kick off the elbow. This serves as a defense structure, biologically. Aesthetically, it suggests an elbow length glove and helps extend the graceful line of the arm back from the figure (Figure 7.66).

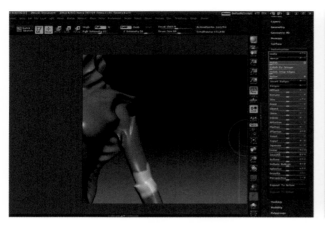 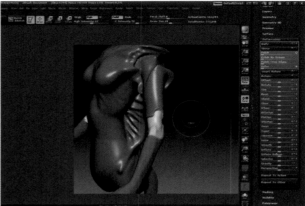

*Figure 7.65: Using a mask to create detail in the joints at the elbows*

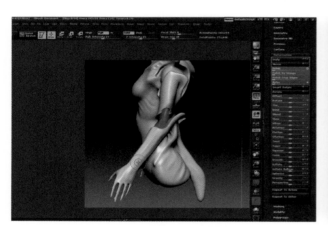 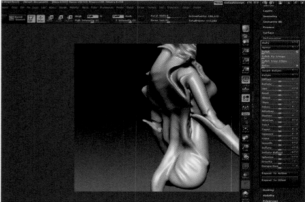

*Figure 7.66: Using the Move brush, pull a spike from the elbow—this suggests a defensive structure and helps to create an elegant line in the arm.*

All the various parts of the figure are in place—we now want to move on to detailing the figure. The first step will be to turn off Dynamesh.

## Adding Final Details

At this phase, we are done with the need for Dynamesh. While we could execute Dynamesh with a higher resolution setting to get more detail, in my experience this is an inefficient way to work. I like to use Dynamesh to establish the primary and secondary forms of the character and then switch into normal subdivision level sculpting to further refine the forms. This allows us to have a range of subdivision levels to move between as we work. Turn off Dynamesh by clicking the Tool ➤ Geometry ➤ Dynamesh button. Now we will start to finesse the figure by adding finer lips and other details.

### Sculpting the Lips

Now that we are out of Dynamesh mode, we can start to add subdivision levels and include more fine detail in the model. In this section, we will refine the lips. The lips and eyes are the central humanizing features in this character—it is the point of reference where the viewer will try to relate to the figure. For this reason, I try and introduce as much character as possible in this area.

1. Add a subdivision level by pressing Ctrl + D. This gives us the level of resolution we need to add the subtlety required for the lips. I choose not to add much detail to the face. I want it to keep its primary general form with subtle shifts in planes to help create a sense of delicate beauty rather than creepy detail.

2. Use the Standard brush to sketch in the gesture of the upper lip line. This is the ledge of the lips where the face meets the soft tissue of the lip itself (Figure 7.67).

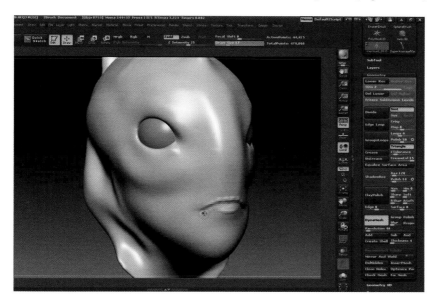

*Figure 7.67:  Tracing the lip line*

3. Select the Clay Tubes brush with the alpha off, and set the ZIntensity to a low value near 20. Use this brush to add some fleshy mass to the upper lip. Extend this fleshiness to the corners of the mouth. Pucker the forms here around the points where the lips end. These soft round shapes are called the nodes of the lips and they are an important landmark to make the lips look realistic. These shapes are visible on your own mouth—use a mirror for reference as you work on this area (Figure 7.68).

The nodes of the lips form a puckering, circular shape at the corners of the mouth

*Figure 7.68:  Puckering the shapes around the nodes of the lips*

4. Use a mask to isolate the lower lip from the upper lip. Select the Inflate brush and set the ZIntensity low. Inflate the lower lip to give it a sense of supple fullness. We will try to make these lips feel full to add a sense of softness to the face. A typical feminine facial feature is a larger lower lip. This is one of many visual cues I will try to introduce to this non-human face, to communicate specific human and gender cues (Figure 7.69).

5. Invert mask and use the Move brush to further shape the bow of the upper lip—for a feminine character such as this, the gesture in the lips is very important to get right. You may find as you work that just the slightest movement in any direction can throw the expression off. It will take time to get the eyes and lips just right, so be patient (Figure 7.70).

*Figure 7.69: Masking the upper lip*

*Figure 7.70: Working the upper lip*

6. Select the Standard brush and Alpha 01. Dial down the draw size and deepen the line between the lips. Be sure to pick out a bit of shadow in the very corners of the lips (Figure 7.71).

7. Use the Clay Tubes brush with no alpha to build up the form of the upper lip. I blend this area up in the the area of the skull between the eyes. While there is no nose on this character, I want a prominent ridge between the eyes, as it mirrors the structure of an ichthyoid skull (Figure 7.72).

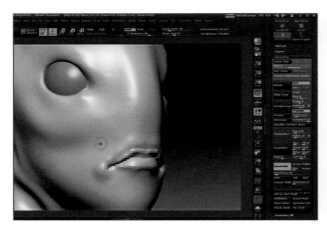
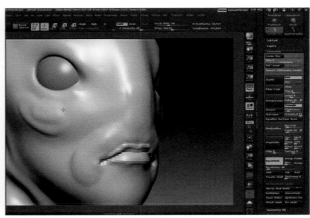

*Figure 7.71: Deepen the line between the lips.*

*Figure 7.72: Building form with the Clay Tubes brush and no alpha*

8. Use the same brush to add a subtle brow bone and mass in the cheekbones. Notice how the cheeks curve in and up—this is a very feminine facial feature compared to more angular or defined cheeks. A more masculine face would have cheeks that angle in and down as well as a wider jawline (Figure 7.73).

9. Using the Standard brush and the Move brush, add further refinements to the eyes. In Figure 7.74, you can see how the lids are shifted to conform to the sphere and the tear duct has been sculpted. These are not structures that would be present on an ichthyoid animal, but I am taking artistic license to create a more humanoid eye.

## Final Detail Pass

We are now at the final stages of the figure. We have completed the majority of the work on the primary and secondary forms. At this point, we will add the last details to tie the character together. Since we have suggested that some parts are hard shelled and exoskeleton, like the arms, we will add some finer details like bumps and ridges that help accentuate the feeling of a hard, armored surface in those areas.

1. At this stage, I add ridges to the body with the Standard brush (Figure 7.75). This creates more interesting surface details and helps create a series of graceful lines flowing around the surface of the body.

2. Zooming into the face, I now add some subtle details to the lips and wrinkles in the face (Figure 7.76). Details like these will catch light and shadow and give a more natural and interesting look to the face.

3. From the Lightbox Brush menu, I select one of the Scales brushes (Figure 7.77). This is used to quickly suggest scale texture on the body. I chose the ScalesLizard brush as well as ScalesFish and combined them on the body in different areas (Figure 7.78). These brushes allow you to quickly stroke a repeating scale texture along the surface of the model.

That completes this lesson. Figure 7.79 shows the final posed figure. The pose was created using Transpose and the render was accomplished by using

The upward curve in the cheek suggests a more feminine facial structure

*Figure 7.73: Adding the cheekbone curve*

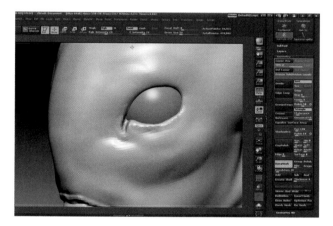

*Figure 7.74: Detailing the eye*

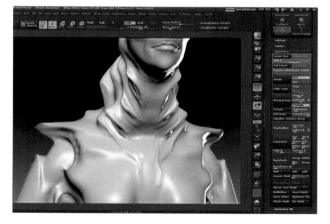

*Figure 7.75: Adding ridges to the body*

ZBrush's built in BPR tools and Photoshop post processing. I posed the character using the Transpose tools and added some spines along the fins with the Snakehook brush. Using the same Photoshop techniques we supply to the Interdimensional Traveler and Forest Spirit characters, I created the image seen in Figure 7.79. See the DVD or download files for a copy of this image with all the Photoshop layers intact.

In this chapter we have learned how to create a feminine creature using Dynamesh to build our forms from basic building blocks. By building up shapes in digital clay and combining them together, we were able to develop the figure in a process very similar to traditional sculpting. Dynamesh is one of the most powerful new ZBrush tools in R2 and should become indispensable to anyone who needs to quickly develop a character in ZBrush without feeling yoked by the concerns of generating a base mesh or suitable topology.

See the DVD or download files for the associated source files and a narrated video of this design process. There you will find more tips and details that we didn't have space to cover in the chapter.

*Figure 7.76: Adding facial details*

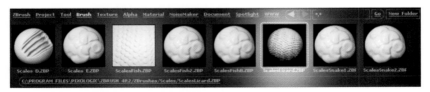

*Figure 7.77: Select one of the Scales brushes from the Lightbox to add scale texture to the body*

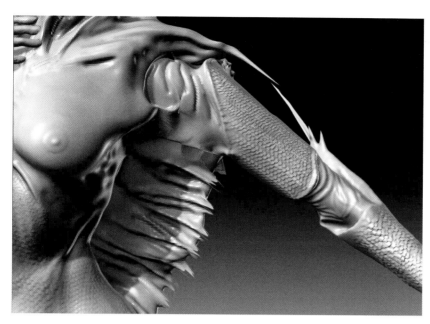

*Figure 7.78:  Adding scales with the Scale brush*

*Figure 7.79:  Final painted image*

eight

# Sculpting the Forest Spirit

In this chapter, we will *be creating a character I call the Forest Spirit. This being is based on the ancient mythological character Pan and appears as a hybrid between human and animal forms. This lesson is a good exercise in anthropomorphism, the practice of ascribing human traits to non-human creatures. We will look at how to use human photo reference and animal reference to blend elements between the two. We will look at how to use shape language to create a softer character with a more empathetic look rather than one who communicates malicious intentions. We will also see how we can use the ZBrush brush set to create the sagging forms of an older body rather than a more fit anatomical form.*

## Using Reference as Inspirational Material

In this chapter, we will make extensive use of reference materials. These consist of photos of two elderly men as well as photos of a goat and a ram. These will not be used to create an exact likeness. Rather, I will use elements from each photo to help add interest to my design. I will look at parts of the human head that would work well combined with the ram's and then combine the elements in my sculpture. It's always important to use reference whenever possible, as it helps you break your own habits and preconceived notions when working. It also opens new and interesting avenues in the design and of course adds a level of realism to your work.

Figure 8.1 shows some of the reference photos I used for this project. The photos all came from the exceptional photo reference site www.3D.sk. The site has been kind enough to allow me to supply you with several photosets on the DVD or download files including those images we use as reference here. I highly recommend investing in a subscription to 3D.sk and the sister site www.photo-reference-for-comic-artists.com/ (Figure 8.2).

## The Brief: Forest Spirit

The brief for this chapter is to design a character called "The Forest Spirit." This wise old man is a cross between a human and a goat or ram. He is a magical being but almost always appears in corporeal or solid form. The Forest Spirit is ancient and kind, although he can be a fierce defender of his forest home. The spirit should have elements of an old human man and a ram mixed together. Reference images of the god Pan are provided for inspiration.

*Figure 8.1: Here you can see the various photo reference images used for this character loaded into Spotlight in ZBrush.*

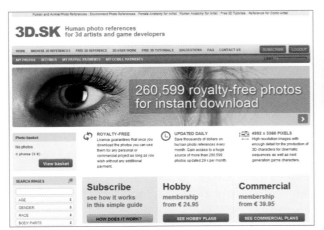

*Figure 8.2: The sites* 3D.SK *and* www.photo-reference-for-comic-artists.com

When using photo reference while you work, you have a couple of different options. You can load it in your favorite photo browser outside of ZBrush and switch between ZBrush and your viewer as you work. Alternatively, you may choose to load your reference into Spotlight within ZBrush. Spotlight is a ZBrush texturing tool that allows you to load and store several high-resolution photos and view them in the document window as you work. While it is primarily a texturing tool, it can also be used to store and use photo references. Follow these steps to load your reference images into Spotlight. Please see the DVD or download files for a video tutorial on the Spotlight interface and its uses.

1. In ZBrush, click the Texture Import button and load one of the reference images supplied on the DVD or download files. The image will automatically load into the texture palette (Figure 8.3)
2. Under the Texture menu, click the Add to Spotlight button (Figure 8.4). This causes the image to load into the Spotlight tool. The image will now be added automatically to the spotlight interface that appears over the document window (Figure 8.5).

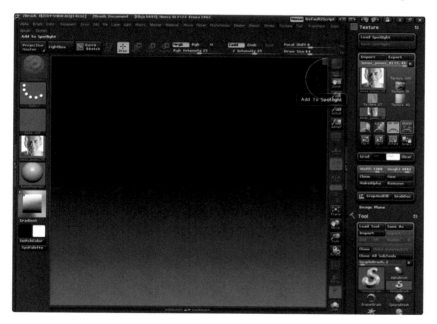

*Figure 8.3: Import an image into the texture palette.*

*Figure 8.4: Click Add to Spotlight to add the image to the Spotlight tool.*

3. Now press Import again and select several more pieces of photo reference. They will all automatically be added to the Spotlight when you click the Open button on the file browser window (Figure 8.6).
4. To organize the images clearly in the document window, press the Tile Unified button on the spotlight ring (Figure 8.7). This will cause all the images to be tiled at the side of the screen. You may click and drag photos in the Spotlight interface. Scale up by clicking on the Scale icon and dragging clockwise, and scale down by dragging the icon counterclockwise in the Spotlight dial. Note that the selected image is outlined in red in Spotlight (Figure 8.8). If no image is selected, then you will move all the images at once.

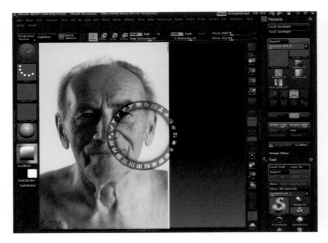

Figure 8.5: *The image will now appear over the document window along with the Spotlight circle control.*

Figure 8.6: *Multiple images can be added to Spotlight at once.*

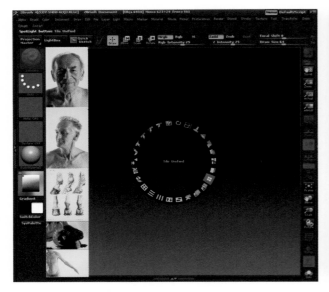

Figure 8.7: *Press the Tile Unified button to organize the images to the side of the screen.*

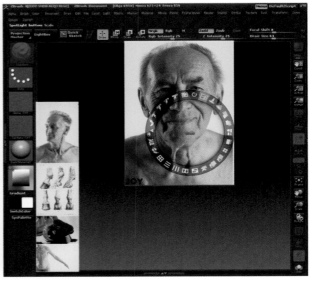

Figure 8.8: *Click on the image to move and scale it over the document window.*

5. You may press the Z key to exit the Spotlight interface and leave your reference open while you work (Figure 8.9). The ring will disappear while the photos remain visible, and you are able to sculpt and paint on your model. If you want to make the reference partially transparent, adjust the opacity option on the Spotlight ring by clicking and dragging the icon (Figure 8.10).

It is very important to note that if you want to sculpt a surface while spotlight images are visible, they have to go into the Brush menu and turn off the Spotlight Projection button in the Samples subpalette. Otherwise only the Move brush works and none of other brushes work. This is because Spotlight is using the images as a projection mask. Thus, if the images are pushed off to the side, then ZBrush acts as if the whole surface is masked.

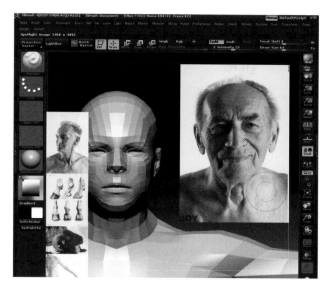

*Figure 8.9: Press Z to sculpt with spotlight open.*

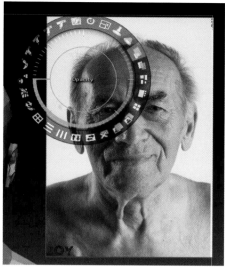

*Figure 8.10: Click and drag the opacity icon to change the transparency of the reference image.*

Spotlights are loaded under the File ➤ Spotlight menu. Spotlights cannot be saved with Project files and must be saved and loaded separately. While a Spotlight is loaded, you can enable and disable it with the Shift Z hot key.

6. You can save the Spotlight file for future use by clicking the File ➤ Spotlight ➤ Save Spotlight button (Figure 8.11). This will store a file that contains all your reference images at full resolution. This can be loaded back into any scene at a later date. Spotlights must be saved on their own as they will not be stored within a project file.

*Figure 8.11: Save a Spotlight file for use later.*

# Sculpting the Body

We will begin this sculpture using a generic human ZTool from Pixologic. This model is available on the DVD or download files as basemesh.ztl. This mesh I use often for my generic bipedal characters because it has a nice even edge layout—it does not have too much detail—and lends itself well to being divided to a high subdivision level when the computer RAM can handle large models. Follow the steps below to load and start to modify this mesh. Be sure to see the DVD or download files for this full process captured on video for more tips and techniques.

1. Load the basemesh.ztl file from the DVD or download files. This is a generic male figure of average build (Figure 8.12).
2. Immediately I want to relax the pose, as I find the arms outstretched in a T formation, while sometimes preferable for rigging, is far too stiff. Many

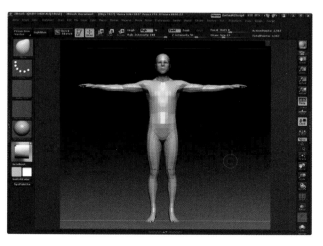

*Figure 8.12: Load the basemesh.ztl file. The figure is an average male in a very rigid pose.*

setup artists actually will prefer to have a copy of the model in a more natural relaxed pose, but since we are concerned here with design rather than technical considerations, we will focus on posing the character in a natural, appealing manner. Select the Transpose Rotate brush by pressing the R hot key. This will select the Transpose Rotate brush.

3. Using the masking brushes as well as Transpose Masking, make sure the body is masked and the arms are unmasked. Ctrl + Click on the masked area to feather the masking edges. Draw a transpose line from the shoulder to the middle of the arm (Figure 8.13). Click and drag on the last circle of the line to rotate the arm down (Figure 8.14). The mesh will get slightly distorted as you rotate and shift the arm geometry. Don't let this worry you—it will be fixed easily with the Move brush later.

4. Select the Move brush and correct the volume of the torso mass. This has collapsed as a result of rotating and lowering the arms (Figure 8.15).

5. At this stage, I want to start to bring in elements from my photo reference. I like the figure proportions and posture shown in Figure 8.16. The figure in the reference has an unusually short torso, which I want to bring into the character we are working on here. Part of this compressed distance is the stoop in the man's posture.

*Figure 8.13: Isolate the arms with a mask to facilitate transpose rotating them down.*

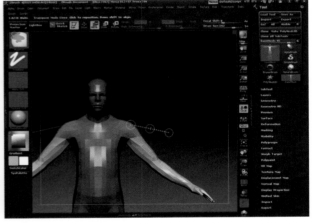

*Figure 8.14: The arms are lowered into a more relaxed position.*

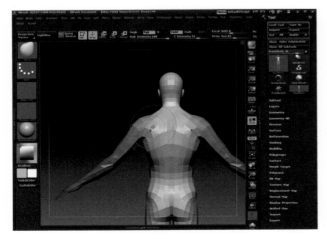

*Figure 8.15: Correcting the torso mass with the Move brush*

*Figure 8.16: We will now try and recreate elements of the torso seen here in this photo reference from 3D.SK.*

In addition to the abbreviated proportion of the torso, I also like the sagging slushiness of the fat and muscles. Figure 8.17 shows the features that I will try to bring into the sculpture as we progress. Notice the fold of flesh at the abdomen as well as the heaviness in the chest fat contrasted with the very sinewy arms. This model shows a marked lack of skin elasticity and a sinewy muscle definition. This is common in old age, when muscle mass diminishes and the skin and fat starts to sag across the form. It creates a blend of high definition in some areas and a loose fattiness in others. Some specific points of interest are the bony landmarks of the scapula (shoulder blades) and acromion processes—or the point where the skeleton is closest to the skin at the top center of the shoulder (Figure 8.18). By accentuating shapes like this, you can reinforce the lack of soft tissues to the viewer.

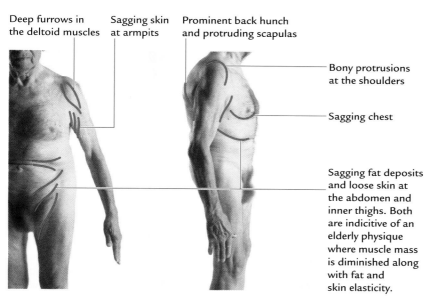

Deep furrows in the deltoid muscles

Sagging skin at armpits

Prominent back hunch and protruding scapulas

Bony protrusions at the shoulders

Sagging chest

Sagging fat deposits and loose skin at the abdomen and inner thighs. Both are indicitive of an elderly physique where muscle mass is diminished along with fat and skin elasticity.

*Figure 8.17: These elements are interesting features I want to incorporate into my sculpture.*

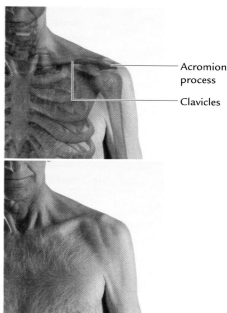

Acromion process

Clavicles

*Figure 8.18: Bony landmarks like the acromion process help accentuate the emaciated aspect of the figure by calling attention to the underlying skeletal form.*

We will exploit other skeletal landmarks like this as we work on this figure as well as various major muscle forms. Points on the skeleton like the acromion process, thoracic arch, and epicondyles of the humerus all help us reinforce the sense of skeletal structure under the skin. Figure 8.19 shows many of the muscular and skeletal forms we will be working with.

By knowing where these landmarks are, you can choose how much to accentuate them. The more prominent all the bony landmarks and the more frequent their appearance, the more emaciated the figure becomes. Combined with prominent muscle forms, the figure takes on a more fragile or undernourished appearance (Figure 8.20).

With the above anatomical guidelines in mind, we will now start to adjust the form of the figure. At this stage we will alter both the proportion as well as the general silhouette to give more of a compressed, heavy, and stooped appearance. Follow the steps below.

1. Use the Move brush to pull the scapulas out and shift the shoulders forward. This will help create the hunched-back appearance seen in the photo reference (Figure 8.21).

2. The head needs to be slung further forward to give a sense of weight and strain on the neck muscles. If this figure holds his head too high, he will not appear as old or stooped as we want. Remember as well he will likely have large horns that would also be a weight on his head. Transpose the neck down and use the Transpose Rotate brush to adjust the relationship between the head, neck, and shoulders (Figure 8.22).

3. By using the Move brush to pull the chest muscles down and forward slightly, a sag is created in the whole upper body (Figure 8.23).

4. We will now squash the torso proportion slightly by compressing the distance between the ribs and pelvis. Mask the upper body and select the Transpose Move brush. Draw a transpose line down the legs from the side view (Figure 8.24).

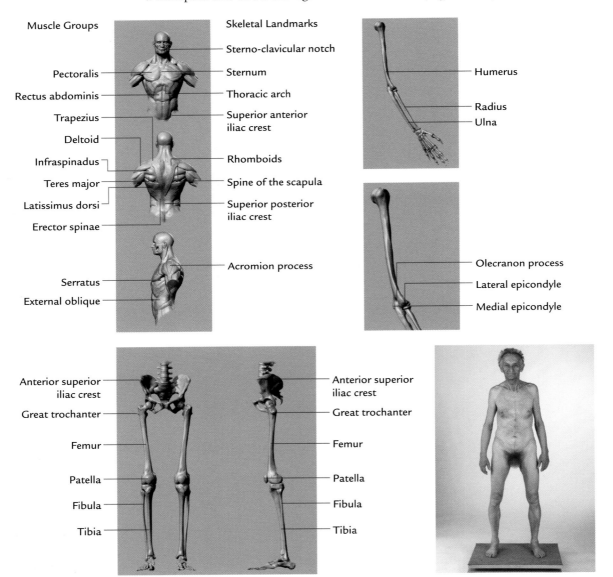

Figure 8.19:  Bony landmarks on the figure

Figure 8.20:  A figure with both well-defined muscle forms as well as prominent skeletal landmarks appears undernourished but sinewy to the viewer.

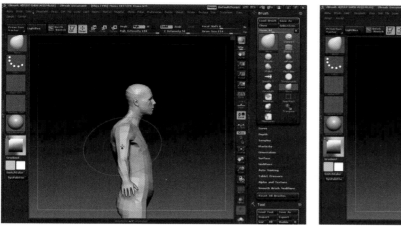

*Figure 8.21: Pulling the scapulas back and shoulders forward with the Move brush to hunch the back*

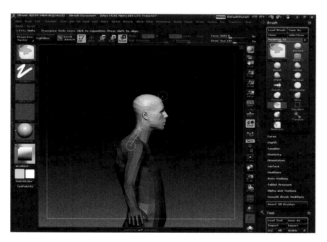
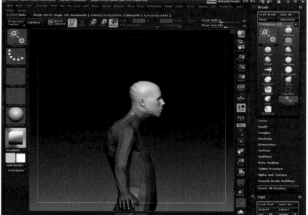

*Figure 8.22: Use Transpose Rotate to bring the head and neck forward.*

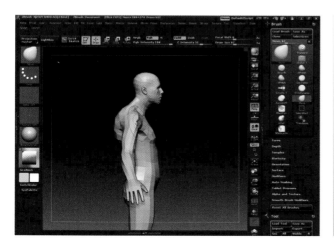
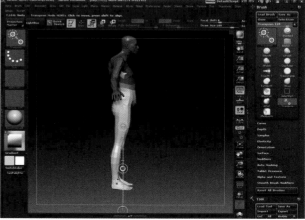

*Figure 8.23: Pull the chest forms out slightly and down to create a sense of sag in the chest fat and muscle.*

*Figure 8.24: To compress the torso, mask the upper body and draw a transpose line down the leg.*

5. Click and drag in the transpose circles to shift the pelvis up slightly toward the ribs. Switch to the Move brush to further adjust the shapes in the hip area (Figure 8.25). I have widened the hips as well as brought them up. Take care not to lengthen the legs too much as you stretch with the transpose line.

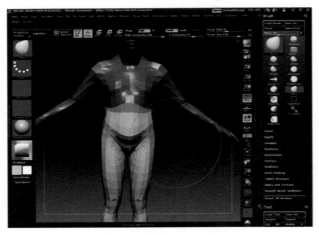

*Figure 8.25: Making further adjustments to the torso proportion with the Move brush*

6. Figure 8.26 shows the model at this stage with the gross-form changes introduced. We will continue to refine the forms and their relationships in the next sections. With the Move brush, some more subtle changes are introduced, including more weight to the belly and very slight overhangs where the love handles will be (Figure 8.27).

7. Zoom into the neck. With the Move brush, shift the area of the collarbones down and lower the back or trapezius muscles (Figure 8.28). This helps create a longer and more graceful neck. This will help attain a more appealing character when the large horns are added later. A long neck is also helpful in keeping with the look and character of a goat, helping to blend the human and animal anatomies.

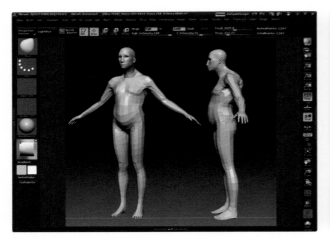

*Figure 8.26: The basic proportions of the torso blocked in with the Move and Transpose tools*

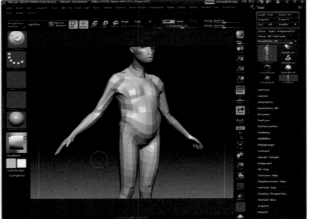

*Figure 8.27: Subtle mass additions to the flanks and belly with the Move brush create more of a sense of weight and gravity to the figure.*

Take note that so far we have not divided the mesh at all. The shapes we are making are large general forms and are best considered with as little geometry as possible. This helps keep you from becoming lost prematurely in too many details, it also helps you create broad, appealing form relationships because the mesh is light and responds well to big shape changes with the Move and Transpose tools. Lower-resolution meshes make it much easier to see and manipulate large-scale form changes. I recommend always staying at the lowest possible subdivision level to support the type of shape you are creating at that time. We will now move on and start to change the shape of the head.

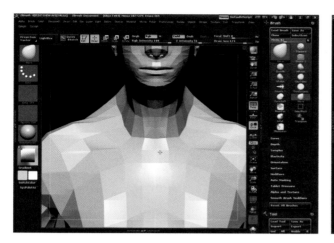 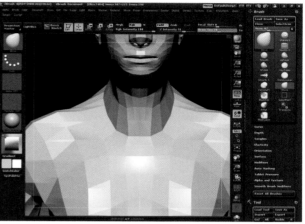

*Figure 8.28: Lower the clavicles and reduce the trapezius muscles to lengthen the neck.*

## Sculpting the Head Shapes

As we work on this character, we are constantly trying to incorporate elements from our photo references of animal and human anatomy into a unified whole. It's important that the piece be unified and not just animal features stuck on a human body.

1. With the Move brush, elongate the "muzzle" shape of the mouth and nose from the side view (Figure 8.29). We want to mirror a shape similar to the ram seen in Figure 8.30. We want to give the face the same overall length—especially between the eyes and the end of the nose. The nose and lips will remain close together—this proportion between the features will ultimately trigger the viewer to associate the animal with features common to the bovid animal family (goats, rams, and other horned quadrupeds).

2. Next, we will adjust the shapes of the cartilages of the nose to integrate it more with the upper lip in a manner similar to the animal reference. We will also round out the lower jaw to get a smoother transition from the lip to the chin (Figure 8.31). Using the Move brush, shift the shapes of the nose and lower jaw as seen here (Figure 8.32).

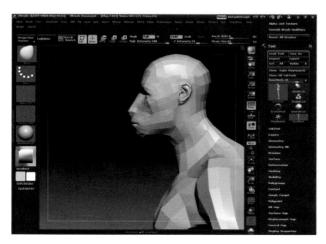 

*Figure 8.29: Elongate the mouth and nose bridge with the Move brush to give a muzzle form to the lower face.*

*Figure 8.30: The photo reference of the Ram from* 3D.SK

*Figure 8.31: Features of the nose and mouth on the photo reference we want to incorporate. Notice how the nose and lower jaw integrate into the form of the lips. Also notice how close the nose is to the upper lip, essentially meeting it.*

**3.** We are taking care here to create large blunt shapes in the face. Figure 8.33 shows the snout being slightly broadened and flattened with the Move brush. I had noticed it was looking rather sharp from the top view, creating a harsher appearance to the face. We will follow this same design methodology of blunting forms though the whole body, as these blunt forms are less aggressive than angular or sharp shapes. They are also in keeping with the shape language inherent in the face of a goat or a ram. While the overall facial wedge might be angular, the internal forms of the snout, teeth, and eyes tend toward broad, flat forms, softening the viewer's reaction.

**4.** At this stage, I check my photo reference to determine what human features I want to use to inspire the shapes of the head. Open the Spotlight file that contains our photo reference, or use it in a separate viewer on your screen (Figure 8.34). The spotlight file used here is available for you on the DVD or download files.

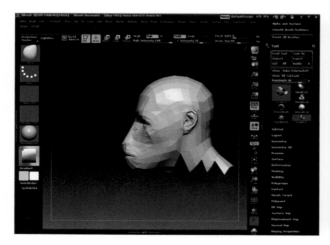
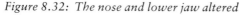

*Figure 8.32: The nose and lower jaw altered*

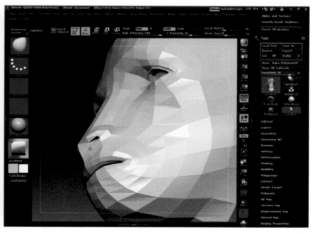

*Figure 8.33: The snout is broadened and blunted with the Move brush from a three-quarters up view.*

Looking at the reference, I am interested in incorporating this man's broad cheekbones and flattened head. These features both lend themselves to the facial structure of the animal and allow me to find a common point of morphology to anchor both the animal and human aspects of the face (Figure 8.35). Areas of interest are the broad, blunt cheekbones, the rounded shapes of the brows (which, while furrowed, do not express anger due to their soft shape and angle), the broad upper lip, and the rounded chin.

Figure 8.34: *The photo reference open in Spotlight*

Figure 8.35: *The large, broad shapes seen in this image lend themselves to the animal reference. I will try to incorporate these into the character's head as anchors between the animal and human facial structures.*

At this stage, I need to polygroup the ears separately from the head to make it easier to shape and move them into a new form. I know this character will have vastly different ear shapes than those on a human head. To polygroup the ears, follow these steps.

1. From the Brush menu, select the Lasso brush. Isolate the ears as seen in Figure 8.36.
2. With the ears isolated on screen, go to Tool ➤ Polygroups ➤ and Click Group Visible (Figure 8.37). This will assign a new polygroup to just the ear faces. This group will display a different color when the model is in polyframe mode (Figure 8.38). You will not be able to see the backside faces of the ear in ZBrush unless you turn on double-sided view. To do this, go to Tool ➤ Display Options and turn on the Double button.

This new polygrouping makes it much easier to select and mask the ears from the head. All you need do is Ctrl + Shift + Click on the polygroup and it will be isolated on the screen. This saves you the trouble of having to lasso it out each time you want to hide the head.

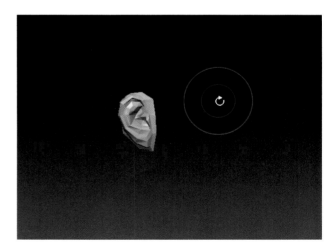

Figure 8.36: *Use a selection Lasso brush to isolate the ear geometry from the head.*

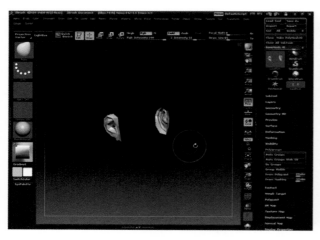

*Figure 8.37: Click Group Visible to polygroup the geometry on screen*

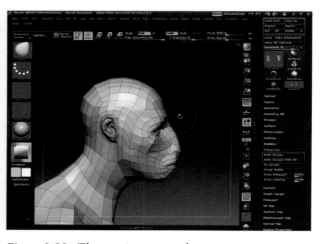

*Figure 8.38: The ears in a new polygroup*

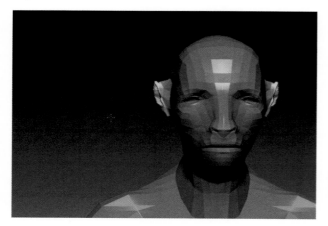

*Figure 8.39: Manipulating the ears with the head masked*

3. Ctrl + Shift + Click the new ear polygroup to isolate them on screen. Mask the ears then Ctrl + Shift + Click on the background to show the full model again.

4. Ctrl + Click on the backdrop to invert the mask so the head is now masked and the ears unmasked. Use the Move brush to alter the shape of the ear. Note that the mask will protect the head geometry from unintentional changes (Figure 8.39).

We will move on from the ears for now and address the face. The ears are now polygrouped and shifted from the head geometry so we can easily create new shapes from them later in the process. We will now start to make some changes to the head based on the photo reference we stored in the Spotlight.

1. Open the photo reference Spotlight to view the head reference again. If you want you can load the spotlight file Spotlight.ZSL off the DVD or download files. Looking at the photo of the model Jonas (Jonas_poses_0135.JPG from the DVD or download files), I am looking at the crests of the cheekbones and the temporal ridge of the skull. These are very particular lines in the man's face and, using the Move brush, I start to introduce them on the character's head.

2. I also use the Move brush to round out the lower jaw based on the photo reference (Figure 8.40). I also start to suggest the loose skin that will sag beneath the chin by pulling some of the points in the mesh down under the jaw line (Figure 8.41).

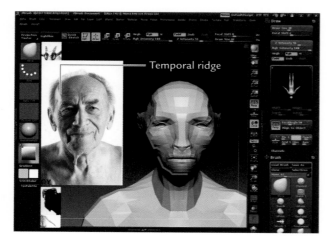

*Figure 8.40: Shaping the cheekbones, temporal ridge, and lower jaw based on the photo reference*

3. Be sure to work the head from multiple views. If you spend the whole time working from the front view, it will cause you to overlook shapes and problems from other sides. Figure 8.42 shows the head rotated into a down view, which I use while I smooth back the cheekbones slightly.

4. Use the Move brush now and zoom in on the eye areas. Enlarge the eyes by pulling at the edges with the Move brush (Figure 8.43). I also want to rotate the eyes so they are on a different angle than a human eye—more in keeping with the angle of the ram's eye (Figure 8.44).

5. To rotate the eyes, mask out the eye area and then invert the mask. Next, draw a transpose rotate line from the center of the eye out. Click and drag in the outer circle to rotate the eye geometry. (See Figure 8.45.)

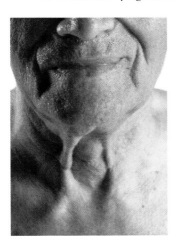
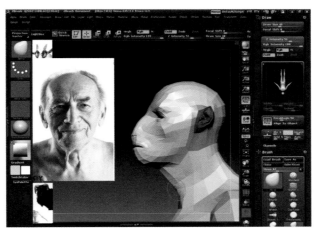

Figure 8.41: *Suggesting the waddles beneath the chin*

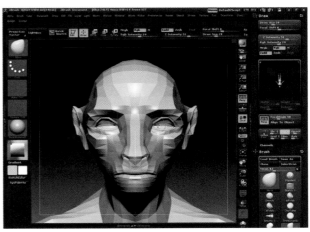

Figure 8.42: *Be sure to work the sculpture from multiple angles to maintain coherence between all your shapes.*

Figure 8.43: *Enlarging the eye with the Move brush*

Figure 8.44: *We will rotate the eye geometry to match the angle closer to the ram's eye angle.*

Figure 8.45: *The eye area isolated with a mask in preparation for rotating the geometry. A transpose line is then drawn from the center of the eye out and used to rotate the eye shape.*

## Refining the Face

Now that we have the general form of the face roughed in, we may start to focus in on more facial details. Divide the mesh once, so we can have more subdivision levels to carry the finer forms of the figure.

1. Divide the mesh by pressing the Ctrl + D hot key or click Tool ➢ Geometry ➢ Divide.
2. Open the Spotlight with your photo reference and enlarge the ram photo (Figure 8.46). If the Spotlight is already loaded, it can be enabled by pressing Shift + Z.
3. From this image, we will be looking at the character of the mouth and nose (Figure 8.47). To make changes to the mouth, we will need to move the lips independently of each other. This will require the use of a specialized brush. From the Brush menu, select the Move Topological brush.

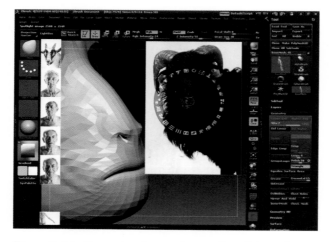

Figure 8.46: *From the photo reference Spotlight, enlarge the ram photo*

Figure 8.47: *This photo shows an interesting view of the mouth and nose we will use for reference.*

The Move brush tends to grab any and all geometry under its falloff range. This makes it unsuitable for pulling one lip over another or working in the mouth area. The Move Topological brush has a topological masking function applied, which allows it to grab only those faces adjacent to the one beneath the center of the brush. Figure 8.48 shows the effect of the normal Move brush compared to the Move Topological one. I have set the brush to also apply color so you can clearly see the area being impacted when topological masking is on and off.

The topological masking function is found under Brush ➢ Auto Masking and can be applied to any of the brushes. The Move Topological brush is a preset brush with topological masking already applied. Depending on the scale of your model, you may need to lower the Range slider as small as .5 for best results. Try to reserve this brush for low-resolution meshes as it tends to get bogged down on dense models.

4. Using the Move Topological brush to shift the upper lip over the lower. This keeps the mouth from looking like just a slice into the head but gives it form and depth as well as the potential for expression (Figure 8.49). Select the Standard brush and with ZSub on and a small draw size, add the split that runs from the nose through the upper lip. This split is called the philtrum (Figure 8.49).

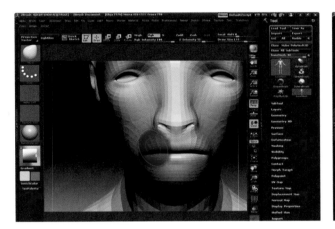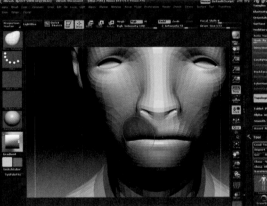

*Figure 8.48: The image on the left shows the Move brush; the right image shows the Move Topological brush. The topological masking function allows you to isolate the brush's effect to just those faces adjacent to the center of the brush.*

*Figure 8.49: Shift the upper lip over the lower lip with the Move Topological brush. Then with the Standard brush, add the philtrum, or spit from the nose to the mouth*

5. Select the Inflate brush. Gently, inflate the mouth and nose area to pucker the forms together. Don't overdo this pass—it's just to give some mass to the lips and nose and help them look fleshier (Figure 8.50).

6. At this stage, eyeballs are added from the Polysphere ZBrush primitive just as we did in Chapter 2, "The Character Portrait: Sculpting the Alien Mystic." Please see the DVD or download files for this process in action.

7. The eyelids are conformed to the spheres using the Move brush. I droop the eyes to give an older, softer look to the face (Figure 8.51).

8. We will now add some more detail to the face. Add a subdivision level with the Ctrl + D hot key.

9. We will now add the fold of fatty tissue next to the nose, known as the nasolabial fold (Figure 8.52). Isolate the area with a mask as seen in Figure 8.53. This fold of skin is particular to the physiology of a human face and the manner in which the mouth and nose interact during speech. Adding it to this creature's head further ascribes human-oid qualities to his face.

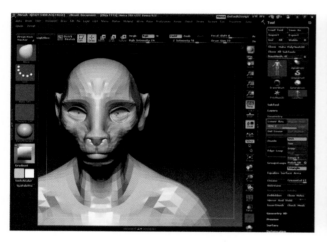

*Figure 8.50: Use the Inflate brush to add a sense of mass and fleshiness to the upper lip and nose.*

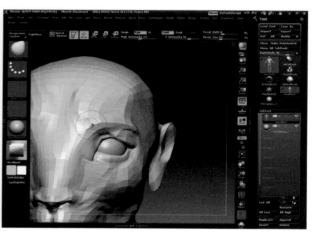

*Figure 8.51: Drooping the eyelids over the sphere of the eye*

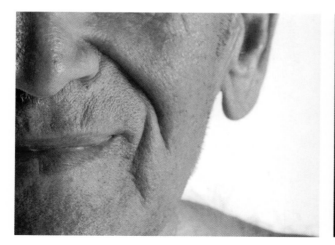

*Figure 8.52: The fold of fatty skin next to the nose is called the nasolabial fold.*

*Figure 8.53: Isolate the area of the fold with a mask.*

10. Using the Move brush, pull the nasolabial fold out. Smooth the hard edges and refine the form further with the Standard or Inflate brushes (Figure 8.54). Be sure to use the Clay Tubes brush to flesh out the space between the fold and the cheekbones. This area is filled out with muscles of facial expression and fatty tissue. We need to suggest this muscular anatomy exists to justify the existence of the nasolabial folds. This is because these folds of skin exist partially as a result of pulling of muscles over time from the cheekbone to the corners of the mouth.

11. Moving up to the eyelids, I want to give the impression of puffy soft skin around the eyes. Mask the brow line as seen in Figure 8.55 and with the Clay Tubes brush, add a sock pucker form to the upper lid. Remember to make sure the alpha is off on the Clay Tubes brush. This soft fleshiness will help suggest the drooping, older eyelids. Note the eyes in photo reference (Figure 8.56) have a soft puffiness.

12. Isolate the ear polygroup by Ctrl + Shift + Clicking on it. Select the Move brush and pull the shape of the ear out from the sides of the head (Figure 8.57). Use the Move brush to shift the points of the ears to fall downward with gravity—giving them a loose floppy look.

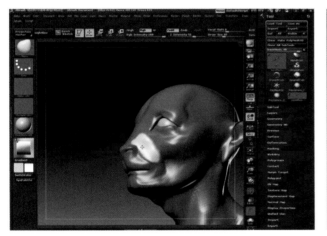

*Figure 8.54:  Pull the nasolabial fold out with the Move brush*

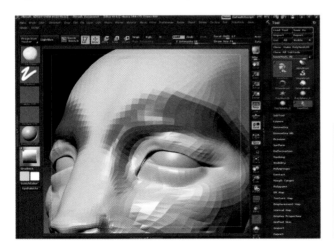

*Figure 8.55:  With the Clay Tubes brush, add a sense of fleshiness to the eyelid.*

*Figure 8.56:  The eyes in the photo reference show a soft puckering like what we are trying to introduce in the model.*

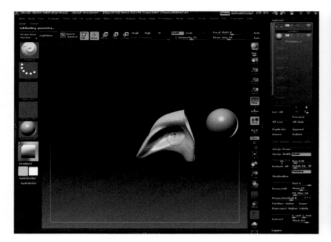
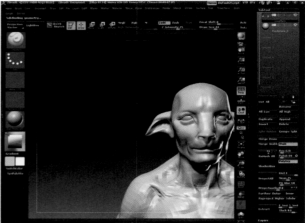

*Figure 8.57: Changing the shape of the ear with the Move brush*

The head will go through many changes before we arrive at the final character. I will step away now and look at the body. Later, we will return to the face and make some further form changes before the project is completed.

## Refining the Body

With the head and face refined, we will now return to our general form and start to give the body and limbs much more detail. We will pick out skeletal landmarks as well as suggest the knotted sinewy muscularity seen on the photo reference. Remember that when you combine the look of prominent bony landmarks with muscle groups you give the impression of a figure with very little body fat. If you add rounded fatty forms at the bottom of key areas like under the arms, buttocks, and chest you give the impression of elderly sagging skin over a body losing muscle mass. In the following section, we will look at how I give the body much more detail and character.

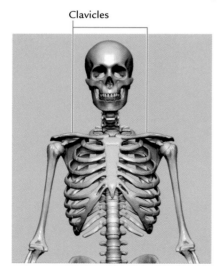

Clavicles

*Figure 8.58: The first bony landmark will be the clavicles.*

The first skeletal landmark we want to sculpt are the clavicles, or collarbones (Figure 8.58). The collarbones will be the skeletal landmarks that allow us to place the deltoid muscles, the shoulder blades, and even the major muscles of the neck. It is a central bony landmark that is extremely important to get accurate and early in the process. A pronounced set of clavicles also helps a neck look thinner.

1. Select the Clay Tubes brush from the Brush menu. Turn off the alpha and dial down the ZIntensity. Sketch in the sternomastoids and clavicles as seen in Figure 8.59. I also build up the chest fat over the pectoralis muscles and tug it down with the Move brush to add a sense of sag to the area.

2. Checking the photo reference, I decide to address the silhouette of the arms. I want this character to have very thin arms with prominent furrows between the musculature, as seen in Figure 8.60.

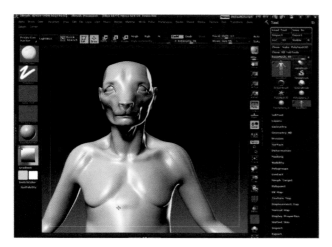

*Figure 8.59: Sketching in the clavicles and sternomas-toids with the Clay Tubes brush*

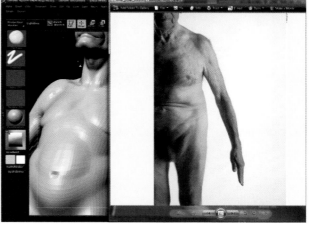

*Figure 8.60: Compare the arms of the figure to your photo reference.*

3. Using a combination of the Move and Claytubes brushes, define the outer edge of the deltoid and bicep muscles. Make sure to get the brachio-radialis of the forearm where they originate from the humerus and flow down the forearm (Figure 8.61).

4. Use the Claytubes brush to build up fatty tissues on the belly and sides of the ribcage (Figure 8.63). I find the Claytubes brush with no alpha is the best tool for building up fat mass. It adds form in a subtle manner perfectly suited for this kind of shapes.

5. Always try to consider the effect of gravity on any fleshy form but especially those that are intended to be soft and fatty. When sculpting fat, a useful technique is to use the Move brush to tug the fatty forms down into crescent shapes. See Figure 8.64 for an example of how forms are made to feel heavier and more sagging by pulling slightly on the bottom edge of any form. Often I will mask part of the surface and then pull forms over the masked area to create the appearance of folds of flesh.

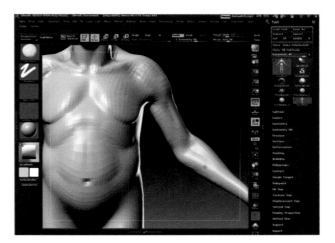

*Figure 8.61: Roughing in the arm anatomy*

6. Mask the clavicles. We will now sketch in the part of the pectoralis muscle that attaches to the clavicles. It's called the clavicular head of the pectoralis. By showing the definition between the various heads of the chest muscles, you can accentuate the emaciated look of the figure. Fatty tissues usually fill out the spaces between the muscle heads. The same form is very subtle but visible on the photo reference here (Figure 8.65).

7. Using the Standard brush, deepen the hollows between the muscles of the neck. Here you can see the two heads of the sternaomastoid muscle attaching to the sternum and clavicle (Figure 8.66).

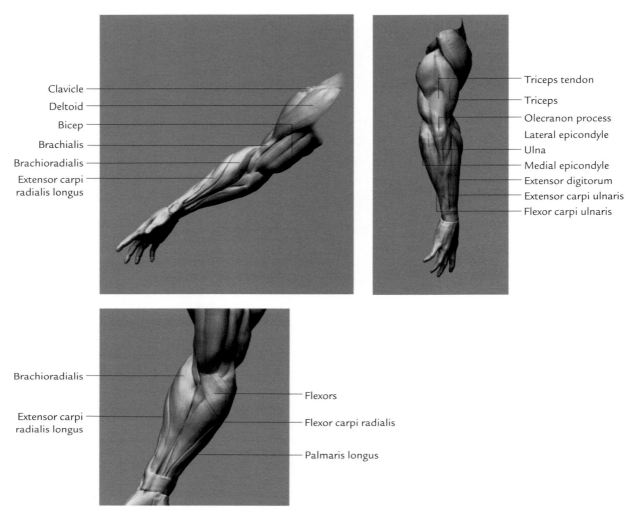

Clavicle
Deltoid
Bicep
Brachialis
Brachioradialis
Extensor carpi radialis longus

Triceps tendon
Triceps
Olecranon process
Lateral epicondyle
Ulna
Medial epicondyle
Extensor digitorum
Extensor carpi ulnaris
Flexor carpi ulnaris

Brachioradialis
Extensor carpi radialis longus

Flexors
Flexor carpi radialis
Palmaris longus

*Figure 8.62: This image should be helpful when identifying the anatomy of the arm—keep in mind this figure will have the same muscle forms but the mass will be greatly reduced due to the age and physique of the character.*

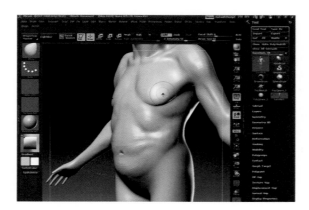

*Figure 8.63: Adding fat with claytubes*

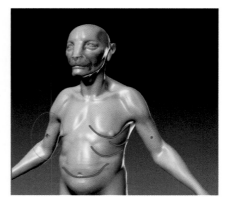

*Figure 8.64: Adding sag to the fatty form with the Move brush.*

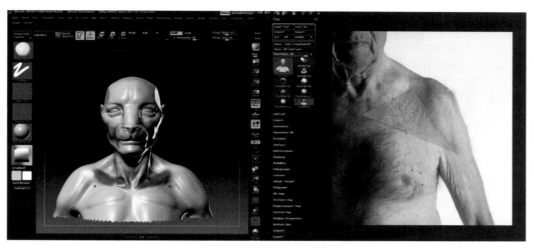

*Figure 8.65: Sculpting the clavicular heads of the pectoralis muscles. The clavicles here are masked out.*

8. Rotate to the back view and sketch in the scapulae (Figure 8.67). Also, be sure to add the bony landmark of the seventh cervical vertebra. This is the prominent part of the spine that's at the base of the neck on your back. The thinner a human is, the more pronounced this vertebra will become. It's also an important visual landmark to place the other relevant muscles of the back.

9. With the Standard brush on ZSub, I knick out a hollow between the two pillars of the trapezius muscles where they attach to the base of the skull (Figure 8.68). Again, by catching a shadow here with this hollow, you help add interest to the shapes of the back as well as a sense of anatomical veracity. While the viewer may not know anatomy, they will have an instinctual eye for what "feels right," as we observe people every day. Accurate forms on a fantasy character are extremely important since they help add realism to an otherwise fantastic form.

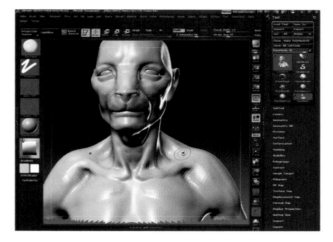

*Figure 8.66: Accentuate neck muscles*

10. With the Standard brush, I etch in a division between the sterna and clavicular heads of the pectoral muscles (Figure 8.69). This kind of deep anatomical detail is only visible on one who is exceptionally fit or old, as it is only visible when the fatty tissues between the muscles break down.

11. Rotate to focus on the neck. Here I will use the Standard brush in conjunction with the Clay Tubes brush to stroke across the anatomy that has already been sculpted in place. The idea is to create strokes that traverse across the larger muscles and bones to give the impression of skin and tendons stretching over the anatomy. By "obscuring" the shape of the clavicles, for example in the areas where the strokes cross over the form, it gives the impression of a drape of skin over the bone. If the bone were clearly outlined with no "lost" edges, it would look sculpted and less interesting (Figure 8.70).

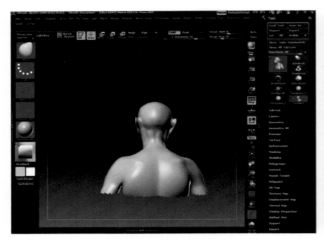 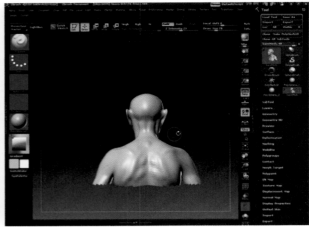

*Figure 8.67: Sketching in the scapulae*

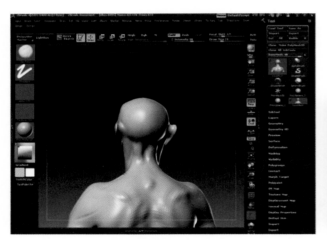 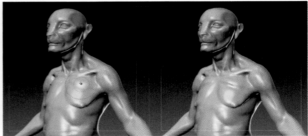

*Figure 8.68: Adding a hollow between the pillars of the trapezius that attach to the base of the skull*

*Figure 8.69: Etching in a division between the sterna and clavicular heads of the pectoral muscles*

Stroke across the anatomical forms

*Figure 8.70: Stroking across the clavicles to lose the shape in some areas and suggest skin draped over the bone*

Don't be afraid to lose the shape of the sculpture in some areas. If every bone and muscle is clearly defined by a shadow, it will look carved out and generally unconvincing as organic form. You create the impression of skin by allowing your muscle and skeletal forms to be lost in some areas by stroking your brush across them, filling in areas and making it look like the underlying shapes are covered by a drape of skin and fat. Take any recognizable shape and drape a sheet over it or stretch a balloon across its surface. Notice how the forms are still visible but the deepest areas are filled out by the stretch of the material across it. This is how skin and fat behave over bone and muscle.

12. Looking at the chest, I feel the space between the pectoral muscles is unnaturally deep. I select the Clay Tubes brush with no alpha and stroke between the pecs to create more of the sternum (Figure 8.71). Also note that I spread the space between the sternomastoids slightly to create a more natural pit to the neck. The hollow at the base of the neck is properly called the sternoclavicular fossa.

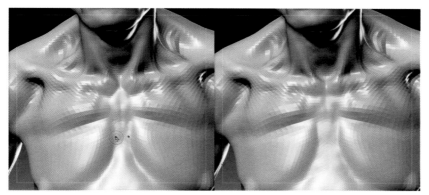

Here a subtle change is made to the sternum using the Clay Tubes brush. I fill out the space between the pectoralis muscles and widen the sternoclavicular notch at the pit of the neck.

*Figure 8.71: Adding sternum*

13. I decide to add weight to the chest fat over the pectoral muscles with the Inflate brush. Stroke along the bottom edge, massing out the lower portion. This will create the sense of fat settling with gravity and being pulled down the chest causing the skin to sag and pucker. Mask out the underside of the chest fat to help create the fold of flesh (Figure 8.72).

14. At this point, I notice the gesture of the clavicles seems off. With the Move brush, adjust the shape of the clavicles so they sweep out with a more graceful line, as seen in Figure 8.73.

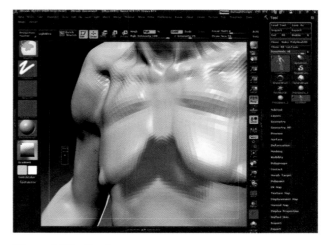

*Figure 8.72: Pec fat*

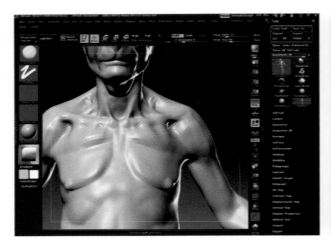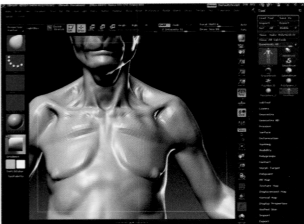

*Figure 8.73: Adjust the clavicles*

## More Facial Refinements

As I have been working on the body, it has become apparent the head is too short and too feline. At this point I revisit the head to make some changes. Remember that sculpting and design is best approached holistically. Always move around the sculpture and work from multiple angles and keep circulating among the different parts of the figure. For this reason, we continue to develop at different stages and revisit areas to bring them into the next stage of development. Always avoid working on one part of the figure for too long—it causes the overall look of the character to become unbalanced, with one piece far further developed than the rest. The steps below detail how I made the necessary changes to the head.

1. Using the Move brush, create the two crests on top of the head seen in Figure 8.74. These will be the points of origin for the horns later in this chapter.
2. Isolate the lower face with a mask and use Transpose to shift the top of the head up, lengthening the form (Figure 8.75)
3. Step down to the lower subdivision levels. With the Move brush, spread the eyes and make them smaller (Figure 8.76). I also lower and round off the top of the head to give it a blunt form. Later in this chapter we will look again at how I try to keep many broad, blunt shapes in this design (Figure 8.77).

After some more enhancing with the Move brush, Figure 8.78 shows the new face shape. I prefer this as it feels less cat-like and far more in keeping with the character of the animal reference. Originally I thought larger eyes would be a good design choice—large eyes tend to create empathy with a character—but in this case, large eyes are too far off the model of a goat or ram—a feature of those animals are small, wide-set eyes. Smaller eyes also help give an older look to the face while larger eyes feel more childlike. By shrinking the eye size, the character immediately starts to look more goat-like. I also push the ears in closer to the head with the Move brush—this will be even more important in the next step, when we create the large spiral horns. The ears need to be falling, out of the way of the horn geometry.

*Figure 8.74: With the Move brush, create the two crests seen here—this will be the point of insertion for the horns*

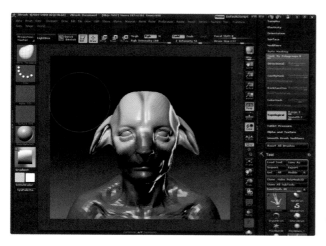

*Figure 8.75: Stretching head*

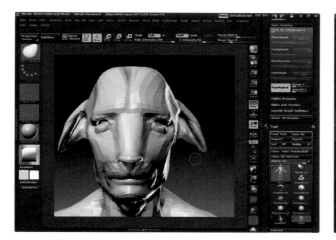

*Figure 8.76: Spreading the eyes apart and making them smaller*

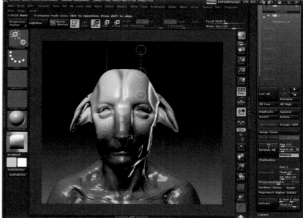

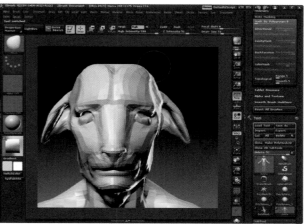

*Figure 8.77: Lowering the top of the head*

## Creating the Horns

The horns for this character will be a spiral configuration—very similar to ram horns but with some fantasy elements. The horns are best created using ZBrush primitives. ZBrush has a wide array of primitive shapes that can be manipulated to create all manner of basic models for use in your designs. Follow these steps to create the horns.

1. From the Tool menu, select the ZBrush primitive Helix3D (Figure 8.79).
2. The tool will initially look like a spring with tapers on each end. We will need to customize the shape. To do this, open the Tool ➢ Initialize menu to access the settings that determine the overall shape of this primitive (Figure 8.80).

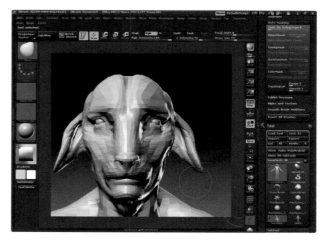

*Figure 8.78: Altering the face shape*

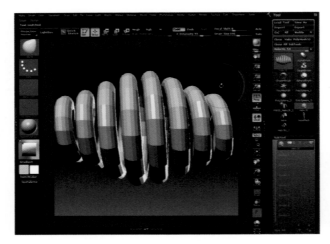

Figure 8.79: *Select the Helix3D ZBrush primitive to create the horn.*

Figure 8.80: *Open the Initialize menu to customize the helix shape.*

3. Set the coverage slider to 1.96. The rest of the geometry is controlled by curves. Figure 8.81 shows the curve settings for each of the following parameters: Profile, Radius, Thickness, Zoffset, and Twist. The settings will result in a horn shape like the one seen in Figure 8.82. We are now ready to import this geometry into the character SubTool stack.

4. When you selected the Helix3D tool, the character was automatically deselected. From the Tool menu, select the figure once again.

5. Under the Tool ➤ SubTool menu, click Append and select the Helix3D tool that we have modified. You should be able to tell it from the thumbnail (Figure 8.83).

6. ZBrush will automatically convert the ZBrush primitive into a polymesh so that you can sculpt it using the sculpting brushes. We will now need to scale and position the horns in relation to the head (Figure 8.84).

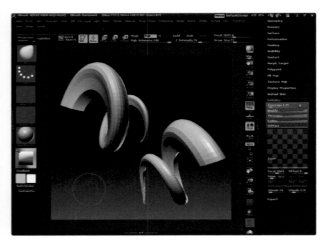

Figure 8.81: *Adjust the curves under Initialize to reflect those shown here.*

Figure 8.82: *The final horn shape will look like this.*

*Figure 8.83: Select the helix SubTool.*

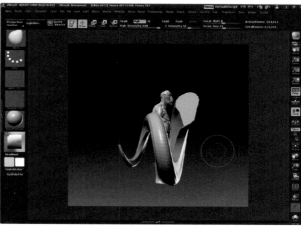

*Figure 8.84: The horns appended into the stack, but the size and placement needs to be corrected.*

7. Make sure the horn is the active selected SubTool from the SubTool menu. Press the E hot key to enable the Transpose Scale brush. Scale the horn down to a more manageable size. Use Transpose Move (the W hot key) to shift the horn into position on the head (Figure 8.85).

8. When the horn is placed correctly, use the mirror function in the SubTool master ZScript to mirror it across the X axis (Figure 8.86). Figure 8.87 shows the figure so far. We are now ready to move on to looking at the arms and legs of the character. We need to bring the same level of attenuated musculature and saggy skin to the rest of the body.

The horns are divided and detailed with the standard brush and a variety of masks. For the process in detail, see the accompanying video on the DVD or download files. There you can see the process I followed to create texture and detail on the horns.

*Figure 8.85: Scale the horn down.*

*Figure 8.86: The horns mirrored*

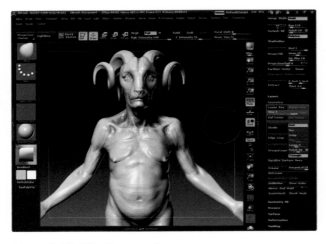

*Figure 8.87: The figure so far*

At this stage, I check the figure proportions using the transpose line as a measuring tool. The figure is close to six heads tall and with the horns added is starting to look a little too heavy. I adjust the body-to-head ratio so the character is approximately seven heads tall. To see this process in detail, please see the narrated video on the DVD or download files.

## Refining the Legs

At this point, I decide to change the overall structure of the legs. I will break the normal human leg forms and alter the character's legs to be more of an ungulate leg formation. Ungulates, which means "being hoofed" or "hoofed animal," are several groups of mammals, most of which use the tips of their toes, usually hoofed, to sustain their whole body weight while moving. Figure 8.88 shows a bit of reference for this kind of leg. This etching is from the classic animal anatomy book *Atlas of Animal Anatomy for Artists* by W. Ellenberger, H. Dittrich, H. Baum (Figure 8.89). This is one of my favorite animal anatomy books and I highly recommend it as a low-cost and highly informative reference book. The following steps detail how I convert this character's leg formation from a human, or plantigrade structure to an ungulate, or hoofed-leg formation. It is always good practice to try doing animal sculpture from reference like this. By careful study of living animal anatomy, you can create a better base of knowledge to pull from for your fantasy characters. Figure 8.90 shows an exquisite equine sculpture by artist Hardh D. Borah. This figure was created in ZBrush and 3D printed.

1. Isolate the legs from the body with transpose masking (Figure 8.91).
2. Use Transpose Rotate to bend the legs at the three key joints shown in Figure 8.92.

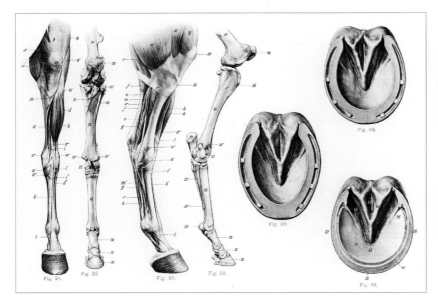

*Figure 8.88: Ungulate leg ref*

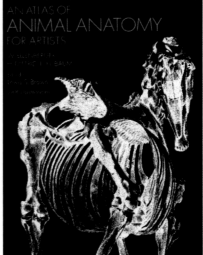

*Figure 8.89:* Atlas of Animal Anatomy for the Artist *is a classic text and one of my favorite animal anatomy books.*

Figure 8.90: *Creating animal sculptures from reference is a good way to practice and to add to your knowledge base of animal physiology for use in fantasy characters.*

Figure 8.91: *The legs isolated from the body with a mask*

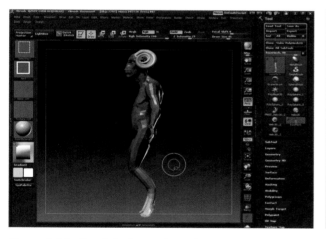

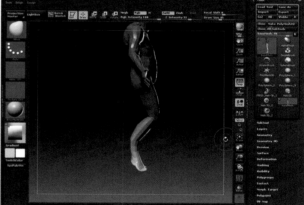

Figure 8.92: *Bend the leg at these three points.*

3. Shape the foot into a hoof form, taking care not to distort the toes. We don't need the actual toe geometry so we will delete them in the next step (Figure 8.93). Figure 8.94 shows the shape of the legs at this stage.

## Using GoZ to Reform the Foot

We will now look at how to delete the toe geometry without losing the sculpted detail of our mesh. To do this, we will use the free ZBrush plugin GoZ. GoZ allows you to transfer your lowest-resolution mesh into a compatible polygon-modeling software, such as Maya, Modo, 3dsMax, or Cinema, make changes to the geometry, then return to ZBrush, and retain all your sculpted subdivision levels. We will follow these steps to delete the toes and create a foot shape more suitable for sculpting a hoof.

1. With the body as the active SubTool, press the GoZ button, located under the Tool menu (Figure 8.95).

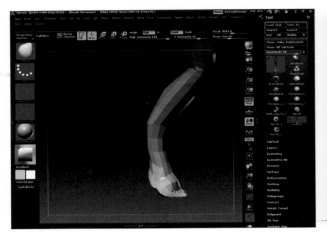

Figure 8.93: *Shape the feet into hooves*

Figure 8.94: *The legs at this stage*

Figure 8.95: *Press the GoZ button to transfer the body mesh to Maya.*

2. The body will now export from ZBrush and open in Maya ready for editing (Figure 8.96). Focus in on the foot geometry and delete the toe facts, as seen in Figure 8.97.

3. Select the edges shown in Figure 8.98 and collapse them. Be sure to do this on the top and bottom of the foot.

4. Select an edge along the hole in the foot. Use the Mesh ➤ Fill Hole function to close the hole (Figure 8.99). Select the Edit Mesh ➤ Split Polygon tool and cut new edges, connecting the edge flow from the top to the bottom of the foot while maintaining the all-quad layout of the mesh (Figure 8.100).

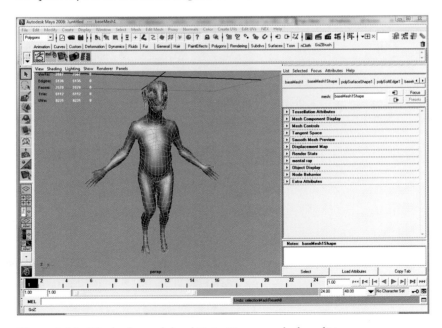

Figure 8.96: *The body mesh loads into Maya, ready for editing.*

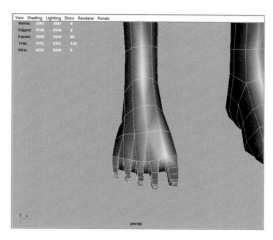
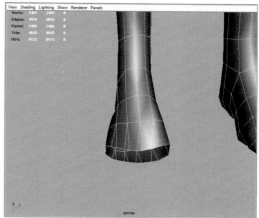

*Figure 8.97: Delete the toes from the mesh, as seen here*

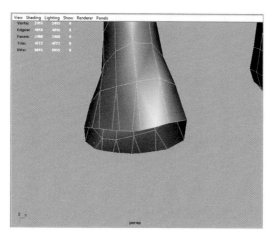
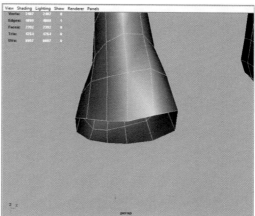

*Figure 8.98: Collapse these edges*

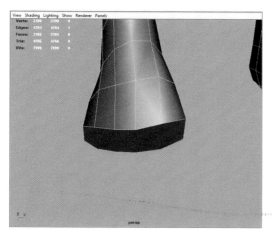

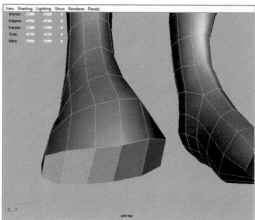

*Figure 8.99: Fill hole*          *Figure 8.100: Split poly*

*Figure 8.101: Press the GoZ Shelf button to return to ZBrush.*

5. When this is done for both feet you are ready to export back to ZBrush. Make sure the mesh is selected in Object mode and press the GoZ Shelf button (Figure 8.101).
6. The mesh will transfer back into ZBrush. A dialogue box will ask if you want to transfer the high-resolution details. Select Yes (Figure 8.102).
7. Back in ZBrush, use the Move brush to reshape the hoof based on the reference materials (Figure 8.103). GoZ will apply a mask to any unaltered areas of the ZTool when you return to ZBrush. Be sure to clear this mask before you continue.

The mesh is now updated. The ZTool has no toes and in their place are quad faces ready to be sculpted into hooves. For the remainder of the legs process, please see the DVD or download files for a fully narrated video showing the sculpting process for this character. We will now move on to the arms and hands.

*Figure 8.102: When transferring back into ZBrush, a dialogue box will ask if you want to transfer high-resolution details. Select Yes.*

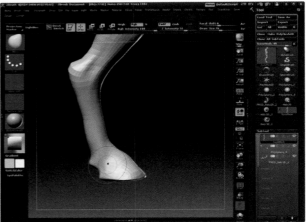

*Figure 8.103: Reshape the hoof according to the reference materials*

## Refining the Arms

Like the rest of the body, the arms will be based on the human photo reference. As before, it is important to get the muscular quality of the arms while retaining their thin and sinewy appearance. This will be accomplished by keeping the muscle mass low and the fatty tissues concentrated in the undersides of the limbs, as if they are being pulled by gravity. The following steps show the arms in progress.

1. Isolate the area for the bicep muscle with a mask. Using the Claytubes brush, stroke the bicep, taking care to get the flow of the muscle correct from beneath the deltoids and pectoral muscles (Figure 8.104).
2. Isolate the area for the triceps muscle with a mask (Figure 8.105). Using the Clay Tubes and Inflate brushes, rough in the three heads of the triceps muscles. Don't get too specific at this time, we just want to get the general form suggested. The arm anatomy, like the rest of the figure, is best developed in passes, as you work around the figure (Figure 8.106).

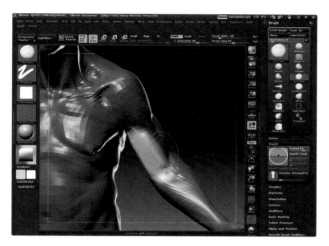

*Figure 8.104: Sculpt the biceps.*

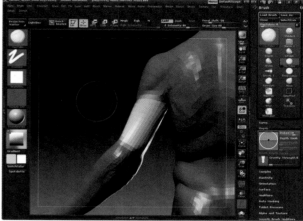

*Figure 8.105: Isolate the triceps with a mask.*

3. On the forearm, be sure to get the angle of high points accurate from the front view. This represents the relationship between the crest of the extensors on top of the arm and the crest of the medial epicondyles on the bottom. These two landmarks help us get the correct shape of the arm in silhouette (Figure 8.107).

4. On the elbow, make sure to get the landmark of the olecranon process as well as the V shape created by the origin of the extensor muscles of the forearm (Figure 8.108).

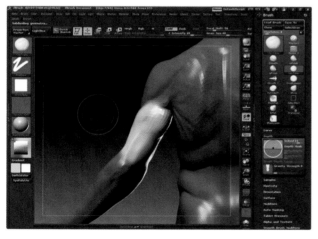
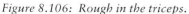

*Figure 8.106: Rough in the triceps.*

*Figure 8.107: Correct crests in silhouette*

The key points above are of great importance when working the arm. For a full look at the process of sculpting the arm as well as the hand, see the video on the DVD or download files. We will now look at the process I used to add some tertiary details like wrinkles around the joints, fat deposits, and other surface features. If you are interested in a more in-depth look at these topics as they apply to the human figure, please check out my book *Digital Sculpting Human Anatomy*, where I address figure sculpting and anatomy in detail.

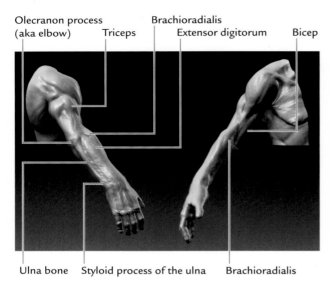

Olecranon process (aka elbow)   Triceps   Brachioradialis   Extensor digitorum   Bicep

Ulna bone   Styloid process of the ulna   Brachioradialis

*Figure 8.108: Landmarks on back-of-arm elbow and extensors*

## Adding Skin and Fat Details

In this section we will look at how to add wrinkles, folds, and fat deposits to the character. Details like these give the impression that there is skin over the underlying anatomy and add an enormous amount of character to the figure. It is important, even on the most fit of models, to give the impression of fatty deposits pressed together in areas they would naturally be fatty. Details like this make the figure appear to be flesh and blood rather than polygons carved into anatomical shapes.

Masking is used extensively when trying to create folds of fat and flesh. Often I will mask an area, then sculpt against the mask to create a sharp overhang where a fold of fatty flesh or a wrinkle overhangs. This helps create a realistic undercut where the folds of flesh resides. Let's take a look at some of the techniques I used to create the fleshy details of this model. Again, be sure to watch the video on the DVD or download files for the whole process.

1. To create the folds of back fat follow these steps. In the back view mask under the pads of fat commonly called "love handles." Use the Inflate brush to stroke along the masked edge increasing the mass of the love handles (Figure 8.109).

2. Extend the mask over the love handles. We will now add a layer of back fat. Again, use the Inflate brush to stroke along the masked edge and use the Move brush to tug the newly inflated fat roll down to give a sense of gravity pulling at the fatty tissues (Figure 8.110).

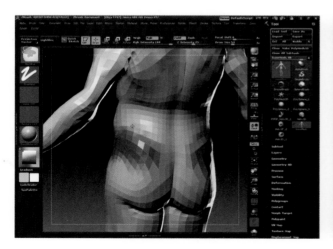

*Figure 8.109: Sculpting the oblique fat pads aka "love handles"*

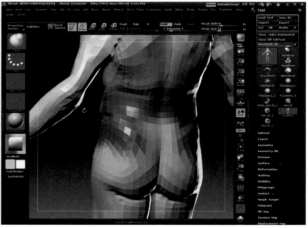

*Figure 8.110: Inflate fat tug move*

3. Step up a subdivision level so we can add more specific wrinkles. Using the Standard brush, I etch folds in under the scapulas and the roll of back fat directly beneath the shoulder blades (Figure 8.111). Use the Inflate brush with the gravity modifier on to

add weight to the folds (Figure 8.112). The gravity modifier is found under the Brush ➤ Depth menu (Figure 8.113). Point the arrow down for the direction of pull and set the strength slider until the effect is acceptable. Gravity will pull the mesh in the direction of the arrow while the brush affects the surface. When used with the Inflate brush, it will tug down on the faces while inflating them automatically, adding sag to the flesh.

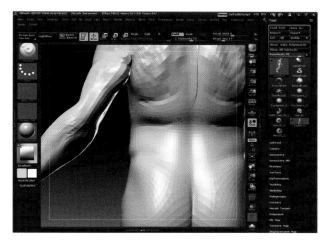

*Figure 8.111: Using Standard brush to accentuate folds*

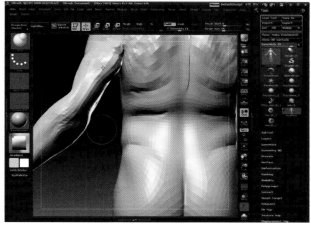

*Figure 8.112: Inflate with gravity*

4. A sag is created at the buttocks by inflating along the lower edge of the gluteus, allowing the flesh to sag slightly over the back of the thigh. Smaller wrinkles are added in, using the Standard brush with alpha 1 set to ZSub (Figure 8.114).

Some areas of the photo reference show area areas of finely concentrated wrinkles that give the impression of thin tissue—like skin (Figure 8.115). The armpits and the back both feature concentrated raised wrinkles that give the skin a loose, gathered look. To create wrinkles like this, use the standard brush with alpha 58 and ZAdd. Figure 8.116 shows the wrinkles at the armpit created with this technique.

*Figure 8.113: The gravity slider*

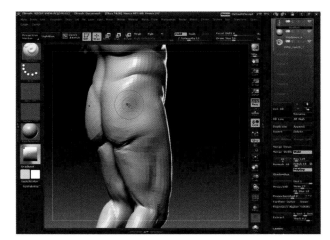

*Figure 8.114: Sagging the buttocks*

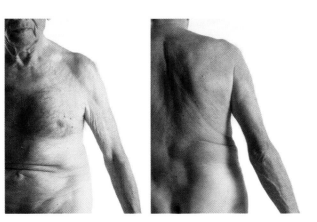

*Figure 8.115: Raised wrinkles such as these gather at the areas where the skin is sagging most. It creates a sense of loose tissue skin.*

*Figure 8.116: The wrinkles seen here are created by using the Standard brush with alpha 1 and ZAdd mode on to build up layers of wrinkles that are raised rather than etched into the skin.*

## Analyzing the Shape Language

Throughout the process of working on this character, I have tried to maintain a consistent shape language. The face and body all maintain a consistent series of broad, blunt shapes designed to soften the perception of the character and make him seem less intimidating. These broad forms were inspired by those already occurring in the face of a ram.

Figure 8.117 shows the face of the figure with the broad shapes highlighted. See how the consistent shape is a broad, blunt form from the top of the head down to the nose and shin. The crests of the head where the horns insert are rendered with a slight softness to the edge, to keep them from becoming too angular.

Taking the same idea into the body, see how the torso is essentially the same kind of shape? As we have seen in Chapter 1, "ZBrush as a Character Design Tool," always consider characters as their most basic shape relationships. Here you can see the same shapes echoed into the body from the head (Figure 8.118).

*Figure 8.117: The shape language for the character face*

*Figure 8.118: The shape repetition on the torso consists of multiple broad blunt forms*

The hands as well carry this same language. The fingers are broad and blunt as opposed to long and tapered, even the shape of the hand itself is a broad and flat wedge (Figure 8.119).

Here you can see the teeth are also considered in the same way (Figure 8.120). While a goat or ram would have large broad, flat teeth anyway, I find it important to mention that these shapes echo all the way to the dentals.

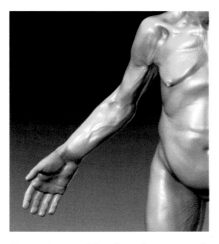

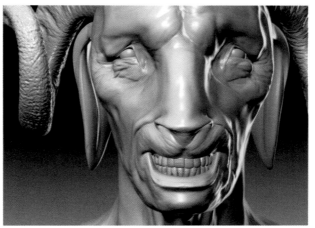

*Figure 8.119: The shape language of the hands*

*Figure 8.120: Teeth shape language*

That completes this chapter's lesson on designing the Forest Spirit. Figure 8.121 shows the final figure sculpture for this chapter. In this chapter, we further explored shape language, repetition of forms, using photo reference for inspiration, and sculpting techniques for fat and fleshy folds. In the next chapter, we will pose, compose, and paint the final presentation image in Photoshop.

*Figure 8.121: The final figure sculpture*

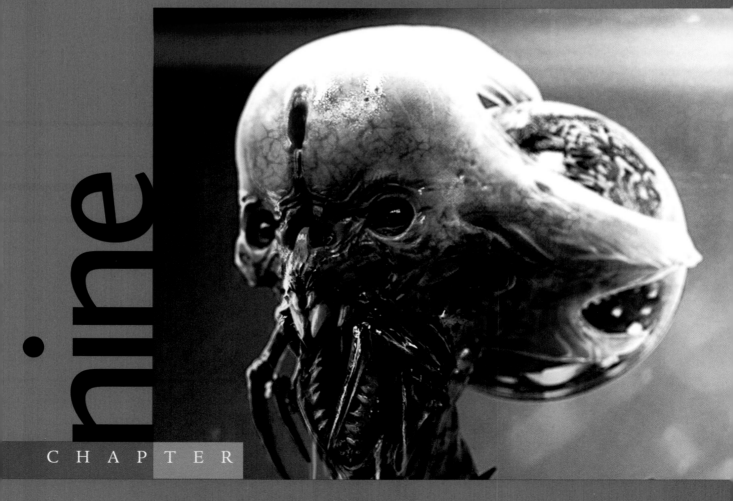

nine

# Painting the Forest Spirit

**In this chapter we will** *pose and paint the Forest Spirit character we created in Chapter 8, "Sculpting the Forest Spirit." We will look at some of the considerations I used when posing the figure. We will also look at how to render base images outside of ZBrush. This requires touching on the ZBrush plug-in Decimation Master, which we cover in depth in Chapter 11, "ZBrush for Digital 3-D Printing." We will then take our model to Maya, where we will create a scene file, lighting, and render passes using Maya render layers. These layers will be composited in Photoshop. Once in Photoshop, we will look at how to create an interesting character illustration using a limited palette.*

*We will keep the color unsaturated and monochromatic. This is often desirable when you want to communicate a design without addressing questions of color. Some directors can be quite sensitive to color choices and as a result of this it can sometimes be beneficial to address a design in a more desaturated color space to help the viewer see and evaluate the character independent of any color choices. This allows the sculpture and form to be evaluated before the extra element of color is added to the mix. I have seen designs dismissed because the color choice was not suitable. Often you have only a few moments in the first viewing to capture attention and appeal. The Forest Spirit lends itself to this approach since unsaturated earth tones suit an earthy character like this. While we are in Photoshop, we will look at how I paint hair and fur on a character as well as an extremely fast technique for painting eyes.*

## The Brief: Forest Spirit in Color

The brief for this chapter is to execute a character illustration from the Forest Spirit model. We want to give this character a desaturated, muted color language. Try to avoid any overpowering color choices so the viewer can concentrate on the formal elements of the design. We will look at how to create a moody image with dynamic presence while minimizing the amount of painting required. We will give this character a hirsute quality by painting in thickets of coarse hair.

# Preparing the Model in ZBrush

*Figure 9.1: The posed figure*

Before we can render our images outside of ZBrush, there are some things we need to think about and establish. Firstly, we will need to pose the figure. In the Interdimensional Traveler character, we opted for an evenly balanced pose. This time we will experiment with offsetting the weight of the character in what is called *contrapposto*. We will also need to look at how to get the detailed figure outside of ZBrush for rendering. To accomplish this we will learn about Decimation Master, a plug-in for ZBrush.

## Posing the Figure

As we have seen in other projects so far, the model has been posed in a manner that helps communicate the character and disposition. This helps create a far more dynamic presentation than a mere neutral pose that communicates very little about a character's attitude. Since I had considered this particular character to possess a softer, more gentle personality, I attempted to give him a more introspective pose. I accomplished this by giving a slight tilt to the head and raising his eye line rather than making direct eye contact. With this I intended to give him a thoughtful presence rather than a direct engagement with the viewer (Figure 9.1).

### Contrapposto

When posing this figure, I have used the technique of creating a contrapposto pose to make the figure feel more dynamic, interesting, and alive. *Contrapposto* is an Italian word meaning counter pose. It describes a figure where the weight is shifted to one leg or the other and not held equally distributed between the legs. This causes a rhythmic offsetting of the masses in the body expressed by contrasting angles between the knees, hips, and shoulders. Contrapposto was very common in Renaissance art—it is seen most famously in the figure of David by Michelangelo. In Figure 9.2, I have illustrated contrapposto in the figure of a giant sculpted by Jim McPherson.

For the Interdimensional Traveler, we allowed the weight to remain between the feet. The dynamics of the pose were achieved by offsetting the figure in a spiral composition. For the Forest Spirit, we will keep the figure facing forward but we will offset the weight between the hips and shoulders to create a more interesting effect (Figure 9.3).

Blue line represents center of balance

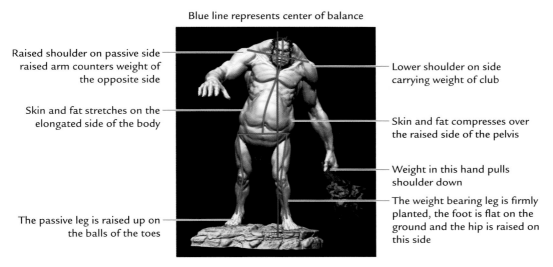

Raised shoulder on passive side raised arm counters weight of the opposite side

Lower shoulder on side carrying weight of club

Skin and fat stretches on the elongated side of the body

Skin and fat compresses over the raised side of the pelvis

Weight in this hand pulls shoulder down

The weight bearing leg is firmly planted, the foot is flat on the ground and the hip is raised on this side

The passive leg is raised up on the balls of the toes

*Figure 9.2: This giant sculpture demonstrates the concept of contrapposto and offsetting masses.*

## Exporting from ZBrush

Before we can render this figure outside of ZBrush, we would need to either generate displacement or normal maps with a low-res model or export high-resolution decimated models, which can be rendered outside ZBrush. Normal and displacement mapping is a complicated process which is absolutely necessary if you want to export your figure to a rendering and animation pipeline. Since we will be rendering still images, we can take a much simpler route and decimate the figure. To do this we will use a ZBrush plug-in called Decimation Master. We cover Decimation Master in much more detail in Chapter 11 but I will give you the basic steps for its use here.

### Decimating the Figure

Decimation Master is used to reduce the overall poly count of the figure while retaining the details. The posed Forest Spirit model, exported at full resolution would be far too heavy to open and manipulate in Maya successfully. The system would be unstable and memory would likely crash. By reducing the poly count with Decimation Master, you reduce the file size. The original ZTool is 275 megabytes and several million polygons. After Decimation Master the resulting model is 38.1 megabytes and 999,000 faces. This polygon count and file size is perfectly suited for rendering in Maya. By decimating the model you will retain all your detail without having to resort to complex shader networks to render normal maps or displacements in mental ray.

*Figure 9.3: The Forest Spirit pose with lines overlaid on the angles*

If you want to know more about rendering displacement and normal maps, I have included some bonus videos on the DVD or download files that deal with this.

*Figure 9.4: The body is the active SubTool selected in this screenshot.*

*Figure 9.5: The Decimation Master submenu*

*Figure 9.6: The k Polys slider sets the target polygon count of the final mesh in thousands of polygons.*

Follow the steps below to export the decimated figure.

1. Load the ZProject file goatman_posed.ZPR containing the posed figure from the DVD or the download files into ZBrush.

2. Make sure the body SubTool is currently selected under Tool ➤ SubTools (Figure 9.4). You also want to be sure you are at the highest subdivision level so all of the model's detail is visible. Open the ZPlugin menu from the top of the screen and click the radial icon to dock it to the side of the interface. From the ZPlugin menu open the Decimation Master submenu (Figure 9.5).

3. Under the Decimation Master menu click the Pre-process All button. This will cause ZBrush to run the initial computations on the mesh for each SubTool and allow us to decimate in the next step. This stage of pre-processing may take a few minutes depending on your computer's speed. ZBrush is writing a cache file to disk for each SubTool, which will allow it to perform the mesh reductions required for decimation.

4. Once the mesh is preprocessed, we will set the level of decimation. Set the k Polys slider to 999. This value specifies a mesh with 999,000 polygons. Maya tends to work best for me with meshes of 1 million polys or less. This varies from system to system depending on your hardware specs. For this section, we will decimate the figure to 999,000 polygons. This level will give us good detail while creating a model which can be easily loaded into Maya without crashing the system.

5. Press the Decimate Current button and ZBrush will start the decimation process (Figure 9.6). This stage may take a few moments but most of the heavy computation was completed in the Pre-process mesh step. When the model is decimated you will be able to zoom in and examine the details. Turn on Polyframe mode with Shift + F to see the level of decimation (Figure 9.7).

6. Now that the mesh is decimated you can export the OBJ file. Under the Tool menu, click the export button and save the mesh as body.obj. We will need to repeat the process for the horns.

7. Select the horn SubTool and be sure you are at the highest subdivision level. Open the ZPlugin ➤ Decimation Master menu. We don't need to preprocess the horns at this stage because we clicked Pre-process All before, which wrote a cache file for each SubTool. Set the k Polys slider to 200. This will decimate the horns to 200,000 faces.

8. Export the horns as horns.obj. You will also want to manually export the eyes and teeth respectively. These are not detailed ZTools so the objs can be exported without decimation.

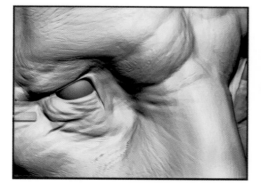 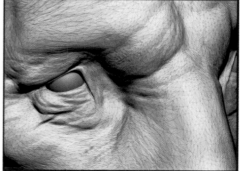

*Figure 9.7: Here you can see a decimated mesh in gray shade as well as frame mode. In frame mode, the selective triangulation performed by Decimation Master is apparent.*

Now that the decimated meshes are exported to disk as OBJ files, we are ready to move to Maya. In the next steps, we will import these models, create a lit environment, and render passes for compositing in Photoshop.

## Loading the Models to Maya

At this stage, we are ready to load our decimated meshes into Maya. This will allow us to render passes of the character, taking advantage of Maya's light and camera settings as well as the indirect lighting options available in Mental Ray for Maya. We will use Maya's render layers to help organize the scene and create the required render passes for compositing. Follow the steps to prepare a Maya scene.

1. With Maya open, go to File ➤ Import ❏ and from the File type drop-down select OBJ (Figure 9.8). At the bottom of this window, in the File Type Specific Options section, make sure the radial button next to Single Object is selected.

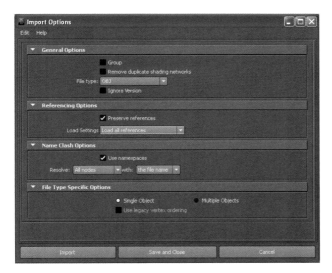

*Figure 9.8: The Import Options menu*

2. Click the Import button and browse the the body.obj file. Import this into Maya (Figure 9.9). The geometry will likely come in upside down. Do not move or scale it yet. We need to import the other SubTools.
3. From the same Import menu, bring in the eyes and horns SubTools. The teeth can be left out since the character's mouth is not open. When all the objects are imported, they will align in the correct space. Click and drag a selection marquee around the models to select them all. Press the Ctrl + G hot key to group them together.
4. We now want to center the pivot of the group to make manipulating the size and placement of the figure easier. Click Modify ➤ Center pivot. (Figure 9.10).
5. Press the E key to enter rotate mode while the group is still selected. If you accidently deselect the group, select any object that is a member then press the up arrow on the keyboard. This will select the group again. Rotate while holding down the J key to snap the rotation to degree increments. This helps you rotate the model exactly. Figure 9.11 shows the model rotated to the correct world space.
6. Press the W key to switch to Move from Rotate. Move the model up in Y so the figure is standing on the ground grid.

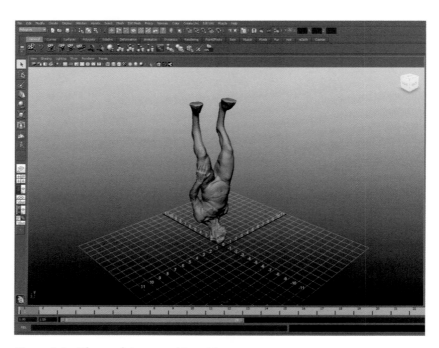

*Figure 9.9: The mesh imported into Maya*

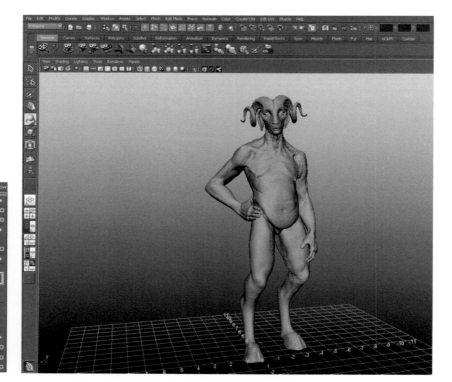

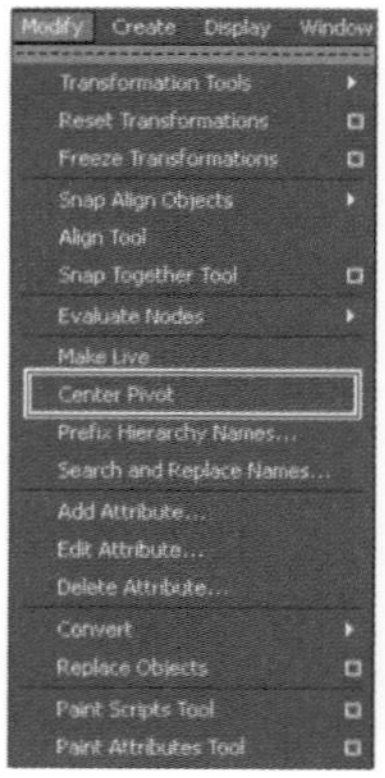

*Figure 9.10: Centering the pivot point*

*Figure 9.11: The model rotated into correct orientation*

# Preparing the Scene, Lighting, and Background in Maya

We have now imported the meshes themselves and oriented them in the scene. The next step is to create an environment for the figure to be lit. Since the purpose of this image is to showcase the character, we will chose a simple photo studio setup. This allows us to focus entirely on the figure and his silhouette.

## Creating the Backdrop

In the steps below, we will create the studio backdrop as well as the basic lighting setup.

1. From the main menu at the top of the screen click Create ➤ Polygon Primitives ➤ Plane ❏. Reset the settings by going to Edit ➤ Reset settings on the window. Set the height and width to 35 and the width and height divisions to 3 (Figure 9.12).

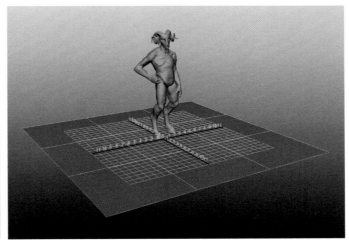
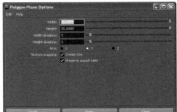

*Figure 9.12: The create Polygon Plane options are shown on the left of the screen here. The polygon plane moved to the level of the feet to serve as a ground plane.*

2. With the plane selected, press the F9 key to enter into the vertex selection mask. Select the back row of vertices as shown in Figure 9.13.
3. Press W to enter move mode and drag those vertices up in the Y direction. Invert the selected vertices by going to Edit ➤ Invert selection. Now the other control vertices will be ready to move. Shift these back in Z until the backdrop looks like Figure 9.14.
4. Press the F8 key to return to Object Select mode from Vertex mode. Make sure the selection mask in Maya is set to Polygons (Figure 9.15). If this part of the UI is not visible, go to Display ➤ UI Elements ➤ Show All UI Elements (Figure 9.16). Alternatively, you can open the hotbox by holding the spacebar and then click in the left region to bring up menu masks. Select polygons from there to switch the main menu to polygon model (Figure 9.17). Now the main menu at the top of the screen will display the polygon modeling options.

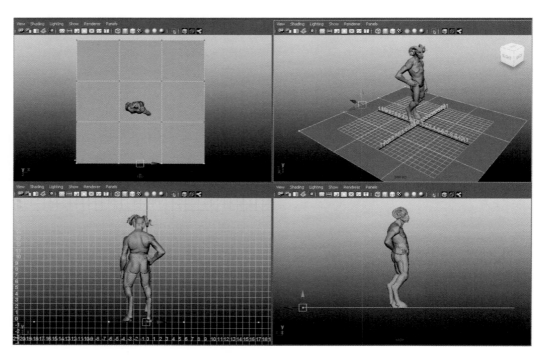

*Figure 9.13: The back row of vertices selected*

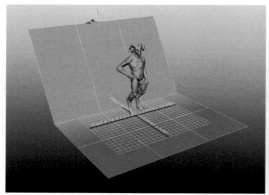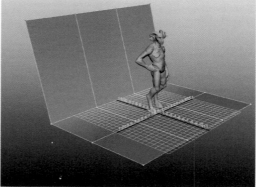

*Figure 9.14: On the left you can see the vertices moved up in the Y direction. On the right the vertices are moved back in Z.*

*Figure 9.15: The polygons menu mask*

5. With the backdrop geometry selected, go to Mesh ➢ Smooth ❑. Reset the settings. Set divisions to 2 and then uncheck Geometry Borders under the Preserve section. Click Smooth and the backdrop will smooth (Figure 9.18).

6. The backdrop is now finished. We can add this to a layer and set it to reference to keep it from being selectable while we work. To do this, click the new layer icon at the right side of the screen as seen in Figure 9.19. Double click the layer name to bring up the Edit Layer box. Here you can rename the layer to backdrop (Figure 9.20).

*Figure 9.16: The display all UI elements menu*

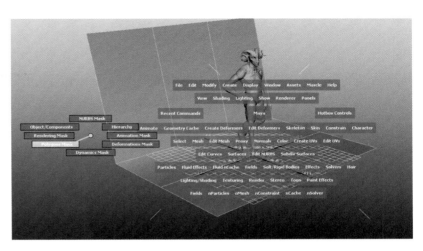

*Figure 9.17: Selecting the polygon menu mask from the hotbox*

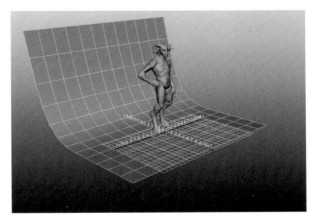

*Figure 9.18: The backdrop geometry smoothed*

*Figure 9.19: Create a new layer by pressing the new layer icon shown here*

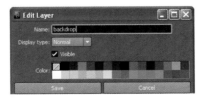

*Figure 9.20: Double clicking the layer name will open this dialogue box and allow you to rename the layer.*

7. Select the backdrop geometry and right click the layer name. From the popup menu select add selected objects (Figure 9.21). With the layer selected, click the Layers menu item. Set selected layer ➢ Reference to set the layer to reference mode. This means you cannot select the backdrop accidently while you work. To easily select the backdrop again simply right click on the layer name and select objects to select the backdrop (Figure 9.22).

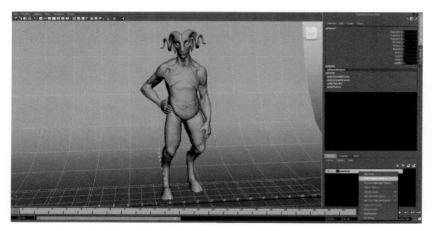

*Figure 9.21:  Add Selected Objects to layer*

*Figure 9.22:  Use the Select Objects menu to select the contents of a layer set to reference mode.*

## Setting Up Lighting

With the backdrop in place, we are now ready to create the lights for our scene. Follow these steps to create a key and backlight using Maya's directional lights.

1. Create a directional light by clicking create ➢ lightsDirectional. Press E to enter Rotate mode. Press the number 7 at the top of the keyboard to display lighting in the viewport and rotate the light at an angle similar to what's seen in Figure 9.23.

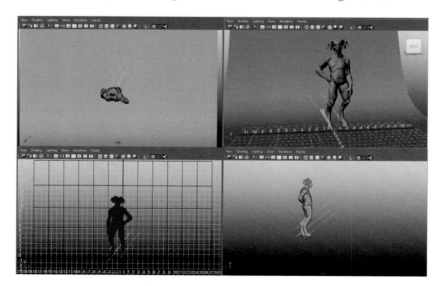

*Figure 9.23:  The light angle menu*

2. Press Ctrl to open the Attribute Editor. Open the shadows options. Set the angle to 10 and the rays to 50. A lower angle setting creates a sharper shadow and more rays reduce the graininess but will also increase the overall render time (Figure 9.24).
3. Duplicate this light by pressing Ctrl + D and rotate the second light to point at the figure's back—this will be the rim light (Figure 9.25). The Attribute Editor should still be open. If not, press Ctrl + A while the light is selected.

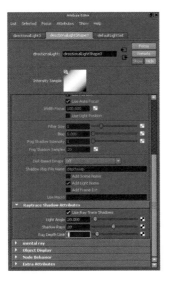
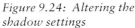

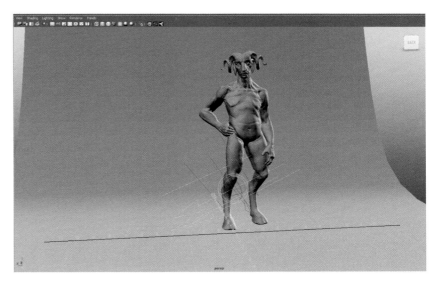

*Figure 9.24: Altering the shadow settings*

*Figure 9.25: Setting up the rim light*

4. Pressing Ctrl + A will open the Attribute Editor for the rim light. Set the light intensity to 3.71 (Figure 9.26). We want to give the rim light a cooler hue. To do this, we will assign a color to the light. Click the color box in the Attribute Editor and set the color to a pale blue (RGB 0.687 0.844 0.922). This will help differentiate the rim light from the key. The cooler light will help make these areas recede but the impact of the rim light will help define the character from the background.

## Setting Up Materials

Now we will set up materials on the body, eyes, and horns. These will be fairly standard blinn shaders with slight modifications. We are most concerned with getting a variation in specular quality between the skin, eyes, and horns since these are three distinct materials.

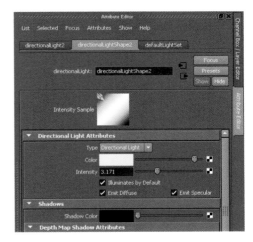

*Figure 9.26: Setting the light color*

1. Select the body mesh. Click and hold the right mouse button and select Assign Favorite Material ➢ Blinn. This will assign a blinn shader to the body, and if the Attribute Editor is still on, the settings will be visible (Figure 9.27). If the Attribute Editor is not open, right click and hold and select material attributes from the Marking menu (Figure 9.28).
2. We want to adjust the specular shading settings. To allow us to see the change on the model, click the Select button at the bottom of the Attribute Editor window. This will allow you to keep the material node selected while deselecting the geometry in the viewport. That way, changes made to the shader are visible in the window (Figure 9.29).

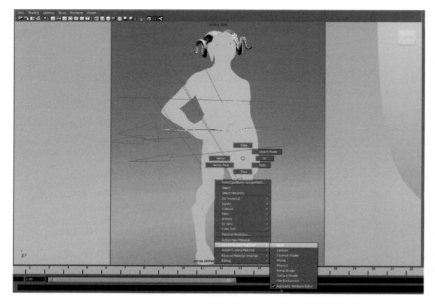

*Figure 9.27: Assign favorite material*

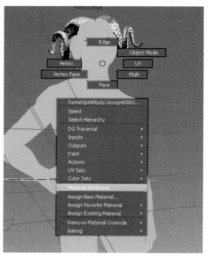

*Figure 9.28: The material attributes menu*

**3.** Click in the color swatch and set the RGB value to 0.500 0.500 0.500. You may need to set the color drop-down box to RGB on the lower right corner of the window (Figure 9.30).

**4.** In the Specular Shading Settings, adjust the Eccentricity setting to 0.281, Specular Roll Off to 0.273, Specular Color to RGB value 0.248 0.248 0.248, and Reflectivity to 0. These settings can be seen in Figure 9.31. This will give the skin a general shine with no sharp, refined specular highlights. This is more suitable for a skin like this that should not appear particularly moist or shiny. The eyes and horns will have a much stronger specular highlight by contrast.

*Figure 9.29: The select button allows you to select and alter the material node while seeing the material change on the model in the viewport.*

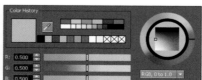

*Figure 9.30: Setting the color value of the light in the color history menu*

5. Select the horn geometry. Right click and hold, and from the Marking menu, select Assign Favorite Material ➤ Blinn. Click the color swatch and set the RGB value to a darker gray than the skin, in this case RGB 0.317 0.317 0.317.

6. Under the Specular Shading settings, set Eccentricity to 0.260, Specular Roll Off to 0.756, Specular Color to RGB 0.309 0.309 0.309, and Reflectivity to 0 (Figure 9.32). This will create a nice color and specular contrast between the horns and the head (Figure 9.33).

*Figure 9.31: The specular settings for the material node*

7. Select each eyeball. While the main menu is in polygon mode, click Mesh ➤ Combine, to combine the two spheres into a single object (Figure 9.34). Click and hold the RMB and assign a blinn shader as before.

8. Set the color of the blinn to 0.600 0.600 0.600 to give the eyes a lighter gray than the skin and horns. Under the Specular Shading section set Eccentricity to 0.209, Specular Roll Off to 1, Specular Color to RGB 0.683 0.683 0.683 and Reflectivity to 0.

*Figure 9.32: Set the specular color for the horns to help control the level of shine*

*Figure 9.33: The horns and skin have varied levels of shininess due to their different specular settings*

*Figure 9.34: Combine the eye meshes*

9. Lastly we will assign a Lambert shader to the backdrop. We assign a Lambert shader to the backdrop so there are no specular reflections/highlights on the background itself. The Lambert shader is flat shading, only with no shine. Click the Channel box tab at the right side of the screen or press Ctrl + A to switch from the Attribute Editor to the channel box. Under the Layer menu at the lower right corner of the screen right click and hold on the backdrop layer and, from the popup menu, select Objects.

10. The backdrop is now selected. Remember we cannot directly click on the backdrop geometry to select it at this time because the layer is set to reference. Right click and hold on the backdrop in the viewport menu. From the popup menu, select Assign Favorite Material ➤ Lambert. The shader will appear in the Attribute Editor on the right side of the screen. Set the color to RGB 0.453 0.453 0.453.

That completes the shader assignments. We are now ready to create render passes to ensure that we get the images from Maya we need for export.

## Setting Up Render Pass Layers

Maya allows you to create various render layers that control the type of image output by the renderer. We will use these render layers to create a normal base render, an ambient occlusion pass, and a matter pass for our render.

1. Press Ctrl + A to exit the Attribute Editor and show the Channel box. Alternatively, you can click the Channel box tab at the right side of the screen. In the Layers menu at the bottom, click the Render tab. This is where we will create and edit render layers (Figure 9.35).

2. By default, you have a master layer that renders the basic scene with lighting. We will create another render layer that is set to generate an ambient occlusion pass. Ambient occlusion helps define the shadows on the figure and is very useful in Photoshop for giving more depth and intensity to the lighting. Select the figure, pressing the up arrow on the keyboard so the whole group is selected. Holding down Shift, drag a marquee around the lights to select them as well.

3. With this selection, click the Create New Layer and Assign Selected Objects button, shown in Figure 9.36. This will create a new layer called layer1 (Normal) and assign the figure and lights to it. Double click the layer name and rename it Occlusion.

4. Right click on the layer name and from the popup window, select Attributes. This will open the render layer attributed in the Attribute editor. Click and hold the right mouse button over the Presets button in the Attribute editor. Here you will find several layer types listed. Select Occlusion, and Maya will automatically set up the render layer to generate an ambient occlusion render (Figure 9.37).

5. Now we will create a matte layer for the figure. Select the figure again. Press the up arrow so the whole group is selected. This time you will not select the lights. Again, press the Create New Layer button to generate a layer and add the selected geometry. Double click this layer and name it "Matte."

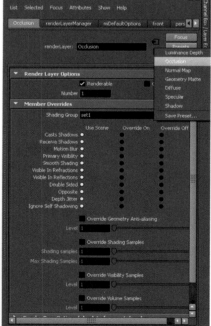

*Figure 9.35: Create render layers.*

*Figure 9.36: Create new layer and assign the geometry and lights.*

*Figure 9.37: Selecting the attributes for the Occlusion render layer*

**6.** Right click the menu name "Matte" and from the popup menu, select Attributes again. In the Attribute Editor, click Presets and select Geometry Matte. This will create a matte render layer. Note that the figure will appear blacked out on the screen now; select the master layer and your regular shading and lighting will reappear (Figure 9.38).

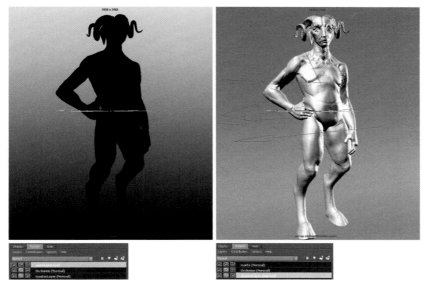

*Figure 9.38: The figure will appear in silhouette when in the geometry matte render layer, as we see on the left. When you select the master layer, the regular lighting will reappear, as shown on the right.*

## Setting Up Camera and Render

Now we are ready to set up our camera view for rendering. In this section, we will look at how to enable the rendering camera and set up all our render options so we get the images we need from Mental Ray.

*Figure 9.39: The Render Settings button*

**1.** From the top of the screen, press the Render Settings button (Figure 9.39). Alternatively, you can access the render settings by clicking Window ➤ Rendering Editors ➤ Render Settings (Figure 9.40).

**2.** In the render settings window, set Mental Ray in the Render, using the drop-down box. This selects Mental Ray as the renderer (Figure 9.41).

**3.** Under the Common Settings tab, open the File Output menu (Figure 9.42). Set the image format drop-down box to tiff. Under Renderable Cameras, select Perspective (Figure 9.43). This will set the perspective camera as the rendering camera and the file type output will be tiff.

**4.** Next we will set the resolution. I chose a high-resolution final render in a portrait proportion, that has a longer height than width. Uncheck Maintain width/height ratio and set the image to 1920 × 2650. Set Resolution to 300, so the image is suitable for print (Figure 9.44). Figure 9.45 shows the render window as a whole.

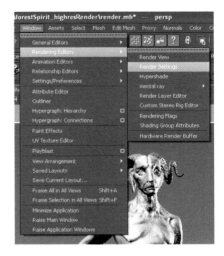

*Figure 9.40: The Render Settings menu*

*Figure 9.41: Set Mental Ray as the renderer*

*Figure 9.42: File output*

*Figure 9.43: Setting the Renderable Cameras to perspective*

*Figure 9.44: Image Size settings*

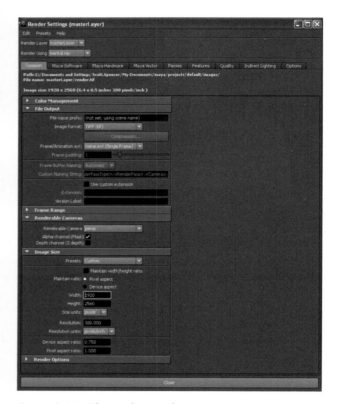

*Figure 9.45: The render window*

## Some Special Settings for Rendering Multiple Views

If you choose to keyframe multiple camera positions or model positions with the intention of rendering multiple options from Maya, you will need to set a couple extra render global settings. Under the File Output section, set Frame/animation ext to name.number.ext. This ensures that each individual frame is rendered and named with its own number in the filename. Set the frame padding slider to 2. Under the Frame Range submenu, you will need to set Start and End frame. If you set keyframes at 1–5, you want to set your Start to 1 and End to 5. With these settings in place, Maya will render a pass for each frame, number the image accordingly, and store it in the appropriate folder, as we see in the next section.

5. Next we will set up the anti-aliasing settings to give the best image quality. Go to the Quality menu tab in the Render Settings and choose the "Production" preset. This allows the anti-aliasing settings to be automatically created. You must be sure to do this before turning on Final Gathering in the next step.

6. Next we will enable Final Gathering. This will give a very nice, soft lighting and shadow effect on the final image. Click the Indirect Lighting tab at the top of the Render settings window (Figure 9.46). Open the Final Gathering submenu and click the Final Gathering checkbox. Set accuracy to 100, Point Density to 1, and Point Interpolation to 10. You can increase Accuracy to 200 for a higher-quality result, but the render will take longer. Remember we will be using this as a basis for painting in Photoshop, so you can afford to reduce some quality for speed.

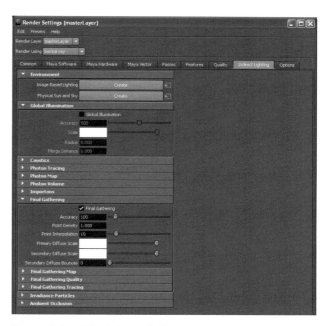

*Figure 9.46: The indirect lighting options*

Click the Close button at the bottom of the menu. Your render settings now are stored. Now we will enable the necessary camera settings so we can frame the image for composition.

*Figure 9.47: The select camera icon*

1. Select the perspective camera by clicking the camera icon in the toolbar along the top of the perspective viewport window (Figure 9.47).

2. We will now want to display the resolution of the image the camera is set to render. This is called the resolution gate, and it is enabled by clicking the View menu in the perspective viewer toolbar, under View select Camera Settings ➢ Resolution Gate (Figure 9.48). A rectangle will appear in the viewport now—this rectangle is determined by the image dimensions set in the render global.

3. If the borders are offscreen, with the camera selected, open the Attribute Editor. Under the Display Options settings, raise the overscan value until the resolution gate is visible in the viewport. This helps to accurately frame your render (Figure 9.49).

4. Orient the camera to the figure to get the best possible composition. You may choose to keyframe several camera positions. You can also rotate the group node containing the figure to get various angles. These rotations can be keyframed as well. Check the sample scene file on the DVD or download files for an example of how keyframes have been set for the camera as well as the figure group.

5. Save your scene file before moving on to the next steps. Create a new project by going to File ➢ Project ➢ New. Name the project "forestSpirit Render." Note the fact that there are no spaces in the project name. In the new project window, click the Use Defaults button, to fill in the directories (Figure 9.50).

6. Click Accept and then save your file as "render.mb." Take notice of where your project folder is located. Your final renders will store here in the image subfolder. We will need to get them for the Photoshop stage.

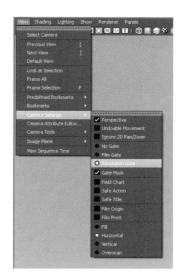

*Figure 9.48: The Resolution Gate shows a rectangle representing the image resolution set in the render globals.*

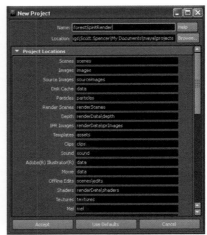

*Figure 9.49: The overscan value can adjust the visibility of the resolution gate.*

*Figure 9.50: Create a new project.*

## Rendering the Image Passes

We are now ready to render images from Maya. Follow these steps to create separate render passes on disk.

1. Under the Render Layers menu, make sure all layers are set to render. The first little icon on the layer should have a green checkmark (Figure 9.51).
2. Change to the Rendering Menu Mask at the top left of the screen (Figure 9.52).
3. From the top menu bar, click Render ➢ Batch render. This will start the rendering of your three layers. You can watch the render in progress by opening the Script Editor, clicking the icon in Figure 9.53 or going to Window ➢ General Editors ➢ Script Editor.
4. Change to the Rendering Menu Mask at the top left of the screen (Figure 9.54).

*Figure 9.51: Set to render*

*Figure 9.52: Rendering menu mask*

*Figure 9.53: Script editor button*

*Figure 9.54: Script Editor menu*

When the render is complete, you will find the passes stored in the Maya project directory, in the Images folder, in subfolders named for each layer. If you rendered multiple frames, each folder will have an image numbered for each frame. This will help you identify and composite the associated layers in Photoshop.

# Compositing and Painting in Photoshop

Now that we have completed the technical stages to render out images, we are ready to start painting in Photoshop. This section is where we pull out the tips and tricks to really make this image come alive. With just a few simple techniques, I will show you how to give these renders a textured, illustrative feel as well as how to add light and life to the eyes with just a few passes of light and shadow.

Make sure your brush set that came with this book is loaded into Photoshop. This can be appended to your favorite brushes or replace them entirely. We will be using soft round brushes for most of the work in this chapter with the exception of some specific hair brushes. We will discuss the hair brushes as they come up later. If you rendered multiple keyframes in the previous example, pick one of them to follow these steps or use the render passes supplied on the DVD or download files.

## Composite Layers in Photoshop

To composite the layers, we will use the same script as seen in Chapter 5, "Painting the Interdimensional Traveler." In Photoshop, open the menu item File ➢ Scripts ➢ Load Files Into Stack.

1. From the Load Layers menu, click Browse and locate the render passes. Maya stored them in the Images Subfolder of your project folder. The renders will be stored in folders called MasterLayer, Occlusion, and Matte. If you rendered multiple keyframes, each folder will have a file named with a number that corresponds to the keyframe it represents. For the first frame you want to only load the passes numbered 01.

2. Browse and load the masterLayer, occlusion, and master images for frame 001 (Figure 9.55). When this is done, click OK on the Load Layers dialog box, and Photoshop will create a new layered document from the files selected.

3. Arrange the masterLayer image on the bottom of the layer stack with Occlusion and Matte above it. Rename the layers "figure," "occlusion," and "matte" for clarity later, as we need to work with specific layers (Figure 9.56).

4. Select the occlusion layer. Set the layer blending mode to multiply (Figure 9.57).

5. Use the magic wand to select the body on the matte layer. Make sure layer visibility is on and click on the character's body with the magic wand tool. You will get marching ants around the figure silhouette (Figure 9.58).

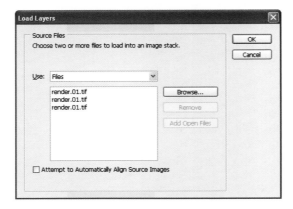

Figure 9.55: The render passes selected in Load-Layers

Figure 9.56: Arrange the renamed layers as seen here with Occlusion and Matte above the figure layer

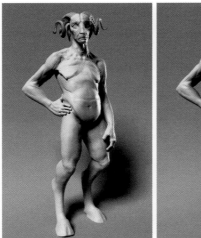

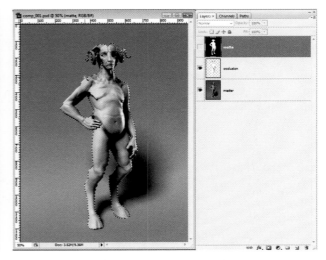

Figure 9.57: The image on the left is the figure without the occlusion layer. On the right is the figure with the occlusion layer set to multiply.

Figure 9.58: Selecting the figure with the matte

6. Since we have the figure matte selected now, we can separate it from the background. This will make it easier to generate a selection later. All you will need to do is Ctrl+Click on the layer and it will automatically select just the pixels of the figure. Press Ctrl + J to jump the selection up into a new layer. Name this new layer "figureMatte" (Figure 9.59). You can turn off visibility on both the matte and figure matte layers now. This will make isolating the figure from the background much easier. All you need to do is Ctrl+Click on the layer itself to select the figure. The layer need not be active or visible for this to work.

7. Create a new layer by going to Layer ➤ New ➤ Adjustment Layer ➤ Levels. This creates a levels adjustment layer at the top of the stack (Figure 9.60). When the layer is created, the Levels control window will appear in the Photoshop interface, allowing you to adjust the levels of the image (Figure 9.61). This allows you to apply changes to the lightness and darkness of the layers beneath this adjustment layer. Darken the image using the layers control sliders. At this stage, the entire image is darkened by the levels control (Figure 9.62).

8. We now want to create a falloff, so the darkening effect appears to increase toward the bottom of the image. This will help create the impression of a key light falling off toward shadow and increase the contrast and atmosphere of the image. The adjustment layer comes with a layer mask by default (Figure 9.63).

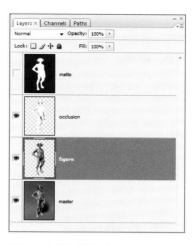

*Figure 9.59: The figure layer*

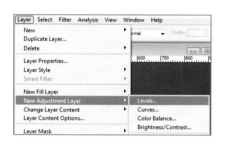

*Figure 9.60: Create an adjustment layer for level control.*

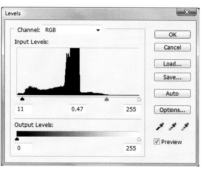

*Figure 9.61: Adjust the histogram to darken the image as seen here.*

*Figure 9.62: The entire image is darkened by the levels adjustment layer.*

9. Click in the mask so it is active. From the tools, select the Gradient tool. The Gradient is located under the paint bucket so if you do not see the gradient icon, click and hold on the paint bucket to select it (Figure 9.64).

10. With the Gradient tool selected, click and drag from the upper left to lower right corners of the image. This will add a gradient to the mask layer causing the lighting effect to grow in intensity toward the feet, giving the impression of light falling off to shadow. If you see the actual gradient in your image, you are not currently painting into the layer mask. To fix this,

*Figure 9.63: The adjustment layer comes with a layer mask attached as seen here. Click in the white rectangle to select it and make it editable.*

*Figure 9.64: Select the Gradient tool.*

undo with Ctrl + Z, make sure you click on the mask in the layer menu, and draw the gradient again (Figure 9.65).

Figure 9.65: *Create an adjustment layer to control the levels and selectively darken parts of the image*

## Adding Noise Layers for Skin Variation

We will now add a layer of visual noise to the figure itself. This will break up the perfectly gray surface and help to suggest irregularities and texture in the skin.

1. From the DVD or download files, load the image noise.tif. We will add this as a noise layer over the whole image. We will add this as an Overlay layer to introduce skin texture variation (Figure 9.66).
2. Select the image with Ctrl + A, then press Ctrl + C to copy it into memory. Return to the character image and paste the noise image in by pressing Ctrl + V. It will paste as a new layer. Rename the layer to "skinOverlay" and arrange the layer so it is above the MasterLayer. Set the skinOverlay blending mode to Overlay (Figure 9.67). You may want to reduce the layer opacity if the effect is too strong.

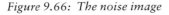

Figure 9.66: *The noise image*

Figure 9.67: *The skin with the noise overlay applied—notice the broken up texture patterns*

3. We want to remove the overlay image in the areas that overlap the background. We want to concentrate this noise pattern on the figure itself. Ctrl+Click on the figureMatte layer to select the figure pixels. Do this while the skinOverlay layer is still selected.
4. Press Ctrl + I to invert the selection and press the delete key to remove the noise that falls outside the figure (Figure 9.68). Clear the selection by pressing Ctrl + A.
5. At this point, I select the eraser with a soft round brush. Enlarge the brush size and set the opacity to 50%. Erase sections of the figure texture. While on the skinOverlay

layer, press Ctrl + A and then Ctrl + J to copy and jump the layer up (Figure 9.69). This will cause the texture effect to be stronger, as it effectively doubles the noise effect. Continue to erase areas to create variation (Figure 9.70).

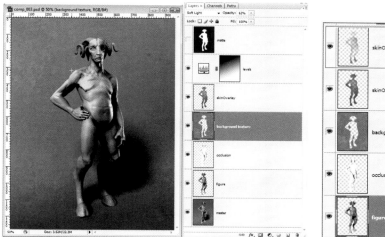

*Figure 9.68: Background noise removed*

*Figure 9.69: Duplicated layer of noise*

6. Press Ctrl + Alt + Shift + N to create a new layer. Name this layer "highlights."
7. Ctrl+Click on the figureMatte layer, to create a selection from the body. You can hide the marching ants while keeping the selection active by pressing Ctrl + H.
8. Select a soft round brush and from the color picker, select a cool white (RGB 236 245 246).
9. Set the opacity to 20% and paint along the edge of the figure. Build up a rim light along one side (Figure 9.71).

*Figure 9.70: Effect of duplicating and erasing out the layer*

*Figure 9.71: Painting rim light*

10. Pick out areas of highlight along the eyes and horn with a harder round brush. White highlights with a sharper edge give the impression of shiny harder material. Softer edges on highlights create the impression of softer, less wet, or polished materials. Suggest the eye that's hidden in shadow by painting in some highlights along the lower eyelid. This brings some interest to what would otherwise be a dead space of dark in the image (Figure 9.72).

*Figure 9.72: Picking out highlights in the face*

## Painting Hair

We will now paint in hair on the character. While we want to give him a hairy appearance, it is not necessary to paint every hair on his body—doing so would create a noisy or unappealing character. In this section, I will show you a painterly approach to the character's hair, using some special brushes in the brush set supplied on the DVD or download files.

### Painting the Beard

We will start by painting a goatee on the character. I had always envisioned his face with a long, pointed goatee. You will see how the addition of this form will further complete the shape language of the character's head bringing the angles of his face to a much more acute point (Figure 9.73).

1. Create a new layer and name it "goatee." In the Brush menu, click the arrow in the upper right of the menu to open the options.

*Figure 9.73: Notice how the addition of the long pointed beard alters the angles of the face. It tends to lengthen the long triangle of the face and changes the overall appearance of the character*

2. Sketch in the general shape of the center long hairs with the same brush (Figure 9.74). Select the brush hard round 1 #2. With this brush we will sketch in single strands of hair. Dial back the opacity of the brush to 50% and sketch in stray hairs (Figure 9.74). You may also want to sketch hairs along the jaw line as well (Figure 9.75).

3. Select Large List to see the full brush names. Select the brush called streaks from the brush presets (Figure 9.76). Dial back the opacity to 65% and select a light gray color. You can hold the Alt key to invoke the color sampler and actually sample a light value from the image itself.

4. Lower the brush diameter. We want to start to suggest short choppy stubble along the jaw line but the brush is at the wrong angle. Open the Brush menu by clicking the icon here or clicking Window ➤ Brushes (F3 hot key) (Figure 9.77). Click the Brush Tip Shape menu and you will be able to adjust the brush tip angle by clicking and rotating the crosshair. Rotate the brush to an angle congruent with the jaw line (Figure 9.78). With shirt strokes suggest choppy hairs along the jaw line.

*Figure 9.74: Sketching in the center of the goatee*

*Figure 9.75: Adding hairs to the jaw line*

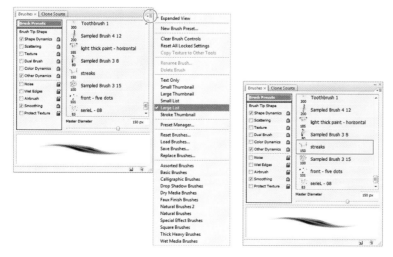

*Figure 9.76: Here the Large List option is enabled in the Brush menu. Select the brush named streaks*

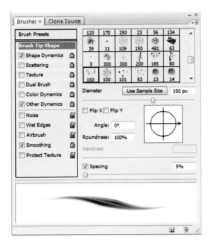

*Figure 9.77: Open the Brush Tip Shape menu here.*

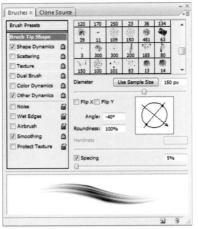

*Figure 9.78: Choppy hairs on jaw line created with rotated brush—sketch in center of goatee with long strokes.*

5. From the Brush menu, flip the brush angle so it follows the other side of the jaw. Press and hold Alt and select a very light color from the rim light side of the figure's face (Figure 9.79). We want the hair on this side to be brightly lit like the face itself. This will make it have less detail but you will still be able to see the ragged edge of the hairs (Figure 9.80).

6. We want to add some contrast. Duplicate the goatee layer by pressing Ctrl + J. This copies the layer above itself into a new layer. The effect will brighten the beard considerably. Set the blending mode to Multiply and name the layer "goatee multiply" (Figure 9.81). You will see that this now darkens the beard and adds contrast.

7. Dial back the layer opacity to 65%. Select the eraser with a soft round brush. Set the eraser opacity to 10% and erase areas that are too strong. The purpose of this Multiply layer is to add contrast to the beard.

*Figure 9.79: Paint in highlights with brighter white.*

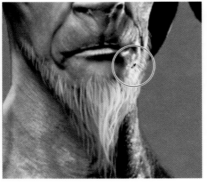

*Figure 9.80: Sample light color from the rim light side.*

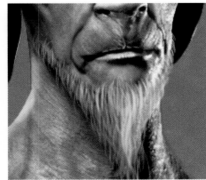

*Figure 9.81: Add layer as multiply.*

8. Select the goatee layer again and select the Blur brush. Set the opacity to 15% and blur the edges of the hairs. Do not overdo this—you just want to add a sense of fuzziness to the hair so they are not all like crisp strands of spaghetti (Figure 9.82).
9. Group the layers of the goatee together and call this group "beard" (Figure 9.83).

That completes the goatee (Figure 9.84). We will now look at using some more specialized brushes to create body hair on other areas of the character.

Figure 9.82: *Use the Blur brush on the hair.*

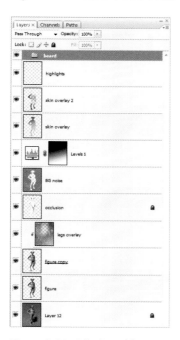

Figure 9.83: *The beard layers grouped. The group folder is closed in this image. Click the arrow next to the folder to expand it and view the contained layers.*

Figure 9.84: *Final goatee*

### Painting the body hair

1. In the Brush menu, select Replace brushes and browse to the hairbrushes.abr brush set, supplied on the DVD or download files. This will replace the current brush set with the hair brushes we will use for this section. Make sure you have your current brush set saved and easily accessible to reload later (Figure 9.85).

*Figure 9.85: The specialty hair set hairbrushes.abr*

2. Select the brush Hair 06. Using this brush, sketch in the mass of hair at the midsection. Try to keep in mind a growth pattern that trails up to the navel. When painting hair, I try to sample color directly from the image by pressing the Alt key while in the brush tool. This invokes the color picker. Select light gray values for the hair and then shade with darker values (Figure 9.86).

3. The shape of the groin hair is a large inverted triangle. It is intended to help mirror the shape of the head and facial hair, continuing the repetition of triangles down into the body.

4. Sample a lighter value and paint in highlights to the groin hair. Use the round brush with a low diameter setting and manually sketch in each hair. Blur the edges of the hair with the Blur brush (Figure 9.87).

5. Use the soft round brush, turn down the diameter until it is a very fine brush, and sketch in small hairs along the far edge of the belly (Figure 9.88).

6. For the leg hair, use the Fuzz brush. Select a light gray value and with the brush sketch in the woolly leg hairs. Be sure to sample both light and dark values to give contrast to the hair (Figure 9.89).

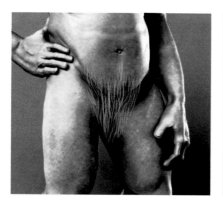

*Figure 9.86: Painting midsection hair. Use the brush hair_6 to sketch in the hair at the midsection*

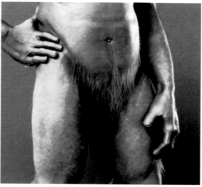

*Figure 9.87: Highlighting groin hair*

*Figure 9.88: Painting hairs on the edge of the bell*

**7.** Sample the blue rim light and paint along the edge of the leg hair. This gives the impression the light hits the hair as well, creating a cool fringe of light. This helps marry the hair to the image and combat the impression of strokes painted on top of the image that do not incorporate the lighting (Figure 9.90).

**8.** Using the same Fuzz 1 brush in conjunction with Hair 06, paint in forearm hair and underarm hair. Just suggest the hairs here—try to avoid making too many detailed strands, as these would be distracting and unpleasant. By breaking up the edges of the figure with hair fringes, you can suggest the hairiness without being too specific (Figure 9.91).

**9.** Figure 9.92 shows the final hair. Be sure to see the video on the DVD or download files for more tips and tricks to painting the body hair.

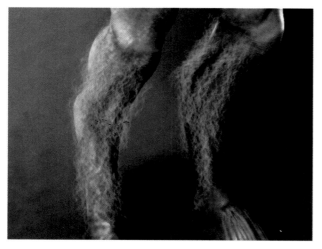

*Figure 9.89: Painting hair fringe on legs*

*Figure 9.90: Detailing hair fringe on legs*

*Figure 9.91: Body hair*

*Figure 9.92: The final hair*

## A Quick Approach to Painting Eyes

Now I would like to share a very quick way you can paint a realistic eye in the fewest possible steps. This approach has served me very well when I needed to show a quick gray render but I needed to introduce some life to the character beforehand. With only minutes before a presentation, little touches like this can really help push an idea to the forefront because a character with "light" in the eyes will always be more appealing than one with smooth gray spheres for eyeballs!

See the DVD or download files for a video demonstrating this process on the image here as well as a separate video tutorial on painting eyes on a close-up render of this Forest Spirit character.

1. Create a new layer with the Ctrl + Shift + N hot key. Name this "layer eyes."
2. Select the brush hard round 9 #3. Set the diameter to be the size of the iris for the eye. Don't worry if the iris overlaps the upper and lower lids, just get the right diameter. Set the brush hardness slider to about 70%.
3. Select a dark color like RGB 0.14 0.14 0.14 and create a circle for the iris with the brush (Figure 9.93). Select the eraser and erase any parts that overlapped the eyelids (Figure 9.93).
4. Create a new layer with Ctrl + Shift + N and name this one "iris color." Select a lighter amber color like RGB 142 121 59. Use the same brush but dial back the hardness to 50%. Ctrl+Click on the iris layer to select the pixels of the iris. The irises will be highlighted by the marching ants marquee. You can hide this selection with Ctrl + H. This will constrain the brush strokes on this layer to just the area covered by the iris.
5. Stroke along the bottom of the iris selection. This will concentrate the brightest values at the bottom of the eye. Based on the angle of the light, this is where the light would be hitting the iris directly. The upper iris is shaded by the brow ridge and eyelid (Figure 9.94). Once this light is painted in, it should look like a crescent of light in the eye.

*Figure 9.93: Creating a black circle for the base of the iris*

*Figure 9.94: Concentrating lightest color at bottom of eye*

6. Create a new layer and name this layer "pupil." Dial back the draw size and create a pupil. Make sure the pupils are consistent and do not look walleyed or cross-eyed (Figure 9.95).

7. Create a new layer named "highlight." Dial back you brush diameter and select white. Pick out a highlight in the areas shown in Figure 9.96. Make sure the highlight over- laps the dark of the pupil.

8. You may also choose to tint the inner corner of the eye. This pinkish area is called the tear duct, or more properly, the caruncle. You can color the edge of the eye with the same brush. Create a new layer and name it "eye tint." Dial back the opacity slightly and keep your edges hard for wet shiny highlights. Select a rose color like RGB 161 66 66. Set the blending mode to Overlay. At this stage, we have several layers built up to create the look of the eye. For clarity, the layer stack is shown in Figure 9.97. You may also choose to tint the lips and nostrils as well. Here you can see the final effect (Figure 9.98).

This is a very simplified, quick approach to the eye. It is extremely effective and you can even change the color by doing a hue saturation adjustment on the iris layer.

*Figure 9.95: Use a hard round brush with a dark value and add the pupil.*

*Figure 9.96: Create highlights here.*

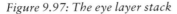

*Figure 9.97: The eye layer stack*

*Figure 9.98: Tinting the eyes*

## Adding Atmospherics

In this section, we will add the final pass of atmosphere to the character. We will create a key and fill light effect where a warm and cool light are both shining from different sides of the image. This is the same process we used to light the Interdimensional Traveler in Chapter 5. I will touch on the steps here. Please see Chapter 5 for a more in-depth approach or, alternatively, view the video for this chapter. We will create a depth-of-field effect in this demonstration in a slightly different manner. While we used a depth pass render in Chapter 5, here we will use a Gaussian Blur filter and selective erasing to create a similar effect.

1. Create a new layer and call this layer "key warm."
2. From the Tool menu, select the Gradient tool. If you do not see the Gradient tool, click and hold the left mouse button on the paint bucket and the gradient will appear. Set the gradient type in the Gradient Editor to "Foreground to Transparent" (Figure 9.99).
3. From the Color menu, select a warm color like RGB 138 120 62. Draw the gradient from the upper left to lower right, as seen in Figure 9.100.

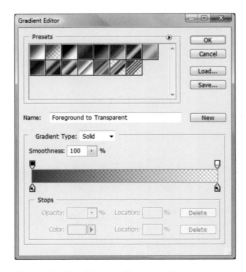

*Figure 9.99: Set gradient to "Foreground to Transparent"*

*Figure 9.100: Gradient drawn in normal blending mode*

4. Set the blending mode to overlay and your image will look like Figure 9.101. You may want to dial back the layer opacity. If you want to further adjust the color, use the Hue Saturation controls by pressing the Ctrl + U hot key.

5. Create a new layer and call this "fill cool." Select a cool color from the Color menu, like RGB 100 142 142. Repeat the process and draw a gradient from the lower right to upper left of the screen. Dial back the layer opacity and set the blending mode to overlay. Your image will now look like Figure 9.102.

*Figure 9.101: Gradient layer changed to Overlay blending mode*

*Figure 9.102: Both warm and cool light gradients help create a temperature contrast in the image, adding to visual interest.*

## Creating Lens Blur with Gaussian Blur

Now we will create a lens blur effect similar to what we did in Chapter 5. In Chapter 5, we used a depth pass rendered from ZBrush to calculate accurate lens blur using the Lens Blur Photoshop filter. While this is a highly accurate and effective way of creating atmospheric perspective and depth of field, we will now look at a fast way to mimic the same effect. In this lesson, we will use the Gaussian blur filter to selectively soften areas of the image while keeping the center of interest in sharper focus. While not as accurate as the Lens Blur filter, this technique is fast and effective for creating a soft-focus, painterly style.

If you prefer to use a ZDepth pass for this effect, as we did in Chapter 5, simply render depth from Maya. A ZDepth pass can be enabled by clicking the checkbox Depth channel (Z Depth) under the Renderable Cameras section in the Common tab of the Render Settings window.

1. We will now collapse all the layers into a new layer copy. This essentially flattens the document to a new layer while keeping all the previous layers beneath in the stack. Press Ctrl + Alt + Shift + E. You now have a new layer. Name it "flattened."
2. Duplicate a new copy of the layer by selecting all with Ctrl + A and jumping up with Ctrl + J. This creates a copy of the layer above the original. Add a blur to this layer by going to Filter ➢ Blur ➢ Gaussian Blur. Set the blur to approximately .9 (Figure 9.103).
3. Use a soft eraser brush set to 20% opacity to erase the areas you want to remain in focus. This is a kind of depth-of-field cheat that also helps focus viewer attention. Figure 9.104 shows how I have brought portions of the image into sharper focus while letting others fall slightly into blur. Figure 9.105 shows the final image.

*Figure 9.103: The blurred layer*

*Figure 9.104: Image with DOF*

*Figure 9.105: The final image*

That completes this lesson in painting the Forest Spirit. We have learned how to render base images from Maya for use as Photoshop layers. We have also looked at how to create an unsaturated character design illustration, how to paint realistic eyes quickly, as well as how to approach painting hair and fur.

Before we move on to the next chapter, I'd like to share this space with a good friend and artist I greatly admire. Jerad Marantz has designed on some of the biggest films in the past few years and his art is always inspiring (see Figure 9.106 for a great example). Follow along as he shows some of his process for the Space Ghoul image.

## Designing the Space Ghoul with Jerad Marantz

Thanks to Jerad Marantz for contributing to this section! Marantz is a freelance concept artist and teacher based in Sherman Oaks, CA. He has designed for several practical FX houses, visual FX studios, and video game companies, and is currently the lead artist at the Aaron Sims Company.

This concept started as a loose sketch. I wanted to design something wacky that was also disturbing. I played around with the proportions and the idea of an orb somehow tethered to the back of a creature's head. As a concept artist, I spend a lot of time in Photoshop and ZBrush, but I always try to keep up my drawing skills. I find that out of every tool I've adopted for my pipeline, drawing is the first thing that suffers if I don't practice, so I do it every day.

Before going into ZBrush, it is essential that you have 60% of your design resolved. This is important because you need set up the geometry according to where you will need your detail. A good sketch is a solid foundation (Figure 9.107).

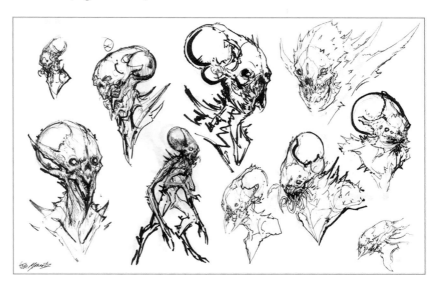

*Figure 9.106: A sample from Jerad's portfolio of work. I'm sure you will find his creatures as amazing and inspiring as I do!*

*Figure 9.107: Sketches*

### Sculpting the Space Ghoul

I started from scratch and built the sculpt in ZSpheres. At this point, I'm setting up my geometry and determining where I'll need the mesh to be the densest. For the eyes, I added ZSpheres and inverted them to accommodate the edge loops for the eye sockets. I constantly preview the adaptive skin to make sure the geometry is doing what I want it to do by hitting the A key. During this stage, I realized that I could get more resolution out of the model if I sculpted the mandibles separately as independent SubTools. I appended a new ZSphere and quickly set up the mesh for the mandibles. Once everything was in place, I created the adaptive skin and started sculpting (Figure 9.108).

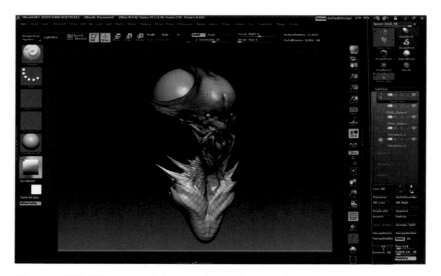

*Figure 9.108: The base subdivision level of the mesh*

When sculpting in ZBrush, I use these brushes primarily: the Move brush, Clay Tubes, Dam Standard, Standard, Clay, Trim Dynamic, and the Rake brush. For the first step, while the mesh is at subdivision 2, I use the Move brush to pull out my main forms: the forehead, cranium, jaw, muscle, and cheek bones. Then I push in the eye sockets, mouth, and nasal cavities. By working at this level, I am taking advantage of the low geometry and am able to define the sculpt in simple planes. I always try to take the model as far as I can before using any of the other brushes or sculpting on high subdivisions. One of the biggest issues I've noticed in beginners' models is that their sculpts tend to feel "baggy." The anatomy seems to hang loose and there is a lack of structure. This is often caused by starting the sculpt in the higher subdivisions.

At subdivision 4, I then start to lay more complex anatomy with the Clay Tubes brush. Clay Tubes has a wonderful edge to it as it builds up the forms and allows you to maintain structure (Figure 9.109).

Once I've gotten the sculpt where I want it with Clay Tubes, I use the Rake brush to refine the sculpt. I use this brush in additive and subtractive ways. Rakes in traditional sculpting are used to remove excess clay by averaging out the surface and refining the sculpture. The Rake brush in ZBrush can work the same way, but it pushes and pulls the mesh instead of actually carving into it like clay. I use the Rake to refine the model and add more detail to the forms. I always start to use the Rake at a large diameter, and as I'm refining the sculpt I shrink the diameter down and focus on resolving more of the complex forms (Figure 9.110).

Once I've reached a certain point with the Rake brush where I'm happy, I start to smooth out areas by hitting Shift. I then use my Trim Dynamic brush to find edges that I may have lost, especially in the cheek bones and other under planes. Then I move on to the Standard and Dam Standard brushes. Dam Standard is phenomenal for carving in details like fine wrinkles and delicate areas, whereas Standard helps you to build up your tertiary detail.

Once the sculpt has reached a level at which I'm content, I then bring the entire model to a low subdivision and pose it, masking off areas and moving or rotating them. In the case of this sculpt; I just turned the head slightly. It's amazing how a subtle pose will bring a character to life. Once I'm done posing my model, depending on the model's resolution, I will decimate it if I intend to render outside of ZBrush. I accomplish this with the Decimation Master plug-in. My favorite thing about Decimation Master is that before you decimate your model, you can mask out the areas that you want to retain the most detail and Decimation Master will leave those areas at a higher resolution (Figure 9.111).

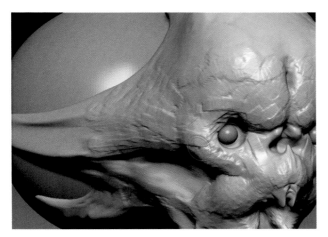
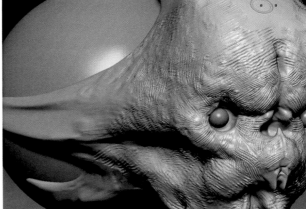

*Figure 9.109: Clay Tubes brush in use*          *Figure 9.110: Rakes in use*

I created these render passes outside of ZBrush using the same techniques Scott discussed earlier in this chapter. I used a very simple skin shader for one of my passes. Pretty much any rendering engine will have some kind of skin shader these days. If you choose to use ZBrush for your render passes, check in Chapter 10, "Rendering the Enforcer," for a demonstration of how to render skin materials in ZBrush. When I'm rendering my character, I always make sure that the lighting is dramatic. Dramatic lighting guarantees a dynamic image. I rendered several material passes. I first selected a translucent skin material and went into the material's properties to change the color to a green hue (Figure 9.112).

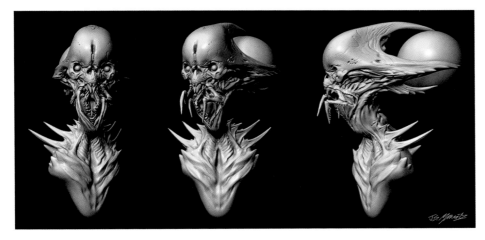

*Figure 9.111: Posed head*          *Figure 9.112: Base render*

Then I did pass of a matte material that really showed me all of the detail in the sculpt. I also took a pass of a very black and shiny material that I used for the creature's black pattern on the mandibles, chest, and spikes. Finally, I render a flat material pass that is a solid white silhouette. This is a pass that I'll use as a mask when I start to bring the design into Photoshop (Figure 9.113).

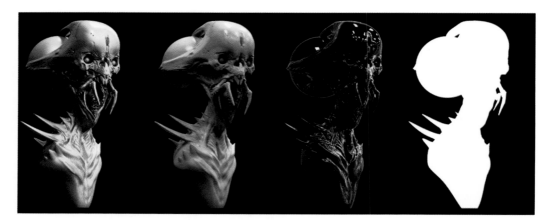

*Figure 9.113: Materials matte black and flat mat*

## Finishing in Photoshop

I bring the material renders into Photoshop and stack them one on top of the other in the same document, making sure that they are all lined up. I then experiment and see how the materials work with each other. I turned the translucent skin pass into a Soft Light layer and put that on top of the matte material layer. This became my base for the painting. Then I placed my shiny black material on the top layer and used a mask to paint the patterns on the chest, mandibles, and spikes (Figure 9.114).

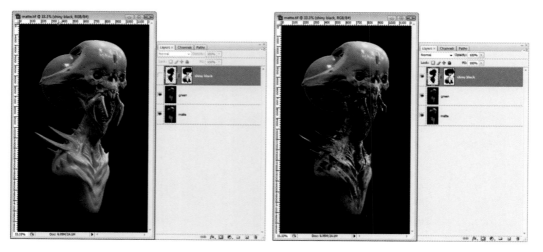

*Figure 9.114: Using the shiny black material*

In Photoshop, I can continue to design. If I want to significantly alter the model, I can liquefy it or I can paint directly over the image. I do tend to paint over my 3-D renders quite a bit, using a soft brush to maintain the illusion and consistency of the image. You'll notice that I didn't take the time to sculpt the creature's eyelids in the model. When I brought the renders into Photoshop, I decided to paint them in, giving the creature a slight sympathetic quality (Figure 9.115).

To break up the color of the face, I lightly painted some pinks around the eyes, nose, and mouth on a soft light layer (Figure 9.116). I wanted the creature to be really fleshy and translucent, so I spent time panting in veins. To accomplish the effect in the forehead, I used a photograph of a human brain on another Soft Light layer. The translucency of a soft light layer works really well in creating something that looks like it's under the skin (Figure 9.117).

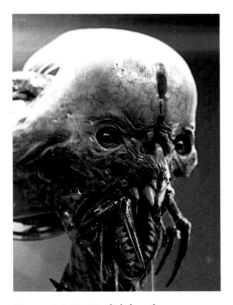

Figure 9.115: Eyelid detail          Figure 9.116: Pinks around face

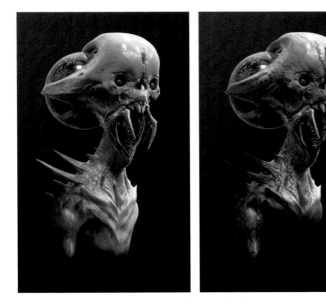

Figure 9.117: Soft light veins before and after

With Photoshop you can easily adjust and change the color of your material renders by using Color Balance and Hue Saturation. You are not limited by the color of the original renders.

Finally, I added atmosphere to the design using a soft brush on a normal layer and painted in the lighting effects to indicate a vague environment, just to place him somewhere (Figure 9.118). These were placed on a Linear Dodge (Add) blending mode to create a blown-out lighting effect. Figure 9.119 shows the final image.

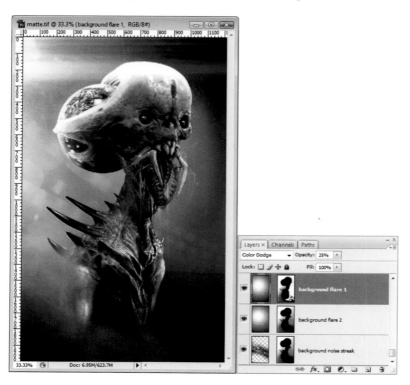

*Figure 9.118: Light effects layers*

*Figure 9.119: The final image*

ten

# Rendering the Enforcer

For this chapter, I have *invited ZBrush and Maya expert Eric Keller to share his knowledge of the BPR rendering system. Eric has extensive experience with rendering for production across various platforms. His work with the ZBrush rendering system has been very impressive. You may know Eric from his books* Mastering Maya *as well as the staple ZBrush book,* Introducing ZBrush. *I am excited to have him sharing his techniques in this chapter!*

*This chapter covers techniques for rendering a creature directly in ZBrush using its advanced "BPR" (Best Preview Render) technology. ZBrush's rendering capabilities have taken a massive leap forward with the recent release, giving you many creative options for generating amazing images entirely within ZBrush. This eliminates the need to export your models to other 3-D software for rendering. Figure 10.1 shows a render of the Enforcer character created with BPR in ZBrush.*

*Figure 10.1: The rendered enforcer*

## The Brief: The Enforcer

This character is named "Ph'nglui mglw'nafh of Venus" or simply, "The Enforcer." He is an all-purpose tough guy who wanders from spaceport to spaceport picking up work as a hired gun, bouncer, or bounty hunter. He is generally a tough character but has a fondness for Yuggothian rabbits, which he raises in a climate-controlled hutch back on his ship.

### LOOK DEVELOPMENT IN ZBRUSH

Often you will find that a director wants to see some variation in materials and color before they make a decision on the final character. This is often called "look development" or "look dev." The brief for this chapter is to explore some variation in skin and material representations on the Enforcer character. Using the ZBrush material menus, explore how to create and apply material representations to the Enforcer character and produce some final showpiece renders.

# Advantages of BPR

The primary advantages of rendering in ZBrush are speed and flexibility. While the ZBrush rendering system is not a physically based photorealistic renderer such as V-Ray or Mental Ray, I consider it an excellent "artistic" rendering option. In other words, your goal when rendering in ZBrush should be to make a pleasing composition that shows off the model as opposed to creating a photorealistic one through the simulation of physical light properties, which is a task better suited for external rendering systems.

This means that if you're used to working in Maya's Hypershade or in 3dsMax's material editor or any other integrated 3-D animation and rendering package, you're going to find that the ZBrush approach is very different if not altogether alien. So expect a little "quirkiness" when rendering in ZBrush, but if you've come this far with ZBrush, a little quirk should come as no surprise.

ZBrush offers options for rendering realistic and stylistic lighting such as ambient occlusion, subsurface scattering, depth of field, and image-based lighting. But these features are not based on physical simulations of light—rather, ZBrush uses some special "cheats" to achieve these effects, which are designed to create an artistically acceptable result. This is why I consider ZBrush as an "artistic" rendering solution. The approach to designing lighting and materials is very flexible and fast and even fun once you get the hang of how all of these elements work together in ZBrush. While this chapter is not intended to be a comprehensive guide to every single feature, it should give you a good sense of how powerful ZBrush rendering is as well as some ideas you can use for your own projects.

This project uses Scott's Enforcer model as the subject. Our goal is to use the ZBrush lighting, material, and rendering toolset to help make the character look believable and impressive. The final image should be portfolio quality, and we'll see just how far we can go without leaving the ZBrush environment.

You'll find that ZBrush's rendering tools are great for look development because you can test, tweak, render, and create variations very quickly. In a production environment, speed is of utmost importance. If you can pump out 10 different options for your director to review in the time it takes to render a single still in another 3-D program, clearly you'll have a competitive advantage over many other artists.

# Establishing the Lighting Using LightCap

One of the most interesting tools introduced in ZBrush 4 R2 is the LightCap lighting editor. This interface is meant to augment the existing lighting interface with more advanced options so that you have more specific control over how the simulated lights interact with the surface properties of your model.

Lighting, rendering, and material development all work together in Zbrush, so often you'll be moving back and forth between various palettes as you tweak settings. That being said, I think it's easiest to start by setting up a basic lighting scenario and go from there. While working on the lighting, there are a few things you can do to make the process a little faster. The Enforcer model is fairly dense and, while ZBrush renders are fast, you can save some time while tweaking lights by making adjustments in the Render palette.

1. Open up the Enforcer_start.ZPR project located in the Chapter 10 folder on the DVD or download files. The model looks very blocky because all the SubTools have been set to the lowest subdivision level. This helps speed up the performance of ZBrush while working. Scott has modeled all the elements and polypainted details on the surface.
2. In the SubTool subpalette of the Tool palette, select the enforcer_body SubTool, which is at the very top of the SubTool stack. Press the Solo button on the right shelf so that all other SubTools are hidden from view.
3. The body has a total of seven subdivision levels, and at subdivision seven the point count is about 3.35 million. While establishing the lighting, we don't need to be at the highest SDiv level. Set the SDiv slider to level 4. At this level the body has 52,224 points, just enough so we get an accurate read on the silhouette and major details, while at the same time the performance of ZBrush is not compromised.
4. Open the Render palette and place it in a tray for easy access. Under the Render Properties subpalette, set the Details slider to 1 and turn on the Smooth Normals button (see Figure 10.2).

    *Figure 10.2: Adjust the Details slider and turn on Smooth Normals in the Render palette.*

    The Details slider controls the resolution of the maps used by the lights to create shadows and the overall quality of the lighting, which you'll be setting up in a moment. While establishing your initial lighting scenario, you can set this to 1, and then, as you get closer to a final render, you can raise this setting to improve quality. A lower setting means a faster render, a higher setting means higher quality but increased render time.

    The Smooth Normals button softens the edges where polygons meet so that the surface looks nice and smooth at lower subdivision levels when you render with BPR. Activating this feature is another great way to speed up a render while testing because it allows you to get a good sense of what the final high-resolution render will look like even while working at a lower subdivision level.

5. In the SubTool subpalette, turn off the little eyeball icon. This disables polypainting, which will hide the colors and details on the model. This way we can see how the lights interact with the surface without the interference of the colors on the model.
6. Set the color in the Color palette to white.
7. Press the BPR button at the top of the right shelf (hot key = Shift + R). The model renders in a few seconds. The skin looks gray. Because of the basic material, you can see some shadows but overall it looks pretty boring. That's a perfect place to start (Figure 10.3)!

*Figure 10.3: A starting place for lighting the model has been established.*

*Figure 10.4: Turn off the Lightbulbs in the Light palette and set Ambient light to 0.*

8. Open the Light palette and place it in the left tray. The Material palette is already there by default. There are two lights activated in the basic light options at the top of the Light palette. Click on both of these lightbulb icons to turn them off (the icons are orange when they are on and gray when they are off). The model will turn black, indicating that the lights are off.

9. Set the Ambient slider below the lightbulb icons in the Light palette to 0; this way you can be sure that no additional light is affecting what you see on the canvas (Figure 10.4).

10. We're going to work in the LightCap editor, which I think is a much easier and more powerful interface for designing ZBrush lighting than the classic ZBrush lightbulb interface. Expand the LightCap subpalette of the Light palette.

LightCap is a term invented by Pixologic to refer to their unique lighting technology; "LightCap" is short for "light capture." LightCap creates a texture file that stores the lighting information that you create for the scene. This texture is mapped to a virtual sphere that surrounds the model. The color, position, and intensity of the lights are contained in this texture. The Details slider that you adjusted at the start of the exercise controls the resolution of the texture, so higher setting creates more detailed lighting. You don't need to work with the texture file directly—instead you'll use the LightCap interface to add, edit, and remove lights from the scene. The interface and its controls are found within the LightCap subpalette.

Lights in ZBrush do not appear as 3-D elements like they do in most 3-D packages. You won't see the light source on the canvas—instead the position of the lights is determined by where you place dots on the sphere shown in the LightCap interface.

11. Press the New Light button in the LightCap palette. The new light appears as a red dot surrounded by a fuzzy gray area (see the left image in Figure 10.5). Also the model appears on the canvas dimly lit. The new light is shining directly at the model.

12. Drag the red dot in the LightCap interface up to the left. You'll see the lighting update on the model as well. Increase the Strength slider and the light becomes brighter. This light will be the key light for the moment.

13. The Aperture slider sets the overall size of the light as it spreads across the surface, the Falloff adjusts the softness of the edge of the light (you can create an interesting "graphic novel" style of lighting by setting the Falloff to 10 (see the left image in Figure 10.6). Let's start by creating a basic but realistic style of lighting. Set Strength to 1.5, Aperture to 90, and Falloff to 10 (see the middle image in Figure 10.5).

14. Click the New Light button to add a second light. You'll use this light to create rim lighting. Drag this light off to the lower right corner until it is all the way off the sphere.

Increase the strength to 0.8. The rim light does not need to cast shadows so set the shadow slider to 0.

15. Add a third light to create side lighting. Move this light down to the right corner. Set the Strength to 0.3 and Aperture to 45. Click on the color swatch and set the color of the light to a cool pale blue (see the right image in Figure 10.5).

16. Press the BPR button to render the scene (see the right image in Figure 10.6).

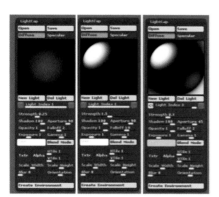

*Figure 10.5: Use the LightCap interface to add and edit lights. You can create a basic three-point light setup as a starting place in LightCap.*

*Figure 10.6: Set the aperture of the light to 0 to create a "graphic novel" style render (left image). The character is rendered using BPR and a basic light setup (right image).*

You now have a basic three-point light setup. This is a good starting place, which will give you context as you develop the materials. You'll probably revisit these lights frequently as you work. Save the project so you can return to this arrangement later if you need to.

Here are a few tips on working within the LightCap subpalette:

- You can select a light by clicking on its red dot in the interface. However, if you have a lot of lights, you can use the Light Index to switch from one light to the next. You can add as many lights as you want to LightCap, so it can get pretty crowded! The index number is determined by the order in which the lights are added.

- You can edit the specular intensity separately from the diffuse intensity using the Opacity slider. Press the Specular button at the top of the interface to switch to specular mode and then adjust the Opacity slider. If you want a light to have no specular highlight, switch to Specular mode and set Opacity to 0. If you want a light to have a specular highlight but no diffuse light, set Opacity above 0 while in Specular mode and switch to Diffuse mode and set Opacity to 0. Opacity affects the influence of the diffuse or specular component without affecting the intensity of the light (see Figure 10.7).

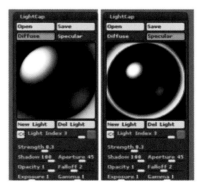

*Figure 10.7: Switch between Diffuse and Specular mode to adjust the opacity of the diffuse or specular component of the selected light.*

*Figure 10.8: You can add alphas and textures to affect the shape of the light.*

- You can use the blend mode to control the quality of the light. The blend modes are similar to layer modes found in programs such as Adobe Photoshop (screen, multiply, overlay, soft light, etc.). A light with a black color and a blend mode set to Mutiply will actually create a dark spot.
- Use the Alpha button to add an alpha texture to the light—this way you can actually shape the light as if a gobo is applied to the light. Textures can also be applied using the Txtr button. This creates the effect of a gel being applied to the light. Use the HTile and VTile sliders to create a repeating pattern for the alpha. Orientation, Scale Width, and Scale Height sliders can also be used to adjust the shape of the light (see Figure 10.8).
- If you create a LightCap arrangement that you want to use in other projects, you can use the Save button in the LightCap subpalette to save it to your local disk using the .ZLD format. LightCap lighting is also saved as part of a project file (.ZPR).

## Create a Skin Material

Now it's time to start developing an advanced material that will make the Enforcer look more realistic in the BPR render. You'll be surprised at how far you can go with ZBrush materials but it takes some understanding of how the material interface works and some patient tweaking. We'll start with the body of the Enforcer so that we can establish the look of his flesh based on the light setup created in the previous section.

### Material Shaders

ZBrush materials are composed of one or more "shaders," which are layered on top of each other. The interface itself lists the shaders from left to right. The shader mixer is used to determine how the shaders are blended together. It can get confusing really fast, so I like to try to work on each component of the material individually to establish the basic properties and then spend some time blending them together.

One of the oddest quirks about materials in Zbrush is that you never create a material from scratch; instead you edit an existing material and then save it under a new name. The same goes for the shaders that make up the material. So there's no "new material" or "new shader" button. You start with a material that has the number of shaders that you need, and then you copy other shaders into the shader slot and then tweak as needed. It is an odd way to work and if you're already confused, don't stress out. Going through the process a few times will make it a bit clearer. It's always best to break it down into its simplest components.

To create a believable skin material, we need three basic elements. I like to separate each of these elements into its own shader and then combine these shaders into a single three-shader material. The shaders we'll need to achieve this are:

**A Diffuse Shader**   This determines how the light is scattered as it is reflected off of the very surface of the skin. This shader is responsible for the overall color when combined with the polypainting. I imagine what dry skin would look like and then create a shader to simulate this look. We'll use the basic shader to handle the diffuse shading.

**A Specular Shader**   This determines how the skin reflects all of the light sources in the scene—in other words, the shiny quality of the skin. This is layered on top of the diffuse shader and is responsible for giving the skin a wet or oily quality. We'll use a standard shader to create the specular quality.

**A Subsurface Scattering Shader**    This shader simulates the luminescent quality of the skin. As photons of light penetrate the layers of skin they bounce around, pick up the color of the deeper layers of tissue, and then exit the skin giving it a kind of glow. This helps make the model look as though it is made up of living flesh. In many 3-D packages, this effect is simulated by more or less replicating the physical properties of light. In ZBrush, the effect is done using a gradient of colors—this is a cheat, but it's an effective one!

## Create the Diffuse Shader

The diffuse shading is pretty straightforward. Using the Basic shader combined with the controls in the LightCap editor, you'll create the overall surface quality of the skin. Diffuse shading simulates what happens when photons of light are reflected off of a rough surface. The tiny bumps on the surface cause the light to be "diffused" back into the environment, in other words, they bounce off of the surface in all directions. Think of sunlight reflected off of concrete. Skin is not as rough as concrete but you can imagine that by adjusting the settings you can give the viewer some sense of the creature's character.

1. Continue with the project from the previous section.
2. Set the subdivision of the creature's body to 7 and turn on the paintbrush icon in the SubTool palette to activate polyPainting. The colors of the skin appear on the surface but you'll also notice that a material has been painted on the creature. Until you remove this material, you won't be able to see your new custom materials update as you work.
3. In the Material palette, select the Flat Color material. On the top shelf, press the M button. In the Color palette press the Fill Object button (Figure 10.9).

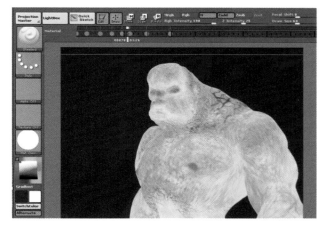

*Figure 10.9: Fill the surface with the Flat shader to remove any materials that have been painted onto the model.*

This fills the surface with the Flat Color material. You'll see the polypainted colors on the creature's skin but the shadows and shiny qualities disappear. By filling the surface with the Flat Color material, you reset the materials on the surface, so now, as you switch from one material to another, the surface will update accordingly. This is a great technique for erasing any materials that have been painted on the surface. It's very important that the M button is active on the top shelf and NOT the Rgb or Mrgb buttons—otherwise you'll erase the colors that have been polypainted on the surface!

4. From the Material library, choose the BasicMaterial shader. Open the Tray on the left side of the canvas and expand the Material modifiers.

There are a lot of sliders here controlling a wide variety of material qualities. If you wanted to, you could use this one shader to control every aspect of the surface—however you're actually going to use this material to control only the diffuse quality, which means that only a few settings need to be adjusted on this shader. By separating material qualities (diffuse, specular, and subsurface) into different shaders, you'll have more flexibility via the shader mixer. It's just one possible approach out of many different strategies.

5. Set the Specular slider to 0.
6. Set the Ambient slider to 0 and the Diffuse slider to 70.

If you expand the Diffuse Edit curve below the Diffuse slider and edit the shape of the curve, you won't see much of a change on the model. Why is this? Well, here's one of the quirks of ZBrush that may cause a little head scratching. The Diffuse slider in the Material modifiers does in fact control the *amount* of diffuse light reflected by the surface. However, the spread of the diffuse highlight on the surface is controlled by the LightCap settings. So you need to return to the LightCap settings in the Light palette to adjust the overall spread of the diffuse lighting.

7. In the LightCap palette, set the Light Index to 1 so that you're editing the key light. Increase the Aperture to 120 and the Falloff to 5.
8. Set the Light Index to 3 so that you are editing the fill light. Set Strength to 0.35 and Aperture to 80 (See Figure 10.10).
9. Set the ColorizeDiffuse slider to 25. At the bottom of the Material palette, click on the Dif color swatch and choose a pale blue. This tints the diffuse light a little (see Figure 10.11). By making the color cool, it desaturates the surface somewhat when combined with the warm colors of the polypainting. A little desaturation helps to make it look more realistic.
10. Create a render using BPR (hot key = Shift + R) to see how the material looks so far (see Figure 10.12).

Figure 10.10: Adjust the LightCap settings to increase the spread of the Diffuse light across the surface.

Figure 10.11: Increase the Colorize Diffuse slider and set the Diffuse color to a pale blue.

Figure 10.12: The results of the diffuse shader rendered with BPR

11. Use the Save As button in the Material palette to save the material as DiffuseShader. ZMT. It's very easy to accidentally overwrite a shader in ZBrush so I find it's a wise practice to save the materials whenever I work on them.
12. Save your project!

## Create the Specular Shader

The specular shader will set the overall amount of specularity for the material. This gives the surface a wet or oily look and also controls how much of the environment is reflected in the surface. The rim lighting you created earlier using the LightCap editor will show up a bit more as specularity is increased.

1. Continue with the project from the previous section.
2. Select the BasicMaterial2 Shader from the Material palette.
3. In the Modifiers for the material, set the Ambient and Diffuse sliders to 0. The model should appear mostly dark and very shiny.
4. Set the Specular slider to 20. The specularity of the overall skin shouldn't be too shiny, at least not yet. Later on, you'll learn how to paint in areas that are shinier than others.

Just as with the Diffuse settings, the Specular edit curve in the Material modifiers doesn't affect the quality of the specularity because the LightCap settings are overriding the curve. To change the spread of the highlights on the surface, you'll revisit the LightCap palette and make a few adjustments.

5. Expand the LightCap subpalette of the Light palette and press the New Light button to make a new light. You will adjust this light so that it will affect only the specular component of the material.
6. Make sure the Diffuse button is on in the LightCap editor and set Opacity to 0. Press the Specular button and move the light to the upper left of the sphere.
7. Increase the Strength to 1.8, Aperture to 140, and set Exposure to 0.65. This creates a sort of broad highlight across the surface of the skin (see Figure 10.13).
8. Use the Save As button in the Material palette and save the material as SpecularShader.ZMT.
9. Save the project.

*Figure 10.13: Edit the LightCap settings to adjust the spread of the specular highlight across the skin.*

## Create the Subsurface Scattering Shader

The last ingredient for the skin shader is the subsurface scattering. This is what helps bring the skin to life by adding that luminescent quality. Working with subsurface scattering (SSS) in ZBrush is a little tricky since there are a few ways to create this effect and the interface is not terribly intuitive. The goal is to add a hint of reddish color that is stronger on the thinner parts of the model. If the effect is too strong, the model will look like wax or plastic.

It is best to develop the SSS shader in isolation so that the influence of other material properties, such as the diffuse and specular highlights, doesn't confuse the result.

1. Continue with the project from the previous section.
2. In the Render palette, enable the Sss button—if this button is not active, the effect will not appear when you press the BPR button (see Figure 10.14).
3. Rendering SSS adds to render time, so lower the SDiv slider to 4 so that testing doesn't take as long.
4. From the Material palette, select the Fresnel Overlay material. This material contains two shaders—a basic shader, similar to what you used for the diffuse and specular shaders, and the Fresnel Overlay, which creates a gradient of colors used for subsurface colors.
5. In the Material modifiers, make sure the S1 button at the top of the palette is selected—this is the first shaders slot. Press the little circle so that it turns into a dot (see the left image in Figure 10.15). This is a switch that turns the basic shader off. This shader will not be used—turn it off so you can focus on just the settings in the S2 slot.
6. Press the S2 button to switch to the Fresnel Overlay shader. Make sure the circle is not a dot so that the shader is actually on (see right image in Figure 10.15).

The color swatches at the bottom control the colors used in the gradient and the sliders at the top control the amount of influence of each color. The shader is essentially a way to mix the colors together. The Fresnel Factor slider controls the strength of the gradient based on the viewing angle of the surface.

Figure 10.14: Turn on the SSS button in the Render palette.

Figure 10.15: In the modifiers for the Fresnel Overlay material, turn the S1 slot off and the S2 slot on, using the circle icons on the buttons.

7. Click on the Inner Additive swatch and choose a deep red color. Set the Inner Additive slider to 0.5 and the Fresnel Factor to 1. You'll see the surface appear red on the parts of the surface that face the front.
8. Click on Outer Additive and set the color to orange, set Outer Additive to 0.25. The edges that face away from the front pick up the orange color.
9. Click on the Inner Blend color swatch and set the color to a dark magenta and set the Inner Blend to 0.3. You'll see that the inner blend color is overlaid on top of the Inner Additive color. As you increase the Inner Blend slider, the influence of the magenta slider becomes stronger.
10. Set the Outer Blend to a lighter magenta and set the Outer Blend strength to 0.35. This adds color to the Outer Additive Color (Figure 10.16).

The colors and values are fairly subjective and you'll most likely want to tweak them as you work. These warm colors are meant to give the impression of tissue beneath the skin. At the moment, the gradient is applied to the entire surface. The Fresnel Factor slider is going to shift the gradient colors toward the edges when it is set to a positive value and toward the center when it is at a negative value. Many of these settings will be tweaked once you start putting the material together, but at least now we have a place to start.

Of course, this is just a gradient—it is not subsurface scattering just yet. To finish the basic effect you need to adjust some settings in the Mixer.

11. Expand the Mixer subpalette below the modifiers. Set the SSS slider to 100. The surface will become very dark.

12. Set the S Exp slider to 0.8. This controls how much of the SSS effect comes through. Lower values mean that more of the effect is visible, indicating a thinner surface. A setting of 0.8 is probably too low for our lumbering Enforcer character, but at the moment, it will help you to see the effect more clearly while you tweak.

13. Set the blend mode to Add and turn on Black. The Black button means that the SSS shader will be composited on top of a black color, which means the other shaders will not affect the quality. In general, this speeds up the rendering of the effect.

14. Press the BPR button to see a rendering of the SSS effect. It looks a little odd, but now that it is working, you can start building the skin material by combining it with the diffuse and specular shaders you've already created (Figure 10.17).

15. Save the material as SSS Shader.ZMT.

16. Save the project.

## Create a Material from the Three Shaders

To create a single material form the Diffuse, Specular, and SSS shaders, you will copy each shader into one of the slots of the TriShader material and then use the Mixer to control the amount of influence each shader has on the material itself.

1. Continue with the project from the previous section. Make sure that the Diffuse shader, Specular shader, and SSS shader are all loaded into ZBrush. If they are not, you can use the Load button in the Material palette to load them from your local disk.

2. Select the Diffuse shader and press the CopySH button in the Material modifiers.

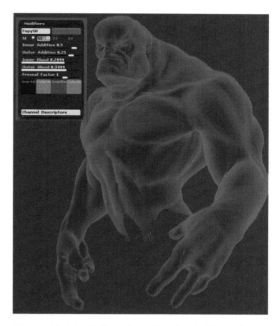

*Figure 10.16: Adjust the colors in the Fresnel Overlay shader to create a gradient of warm colors on the surface of the model.*

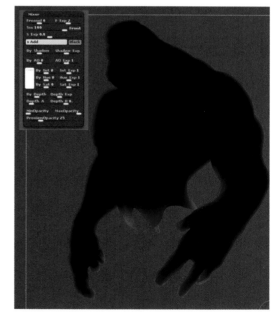

*Figure 10.17: The Mixer determines how the colors of the Fresnel Overalay shader are used in the subsurface scattering effect. Adjust the settings and then render with BPR to see the result.*

3. Select the TriShaders Material from the Material palette, don't worry about the way the model looks at the moment—it will update as you switch materials. Select the S1 button at the top and press the PasteSH button to paste the Diffuse shader into the first slot of the TriShaders material (Figure 10.18).

4. Repeat these steps to paste the S2 shader of the SSS Shader into the S2 slot of the TriShaders material and then the S1 shader of the Specular shader into the S3 slot of the TriShaders material.

5. Save the material as enforcerSkin.ZMT.

Next, you'll do a little tweaking to get the three shaders to work together a little better.

6. Press the BPR button on the right shelf (hot key = Shift + R) to create a render. The left image in Figure 10.19 shows the result. At this point, it is not completely convincing. The SSS effect is too strong, resulting in a red fringe around the edges.

*Figure 10.18:  Copy the S1 shader from the Diffuse shader. Use the PasteSH button to paste it into the S1 slot of the TriShaders material.*

*Figure 10.19:  Turn on the Wax Preview button in the Render palette and adjust the Strength in the Wax Modifies sub-palette of the Material palette.*

7. Open the Material modifiers and click on the S2 slot so that the settings for the SSS shader are available. Set the Fresnel Factor to 10. This pushes the lighter colors of the gradient toward the edges and keeps the darker reds and magentas toward the center of the object.

8. In the Mixer, set the SSS slider to −35. Setting this to a negative number makes the effect more prominent toward the center of the object and will eliminate the odd fringe effect seen in the previous render. It also cuts down on the overall strength of the effect.

Finally one additional "cheat" you can use to sell the look of the skin is to increase the Wax Modifier slider. The wax modifier simulates translucency by adding a warm coloring to the edges of shadows cast on the surface. This gives a slight glow to the skin.

9. In the Render palette, turn on the Wax Preview button in the Render Properties (left image in Figure 10.19). This option just gives you a preview of what the wax modifier effect looks like on the surface. More importantly, it keeps the warning window from appearing every time you adjust the Wax Modifier slider (see right image in Figure 10.19).

10. At the top of the Material palette, set the Strength slider to 60 in the Wax Modifier subpalette of the Materials palette. Create a BPR render. The result is shown in the right side of Figure 10.20.

11. Use the Save button in the Material palette to save the material as enforcerSkin.ZMT. Save the project as well.

*Figure 10.20:  Left image shows a BPR render of the skin material after all the shaders have been combined. The right image shows the render after tweaking the shader values.*

## Paint the Skin Highlights

The skin material is starting to take shape but the specular highlights look very even, giving it a very "CG" look. Skin naturally has variation in the amount of shininess it has, depending on how much oil and sweat is produced by that part of the body.

One way to achieve this variation is to create a similar but slightly more specular version of the skin material and then paint this into areas on top of the original skin material. The materials can then be blended together when rendered.

1. Continue with the last version of the project. Make sure the enforcerSkin material is loaded. Select it in the Material palette. Make sure the Enforcer's body is at the highest SDiv level (should be level 7).

2. You need to fill the current tool with the enforcerSkin material before another material can be painted on top. Make sure the M button on the top shelf is activated. Open the Color palette and press the Fill Object button. The model won't look any different, but at this point the surface should keep the enforcerSkin material, even if you switch to a different material.

3. Open the material library and choose the enforcerSkin material. Press the CopyMat button (left image in Figure 10.21).

4. Select a different material, such as the skinShade04 material. Press the PasteMat button, This overwrites the selected material with the copied enforcerSkin material that has been copied to the clipboard. The only way to create a new material in ZBrush is to copy one material on top of another (right image in Figure 10.21).

*Figure 10.21: Select the enforcerSkin material and press the CopyMat button (left image). Select another material and press the PasteMat button (right image).*

5. Use the Save button to save the material as enforcerSkinWet.ZMT.

6. Make sure the enforcerSkinWet material is selected in the material palette. Select the Standard brush in the brush library.

7. Open the Material palette, select the S3 slot in the Modifiers, and set the Specular to 40. Select the S1 slot and the Diffuse to 60. This makes the material just slightly shinier, creating a wet look (see Figure 10.22).

8. Set the Stroke Type to spray and, from the Alpha palette, choose Alpha 40, which is a tiny dot. In the Stroke palette, set the Placement to 1 and Scale to 0. This increases the distance between each dot in the spray stroke and removes variation in the scale of each dot. The brush will be used to spray small dots of the enforcerSkinWet material on the surface. Turn off LazyMouse.

*Figure 10.22: Set the Specular slider in S3 to 40 (left image). Set the Diffuse slider in S1 to 60 (right image).*

9. On the top shelf, turn off Zadd and Rgb and turn on M. This ensures that only material information is painted on the surface and the colors and surface are not disturbed.

10. Finally, before you start painting the material, you will create a cavity mask so that the enforcerSkinWet material is applied only to the very surface and not in the wrinkles and crevices on the surface. Expand the Masking subpalette of the Tool palette and set the Intensity slider below the Cavity asking button to 100. Adjust the edit curve for the cavity mask so it looks like Figure 10.23.

11. Press the Cavity Mask button to create the mask. The darker areas of the surface will appear darker. Turn off the View Mask button. This hides the mask without removing it.

12. Now you are ready to start painting the material. Set the Draw size to a small value such as 10, zoom in on the head, and use the Standard brush to paint the enforcerSkinWet material on the surface of the skin. Choose areas of the face where the surface tends to be oilier, such as the nose, lips, forehead, and cheeks below the eyes (see upper left in Figure 10.24).

13. Paint on the arms and chest to create the look of damp, clammy skin.

14. Paint a fair amount of the enforcerSkinWet material on the fingernails to make them appear shinier than the surrounding skin (see lower left on Figure 10.24).

*Figure 10.23: Edit the Cavity Profile curve so that it looks like this image*

15. Continue to paint over the surface of the Enforcer's skin. Try to vary the size and placement of the strokes (see Figure 10.24).

16. In the Render palette, set the material blend radius to 4. This setting will blend the materials together, removing the jagged edges where the two materials meet on the surface when rendered. If you set the value too high, the blending might blur the transition too much, and the effect is lost. This setting may need to be adjusted, depending on whether you are rendering the model close up or from far away.

17. Create a test BPR render by pressing Shift + R (see Figure 10.25).

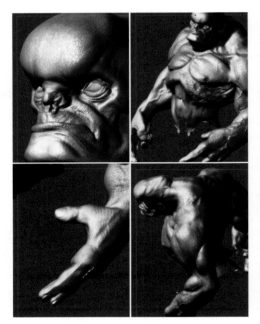

*Figure 10.24: Use the Standard brush to paint the enforcerSkinWet material on the parts of the surface that you want to appear oily or wet.*

*Figure 10.25: The Enforcer body is rendered using BPR. The material Blend property removes the jagged edges between the painted materials.*

18. After you paint the materials on the model, you can continue to edit the settings of either material and they will update.

19. Save the project when you are satisfied that the skin is looking sufficiently realistic when rendered.

ZBrush projects *should* save all of your custom materials as part of the project file. However, in reality ZBrush frequently "forgets" to load your materials. Sometimes when you load a project, your carefully crafted skin shader may appear completely wrong. This is why it is always a good idea to save you materials as ZMT files separately from the project. If you load the project and it looks as though the character's skin has gone haywire, you should be able to fix the problem by loading your saved materials using the Load button in the Material palette.

## Image-Based Lighting

Now that you have a nice looking skin shader all set up, you can move on to other parts of the Enforcer character. However, it might be a good idea to add a little more interest to the lighting, especially if you are going to start dealing with reflective surfaces such as the metallic parts of the model.

You can quickly create a background for the model using a spherically mapped image. This image can also be used as the basis for a more complex LightCap lighting arrangement. In this section, you will download an image from the Internet and use it to create more stylistic lighting for the Enforcer.

## Create a Background Image

A background image of an environment is a great way to quickly add visual interest as you develop the look of a character. Seeing a character in context will also help you make decisions about how to design the materials used in the model. The best background images to use are spherically mapped images. A few example images can be found in the Textures/ Panoramas folder of LightBox. However, these images are a little too pleasant and pastoral for the Enforcer. Another great source of free panoramas can be found online at the sIBL archive at `http://www.hdrlabs.com/sibl/archive.html`.

Because of copyright restrictions, these images can't be included on the DVD or download files that come with this book. However, you are free to download them and use them in your own project. Follow these steps to create a background image for the Enforcer.

1. Open a web browser and go to the following URL: `http://www.hdrlabs.com/sibl/archive .html` (see Figure 10.26).

2. On the front page are a number of archives you can download. I felt the Factory Catwalk images seemed most appropriate for this character. Click on the Factory Catwalk icon to download a zip file containing the images.

3. Once the archive is downloaded, unzip the compressed folder and place it in an easy-to-find location on your local disc.

You can import jpegs and HDR (high dynamic range) images into ZBrush to use as backgrounds and for image-based lighting. High Dynamic Range images contain many levels of exposure, which is why they are often used for image-based lighting in 3-D applications. However, you can get good results using a jpeg as well, and the render will be a little faster.

*Figure 10.26: Point your Internet browser to the sIBL archive to find a number of spherically mapped panoramic images.*

4. In ZBrush, open the Texture palette and click on the Import button. Find the downloaded folder and import the Factory_Catwalk_ Bg.jpg image (Figure 10.27).

5. Open the Light palette, expand the Background subpalette, and click on the button labeled Textu. Select the Factory_ Catwalk image. After a few seconds, you will see it appear behind the Enforcer.

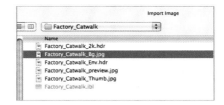

*Figure 10.27: Import the Factory_ Catwalk_Bg.jpg image into the Texture palette.*

6. To align the view of the model and the background, you can adjust the value of the Longitude and Latitude sliders in the Background subpalette of the Tool palette. It helps to turn off Solo, so that you can see the whole model. Turn on the Floor and Persp buttons on the right shelf and adjust the Angle of View slider in the Draw palette (see Figure 10.28).

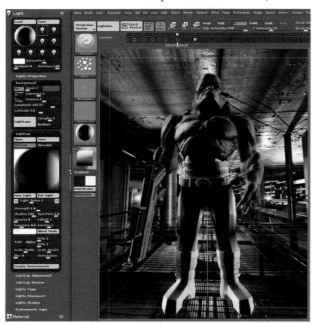

7. Once you have a view you like, press the LightCaps button in the Background subpalette of the Light palette. This creates a new LightCap based on the image (see left image in Figure 10.29).

8. The model looks much darker since most of the LightCap colors are extracted from the ambient lighting of the image. Use the New Light button to add a light to the LightCap. Adjust the Strength, Aperture, and Falloff of this light so that it lights the model in a more pleasing way. Feel free to add a couple of other lights for fill and backlight as well (see right image in Figure 10.29).

9. Once you have a LightCap set-up you like, use the Save button in the LightCap subpalette to save the LightCap as catWalkLights.ZLD.

10. Create a test render using BPR and adjust the lights as needed (see Figure 10.30).

*Figure 10.28: Adjust the latitude and longitude of the image as well as the view of the model so that they look properly aligned*

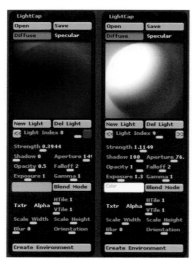

*Figure 10.29: Create a LightCap based on the colors of the image by pressing the Background button (left image). Add lights as needed to make the model more visible (right image).*

*Figure 10.30: Render using BPR to see how well the model is integrated with the lights.*

# Create the Look of Worn Leather

In the last section you learned how to create variation in specular reflections over the surface of the skin by painting a slightly more reflective material on top of a similar, but more diffuse, material. In this section, we'll take a look at a more advanced technique that uses the Material Mixer. This technique uses the intensity of the colors painted on the surface to determine which parts have stronger specular reflection than others. We will use this technique to make the Enforcer's leather corset appear worn and well-used.

## The Material Mixer

The Material Mixer's function is to determine how shaders within a material are layered on top of each other. The advanced settings at the bottom of the Mixer offer controls that set criteria for the strength of the shader based on everything from shadow strength to the hue, intensity, or saturation (or any combination) of the colors painted on the surface. Using these controls, you can create some pretty amazing material effects. This tutorial is going to keep things fairly simple. You will create a two-shaded material: One shader will be very diffuse and the other, very specular. Then you will set the Mixer up so that the specular material is stronger on the parts of the surface that are darker in color and the diffuse shader is stronger on the parts of the surface that are lighter in color. This creates a realistic effect since rough surfaces tend to diffuse reflected light, making them appear lighter than reflective surfaces. Think of a worn leather jacket: the crevices, which are not as exposed to wear and tear, tend to be smoother and shinier than the exposed parts, which become rougher and lighter in color.

1. Open the latest version of the project.
2. In the SubTool stack, find the SubTool named "corset." Select this SubTool and turn on the Solo button, so that the other SubTools are hidden. Set the SDiv slider to the highest setting (see Figure 10.31).
3. In the Light palette, turn off the Background image. This will speed up the performance of ZBrush.
4. Open the Material library and select the DoubleShade1 material. Open the Material Modifiers subpalette.
5. In the SubTool stack, turn on the little paintbrush icon so that polypainting is enabled for the surface—most likely, it is on already and you should be able to see the dark red and orange colors painted on the corset.
6. On the top shelf, make sure the M button is on and Rgb and Mrgb are not on.
7. Open the Color palette and press the Fill Object button. This fills the corset with the currently selected material, which should be the DoubleShade material.

*Figure 10.31: The corset is prepared for editing.*

8. In the Material Modifiers subpalette, click on the circle for the S2 shader, so that it turns into a dot. This means that the S2 shader is off and only the S1 shader is visible in the material.
9. The S1 shader will be the diffuse shader (see left image in Figure 10.32). Make the following adjustments to the settings. If a setting is not listed, then you don't need to change it:

   Ambient: 0
   Diffuse: 90

*Figure 10.32: The shader settings for S1 and S2 of the DoubleShade material*

Specular: 0
Colorize Diffuse: 80
High Dynamic Range: 1.5
Click the Dif color swatch and choose a light tan color.

10. Now switch to the S2 shader. Turn it on by clicking on the dot on the S2 button (See right image in Figure 10.32). Turn the S1 shader off.
11. Make the following adjustments:

Ambient: 0
Diffuse: 0
Specular: 100
Metalicity: 15
High Dynamic Range: 3.5

12. Now turn both S1 and S2 on and make sure the S2 button is highlighted, indicating that it is the selected shader. Expand the Mixer subpalette and make the following adjustments (Figure 10.33):

By Int: −100
Int Exp: 3
By Sat: −60
Sat Exp: 2.5

The By Intensity (By Int) slider sets the strength of the shader based on the intensity or value of the surface colors: setting this to −100 means that the shader is stronger where the surface is darker. The Intensity Exponent (Int Exp) controls the smoothness of the transition of the shader. The By Saturation (By Sat) controls the strength of the shader based on the saturation of the colors on the surface. So by setting this to a negative value, those parts of the surface that are colored with dark, unsaturated colors will be the shiniest parts of the surface.

13. Save the material as "wornLeather.ZMT."

## Paint In the Worn Areas

*Figure 10.33: The Mixer settings for the S2 shader*

Now that the basic material is set up, it is time to start painting in the worn areas. The colors that have already been painted on the surface will serve as a base coat. They are fairly dark reds and oranges and at the moment the surface looks fairly shiny. In this section, you will paint lighter colors over the surface and you will see how these lighter areas appear less shiny than the darker areas thanks to our worn leather material. The great thing about this approach is that the materials are blended smoothly as the colors on the surface transition from light to dark.

1. Continue with the project from the last section. In the Brush palette, select the Standard brush. Make sure the Rgb button on the top shelf is on. ZAdd, ZSub, M, and Mrgb buttons should be off.
2. Set the Rgb intensity to 22.
3. Select the alpha 58.
4. In the Brush palette, set Spin Center to 1 and Spin rate to 5. This rotates the alpha as you paint, which helps to create a nice pattern of overlapping marks.
5. In the color palette, set the color to a light yellowish tan.

6. In the Masking palette, set Cavity Mask intensity to 100 and press the Create Cavity Mask button. Turn off "View Mask" so that the mask is invisible as you paint.

7. Paint the light tan color over the surface of the corset. As you paint, you should see that the lighter areas are less shiny than the darker areas. Paint so that the darker areas are mostly within the cracks of the corset (see Figure 10.34).

8. Paint a dark gray on the studs and add a few oily splotches to sell the worn look. Figure 10.35 shows the corset rendered with BPR.

9. You can adjust the settings in the shaders of the wornLeather materials to fine tune the look after you have painted the surface. Save the project when you're happy with the way it's looking.

*Figure 10.34: Lighter colors are painted on the surface. The remaining darker colors appear shinier than the lighter areas.*

*Figure 10.35: The corset rendered with BPR*

Keep in mind, in this demonstration you used a material containing two shaders and just a couple of settings in the Mixer. Try using the TriShaders or the QuadShaders material and experiment with other Mixer settings. You will quickly realize that there are limitless creative possibilities with these tools!

# Rendering Metals

Metallic surfaces in ZBrush are easy to simulate and, in fact, there are a number of metal materials that come loaded into the ZBrush material library already. In addition, there are a huge number of free material presets that you can download from Pixologic's website. In this section, you'll learn where to find these materials and how they can be used on the metallic parts of the Enforcer character.

## MatCap Materials

MatCap stands for "material capture," just as LightCap stands for "light capture." The idea behind both technologies is very similar. Like LightCaps, MatCap materials use a texture to determine how the material is lit and shaded. The specular highlights, diffuse reflections, and other material qualities are "baked" into a texture and ZBrush references this texture when it renders the image.

*Figure 10.36: The highlights of the rendered model are not aligned with the shadows.*

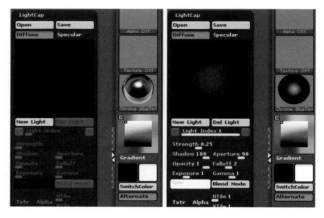

*Figure 10.37: Making changes in the LightCap editor while a MatCap material is selected causes the LightCap info to overwrite the MatCap properties automatically*

*Figure 10.38: The Orientation A (and Orientation B) slider allows you to rotate the texture applied to MatCap materials so that the highlights can be properly aligned.*

There are two key things to watch out for when using MatCap materials:

- Since specular highlights and reflections are baked into the material, it is possible to render a surface in which the highlights are not aligned correctly with the direction of the lights in the composition. Figure 10.36 shows an example where the highlights on the sphere and the torus are not properly aligned with each other and neither highlight is aligned with the shadow-casting light when the scene is rendered with BPR.

- The LightCap editor can be used to create MatCap materials. This is a really great way to design MatCaps. All you need to do is select a MatCap material from the upper half of the Material library and then open up the LightCap editor and make some changes. As soon as you make any changes to the LightCap editor, the lighting is instantly baked into the selected MatCap material. This is great, except that it means that it is very easy to accidentally destroy the current material and Undo is not going to reverse the changes (see Figure 10.37).

The first problem is fairly easy to solve. In the Modifiers for MatCap materials there is an Orientation A slider, which allows you to rotate the MatCap texture so that you can align the highlights with the lights in the scene (see Figure 10.38).

As for the second issue, the best way to prevent this situation form ruining your hard work is to save often. Save your materials when you edit them and save your projects and tools as well. Mind that you do not make changes to the LightCap editor while a MatCap material is loaded in the Material library, unless it is your intention to use the LightCap editor to design a material.

## MatCap Library

To create the materials for the metallic parts of the Enforcer, you will download some MatCap files form the online MatCap library, save them to a LightBox folder, and then fill the surface with the material.

1. Open a web browser and go to the following URL: www.pixologic.com/zbrush/downloadcenter/library/. Here you will find the MatCap library. Click on the link for MatCap metal in the library interface.

2. The materials are listed on the left. As you click on each one, you will see it preview on the troll character to the right (Figure 10.39). When you find a material you like, click on the link below to download it. The file will download as a ZIP archive.

3. Unzip the archive to extract the ZMT file. These files are materials that have been designed by users and uploaded to Pixologic's website for everyone in the ZBrush community to use.

4. Place the ZMT file in the ZBrush 4R2/ ZMaterials folder.

5. In ZBrush, open LightBox and click on the Materials link. You should see your downloaded materials here. For this project, I downloaded sc_tinMan.ZMT, bgs_silvery.ZMT, bgs_brushed_aluminium.ZMT, gk_ultra_oil. ZMT, ok_gunmetal.ZMT, fg_rusted_grey_ metal, and ok_pewter.ZMT. Feel free to download any materials you think will look interesting on the model.

6. To load a material into the current ZBrush session, double click the icon in LightBox (see Figure 10.40).

7. Select the SubTool you want to apply the material to. Turn on the SubTool's paintbrush icon in the SubTool palette to activate polypainting.

8. Set the SubTool to the highest SDiv level and then turn on the M button on the top shelf. You can then either use a brush to paint the material on parts of the surface or use the Fill Object button in the color palette to coat the entire SubTool with the material.

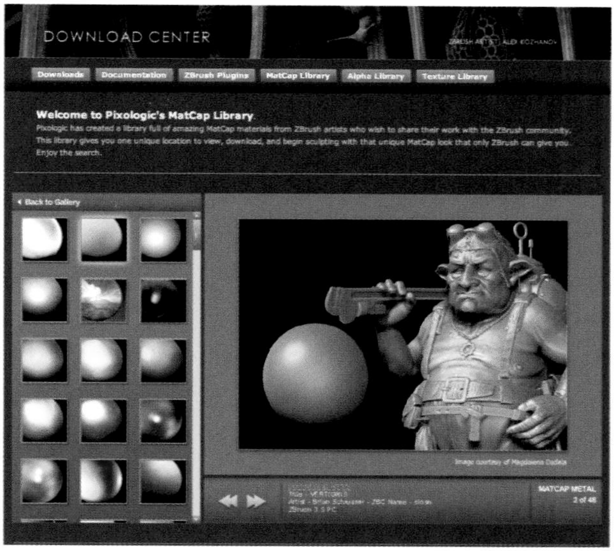

*Figure 10.39: The MatCap library contains a large number of free materials, including many metallic samples.*

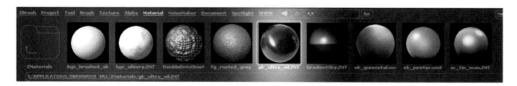

*Figure 10.40: The downloaded materials are available in the Materials folder of LightBox.*

Scott has already applied materials to most of the Enforcer's SubTools but feel free to try applying your own materials as well. Looking at the Modifiers for the materials will help you understand how they work. MatCaps generally base their color information on the texture seen at the bottom of the Material Modifier subpalette and the sliders are used to adjust the various properties of the texture and how they are applied to the surface. Some materials, such as the fg_rusted_grey_metal.ZMT, use shaders to combine both MatCap shaders and standard materials.

## Create the Final Image

The final process for rendering the Enforcer involves making a few adjustments to the render properties, rendering with BPR, and then adding a few post-process effects using BPR Render Filters.

## Render the Enforcer

Once the lighting and the materials have been set up, you are ready to render the image. In this section, you will prepare the project for a high-quality render in ZBrush.

1. Load the most recent version of the project into ZBrush.
2. In the Light palette turn on the On button in the Background subpalette. You may need to reload the background image if it is not available.
3. Spend a few moments aligning the view of the Enforcer with the background. This may require adjusting the Focal Length slider in the Draw palette so that the perspective of the character matches the perspective in the background.
4. Now, to create the final lighting you will want the metallic parts of the character to reflect the background image so that the character looks more integrated with the scene. Turn on the Reflect button next to the LightCaps button in the Background subplatte of the Light palette (see Figure 10.41).
5. Press the LightCaps button. This will replace the LightCap with a new version based on the background image. It does mean that any lights you added will need to be added and adjusted again. If you click on the Specular button you will see the background image has been mapped to the specular highlights of the LightCap lights (see Figure 10.42).
6. This is a good time to save your project and save the LightCap file as well. I saved the LightCap file as catWalkLights02.ZLD.
7. In the SubTool palette of the Tool palette, press the All High button. This sets all of the SubTools to their highest subdivision level. This will take a few minutes to calculate.
8. Open the Render palette and set the Details slider to 3. Make sure Smooth Normals is off.

*Figure 10.41: Press the Reflect button in the Background subpalette of the Light palette.*

*Figure 10.42: The background image has been mapped to the specular highlights in the LightCap editor.*

*Figure 10.43: The BPR render of the scene*

9. Turn on the Shadows, Ambient Occlusion, SSS, and Wax Preview buttons in the Render properties.
10. Make sure Floor is activated on the right shelf and that the grid lines of the floor are aligned with the floor in the background image. BPR will cast shadows onto the grid in the render and, if the scene is aligned with the background image, these shadows will appear integrated with the background.
11. Press the BPR button (hot key = Shift + R). The render will take a while to calculate, so this is a good point to take a break! Figure 10.43 shows the completed BPR render.

After the render is complete, do not change the view of the Enforcer—not only will you lose the render you worked so hard at creating, but it will take just as long to create a new render. However, if you don't change the view, ZBrush stores the ambient occlusion and other render information in a buffer. This means that if you need to redo the render, it should not take as much time, as long as you don't change the view of the scene! This is a great time saver if you need to adjust the lighting or change a material property.

Once the render is complete, you are still not finished. In the next section, you will use the Render Filters to add postproduction effects to the render. This will help separate the Enforcer from the background as well as allow you to adjust the look of the image in real time.

## BPR Render Filters

The idea behind the BPR render filters is similar to Photoshop filters but with the added advantage that the filters take into account 3-D depth information, shadow information, ambient occlusion, and other properties specific to ZBrush renders. This means that you can adjust the image after it has been rendered. As long as you don't change the view of the image, the filters will alter the render in real time. This is an effective time saver and the filters do a lot toward making your BPR render really stand out. This exercise introduces techniques for using the filters on the Enforcer image.

1. Once the BPR render of the Enforcer is complete, place the Render palette in a tray and expand the BPR Filters subpalette.
2. There are eight slots for the filters labeled F1 through F8. The filters are layered on top of each other from the lowest to the highest slot number. Each slot button has a dot in the upper right that is a switch. To turn on a filter, click on the dot so that it turns into a circle. Click on the dot on the F1 button to turn the filter on.
3. By default, the F1 filter is a noise filter. The render now appears brighter and noisy. The settings in the lower half of the BPR Filters subpalette control how the filter is applied (see Figure 10.44).

   It would be nice to separate the Enforcer model from the background image. A good way to do this is to adjust the intensity so that the background is slightly darker than the Enforcer model.

4. Click on the drop-down menu below the filter buttons and set the Filter to Intensity.
5. The Strength slider controls the magnitude of the effect. Set this slider to −0.25. A negative value for Intensity causes the image to become darker.
6. Of course, the filter has been applied to the whole image so everything looks darker. The sliders in the BPR Filters subpalette control how the filter is applied to the image. Set the Mask slider to −1. The Mask slider bases the filter on the alpha of the model. Setting this to a negative value means that the background is filtered while the model remains unaffected. Setting the Mask slider to a positive value reverses this.
7. Turn on the F2 button and set the filter to Saturation. Set the Strength slider to −0.5. This takes some of the color out of the image (a positive value makes the colors in the image more vibrant). Now set the Depth slider to 1. This means that the filter is applied based on depth information so that those parts of the model closer to the font receive less of the filter. Now the Enforcer has a bit more color on the closer parts, which helps to increase the sense of depth in the composition.
8. Turn on the F3 filter and set the filter type to Green. Set Strength to 1. Click on the Blend Mode button and choose Screen from the list. A green color is applied over the model. We want this color to appear only as a very subtle shade to the occluded and

*Figure 10.44: Turn on the F1 filter in the Filters subpalette of the Render palette.*

shadowed parts of the model. Green complements the warm colors of the image and, by using it in the shadowed areas, the shadows will appear less saturated, making the image a little more realistic. Set Shadow to 0.24 and Ao to 0.5. The Ao slider only works when you render the image with ambient occlusion activated.

9. Turn on F4 and set the filter to Fade. The model suddenly looks transparent! The Fade slider blends the model with the background. Set the Fresnel slider to 0.9. This means that the filter is applied to the edges of the model that face away from the viewing angle. Set the Strength slider to 0.15. This makes the effect very subtle. By adding a subtle fade to the edges on the model, you can cheat the look of making the subject more integrated with the background.

10. Turn on the F5 filter. Set the filter to Noise and the blend mode to Add. Set the Radius to 1. This increases the size of the noise grain a little. Set the Depth slider to −0.35 so the effect is stronger at the front of the image. Set the Strength slider to 0.05. Set the Int slider at the bottom to 20 so that the filter is applied based on the intensity of the image. These settings help add a bloom to the highlights in the image, which helps with the contrast, making it look a little more photographic.

11. Finally, add some blurring to increase the depth of field. Turn on the F6 filter, set the filter to Blur, and the Radius to 20. Set the Depth slider to 0.8 and the Strength to 0.5. Figure 10.45 shows the settings I used for each filter.

12. You can go back and make adjustments to the other filters or add more filters as needed. You can tweak until you are absolutely satisfied with the image. Experiment using the other filter modifiers, such as Saturation (Sat), SSS (subsurface scattering), and Hue. The Exponent sliders let you adjust the falloff of the effect. Figure 10.46 shows the render with the filters applied.

*Figure 10.45: The settings for each filter*

As long as the filters are on, each time you render this scene with BPR the filters will be reapplied. This also means that the filters are applied if you render an animation using the Timeline.

Keep in mind that the render passes are also available in the Render palette (Figure 10.47) so you can export these along with the final, filtered BPR render, bring them all into Photoshop to use in a paintover, or just for final tweaking. I felt that, overall, the BPR render was nice but the gun was getting lost in the background, so I took advantage of the render passes to solve this problem in Photoshop.

These images can be further worked in Photoshop using the techniques shown in other chapters. Figure 10.48 shows the Enforcer with a pass of Photoshop paint to help punch up the lighting as well as adjust the overall color temperature.

*Figure 10.46: The BPR render with the filter applied*

*Figure 10.47: The render passes in the Render palette*

*Figure 10.48: BPR render passes further adjusted in Photoshop by Scott Spencer*

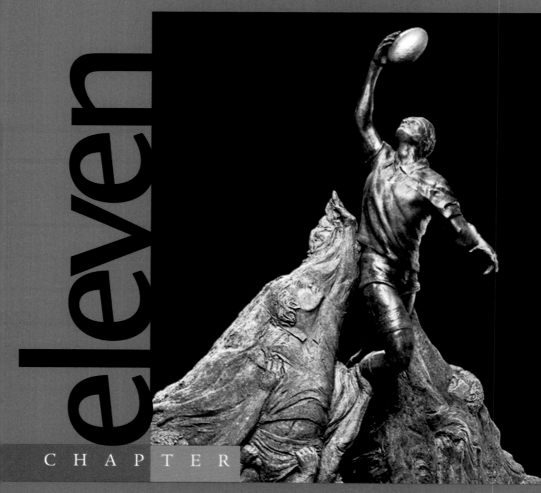

eleven

# ZBrush for Digital 3-D Printing

**As we have seen in** *the previous chapters, ZBrush can*
*be used for all manner of concept design and illustration purposes. One technological innovation that makes ZBrush even more powerful is the ability to create physical 3-D prints from digital geometry. This can be accomplished by various kinds of machines. The two most common are 3-D printers and 3-D mills. 3-D printers are the most common for creating small- to medium-scale figures and parts from 3-D data. 3-D mills are used for making larger-scale objects. In this chapter, we will focus on 3-D printing, as it is the most pertinent to the process of creating design maquettes from 3-D objects. The quality and level of detail in 3-D printing is far higher than what is achieved with 3-D milling technology.*

*The ability to print a physical object from a 3-D model gives designers an incredibly powerful tool, as digital designs on the computer can now be turned into physical objects in a matter of hours. What was once locked on-screen and only visible in the computer can now be placed in a client's hand. A director can see, light, and interact with a character design in a manner that was previously only possible through the use of traditional-sculptor and model-making techniques. This physical maquette can be used throughout the pipeline, helping various departments that need a reference figure of a character.*

Beyond the application of just concept-design maquettes, 3-D printing has allowed ZBrush to become a standard tool in the toy and collectible industry. Gentle Giant Studios, a leader in collectible and toy production, uses ZBrush heavily in their pipeline. I established the ZBrush presence at Gentle Giant in 2005 and we did some of the first work in crating collectible figures entirely using ZBrush. In a few short years, ZBrush sculpting had become the best solution to most projects in the workshop, as opposed to more traditional wax-and-clay approaches. In this chapter, I hope to share some of the workflow I used to create a physical model from digital data.

## The Brief: A Finished Physical Maquette

The brief for this chapter is to create a fully realized physical maquette based on the Interdimensional Traveler design. The 2-D illustration has been approved and now the director wants to see what this character might look like fully finished. To accomplish this, we need to revisit the original model and resolve any unfinished areas to a high level of detail.

In this chapter, we will look at the various methods of creating 3-D objects from digital data. This will include 3-D printing as well as milling. We will focus on 3-D printing technology as it offers much higher detail and is a more common solution for creating small- to midsized-physical objects in high detail. We will examine the various applications of 3-D printing from film and games to collectibles and even fine art. Finally we will look at the process I took to create the final 3-D print of the Interdimensional Traveler maquette.

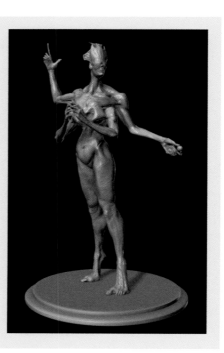

## Methods of Rapid Prototyping

Often you will hear the term *rapid prototyping* used as a catchall to refer to the process of creating physical objects, or prototypes, from 3-D digital data. The two most common kinds of technology used at this time to generate physical objects from a 3-D model are 3-D printing (stereolithography) and 3-D milling (CNC milling). 3-D printing involves the extrusion of micron-thin layers of plastic to build up an object layer-by-layer inside a 3-D printer. Milling is performed by a robotic arm with a cutting head that effectively carves away a shape based on 3-D data.

3-D printing allows for far more delicate pieces and retains fine details. The drawback can be that the size is limited to the size of the printer bed. Milling, on the other hand, works very well for large objects. Because the machine head tends to carve out of foam, your detail can be limited to the size of the smallest mill head. This can work just fine, especially for very large figures where details would actually be much larger than they would be on a smaller maquette. Often a 3-D mill is further finished with real-world sculpting before being molded and cast. A 3-D print may be reworked but often with the newer high-quality machines, the piece off the printer is ready for molding after a light cleaning.

## 3-D Printers

There are a few different manufacturers who produce 3-D printers. The two most common machines I have encountered are 3-D systems Thermojet and the Objet "Eden." I have worked with both and I find the Objet printer to be stunning in its detail and quality of print. Figure 11.1 shows the Objet Eden printer.

These printers work by a process called stereo-lithography. This process involves the extruding of a thin layer of plastic called acrylic-based photopolymer, which is catalyzed by a UV light. Each layer is so thin it must be measured in microns (or micrometers) rather than millimeters. The Eden machines from Objet lay down layers of plastic that are merely 16 µm thick (the symbol µm means microns, or micrometers— i.e., a millionth of a meter; you will encounter this in the documentation for these kinds of machines). As each layer is extruded and cured, a new layer emerges, effectively growing the part from the printer bed (Figure 11.2). The space around the plastic is filled with support material, a waxy substance that washes off later. Because each layer is merely microns thick, a high degree of detail can be reproduced. When a model is properly decimated and oriented on the printer bed, details as small as skin pores are easily reproduced. Decimation is the process of lowering the overall polygon count while retaining all the model details. Decimation is integral to the 3-D printing workflow, and we will look at it in-depth later in this chapter.

On the modern generation of high-end 3-D printers, I have seen models printed with this machine that needed little to no cleanup before being molded for production. Often the single generation loss of detail introduced by the molding process was enough to reduce the remaining surface lines from the build. Figure 11.3 shows a mesh detail from a superhero costume 3-D printed by Gentle Giant Studios. The level of detail here is phenomenal and the build lines are essentially invisible! Build lines are created by the various layers of extrusion material, show up as fine lines on the print, and need to be removed by a light cleanup.

*Figure 11.1: Objet Eden printer*

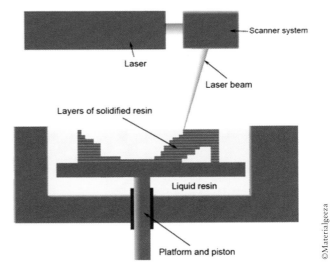

*Figure 11.2: This image illustrates the process by which a part is "grown" in a 3-D printer tray.*

Some printers use a different material than the resin used by the Objet printers. The ZCorp printer line uses a material mix that can also support the printing of some color from the model (Figure 11.4). Figure 11.5 shows a design by Nick Benson printed on the ZCorp Spectrum 510.

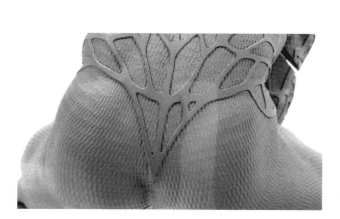

*Figure 11.3: Costume detail from an Objet Eden print at 12 inches tall*

*Figure 11.4: ZCorp color print sample*

Image courtesy of Z Corporation

Artist: Martin Beyer
© Offload Studios Inc.

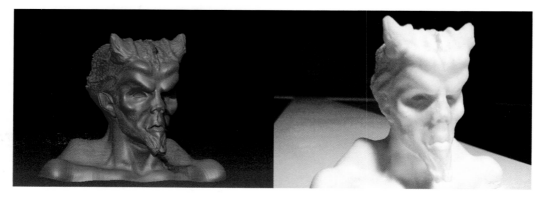

*Figure 11.5: This demon bust was printed by artist Nick Benson on a ZCorp 510 3-D printer.*

## 3-D Milling

3-D mills or CNC milling machines are generally used for larger objects than are possible to print on a 3-D printer. They are somewhat faster and yet reproduce less detail by virtue of the material employed and the fact that a carving approach is used rather than an additive building process. The mill can operate in multiple axes, allowing a movable robotic head to carve away the shape of 3-D data in a block of material (Figure 11.6). 3-D milling is generally used for large-scale objects and the detail is generally limited by the side of the milling head and the quality of base material being milled. We do not focus much on milling in this chapter because you will almost always be printing with a stereolithography machine or a 3-D printer to get the level of detail you will want in your figures.

One drawback to 3-D milling is its inability to reproduce undercuts. Undercuts are areas of a shape that dip back and underneath, like the nostrils or insides of ears

(Figure 11.7). Because a mill carves the shapes out, you cannot mill an undercut as easily as you can print an object with an undercut. Figure 11.8 shows a life-sized King Kong milled by Gentle Giant for the premiere of King Kong in New York City. The data used was the actual Kong model, reworked and detailed in ZBrush. This amazing project was overseen by Gino Acevedo of Weta Workshop for Gentle Giant Studios.

*Figure 11.6: A Comet robot milling machine*

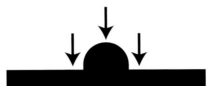

If the arrows represent the milling tool, the shape above can be carved from one direction

Undercut

The undercut cannot be carved by the tool

*Figure 11.7: Undercuts are areas that cannot be accessed by the milling tool—they are areas that curve back and away from the direction of the milling head.*

*Figure 11.8: This life-sized King Kong was milled on a CNC machine from original data of the Kong model.*

# Applications for 3-D Printing

In this section, we will look at the various applications of 3-D printing in the entertainment, art, and manufacturing industries. When I refer to 3-D printing, I am talking about stereo-lithography as opposed to 3-D milling. The combination of ZBrush and 3-D print technology has opened huge new vistas to artists working in this medium. Not only can we use ZBrush to print maquettes as a powerful concept-design tool, but the same technology extends into prop manufacture and even fine art and collectible production based on your digital sculpture.

## 3-D Printing for Digital Maquettes

Here we can see some examples of how a concept design can be taken into the physical realm by printing a 3-D model from the ZBrush data (Figure 11.9). Many times directors will respond better to seeing and holding a representation of the character in their hands. Filmmakers are highly visual people so they will often like to be able to see a character under real lighting conditions even if it is in miniature.

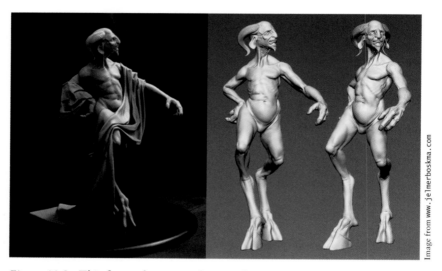

*Figure 11.9:  This figure shows a sculpture of Senator Tumblestone, made and printed by Jelmer Boskma.*

Being able to produce concept maquettes like this has been hugely beneficial beyond just getting design approvals. Once a maquette is approved, it allows other departments to have the figure for reference. The 3-D print can even be painted to illustrate possible skin texture variations.

Concept design is not limited to just the entertainment industry. Figure 11.10 shows a maquette for a monumental piece of public sculpture here in Wellington, New Zealand. The central figure was conceptualized in ZBrush and then milled in foam as basis for the final sculpture. You can see how ZBrush and digital printing is now making headway into the world of fine art, allowing sculptors to develop ideas much quicker and bringing them to life with greater ease.

## 3-D Printing for Toys and Collectibles

In addition to concept maquettes, the 3-D print capability naturally extends to toys and collectibles. Many companies like Gentle Giant Studios will print and market concept maquettes as limited edition releases. Figure 11.11 shows a selection of collectible maquettes by the fantastically talented artist Alterton. 3-D print technology has become available to all artists as its price has fallen. Figure 11.12 shows a bust created by artist Stefano Bernardi from a personal project and a female figure created by independent artist Chris Bostjanick.

*Figure 11.10:  RWC sculpt maquette and on site*

*Figure 11.11:  A selection of sculptures by the ZBrush artist and figure sculptor Alterton*

3-D sculpture data can be easily printed, cast, and painted to create a high-quality collectible prototype in very little time. Figure 11.13 shows this process on two collectible statues by Alterton for Sideshow Collectibles.

In addition to toys and collectibles, artists' reference figures can also be created by loading scan data into ZBrush for cleanup and manipulation. Figure 11.14 shows a selection of 3-D reference prints I use daily. I keep these on my desk as constant sources of reference and inspiration. Many of these figures are taken directly from models that were body-scanned and then cleaned up in ZBrush before printing. The scanning process introduces many artifacts that need to be corrected before the data is usable. Figure 11.15 shows the before and after of using ZBrush standard sculpting and smoothing tools to help clean up a digital scan.

*Figure 11.12: This collectible bust was created in ZBrush by Stefano Bernardi. The helmet is actually removable to reveal the character's face. The Octogirl was sculpted in ZBrush by Chris Bostjanick before being printed in 3-D by Ownage.*

*Figure 11.13: Alterton sculpted these prototypes in ZBrush for Sideshow Collectibles.*

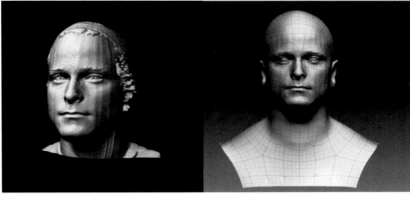

*Figure 11.14: These reference scans are based on 3-D scan data that has been cleaned and printed.*

*Figure 11.15: This head scan has been cleaned and prepared for printing using the standard sculpting and smoothing tools in ZBrush.*

## 3-D Printing and Milling for Props and Manufacture

ZBrush is not limited to just organic models and small-scale maquettes. Artists have been using ZBrush and 3-D printing and milling to create monumental scale set pieces, sculptures, and props and costume elements.

Figure 11.16 shows a lion digitally sculpted by artist Bryn Court. Bryn's digital sculpture was milled and then finished as a faux bronze set piece for the last Harry Potter film. Bryn is a fantastically talented traditional sculptor who is integrating ZBrush into his work as a film artist to cut down on time and increase his ability to generate high-quality work fast.

*Figure 11.16: This lion was designed and sculpted in ZBrush by sculptor Bryn Court. The lion data was milled on a monumental scale and finished in clay before being molded and cast for use as a set piece.*

As we have seen already, ZBrush is capable of creating complex machined surfaces with the new hard surface tools (Figure 11.17). As a result of this capability, ZBrush can be used to conceptualize and create prop designs using a 3-D mill.

*Figure 11.17: This hard surface model was created entirely in ZBrush.*

## How Can I Get My Models Printed?

At this stage, you must be wondering how to get your own models printed. Luckily there are many companies today who are offering this service and the price is dropping. Usually prices are determined by the volume or height of the figure. Price can be lowered by printing the figure laying down rather than standing or by hollowing out the figure and cutting it into parts so it can be more efficiently placed on the printing tray. This means a figure laying down prints faster, but the build lines will be oriented lengthwise down the body.

The following list is a selection of companies who offer 3-D printing services to consumers. I had the Interdimensional Traveler 3-D print for this book printed by Ownage, and I can personally vouch for the exceptional quality of the print as well as the great customer service. I highly recommend you get in touch with them for your printing needs. Desmoda and team will stun you with their high-quality, fast work.

| | |
|---|---|
| **Ownage** | http://ownage.com/ |
| **GrowIt3D** | www.growit3d.com/ |
| **Morpheus** | www.facebook.com/morpheus.prototypes |
| **Offload Studios** | http://www.offloadstudios.com/core/ |
| **Shapeways** | http://www.shapeways.com/ |

One day soon we will have desktop 3-D printing. The Objet company already has the Objet24 and Objet30 personal printers. These machines have a 28 micron layer thickness. That means they will print fine details but not as fine as the 16 µ layers by the Eden line of machines. It is only a matter of time before they become a consumer product. When this happens, manufacturing will be forever changed just like music and film were changed by MP3 and MP4 files. Imagine downloading a toy and printing unlimited copies from home. Imagine being able to scan and replace parts from your vintage toy collections by simply printing them. Imagine scanning your head with your webcam and printing a custom action figure head of yourself. These are all available technologies.

# Prepare the Model for Printing

When printing a model on a 3-D printer, you have to ensure that your object is in print-ready condition. This means checking to see that the object meets certain physical requirements. We will take a look at each here.

## "Watertightness"

An object prepared for printing must be a closed surface as if it were watertight. That means there can be no holes in the 3-D model. For example, Figure 11.18 shows an arm with gloves on—the gloves have no thickness to them—they are only a single layer of polygons. Because of this, they will confuse the machine and will not print. We then see the same gloves with a thickness built in, in the form of an inner and outer shell—they are now objects with a volume that can be printed in the real world.

Sometimes you can resolve water-tightness issues by countersinking objects together. In Figure 11.19, for example, the cylinder is open on one end. These will not print because of the hole in the mesh. If you countersink it into the sphere, the mesh is now printable.

## Workable File Sizes

In addition to being aware of the need for a thickness and watertightness in your models, you must also be aware of file sizes. Many 3-D printers have a file-size limit for the software. This limit improves with each machine but generally an OBJ with many millions of polygons can easily weigh in at hundreds of megabytes of data, whereas an average file-size limit for the printer software might be around 200 megs. You can also speed up the printing process and reduce the chance of the printer crashing in the middle of the process if the file sizes are smaller.

To deal with this discrepancy between file size and software limits on the machine, you will need to decimate the models. Decimation allows the computer to remove polygons in areas of low detail while leaving them in areas of high detail (Figure 11.20). This means you retain all of your fine detail while lowering the overall poly count and file size. As we saw in Chapter 9, "Painting the Forest Spirit," ZBrush uses the plug-in Decimation Master to accomplish this, and we will take a detailed look at it later in this chapter.

Finally, models for 3-D printing need to obey the rules of physical objects. For example, you cannot have floating arms and legs that don't connect to the torso. You also want to avoid very thin or tiny protrusions, as these may not print. Or if they do, they are likely to be very fragile.

# Creating a Maquette

In this section, we will return to the Interdimensional Traveler character. Because we will now be using the model as a final 3-D print and not as the basis for an illustration, we will need to resolve the unfinished areas into a final maquette—we will adjust the pose to work in the round and look at how to compose for 3-D space. We will then decimate and export data suitable for 3-D printing. Let's get started.

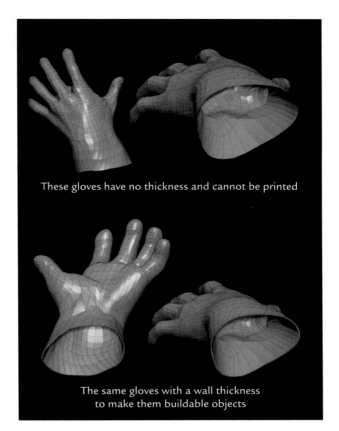

These gloves have no thickness and cannot be printed

The same gloves with a wall thickness to make them buildable objects

*Figure 11.18: These gloves will not print because they are not solid volumes. The same gloves are corrected with a wall thickness, and this makes them real volumes that can be printed. Otherwise, a wall of polygons has no real-world thickness that can be replicated.*

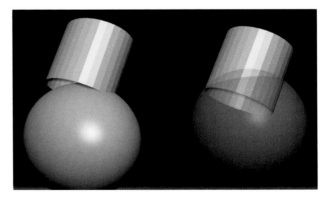

*Figure 11.19: The cylinder here will not print because it is not water-tight. This can be resolved by countersinking the cylinder into the sphere until the hole is contained inside the volume of the sphere.*

## Reconsider the Model as a 3-D Object

In the initial stages of sculpting the Interdimensional Traveler, we took some shortcuts since we knew the design would be painted in Photoshop. Now we have a chance to revisit and resolve the figure in the round. This includes detailing areas we merely suggested before, like the legs, which we knew would fall into shadow. We will also try to redesign some aspects, such as the feet, to make them feel even more alien.

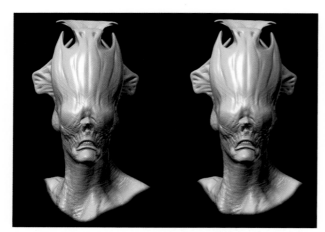

1 million faces          Decimated to 200,000 faces

*Figure 11.20: Here you can see the impact on decimation to the poly count. When performed correctly, the decimation process does not impact the fine details. The head on the left is 1 million faces while the one on the right is decimated to 200 thousand.*

### Readdressing the Back and Scapulae

At this phase, we will start to address some areas that were underdeveloped in the initial sculpt. The back, for instance, needs to be resolved since it was not part of the original illustration.

1. Open the roughsculpt.zpr ZBrush project file from the DVD or download files. From the back view, I start to resolve the shoulder blades (Figure 11.21). The back has been distorted in the process of posing and sculpting the figure for viewing from the front. This was acceptable since we were concerned with quickly creating a 2-D concept image. Now that we need to create a 3-D maquette, we need to resolve areas like this one.

2. The scapulae will swing up and out as an arm is raised, and back toward the middle of the back as the arms are brought back (Figure 11.22). With this in mind, I introduce these forms to the back (Figure 11.23).

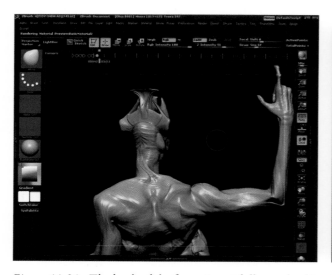

*Figure 11.21: The back of the figure is not fully resolved in the original sculpture. We will need to correct the scapulae.*

The scapula in various arm positions

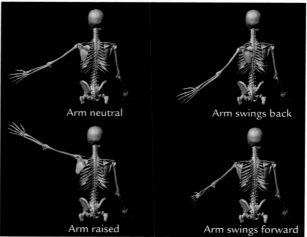

Arm neutral          Arm swings back

Arm raised          Arm swings forward

*Figure 11.22: Scapulae in motion—skeleton reference*

3. Create the impression of skin stretching across the shoulder blades with the Clay Tubes brush. As we have done before, select claytubes and turn off the alpha. Dial down the draw size and stoke across the borders of the scapulae. It will fill into the recessed areas and create the look of skin in tension stretched over bone (Figure 11.24).

4. Since this figure has four sets of arms, we need to make sure to address the second set of scapulae. Using the Standard brush, I sketch in the borders of the shoulder blades (Figure 11.25). A key landmark on a back as sinewy as this would be the traces of the spine. Using the Standard brush I suggest the spinous processes of the vertebrae down the length of the back. This helps reinforce the sense this creature has a very emaciated figure and very thin skin tissue (Figure 11.26).

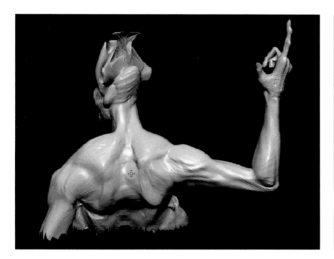

*Figure 11.23: Sculpting the scapulae*

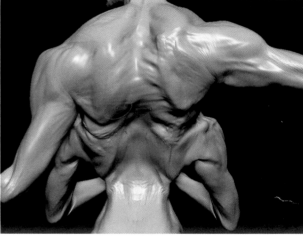

*Figure 11.24: Using the claytubes brush to suggest skin stretching over the bony structure of the scapulae*

In addition to the edits above, I make a few more changes to the anatomy of the figure. Major alterations are made to the buttocks and hands. To see these changes please review the video on the DVD or download files, which shows the edit process narrated in full. We will now move on to the biggest alteration in the design, the feet.

## The Feet

Up until now, the feet were left unresolved in the design. In the original illustration, the legs fall into shadow to allow the focal point to be on the chest, arms, and head. At this point we need to revisit the legs and feet and determine what kind of feet this character will have. I defaulted to a normal human foot shape originally, but this is not something I want to carry into the final design. Since the figure has such a long graceful flow to the stance and proportion, I want a foot design based on a dog leg—a foot that stands on its toe. This leg design

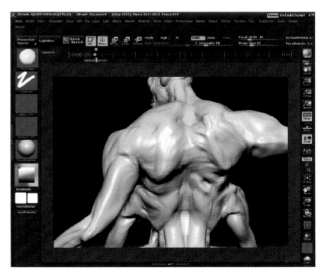

*Figure 11.25: Because this character has four arms, we need to be sure the secondary set of arms has a fully resolved pair of scapulae to allow them to move like the upper arms.*

is called digitigrade. A digitigrade is an animal that stands or walks on its digits, or toes (Figure 11.27).

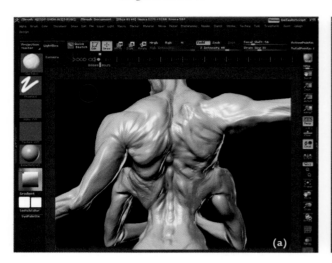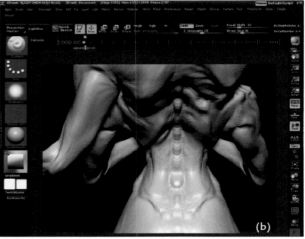

Figure 11.26: *Here I have added in the suggestion of the vertebrae to give the back an even more emaciated appearance. In image a, you can see the scapulae and spine marked in red. In image b, you can see the sculpted spine and scapulae.*

Another benefit to this foot form is that it can lengthen the leg even further, giving a more beautiful sweep to the lower body (Figure 11.28). Follow these steps to create the same foot design. To see this process in full, check the video included on the DVD or download files.

1. Orient the feet to be center screen. Turn on X symmetry by pressing the X key and turn off perspective by pressing the P key (Figure 11.29).

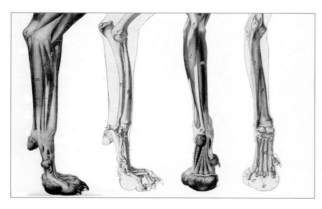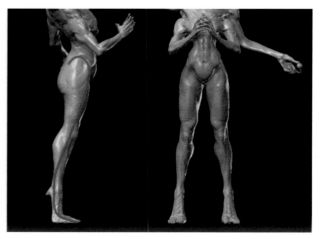

Figure 11.27: *This illustration shows the internal structure of a digitigrade leg.*

Figure 11.28: *Changing the foot design lengthens the graceful sweep of the lower leg even more.*

2. Use transpose masking to mask down to the ankle (Figure 11.30). Orient the transpose line so the last circle is over the ankle. Press R to enter Rotate mode and while holding Alt + Click + drag in the circle to bend the foot down. Alt + Click + dragging in the last circle will activate "bone posing," which allows you to bend the ankle without the mesh collapsing.

3. Extend the mask to the middle of the foot itself. Drag the last transpose circle down to the point where the mask ends (Figure 11.31). Use the same Alt + Click + drag technique to rotate the foot at this angle. I also press W to switch to move mode and shift the toes further down.

4. Using the Move brush, the foot form is further stretched. The ankle and calf are also slightly enlarged to compensate for the longer taper to the leg (Figure 11.32).

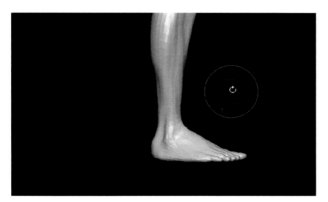

*Figure 11.29: Center the feet on screen.*

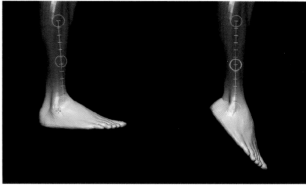

*Figure 11.30: Masking to the ankle the bending with Transpose Rotate*

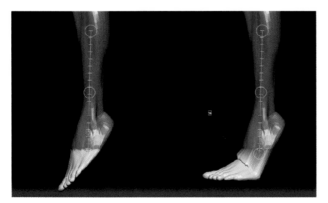

*Figure 11.31: Extend the mask further down the foot to help manipulate the toe shape. Use transpose to shift the toes further from the ankle.*

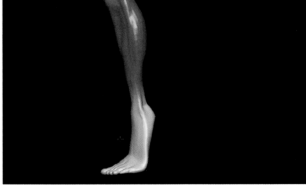

*Figure 11.32: Subtle changes are made to the foot and calf muscles with the Move brush.*

At this stage, the basic foot form is roughed in. We will now turn our attention to the toes. I want to spread the big toe from the others and create a more simian- or chimp-like foot configuration. This gives the impression the foot can grasp or clamp on to surfaces. The other toes are squashed back, making the foot even more inhuman in appearance (Figure 11.33). Follow these steps to create the same look.

1. Step down to the lowest subdivision level so that you have fewer faces to manipulate. We will be making big changes to the foot so detail is unnecessary right now. Mask the leg down to the big toe (Figure 11.34). You may find it helpful to hide the rest of the model except for the feet since our attention will be on this area. Make sure X symmetry is on.

2. Using the Move brush and the Transpose Move tool shift the big toe out from the other digits (Figure 11.35). Rotating to the bottom view will allow you to get a clearer idea of the overall form of the food pad. Shape the toes and the base of the foot from this view as well.

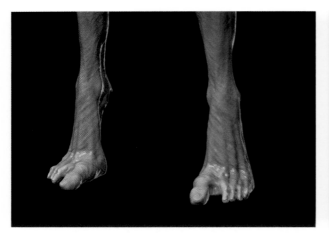

*Figure 11.33: The foot is shaped into a less human form as seen here.*

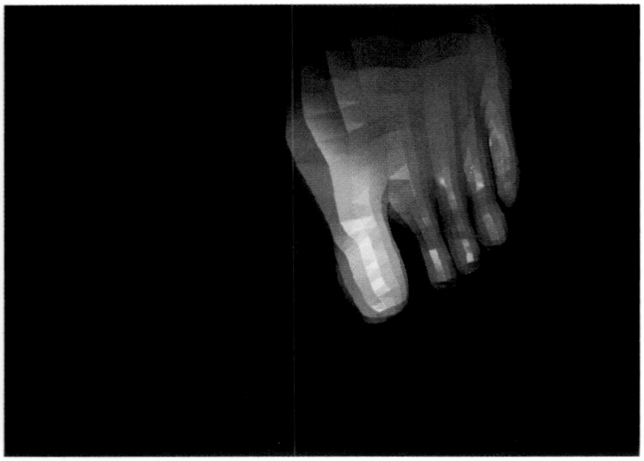

*Figure 11.34: Isolate the big toe with a mask.*

*Figure 11.35: Shifting the big toe away from the other digits and working the shape of the foot from the bottom view*

3. At the ankle, use the Move brush to pull out a claw appendage. This is a kind of vestigial toe that helps add interest to this part of the anatomy and adds another sharp, aggressive element (Figure 11.36). This appendage is suggestive of a dog's dewclaw.

4. At this stage, I need to readdress the calves to site better with this new foot design. As you can see in Figure 11.37, the shape of the calves feels rather uninspired and dull. I select the move brush to alter the overall silhouette of this shape. I will rework the silhouette of the back of the legs to create a more unified rhythm of lines flowing down into the

foot. Using the Move brush, I create a crest in the back of the calf muscle. This sharp line break creates a nice counterbalance to the sweep of the front of the leg (Figure 11.38).

5. Select the Standard brush. We will now start to create the skeletal and muscular anatomy of the foot. As it stands, there is little detail to the forms there, so we need to add secondary shapes to suggest the underlying skeletal and muscular anatomy to add realism to the form. With the Standard brush, sketch in the space between the tarsal bones of the foot (Figure 11.39).

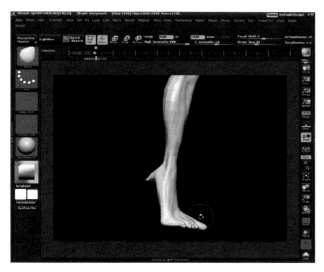

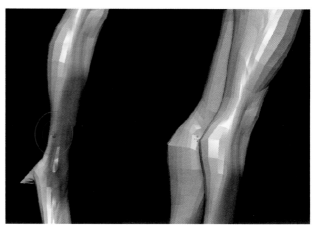

*Figure 11.36: Create a claw form at the ankle.*

*Figure 11.37: Altering the shape of the legs with the Move brush, then pulling out the calf muscles to create a sharper crest in the silhouette*

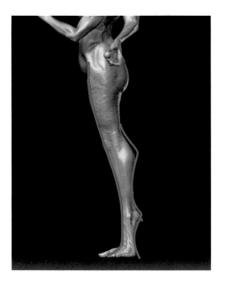

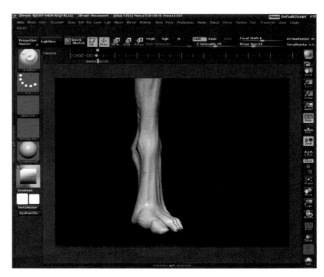

*Figure 11.38: The sweep on the leg from the front is counterbalanced nicely with the crest and break created by the sharper calf silhouette on the back of the leg.*

*Figure 11.39: Sketch in the suggestion of the tarsal bones with the Standard brush.*

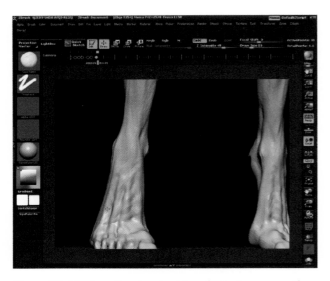

*Figure 11.40: Smaller standard brush strokes across the bony forms help suggest wrinkled skin.*

6. To add a sense of skin stretching across those bones, use the Standard brush. Dial down the draw size and stroke across the tarsal bone forms. This will start to create a series of raised ridges crossing the tarsal bones, which can be resolved into skin. Step up to a higher subdivision level and continue to sketch in raised wrinkles. These will read like tissue skin over the larger bony forms (Figure 11.40).

## Posing for 3-D

This section required that Transpose Master be installed. Transpose Master is a free plug-in from Pixologic for posing models with multiple SubTools. Download and install the files from www.pixologic.com before attempting this section.

In this section, we will repose the figure to be viewed in the round. This is different than posing for a single view because a sculpture, unlike an image, is experienced through a full 360 degrees. We will use a spiral composition for this figure.

Spiral composition is a method of positioning a figure where the masses are each oriented slightly rotated along the Y axis, for example, if the pelvis is facing forward, the shoulders are slightly turned, and the head is turned further (Figure 11.41). This creates a composition where each mass is incrementally turned, which helps create a sense of motion and interest even in a seated or standing pose. This works particularly well for sculpture since it creates interesting shapes throughout 360 degrees of view (Figure 11.42). The steps below show how I use Transpose Master to pose this figure in a spiral composition.

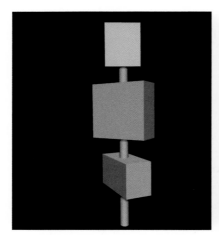

*Figure 11.41: These masses are arranged in a spiral composition.*

*Figure 11.42: The character in spiral composition. Note the offset between each red axis line through the figure.*

We will be using Transpose Master to create this pose. Transpose Master allows you to easily pose characters with multiple SubTools by creating a single proxy mesh that contains all the elements in one model. The pose data is then transferred back to the original model retaining each SubTool. To get the best result, I find it is best to make sure the lowest subdivision level has a fair bit of geometry to support the pose deformation. Transpose Master will create a proxy mesh from the lowest subdivision level of the model. This ZTool has far too little geometry in the hips to support the twisting pose I want to create (Figure 11.43). The figure on the left represents subdivision level 1 while the right is level 3. I want to make level 3 the lowest subdivision level as it has just enough geometry to support thee kinds of pose deformations I need to create.

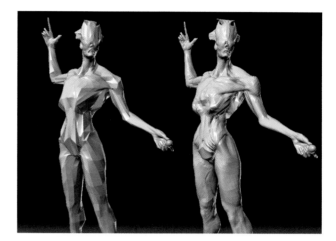

1. Step up to level 3. Form the Tool ➢ Geometry menu click Delete Lower to remove the unneeded lower subdivision levels (Figure 11.44). This will only work if you have no layers in Record mode. If this action fails, be sure to exit Record mode on any layers. You exit record mode by clicking to the right of the record icon. This enables the eyeball icon placing the layer in visible mode with record off. If possible, you may want to collapse any layers you have on the model. Step up to the highest subdivision level and bake the layers by pressing the Bake All button (Figure 11.45). This will permanently apply the layer contents to the model. If you prefer to keep your layers, just make sure to exit record mode on any layers currently active.

*Figure 11.43: In level 1 on the left, there is too little geometry in the waist to support deformation required. Level 3 on the right is a far better resolution for posing.*

2. This creates a level 1 with 102k faces. What's more important than the total face count is the fact the geometry is concentrated in areas like the waist, which I will need to twist to create the pose I want.
3. Start Transpose Master by pressing ZPlugin ➢ Transpose Master ➢ TPoseMesh to create the Posable proxy mesh (Figure 11.46).

Once the model is in TPose, you can use the Transpose tools to pose it. I chose to rotate the torso around the Y axis as well as bring one of the legs back slightly to suggest the anticipation of a forward motion, as if the character might be about to take a step. Follow these steps to create this pose (Figure 11.47).

1. Press R to enter Transpose Rotate mode. Press Ctrl + Click + drag down the model's torso to mask the upper body. Rotate around the figure to be sure everything above the waist is masked. Manually mask in any missed areas (Figure 11.48).
2. Ctrl + Click on the background to invert the mask. Ctrl + Click on the mask itself to feather soften the edge. Press R to enter Transpose Rotate mode and draw a transpose line up the center of the back (Figure 11.49).
3. Rotate to the side view. Click and drag the transpose line to the centerline of the body by clicking on the circle or line itself. Once the line is placed, click and drag inside the center circle to rotate the torso around the Y axis (Figure 11.50).

*Figure 11.44: Delete the lower subdivision levels*

*Figure 11.45: The Bake All button*

*Figure 11.46: Create the Posable mesh.*

Figure 11.47:  The posed figure

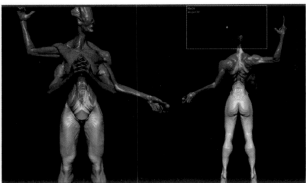

Figure 11.48:  Isolate the upper torso with transpose masking and then manually mask out any missed areas.

Figure 11.49:  Invert the mask and draw a transpose rotate line up the center of the back.

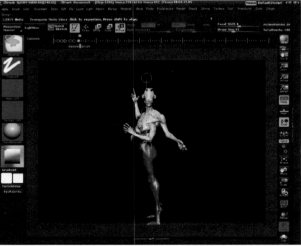

Figure 11.50:  Rotate the torso around the Y axis.

Next we will rotate the legs. We will begin by moving the right leg slightly back from the left. Isolate the right leg so the body is masked and the leg is unmasked. Using the masking pen, adjust the mask edge so it runs along the pelvic bone and the glute muscle is unmasked as well (Figure 11.51).

Draw a transpose line from the hip to the knee. Rotate the leg back slightly. Move the transpose line inside the leg from the front view (Figure 11.52). Click and drag in the center circle to rotate the leg around the Y axis. This rotates the leg in the hip joint and helps make the two feet point down different axes (Figure 11.53)—this helps create a more grounded and natural stance.

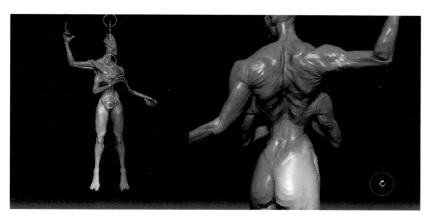

*Figure 11.51: Isolate the right leg with a mask, then manually unmask the glute muscle so it will be included in the deformation.*

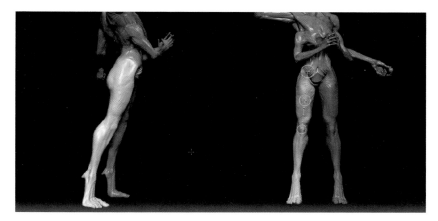

*Figure 11.52: Rotate the leg back slightly and from the front view, shift the transpose line inside the leg.*

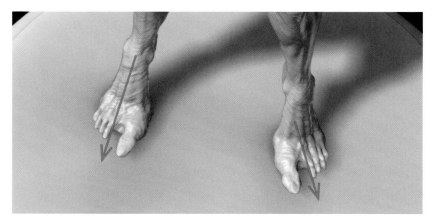

*Figure 11.53: The feet are now oriented down in slightly offset directions. This helps create a more stable stance.*

This completes the pose for the character—notice how the figure suggests a forward motion while at the same time offering an interesting view from each side (Figure 11.54). We will now move on to making a base.

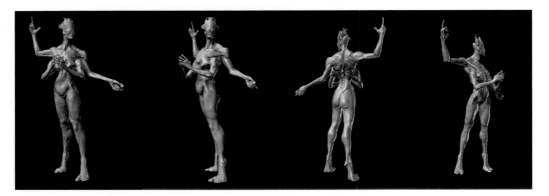

*Figure 11.54: The final pose*

### Create a Base

The figure will need a base so it can stand on a table without danger of toppling over. While it is possible to create such a figure that stands free, a base also allows you the chance to suggest some environment for the character and add other elements. To see this process in detail, please see the video on the DVD or download files.

1. The simplest approach to making a base is to use the ZBrush primitives. With the final posed ZTool open in ZBrush, go to the Tool menu and press the Tool Palette button (Figure 11.55).
2. From the tool palette, select the Sphereinder ZTool. This will replace the maquette as the active tool in the document window.
3. We will need to edit the shape of the Sphereinder to better serve as a base. As of right now, this is not a polygon mesh, it is a ZBrush primitive that has settings under the Tool menu to control its shape and size. Open Tool ➤ Initialize to access the shape controls (Figure 11.56).
4. In the Initialize menu, set the ZSize slider to 15, the TRadius slider to 63, and the TCurve to 50 (Figure 11.57). Convert this to an editable polygon mesh by pressing the Make Polymesh 3-D button under the Tool menu (Figure 11.58). This will create a polygon version of the tool named PM3D_Sphereinder. ZBrush will automatically select the PM3D version of the Sphereinder. We will need to make one more variant of the tool, so be sure to reselect the ZBrush primitive Sphereinder ZTool from the Tool menu. You can easily identify the ZBrush primitive version of the Sphereinder, as it is the one that does not have PM3D_ at the start of the filename (Figure 11.59).
5. Alter the Initialize settings now to the following values: ZSize 5, TRadius 10, and TCurve 100. Click Make Polymesh 3-D to make a poly version of the model. From the Tool menu, select the figure. From the SubTool menu append both PM3D_spheriencer ZTools (Figure 11.60).
6. Hide the other SubTools but the two Sphereinder tools. One of the two Sphereinder disc tools will have a rounded top while the other will be more of a squat flat-topped disc. Select the one with the rounded top and, using the Transpose Move brush, shift it down from the flat top Sphereinder (Figure 11.61).

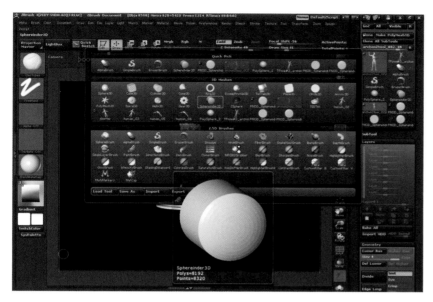

Figure 11.55: Open the Tool palette

Figure 11.56: Open the Initialize menu to access the shape controls.

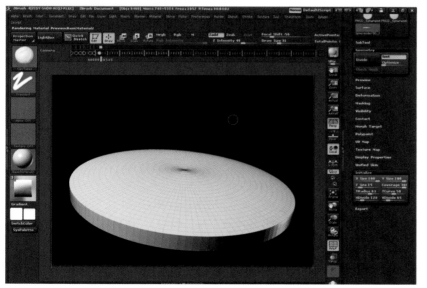

Figure 11.57: Here, you can see the effect of the setting changes.

Figure 11.58: The make PolyMesh 3-D button

Figure 11.59: Select the primitive Sphereinder again—the tool outlined in red is the ZPrimitive, and the others are polymesh copies, as you can tell from the PM3D_ in the filename.

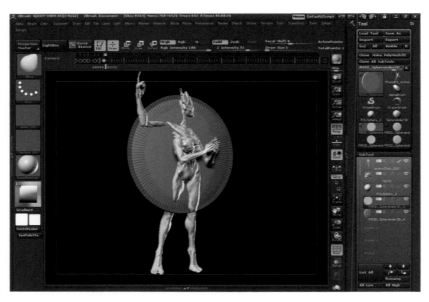

Figure 11.60: Both Sphereinder polymeshes appended

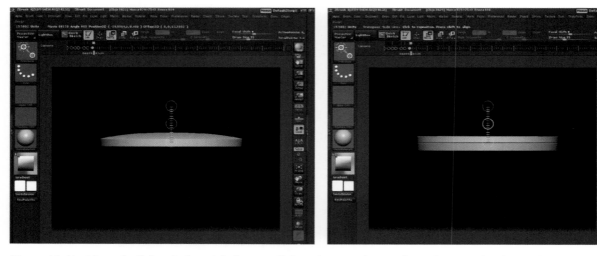

Figure 11.61: Move the Sphereinder with the rounded tip down and away from the second Sphereinder

7. Rotate to the top view. Select the flat top d and press E for Transpose Scale. Draw a transpose line from the center of the Sphereinder. I turn on frame mode to make it easier to spot the center. Scale the Sphereinder down (Figure 11.62).

8. Use Transpose Move to countersink the top disc into the larger base (Figure 11.63). The bottom Sphereinder may protrude because of its convex top. If so, simply use the Clay Tubes brush to push any exposed areas back (Figure 11.64).

9. Merge the two Sphereinders together by selecting the upper Sphereinder SubTool and pressing the Merge Down button under the Tool ➤ SubTool menu (Figure 11.65). Select OK from the popup window (Figure 11.66). Using the Transpose tools, reorient the base under the character's feet (Figure 11.67).

10. To make the feet contact the base, turn on transparency (Figure 11.68). Use the Move brush to shift the pads of the feet to appear to contact the surface of the base (Figure 11.69).

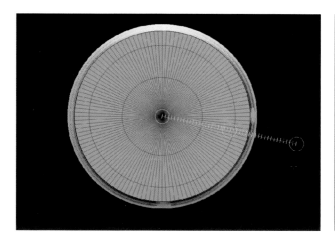

*Figure 11.62: Scale the flatter Sphereinder down.*

*Figure 11.63: Countersink the top Sphereinder into the base.*

*Figure 11.64: The final base*

*Figure 11.65: Merge the two base parts down into one SubTool.*

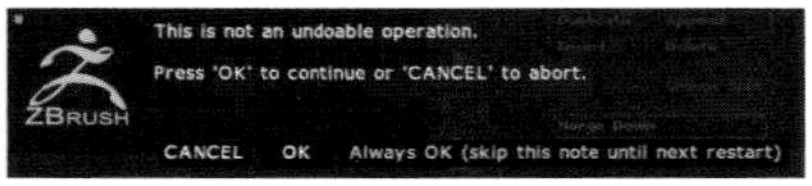

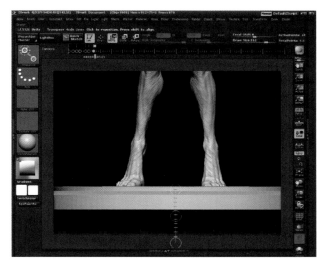

*Figure 11.66: Select OK from the popup menu.*

*Figure 11.67: Orient the base under the character's feet using the Transpose Move and Rotate tools.*

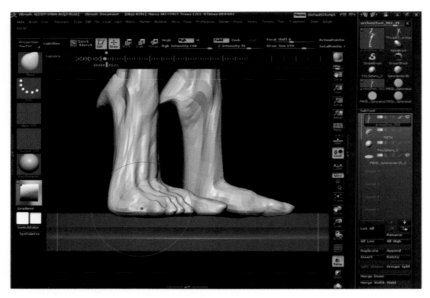

*Figure 11.68:*
*Enable transpar-*
*ency and turn off*
*ghost mode*

*Figure 11.69: Using the Move brush, shape the pads of the feet to the base.*
*Transparency mode allows you to grab the parts of the feet hidden inside the base.*

# Exporting the Geometry for Print

We will now export the geometry for print. Remember that 3-D printers do have a file-size limit. If you were to decimate the subdivision levels to make a smaller file, you would lose resolution—we want to keep detail while lowering file size. Luckily, Pixologic has a free plug-in to do just that— it is called Decimation Master. They also have the 3-D print exporter to allow you to export STL files at a real-world size.

## Decimating the Figure

Decimation Master and 3D Print Exporter are both available from Pixologic.com for free download. Extract them into the ZStartup/ZPlugs folder and restart ZBrush to access them. Here, we discuss how to use Decimation Master.

Before you can complete this section, you need to be sure Decimation Master and 3D Print Exporter are installed.

1. From the DVD or download files, open the ZBrush project posed.zpr.
2. The project will open with the final posed figure including the base and all SubTools. Open the Decimation Master plug-in by clicking ZPlugs ➤ Decimation Master (Figure 11.70). Click the radial button in the ZPlugin menu to dock it to the side of the screen for easier access to the settings.
3. Before any model can be decimated, ZBrush must preprocess it to determine the most efficient way to reduce the poly count while retaining details. This figure has multiple SubTools, but only the figure will require decimation. The sphere, base, and teeth are low enough not to require reduction. With the figure SubTool in edit mode, step up to the highest subdivision level.

*Figure 11.70:*
*Open the*
*Decimation*
*Master menu.*
*Dock it to the*
*side of the screen.*

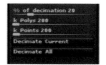

4. From the Decimation Master menu, click the Preprocess Current button. Note that we are only decimating the figure—if you have multiple SubTools to decimate you will click Preprocess All. ZBrush will examine the geometry of the figure and write a cache file on disk for use when it decimates later. This may take some time. When it is complete, you will be able to use the decimation settings to reduce the model.

5. Decimation Master allows three methods of specifying a level of decimation. The three sliders in Figure 11.71 illustrate each of these options. The first slider takes a percentage, the second takes a projected face count, and the third is a projected point count.

7. I find the second slider, number of polys, to be the easiest to use. Generally I will try to keep my mesh around 1 million faces. Since this slider reads in 100k faces, a setting of 200 equals 200,000 faces. I set this slider to 500 for 500,000 faces.

8. Press the Decimate Current button and ZBrush will reduce the model as per your settings. Decimation involves triangulating all the faces of the model, then removing triangles in areas of low detail, and retaining them in areas of high detail. Figure 11.72 shows the figure before and after this decimation operation. The model looks nearly identical. If you look in wireframe (Figure 11.73), you can see how the mesh has been triangulated and reduced in areas of low detail.

*Figure 11.71: The decimation control sliders allow you to define the amount of decimation by percentage, either by thousands of polys (faces), or thousands of points.*

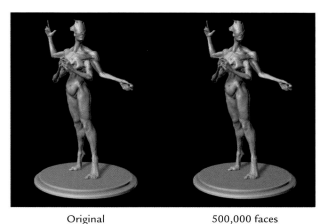

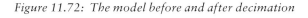

Original                    500,000 faces

*Figure 11.72: The model before and after decimation*

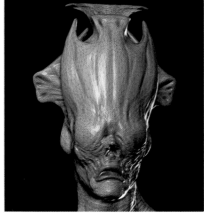

*Figure 11.73: A wireframe view of the decimated mesh shows how the quads have been triangulated and areas of low detail reduced.*

9. At this stage, the figure is decimated and ready for export. You can manually export an OBJ by going to Tool ➢ Export and saving an OBJ file. You will want to export an OBJ for each SubTool, including the sphere, base, and teeth. Each object will export in the correct position in space so they will reload together correctly in the printer company's software.

10. Save your ZTool by going to Tool ➢ Save As and naming the file "figure_decimated.ztl."

As an alternative to the last exporting step, you can use the 3D Print Exporter plug-in for even more control. In the next section, we will look at how to export with 3D Print Exporter.

## 3-D Print Exporter

The 3-D Print Exporter plug-in allows you to export OBJ and STL files from ZBrush for use on a 3-D printer. What makes this plug-in particularly useful is that it allows you to specify an object scale in real-world units, so you can be sure of the object size when it is being sent to the 3-D printer. In the following steps, we will export the figure as both STL binary and ASCII files.

1. From the ZPlugin menu, open the 3D Print Exporter menu (Figure 11.74).
2. If it is not still open, load the decimated ZTool from the previous section.
3. Because the figure consists of several SubTools, we will want to export them all as a single model. Under the section of the plug-in marked 3 Export, enable the All button on the 3-D Print Exporter menu. This will scale and export all the SubTools as a single mesh (Figure 11.75).
4. We will need to reset the size ratios for all the SubTools. To do this, click the Update Size Ratios button (Figure 11.76). Once ZBrush has determined the size ratio between all the buttons, it will enable you to specify a new size in the next step.
5. Select a unit from the two buttons: in. or mm. Most printing companies prefer to work in metric units, but imperial units (inches and feet) will be fine. The stl file has no internal units, so you will need to tell the printer what measurement and unit type you used.
6. I want to export a figure that is 12 inches high. Set the height slider to 12 and press enter.
7. To export an STL file, press the STL button in the Export section of the interface (Figure 11.77). ZBrush will request a filename and export the SubTools as a single STL file. This file can be sent to the 3-D printer or the printing company for output. Some companies will offer a web interface for uploading your data. See the list of service providers earlier in this chapter for companies that can print your figure.

*Figure 11.74: The 3D Print Exporter plug-in*

*Figure 11.75: Enable the All button to export all SubTools as one.*

*Figure 11.76: Update size ratios*

*Figure 11.77: Click the STL button to export a binary STL file of all your decimated tools.*

---

STL binary is the default STL file format. STL binary is the best option as it exports smaller files. Neither STL format supports UVs or textures. VRML will export a model that has a texture and UVs applied to it. This format is ideal for color-printing purposes on machines like the ZCorp, which will print a texture on the model. If you have polypaint on the model and the printer will support vertex RGB, use the ExpColors option to export colored vertices. If you need to export an STL ASCII format, this can be enabled under the Advanced Options of the plug-in.

---

That completes this chapter on 3-D printing and ZBrush. We have seen how to use ZBrush as a tool in conjunction with 3-D printing and milling technology to create physical sculptures on the real world. We have seen the various applications of 3-D printing from concept design to fine art to toys and collectibles. Figure 11.78 shows the final 3-D print produced by Ownage.

*Figure 11.78:  This 3-D print was produced by* ownage.com—*Ownage supplies the best quality for the lowest prices for all your 3-D printing and casting requirements. This figure has been molded for multiple castings.*

# About the Companion DVD

**This appendix summarizes** *the content you'll find on the DVD. If you need help with copying the items provided on the DVD, refer to the installation instructions in the "Using the DVD" section of this appendix.*

## What You'll Find on the DVD

The following sections are arranged by category and provide a summary of the content you'll find on the DVD. If you need help with installing the items provided on the DVD, refer to the installation instructions in the "Using the DVD" section of this appendix.

### Chapter Files

In the Chapters directory you will find all the files for completing the tutorials and understanding concepts in this book. This includes sample files, as well as video files that provide screen recordings of the tutorials in progress. Sculpting, painting, and design is an artistic process that cannot always be described with words alone. You're strongly encouraged to view the movies that accompany some of the exercises in the chapters to see how the example files were created. The video files were recorded using the TechSmith screen capture codes (www.techsmith.com) and compressed with H.264 compression. The videos included will, I hope, help further illustrate the techniques I use in ZBrush and Photoshop to create the imagery for this book. Being able to see a tool in use can better illustrate the concepts than still images alone.

If you purchased an e-edition of this book, you may download the project files by going to wiley.booksupport.com and entering the book's ISBN.

## System Requirements

This DVD does not include the ZBrush software. You will need to have ZBrush 4R2 or higher installed on your computer to complete the exercises in the book.

To complete the core exercises of this book, you need ZBrush version 4R2 or higher. Some sections also include material related to Photoshop and Maya and using these programs together with ZBrush. Hardware requirements are a PC or Mac running ZBrush with a gigabyte or more of RAM. The more RAM you have, the better the results you can get with ZBrush. Make sure that your computer meets the minimum system requirements shown in the following list. If your computer doesn't match up to most of these requirements, you may have problems using the files on the companion DVD.

- A PC running Microsoft Windows XP, Windows Vista, or Windows 7. You can use ZBrush on an Intel-based Mac running Windows emulation software such as Boot Camp or Parallels. However there may be some stability issues with ZBrush plug-ins such as ZMapper (must have SSE2 : Streaming SIMD Extensions 2).
  - Your computer's processor should be a fast, Pentium 4 or newer (or equivalent such as AMD) with optional multithreading or hyperthreading capabilities. ZBrush requires at least a Pentium 3 processor.
  - 2048MB of RAM (4096MB for working with multimillion-poly meshes)
  - Monitor: 1280 × 1024 monitor resolution or higher (32 bits)
- A Mac running Mac OSX 10.5 or newer
  - 1024MB of RAM (2048MB recommended for working with multimillion-polys)
  - Monitor: 1024 × 768 monitor resolution set to millions of colors (recommended: 1280 × 1024 or higher)
- An Internet connection
- A DVD-ROM drive
- Apple QuickTime 7.0 or later (download from www.quicktime.com)

For the most up-to-date information, check www.pixologic.com/zbrush/system.

It is also imperative that you have a Wacom tablet. While it is possible to use a mouse with ZBrush, it is like drawing with a brick. A Wacom or other digital tablet will open the doors for you to paint and sculpt naturally. Personally, I recommend a Wacom Cintiq. There are two variations of this tablet screen available as of this writing: the desktop model with a 21-inch screen as well as a smaller portable model. The Cintiq allows you to sculpt and paint directly on the screen and can vastly improve the speed and accuracy with which you can use ZBrush. It is essential to use some form of Wacom tablet, be it a Cintiq or a standard Intuos, with ZBrush.

## Using the DVD

For best results, you'll want to copy the files from your DVD to your computer. To copy the items from the DVD to your hard drive, follow these steps:

1. Insert the DVD into your computer's DVD-ROM drive. The license agreement appears.
2. Read through the license agreement, and then click the Accept button if you want to use the DVD.

---

Windows users: The interface won't launch if Autorun is disabled. In that case, choose Start ➤ Run (for Windows Vista, choose Start ➤ All Programs ➤ Accessories ➤ Run). In the dialog box that appears, type `D:\Start.exe`. (Replace D with the proper letter if your DVD drive uses a different letter. If you don't know the letter, see how your DVD drive is listed under My Computer.) Click OK.

---

The DVD interface appears. The interface allows you to access the content with just one or two clicks. Alternately, you can access the files at the root directory of your hard drive.

---

Mac users: The DVD icon will appear on your desktop; double click the icon to open the DVD, and then navigate to the files you want.

---

# Troubleshooting

Wiley has attempted to provide programs that work on most computers with the minimum system requirements. Alas, your computer may differ, and some programs may not work properly for some reason.

The two likeliest problems are that you don't have enough memory (RAM) for the programs you want to use or that you have other programs running that are affecting the installation or running of a program. If you get an error message such as "Not enough memory" or "Setup cannot continue," try one or more of the following suggestions and then try using the software again:

**Turn off any antivirus software running on your computer.**    Installation programs sometimes mimic virus activity and may make your computer incorrectly believe that it's being infected by a virus.

**Close all running programs.**    The more programs you have running, the less memory is available to other programs. Installation programs typically update files and programs; so if you keep other programs running, installation may not work properly.

**Add more RAM to your computer.**    This is, admittedly, a drastic and somewhat expensive step. However, adding more memory can really help the speed of your computer and allow more programs to run at the same time.

# Customer Care

If you have trouble with the book's companion DVD, please call the Wiley Product Technical Support phone number at (800) 762-2974. Outside the United States, call +1 (317) 572-3994. You can also contact Wiley Product Technical Support at `http://sybex.custhelp.com`. John Wiley & Sons will provide technical support only for installation and other general quality control items. For technical support on the applications themselves, consult the program's vendor or author.

To place additional orders or to request information about other Wiley products, please call (877) 762-2974.

Please check the book's website at `www.sybex.com/go/zbrushcreaturedesign`, where we'll post additional content and updates that supplement this book should the need arise.

# Index

# T

# John Wiley & Sons, Inc. End-User License Agreement

**READ THIS.** You should carefully read these terms and conditions before opening the software packet(s) included with this book "Book". This is a license agreement "Agreement" between you and John Wiley & Sons, Inc. "JWS". By opening the accompanying software packet(s), you acknowledge that you have read and accept the following terms and conditions. If you do not agree and do not want to be bound by such terms and conditions, promptly return the Book and the unopened software packet(s) to the place you obtained them for a full refund.

1. **License Grant.** JWS grants to you (either an individual or entity) a nonexclusive license to use one copy of the enclosed software program(s) (collectively, the "Software") solely for your own personal or business purposes on a single computer (whether a standard computer or a workstation component of a multi-user network). The Software is in use on a computer when it is loaded into temporary memory (RAM) or installed into permanent memory (hard disk, CD-ROM, or other storage device). JWS reserves all rights not expressly granted herein.

2. **Ownership.** JWS is the owner of all right, title, and interest, including copyright, in and to the compilation of the Software recorded on the physical packet included with this Book "Software Media". Copyright to the individual programs recorded on the Software Media is owned by the author or other authorized copyright owner of each program. Ownership of the Software and all proprietary rights relating thereto remain with JWS and its licensers.

3. **Restrictions on Use and Transfer.**
   (a) You may only (i) make one copy of the Software for backup or archival purposes, or (ii) transfer the Software to a single hard disk, provided that you keep the original for backup or archival purposes. You may not (i) rent or lease the Software, (ii) copy or reproduce the Software through a LAN or other network system or through any computer subscriber system or bulletin-board system, or (iii) modify, adapt, or create derivative works based on the Software.
   (b) You may not reverse engineer, decompile, or disassemble the Software. You may transfer the Software and user documentation on a permanent basis, provided that the transferee agrees to accept the terms and conditions of this Agreement and you retain no copies. If the Software is an update or has been updated, any transfer must include the most recent update and all prior versions.

4. **Restrictions on Use of Individual Programs.** You must follow the individual requirements and restrictions detailed for each individual program in the "About the CD" appendix of this Book or on the Software Media. These limitations are also contained in the individual license agreements recorded on the Software Media. These limitations may include a requirement that after using the program for a specified period of time, the user must pay a registration fee or discontinue use. By opening the Software packet(s), you agree to abide by the licenses and restrictions for these individual programs that are detailed in the "About the CD" appendix and/or on the Software Media. None of the material on this Software Media or listed in this Book may ever be redistributed, in original or modified form, for commercial purposes.

5. **Limited Warranty.**
   (a) JWS warrants that the Software and Software Media are free from defects in materials and workmanship under normal use for a period of sixty (60) days from the date of purchase of this Book. If JWS receives notification within the warranty period of defects in materials or workmanship, JWS will replace the defective Software Media.
   (b) JWS AND THE AUTHOR(S) OF THE BOOK DISCLAIM ALL OTHER WARRANTIES, EXPRESS OR IMPLIED, INCLUDING WITHOUT LIMITATION IMPLIED WARRANTIES OF MERCHANTABILITY AND FITNESS FOR A PARTICULAR PURPOSE, WITH RESPECT TO THE SOFTWARE, THE PROGRAMS, THE SOURCE CODE CONTAINED THEREIN, AND/OR THE TECHNIQUES DESCRIBED IN THIS BOOK. JWS DOES NOT WARRANT THAT THE FUNCTIONS CONTAINED IN THE SOFTWARE WILL MEET YOUR REQUIREMENTS OR THAT THE OPERATION OF THE SOFTWARE WILL BE ERROR FREE.
   (c) This limited warranty gives you specific legal rights, and you may have other rights that vary from jurisdiction to jurisdiction.

6. **Remedies.**
   (a) JWS's entire liability and your exclusive remedy for defects in materials and workmanship shall be limited to replacement of the Software Media, which may be returned to JWS with a copy of your receipt at the following address: Software Media Fulfillment Department, Attn.: *ZBrush® Creature Design: Creating Dynamic Concept Imagery for Film and Games*, John Wiley & Sons, Inc., 10475 Crosspoint Blvd., Indianapolis, IN 46256, or call 1-800-762-2974. Please allow four to six weeks for delivery. This Limited Warranty is void if failure of the Software Media has resulted from accident, abuse, or misapplication. Any replacement Software Media will be warranted for the remainder of the original warranty period or thirty (30) days, whichever is longer.
   (b) In no event shall JWS or the author be liable for any damages whatsoever (including without limitation damages for loss of business profits, business interruption, loss of business information, or any other pecuniary loss) arising from the use of or inability to use the Book or the Software, even if JWS has been advised of the possibility of such damages.
   (c) Because some jurisdictions do not allow the exclusion or limitation of liability for consequential or incidental damages, the above limitation or exclusion may not apply to you.

7. **U.S. Government Restricted Rights.** Use, duplication, or disclosure of the Software for or on behalf of the United States of America, its agencies and/or instrumentalities "U.S. Government" is subject to restrictions as stated in paragraph (c)(1)(ii) of the Rights in Technical Data and Computer Software clause of DFARS 252.227-7013, or subparagraphs (c) (1) and (2) of the Commercial Computer Software - Restricted Rights clause at FAR 52.227-19, and in similar clauses in the NASA FAR supplement, as applicable.

8. **General.** This Agreement constitutes the entire understanding of the parties and revokes and supersedes all prior agreements, oral or written, between them and may not be modified or amended except in a writing signed by both parties hereto that specifically refers to this Agreement. This Agreement shall take precedence over any other documents that may be in conflict herewith. If any one or more provisions contained in this Agreement are held by any court or tribunal to be invalid, illegal, or otherwise unenforceable, each and every other provision shall remain in full force and effect.